Scholarship

WISDOM AND INTELLECT FOR THE 21ST CENTURY

ANTHOLOGY

Zeta Phi Beta Sorority, Incorporated Centennial Commission
1734 New Hampshire Ave. NW, Washington, DC 20009
CentennialCommission@zphib2020.com • www.zphib2020.com

This anthology includes information from personal experiences and historical recollections about Scholarship. These documents are personal contributions intended as a general compilation of thoughts relative to this key principle of Zeta Phi Beta Sorority, Incorporated. The Sorority and the Publisher shall have neither liability nor responsibility to anyone with respect to any loss or damage caused, or alleged to be caused, directly or indirectly, by the information contained in this book. Although the Sorority and the Publisher have made every attempt to ensure accuracy and completeness of information presented, they assume no responsibility for errors, inaccuracies, omissions, or inconsistencies.

Every attempt has been made to cite the specific work and authors and any oversight is welcome for correction so that proper attribution can be made in future publications.

Scholarship: Wisdom and Intellect for the 21st Century; Anthology

Jylla Moore Tearte, Ph.D., Project Director
Doris McAdams Stokes, Editor
Rhonda M. Lawson, Monica M. Leak, M.A., CCC-SLP, MLS, Pam N. Lewis, M. Div.,
  Rosanna Nelson – Copy Editors
Rashida S. Johnson and Geraldine G. Peeples, Proof Readers
Malica Fleming, Cover Design

ISBN 978-1-944663-04-9 (Paperback)
ISBN 978-1-944663-01-8 (Kindle eBook)
ISBN 978-1-944663-03-2 (iPad/Nook/Kobo eBook)

Crystal Stairs, Inc., Publisher
Printed in the United States of America

Zeta Phi Beta Sorority, Incorporated

ESTABLISHED JANUARY 16, 1920

This Anthology
is Dedicated to the Founders

| Arizona Cleaver Stemons | Pearl Neal | Myrtle Tyler Faithful | Viola Tyler Goings | Fannie Pettie Watts |

ZETA PHI BETA SORORITY, INCORPORATED

SCHOLARSHIP – SERVICE – SISTERHOOD – FINER WOMANHOOD

Contents

ZETA DOVES

UPHOLDING THE LEGACY

UNDERGRADUATE SCHOLARS: OUR FUTURE... OUR DREAMS...OUR HOPES

THE SISTERHOOD SPEAKS

THE VOICES OF ZETA

AMICAE TO ZETA: LIGHT BLUE, ROYAL BLUE AND WHITE

SCHOLARSHIP: ACTION THAT SPEAKS LOUDER THAN WORDS

SCHOLARSHIP REGISTRY

ZINGERS, QUOTATIONS AND SAYINGS

ACADEMIC REGISTRY

ACKNOWLEDGMENTS

PERSONAL REFLECTIONS

FOREWORD

Dr. Mary Breaux Wright

Dr. Mary Breaux Wright and
Dr. Algeania Warren Freeman,
President, Wilberforce University

As we celebrate *Scholarship* on our journey to Centennial, I am reminded of my high school business teacher, Ms. Lou Collison, who sowed seeds of strength, determination, and possibility into my life and the lives of a school full of African American students at Holy Rosary Institute in Lafayette, Louisiana. As a white woman in the South during the 1960s, she did not let skin color dictate who was worthy of an education. It was from Ms. Collison that I was given a new perspective on life, on what I could achieve and who I could become.

Unbeknownst to Ms. Collison, she became my role model after which I mirrored my professional career. Upon receiving a B.S. in Business Administration from Grambling State University, I returned to my high school alma mater and introduced my students to the fields of management and marketing for over two decades. Just recently, I accepted an honorary doctoral degree in Economic Justice and Social Sciences from Wilberforce University and could hear Ms. Collison's voice whispering in my ear to "never give up" and "always keep moving forward."

Today, I encourage you to become the Ms. Collison of your time. The need for dedicated role models has never been greater. In a world where "good enough" and "getting by" are the norm, our youth must understand that mediocrity is not acceptable. Competition is global and fierce. Above average grades and test scores are table stakes that will possibly open a door, but will not guarantee success.

Dr. Mary Breaux Wright,
May 8, 2016,
Wilberforce University

Our youth need to be surrounded by "the village," a community invested in their lives, pushing them to excel as early as pre-kindergarten and supportive throughout their college years.

As you read the *Scholarship Anthology: Wisdom and Intellect for the 21st Century,* be renewed by the stories of achievement, even in the face of adversity. Ask yourself, "How can I promote scholarship in the lives of our youth?' We need you to freely share your knowledge and enthusiasm for scholastic achievement. Like Ms. Collison, you never know whose life you may touch.

Our sisterhood will be forever grateful to Dr. Jylla Moore Tearte, 20th International Grand Basileus and Centennial Chair, the Centennial Commission, as well as those members who assisted in the production of this inspiring publication. It is because of their commitment to excellence that we will continue to plant the seeds of wisdom into future generations.

Dr. Mary Breaux Wright
24th International President
Zeta Phi Beta Sorority, Incorporated

PREFACE

Doris McAdams Stokes

Ask any educator and you will be told: Learning occurs in many different ways. This is a universal truth. Scholarship comes in a variety of shapes and sizes and occurs in many different ways and places. Each and every one of us uniquely translates our life experiences into the lessons we learn and retain throughout our lives. The anthology, *Wisdom and Intellect for the 21st Century,* reflects the innumerable facets of our ideal, scholarship.

It is through scholarship that we establish the foundation of all that we, as Zetas, have done or will do. Scholarship was and, to this day, remains the preeminent criteria for membership in the Sorority. With it, many doors can open; without it, much opportunity can be lost. Many authors in this anthology described their quest for knowledge or education as a "journey." And, indeed it is, not a straight forward one, but a journey fraught with twists and turns and mountains and valleys. In this anthology, the second in a series published for the Sorority's Centennial, we hear from and about our Sorors and Amicae. We gain insight about scholarship from Phi Beta Sigma Fraternity, Incorporated, with whom we share the ideal.

The essays, letters, quotes and zingers contained on these pages will assure readers that scholarship is alive and well in the members, chapters and auxiliaries of Zeta Phi Beta Sorority, Incorporated. There are compelling, insightful, thoughtful, gratifying, and amusing stories that reflect our first, and perhaps most important founding ideal.

Our Founders would be pleased with how we have upheld, developed and established this ideal since our founding nearly 100 years ago!

HISTORICAL LEGACIES

Scholarship for Service and Service to Humanity

Brother Jonathan A. Mason, Sr.
34th International President
Phi Beta Sigma Fraternity, Incorporated

The Background

Just a little more than fifty years after the adoption of the Thirteenth Amendment on June 22, 1865, which abolished slavery in the United States, there was great concern among the majority or white population about how the newly freed Negro population could be controlled in the absence of slavery. In the early years of the 20th century, 1900 – 1920, both Phi Beta Sigma Fraternity, Inc. and Zeta Phi Beta Sorority, Inc. came into being.

The earliest Negro fraternities and sororities had been formed to fill the apparent vacuum, as perceived by the majority community, for "leadership" within the Negro community. Actually, several persons advocated various positions for the Negro community such as Prince Hall, an abolitionist; Martin Delany, proponent of Black Nationalism; Edward Wilmot Blyden, father of Pan Africanism; Henry Highland Garnet, political activist; and, Marcus Garvey, political leader. The problem with these leaders was that they were advocating and fighting for full inclusion in the national community or for Negroes to hold positions that were separate from, and sometimes hostile to, the wishes of the white community.

This difference in interests and ideas led the larger white community to suggest that the Negro community needed "leaders" to guide their decisions. The growing number of college or university trained Negroes were viewed as leaders who could and would guide the Negro community in ways that would be non-threatening to the interests of the larger community.

The first Negro fraternities and sororities were seen as the crucible from which the Negro could draw "educated" leadership. Based upon what was being sought, the members of the early Greek-lettered fraternities and sororities with an African heritage began to accept that future Negro leadership would emanate from within their ranks. To a large degree, the early groups saw themselves as a special class whose abilities were above those who they hoped to lead. As a result, the members of the early groups saw themselves as a "Negro elite." Bestselling author Lawrence Otis Graham detailed the ideas and interests of these early organizations in his 1999 book, *Our Kind of People: Inside America's Black Upper Class* (HarperCollins).

It was in this atmosphere that the Founders of Phi Beta Sigma, Inc. and the Sigma men who helped five like-minded women create Zeta Phi Beta Sorority, Inc., found themselves when they sought to create a new and completely different kind of fraternity and sorority.

The Founders of Phi Beta Sigma, in their approach to bring a new organization into being, organized a logical pathway to plot a totally new and different pathway to the future. First, they decided to bind themselves together on one accord to build something larger than themselves and their narrow individual interests. Second, they agreed to "study to show ourselves approved" and to prepare themselves to be good stewards in the community. Finally, they determined that rather than promoting themselves as "leaders" of the community, they must be willing to become "servants" and return their skills back to those who enabled them to obtain a college or university education to assist them in achieving their dreams.

The Three Men – The Three Principles – Walking Exemplars

Each of our predominately African American fraternities and sororities have Founders. Phi Beta Sigma was founded to emphasize Brotherhood, Scholarship and Service. Each of the three Founders was a walking exemplar of one of the three principles around which the fraternity was formed.

The principal Founder, Abram Langston Taylor, a Tennessee native, dedicated himself to service before he arrived on the campus of Howard University. His personal motto "Service to Humanity" was adopted and expanded to the familiar motto "Culture for Service and Service for Humanity" by the fraternity. During his entire life, Taylor sought out places where he could give back to those around him.

Charles Ignatius Brown from Topeka, Kansas, was selected by fellow Founders A. Langston Taylor and Leonard F. Morse because he was respected by the entire Howard University student body with whom he interacted. Given both his knowledge and respect, it was Charles I. Brown who was responsible for selecting almost all of the charter members in 1914. Charles I. Brown was a walking exemplar of Brotherhood.

Finally, Leonard Francis Morse was a walking exemplar of the principle of Scholarship. Prior to entering Howard University, Founder Morse had been the valedictorian of his New Bedford, Massachusetts integrated high school class (prior to 1910), when most of the schools in the country were segregated. At Howard, Morse became the first student in the university's history to graduate in three years. At the time of his transition to Omega Chapter, he had earned or was granted eight degrees. Brother Morse clearly was scholarship personified.

Phi Beta Sigma and Scholarship

Scholarship has been an important principle to Phi Beta Sigma Fraternity, Inc. from its inception. Two of the founding Brothers (Morse and Brown) had achieved a record of high scholarship even before they entered Howard University. Both had been accepted into the prestigious Howard Academy (the preparatory school for Howard University) even before they were admitted to the university. Once founded, the members were held in such high regard that several of their professors agreed to become honorary members of what was then an undergraduate fraternity. Among the professors who joined with their students were Dr. Edward P. Davis (who later became Howard's Dean of the College of Liberal Arts); Dr. Thomas W. Turner (a nationally recognized botanist); Professor T. Montgomery Gregory (a well-known author and theatrical director); and, Dr. Alain Leroy Locke (America's only African American Rhodes Scholar and the Dean of Harlem Renaissance). Based on the high degree of scholarship of both the fraternity's student members and their professors, Howard University recognized Alpha Chapter within four months of the fraternity's founding. This recognition was a singular achievement as Phi Beta Sigma became the first fraternity (or sorority) to be recognized by Howard's Board of Deans on a campus on which other organizations had existed without university recognition for up to seven years.

Scholarship for What? - Scholarship for Service

When the three Sigma Founders conceived the concepts which undergirded Phi Beta Sigma, they took a drastic departure from the pathway set forth by their brother fraternities, and with the founding of Sigma's sister organization, Zeta Phi Beta, a new dimension was set forth in the sorority world as well. Previously, the members of the African American fraternities and sororities saw themselves as an elite class from which the Negro leadership would be drawn. Although all of the previous group members endeavored to be scholars, their scholarship was sought primarily for personal gain and self-promotion. In Phi Beta Sigma, and later Zeta Phi Beta, the attainment of scholarship was sought to give back to the communities from whom the members had come. Both groups saw themselves as stewards of the community and recognized the debt they owed to those who had supported and assisted them in gaining a college or university education. The presence of this ethic in the thinking for both organizations dictated that those who joined hands in the two organizations had to express and adhere to a commitment to the community which did not find quarter in the other organizations.

Leaders give orders. Servants take orders. Given the position taken by the Founders of Sigma and Zeta, rather than members telling the community what to do; the members of Sigma and Zeta have traditionally asked the community to indicate what it desired and then worked tirelessly to provide the requested service. This critical shift in emphasis from the previously existing organizations is what author Lawrence O. Graham, in *Our Kind of People: Inside America's Black Upper Class* identifies as why, in his view, Sigma and Zeta do not fit the society model espoused by those, who like him, see themselves as a Negro elite. He writes:

> *"The smallest and youngest of the fraternities is Phi Beta Sigma, which was founded in 1914 at Howard University. With 650 chapters, the Washington-based fraternity often partners with its sister organization, Zeta Phi Beta......the group has never enjoyed the same prestige as the Alphas, Omegas and Kappas.*
>
> *A great deal of what has determined the prestige of specific fraternities and sororities depends upon the age of the organization, its size, and the wealth and prominence of its members. In fact, many among the old-guard black elite would argue that only three of the fraternities – the Alphas, the Kappas, and the Omegas – and two of the sororities – AKAs and Deltas – actually fit the "society" profile."*

When the Founders of Phi Beta Sigma and Zeta Phi Beta chartered new organizations in 1914 and 1920 respectively, they sought to use their talents and skills to build strength in communities that had few advocates. One hundred years later, the term "community organizers" describes those who dedicate themselves to returning assistance to the community (i.e. – to humanity) from which they have come. The Founders of Sigma and Zeta, and their membership, were community organizers more than one-hundred years before the terminology existed.

Scholarship, the second principle of Phi Beta Sigma (Brotherhood, Scholarship and Service), and the first ideal of Zeta Phi Beta (Scholarship, Sisterhood, Service and Finer Womanhood) define the outreach that points to the rationale for each organization's existence. Each has devoted the full power of its structure to programs such as "Z-HOPE" (Zetas Helping Other People Excel). Helping other people excel is the mission of each organization. The Sigma motto, "Culture for Service and Service for Humanity," could just as well be written, "Scholarship for Service and Service for Humanity".

Phi Beta Sigma Fraternity, Inc. and Zeta Phi Beta Sorority, Inc. have come a long way since each was founded on Howard University's campus in the early 1900s. Times have changed a great deal since those early days; but the organizational purpose of Sigma and Zeta remains unchanged. We are from the community and we are working to make all communities better. We demonstrate on a daily basis that we understand the real value of scholarship is to utilize every vehicle to better the lives of those around us rather than squandering the benefits on just ourselves. Scholarship for What? - Scholarship for Service. This is our mission and the method of our development.

Brother Jonathan A. Mason, Sr. is a graduate of Norfolk State University. He was elected the 34th International President of Phi Beta Sigma, Inc. in 2013.

Howard University: Then and Now

Marjay D. Anderson, Ph.D.

A Perspective: Howard University 1920 – 2020

Then – At the Founding of the Sorority
Now – As the Sorority Approaches Its Centennial

Imagine a post-World War I university campus intellectual environment where a free exchange of ideas flourished. Cultural, socio-economic, scientific, civic, political, creative and performing arts and disciplines of the humanities were all areas that contributed to the higher educational experiences. This enlightened atmosphere provided a rich background for the students enrolled at Howard University. Among the population were five, highly intelligent impressionable young women who later became Founders of Zeta Phi Beta Sorority, Incorporated.

Triumphant Soror Zora Neale Hurston in her essay, *"The Hue and Cry About Howard University (circa 1918-1919)"* assessed the educational experiences; physical facilities; administrative functions; faculty salaries and benefits; enrollment; academic curriculum; and student protests and activism. She concluded that "Katabolism is easy, growth is hard." Triumphant Soror Hurston was Editor-in-Chief of "The Hilltop," the campus newspaper.

Chartered March 2, 1867, the University was established to provide a higher education for post emancipation freedmen in Washington, D.C. As quixotic as the idea seemed at the time, the plans for the creation of the Howard Normal and Theological Institute for the Education of Teachers and Preachers were implemented. The presidents, board of trustees and most of the faculty and the staff were Caucasian. The first students were Caucasian girls.

Later, there were a few Negro administrators and faculty.

The university consistently rejected the proposals of offering industrial, vocational, agricultural and mechanical training as courses of study. Curriculum pathways leading to degrees in the liberal arts and natural sciences, music education, theology, law, medicine and dentistry were offered.

In addition, a rigorous athletics program was prominent with annual champion football classic games and basketball tournaments.

The University is named after General Oliver Otis Howard, founder, civil war hero and Freedmen's Bureau Commissioner. He was president from 1869-1873.

During 1920, the university president was Dr. J. Stanley Durkee and the federal appropriation was $243,000. The first Negro president was Dr. Mordecai Wyatt Johnson (1926-1960).

During the 20th Century, Howard University was at the forefront of civil rights activism and providing legal expertise to the efforts. It also was a beacon of light for the resolution of problems that impeded the progress of humanity - - poverty; illiteracy; social, racial, economic, gender equality. The University led efforts to improve health care and many alumni assumed leadership positions in municipal, gubernatorial and federal offices.

On the eve of the sesquicentennial (150th) anniversary (2017) of the University, the 44th President of the United States of America, Barack Hussein Obama, delivered the 148th commencement address on May 7, 2016. The university awarded 2,300 undergraduate, graduate and professional degrees and certificates.

The University (affectionately known as "The Mecca") remains "on hilltop high . . ." positioned to lead educational institutions in the 21st Century and beyond. Leadership, academic excellence, truth and service are the cornerstones of the University's educational philosophy.

There are many distinguished alumni of the University. These alumni are highly accomplished and are recognized leaders in international and national government; science and healthcare; professional athletics; the creative and performing arts; socio-economic areas; engineering and architecture; information technology and computer systems; business, ancient and modern languages, and social work.

Howard University is the largest comprehensive historically black university in the world. It is rated as a premier tier one research university. It maintains global recognition for its record of academic excellence and the production of leaders.

The University is comprised of seven academic undergraduate and graduate schools and colleges that include Arts and Sciences, Business, Education, Engineering, Architecture and Computer Science and Communications. Professional schools and colleges include Pharmacy, Law, Medicine, Dentistry, Divinity, Social Work, Allied Health and Nursing. It supports a competitive athletics program and multiple co- and extracurricular activities.

The University operates Howard University Hospital, WHUR-FM 96.3, WHU-TV and digital WHBC. The Moorland-Spingarn Center and the Art Gallery are repositories for archival information exhibits on the African American experiences.

Howard University exhibits to the world an institution that dedicates its culture to the preservation of human liberty, freedom and social justice.

Dr. Marjay D. Anderson
A native of Texas, Dr. Marjay D. Anderson is a scientific scholar, a generous philanthropist and humanitarian. Dr. Anderson has been involved in a myriad of scientific, civic, social and honorary societies, organizations and institutions. In 2017, Dr. Anderson will have accumulated fifty years of service as a faculty member in the biological sciences department and as an academic administrator in the College of Arts and Sciences at Howard University.

The Lillian Lincoln Lambert Story

as told to Krysta N. Jones

When Lillian arrived at the Harvard Business School (HBS) in September 1967 (actually she arrived at Radcliffe College graduate dormitory because women were not allowed to live in the accommodations at the Business School), her first thought was "Why am I here!" She had been assured that Harvard was the top business school in the world for training managers and she was encouraged to go there. A key piece of information she did not have was that no other black woman had preceded her. The first class of women was admitted to HBS in 1963. In 1967 out of a total student body of approximately 1,600 students, 35 were women and 9 were black. Upon her arrival, however, the school was still not totally ready to embrace the presence of women. Dormitories were still designed to house men only. Hence, the need for female students to live at Radcliffe, requiring them to walk a half-mile to classes. This began an interesting journey in her life with a dearth of women and black students.

Background

Born on a farm in the segregated South, at the age of 18 and fresh out of high school, she journeyed to New York City and Washington, DC to seek her fortune. With a high school diploma and good typing skills, she thought the world was awaiting her arrival for that dream job as a secretary. After four years of floundering and enduring menial jobs as a maid and typist, she realized her mother was right! She needed more education. First she ventured to Howard University for her BA degree. There her life was forever changed when she met her mentor, Professor H. Naylor Fitzhugh who assured her she was "Harvard material" and encouraged her to apply. She applied for the entering class of Fall 1966. That's when she ran into a brick wall! Her application was rejected because her Graduate Management Admission Test scores were not high enough. She had taken her mentor at his word about being "Harvard material" and did not properly prepare for the admission process. Admission was taken for granted. The rejection letter was an eye opener. Instead of accepting this as defeat, she took it on as a challenge; found out what she had to do to be reconsidered and then took the necessary steps to assure admission. Her persistence paid off and because of it she achieved a historical milestone as the first black woman to receive a Harvard MBA in 1969.

Experience

Four jobs and six years after getting her MBA, she became a barrier-breaking entrepreneur in a male-dominated industry. The company, operating in six states, grew to a $20 million enterprise with more than 1,200 employees. When she started the business in 1976, there were few women entrepreneurs. Most of today's organizations designed to promote female entrepreneurship did not exist then. She gained valuable experience in the building service contracting industry during the three years she worked with a company in that industry. While there she met numerous owners through the industry's international association. All the company owners were men and few women held higher management positions. However, most workers were female. Realizing that her competition would be male owners, she had some questions about her acceptance as an owner instead of an employee of their colleagues. This was an unnecessary concern because she was well received; was invited to serve on the Board of Directors of the Building Services Contractors' Association International, and elected its first female president in 1995. The company was sold after 25 years and she started two other ventures before beginning her career as speaker, author and coach.

A captivating speaker she speaks about the power of persistence, resilience, courage and morality in surmounting hurdles that prevent people from reaching their full potential. She draws on her life experiences from the farm to Harvard, to show how to use obstacles and barriers as stepping stones to higher levels of achievement. Her background, education and experiences have given her insights into what it takes to come from incredibly challenging circumstances and achieve a successful personal and professional life. Using the power of storytelling, she inspires audiences to dream big, act bold and pave their own paths. Her message speaks volumes, offering guidance, hope and inspiration for anyone who is striving to achieve a better life. Her mission now is to serve as an inspiration to others just as so many inspired her as they pushed her further than she thought she could go.

She has received numerous awards and recognitions. In 2003, Harvard Business School awarded her the Alumni Achievement Award, the highest award bestowed on its alumni. The award recognizes recipients for "their contributions made to their companies and communities, while upholding the highest standards and values in everything they do." In 2015, she was recognized by Zeta Phi Beta Sorority, Inc. with its Inaugural Centennial Trailblazer Award. She pledged Zeta with Alpha Chapter in 1964.

Her memoir, *"The Road to Someplace Better: From the Segregated South to Harvard Business School and Beyond"* was published in 2010. The book tells about her journey to find her place in the world, a journey that had many twists and turns and its share of roadblocks. The reader is given insight to what life was like in the segregated south on a small farm and how that experience prepared her for those twists, turns and roadblocks. It describes the paths she took and how she dealt with the adversities she met at various stages of her life - from childhood to adult.

The Smithsonian: Zeta's Perpetual Historical Scholarship Endeavour

Chauntine J. Dorame

The concept of establishing a federally owned museum featuring African American history and culture can be traced back to the year 1915, five years before Zeta Phi Beta Sorority was founded. However the recent efforts for such a building started in the 1970's. After decades of legislative starts and stops, the museum was established in 2003. During the Black History month (February) celebration of 2012 and, after a structure site was selected and the building design approved, the first African American President, Barack Obama, helped break ground for the historical edifice. Recently, it was announced that the museum now named, The National Museum of African American History and Culture (NMAAHC) will open on September 24, 2016.

On Tuesday, May 3, 2016, International Grand Basileus Mary Breaux Wright, Centennial Chair and Jylla Moore Tearte, Ph.D., 20th International Grand Basileus and Centennial Chair along with several undergraduate Sorors, Centennial Visionaries and various members of the Centennial Commission proudly and *Finerly* presented to the Smithsonian National Museum of African American History and Culture a check for $250,000. Our paid-in-full donation was made possible with $125,000 from the 2020 Visionary Campaign, $125,000 from 2014

Boule revenue, and an anonymous gift. As a result, the name of Zeta Phi Beta Sorority, Incorporated will be prominently displayed on the wall of the museum in perpetuity. Not only will Zeta's contribution be highlighted with other major donors but numerous artifacts of Zeta's history will be displayed.

As a center of **SCHOLARSHIP**, the National Museum of African American History and Culture will be a dwelling in which all Americans and world travelers can learn about African American experiences and contributions; what these contributions mean to not only American lives but the world; and, how these experiences helped shape the United States of America and beyond. Throughout the hallowed walls of the NMAAHC, its patrons will learn about the stories and events that rise above our divided boundaries of race and culture.

The Zeta Centennial donation to the NMAAHC emphasizes Zeta's commitment to scholarship and establishes a long-lasting acknowledgment to one of our founding ideologies. Alpha Chapter President, Soror Arayna Spratley wrote the actual check that was signed by International Grand Basileus Wright and Commission Chair Tearte as a tribute to the five Founders of Zeta and as a symbol of passing this legacy on to future generations.

Mr. Lonnie G. Bunch III, (center) Founding Director for the Museum, is pictured with the following members of Zeta (from right to left):

Arayna Spratley, President, Alpha Chapter, Howard University, 2016 Graduate; **Rebecca Jackson**, Zeta IHQ Office Manager; **Charbet Duckett**, Founders' Society Visionary Donor, Atlantic Region; **T Diane Surgeon**, Esq., Eastern Region Director, Diamond Donor Region and 2020 Visionary

Donor; **Ayanha Quwwee**, President, Kappa Alpha Chapter, University of the District of Columbia; **Mary Breaux Wright**, International President, Circle of Pearls Visionary Donor, Southern Region; **Maxine Davis**, President, Sigma Pi Chapter, American University; **Lynette R. F. Smith**, Founders' Society Visionary Donor, Eastern Region; **Jylla Moore Tearte**, Ph.D., 20th Past International President, Centennial Chair and Founders' Society Visionary Donor, Great Lakes Region; **Marjay D. Anderson**, Ph.D., Founders' Society Visionary Donor, Eastern Region; **Janet Y. Bivins**, Esq., Atlantic Region Director, Platinum Donor Region and 2020 Visionary Donor; **Donna Jordan**, DC State Director and 2020 Visionary Donor, Eastern Region; and **Angela Brennan**, Member, Alpha Chapter, Howard University, 2016 Graduate.

The Miss Black USA Pageant

Karen Arrington

Soror Karen Arrington is an award-winning women's empowerment expert and global philanthropist based in Upper Marlboro, Maryland. Karen's coaching, mentoring and`philanthropic work spans over 100,000 hours of service — including her position as a Goodwill Ambassador to Gambia, her work as the co-founder of the first Diabetes Awareness Day in West Africa, and her role as the founder of The Miss Black USA Pageant. She has been recognized by The Lifetime Network and Women's Day Magazine and other major media outlets for her tireless advocacy for women's health, success and empowerment, including an Empowerment Grant from Jones of New York.

Over the past 20 years, Karen has helped over 1,000 women step into powerful careers in media, business, medicine and law, transcending hardship, abuse, financial limitations, and transforming their lives, and subsequently their communities. Today, Karen offers private coaching and global service retreats for ambitious black women who want to live their best lives only better. She has shared information about the pageant and her thoughts about scholarship.

The Miss Black USA Pageant was started in 1986 during the Reagan "Revolution" Administration. At that time, very few mainstream media outlets featured black women. Federal financial aid decreased disproportionately for black girls and women planning to attend college and there was a desperate need for additional resources for people of color to not only pursue higher education, but to stay in school. I grew up reading about black super heroines and they inspired me to use my talents to give back to others. Miss Black USA was founded to fill the void. The first titleholder was Tamiko Gibson, representing the State of Maryland, who was crowned Miss Black USA in Washington, D.C. on June 6, 1987. Since that time, the Miss Black USA Pageant, has grown to state competitions in almost all 50 states in the U.S. and in countries around the world.

Pageant winners receive a prize package valued at $20,000 which includes a $5,000 academic scholarship to any accredited college or university of the winner's choice and travel to West Africa, where Miss Black USA has a library named in its honor. The winner will also travel to and model in Ghana Fashion Week, in Accra. A full year of professional development, career and television appearance opportunities, and wardrobe and styling services complete the package.

Unlike other pageants, Miss Black USA works with each state titleholder for a full year. Contestants don't just compete and win on stage. They are prepared to compete and win in life. As Oscar-award winning actress Viola Davis eloquently stated, "We just need an opportunity." Miss Black USA is a national platform that prides itself on providing a vehicle for its participants to pursue career opportunities that would not be available to them otherwise. We have many success stories with our state and national winners. Eighty-percent of Miss Black USA state titleholders are enrolled in graduate or professional schools. These women are the "Who's who" of the next generation of female leaders. They are smashing the negative images of black women often portrayed on reality television and in mainstream media. To date, $400,000 in scholarships have been awarded to our participants, the largest single source of scholarship funds for black women.

The Miss Black USA Pageant promotes education and scholarship. If you give a woman an education, she can conquer the world. When she can care for herself and her family, she will improve her community and change the world for others. Miss Black USA titleholders know their "her-story." They know of the countless sacrifices that many made who came before them, those who stayed hungry for their education and paved the way for those who came after them, including me. They get it. They understand that education is the new civil rights issue, linked to poverty and social class. Some of our contestants are first generation college graduates and they're determined to change the trajectory and elevation of not only the black women in their family but for generations to come.

Miss Black USA promotes scholarship by giving our titleholders a local, state and national stage. It's powerful to hear and see black women who have beat the odds, who are calling the shots, who are living their dream. Women like Soror Jasmin Alexander, former Miss Black USA 2014, a 26 year old Intelligence Officer and Captain in the US Air Force. Jasmin holds a master's degree in Human Development and Executive Leadership. Another young "she'roe" is Kalilah Allen-Harris, M.D., who won a full tuition scholarship as Miss Black USA 2007 to cover her entire medical school education. She's a physician and full time actress. These women are proof that you can have and do it all.

Unlike other pageants too, there is no swimsuit competition in the Miss Black USA pageant. We have replaced this with a fitness competition which is not based on superficial standards of beauty or body size but rather health, fitness and lifestyle. Contestants wear fitness or athletic wear to showcase their fitness levels. We promote the whole woman, mind, body and spirit. Miss Black USA emphasizes and promotes scholarship and talent, two essential keys to success.

Beauty and brains are compatible in today's world. There are many role today models beginning with our First Lady Michelle Obama. The reigning Miss Black USA is completing her first year at Howard Law School. Oscar winning actress Lupita Nyong'o holds a master's degree in acting from the Yale School of Drama. Beauty and brains is a lethal combination. These women are unstoppable and a force to be reckoned with. And, we need more more like them.

Parents can counteract the media messages portrayed today. I encourage parents to surround their young girls with positive images of black women who embody more than just a pretty face. Support black female organizations like Miss Black USA so that it can further its outreach to young girls and women in our communities and promote the importance of scholarship. Dr. Ian Smith, physician and author said when speaking about the relevance of Miss Black USA today, "Anytime you are part of a sub-culture, it's important to have your own reward system." It's important to a girl's psyche and self-esteem to see positive images of black women that celebrate women of all shades, size, hair textures, and body types. Most importantly, women should showcase that smart is the new sexy.

My career is a perfect match for my college major, psychology as it involves the study of human behavior, and the mental processes that go along with it. I have applied my degree in understanding why some women may under-perform while others may over-perform. The application of my degree in psychology has allowed me to inspire and empower women to fulfill their dreams and reach their God-given potential.

I had no idea twenty years ago that the Miss Black USA Pageant would evolve into the national movement it is today. We attract some of the nation's most ambitious, talented and beautiful women of color. This year's contestant class includes a television producer, a critical care nurse, and students in law school, graduate students, dreamers and world changers. They are leading ladies, leading the change they want to see. We are preparing for our 30 year anniversary in 2017.

I stay motivated because I believe the two most important days in your life are the day you are born and the day you find out why. It wasn't until I stepped on African soil that I found my calling. It was a divine moment. I knew it was the work God called me to do. I've always been told to do that which calls to your soul. Inspiring and empowering girls and women across the globe, to discover their gifts and facilitate their dreams, makes me want to jump out of bed in the morning. When you discover your gift, the world will make room for you.

Karen is a proud member of Zeta Phi Beta Sorority, Inc., Tau Delta Zeta Chapter in Laurel, Maryland. To learn more visit www.karenarrington.com.

The Thurgood Marshall College Fund

Dr. N. Joyce Payne
Contributed by Krysta N. Jones

Meet Dr. N. Joyce Payne, a Soror who has been so busy, many in the sisterhood do not know her. She has two children and four grandchildren, is a native Washingtonian and recently relocated to Rocky Mount, N.C. Dr. Payne founded the nationally recognized Thurgood Marshall College Fund in 1987.

The Thurgood Marshall College Fund (TMCF) is named for the U.S. Supreme Court's 96th Justice and its first African American Justice who served from 1967 – 1991. The TMCF is designed exclusively for exceptional students at the nation's 47 publicly-supported historically black colleges and universities (HBCUs).The organization was established under the leadership of Dr. Payne and in cooperation with the Miller Brewing Company, the NBA and the National Association of State Universities & Land-Grant Colleges. The Fund recently established the Payne Global Initiative in honor of her continued work in promoting study abroad and partnerships with international universities. Because of her work, the Fund has raised and distributed more than $300 million in scholarships, capacity building and programmatic support to its member colleges and universities

In 2008-2009, Soror Payne served as Executive Director of the National Alliance for Public Trust, a new organization committed to advancing principled leadership in American institutions. She accepted this position following her retirement as Vice President, Office for the Advancement of Public Black Colleges and Council of Student Affairs of the Association of Public & Land-Grant Universities (APLU) in cooperation with the American Association of State Colleges & Universities (AASCU).

Before joining OAPBC, Dr. Payne was the president of Global Systems, Inc. and was a senior staff member under the Carter administration with the President's Advisory Committee for Women; President's National Advisory Council on Women's Education Programs, and the White House Conference on Families. She taught at the former Federal City College and at George Washington University.

An authority on women's issues in relation to higher education and labor force participation, Payne has published and presented a number of papers on the pursuit of equality for women and African Americans in higher education. Soror Payne received a bachelor's degree in speech pathology from the former District of Columbia Teachers College and earned her master's and doctorate degrees in education from the former Atlanta University. This year, Dr. Payne was honored at the Black Enterprise Women of Power Summit where she received the Legacy Award for her leadership in higher education. In 2012, she received a Heritage Award from Alcorn State University for her contributions to the School of Agriculture.

She also received a Presidential Medal from Delaware State University and has received honorary doctorates from Lincoln University of Missouri, Lincoln University of Pennsylvania, Kentucky State University, and University of the District of Columbia and in 2012 from Central State University. She was inducted into the District of Columbia's Hall of Fame and the National Black College Alumni Hall of Fame. She served on the Board of Trustees of the University of the District of Columbia for nine years and served for two years as chair of the Board. She serves on the board of directors of TMCF and formerly on the national board of AARP and chaired the AARP Foundation. She served on the distinguished Foreign Service Performance Evaluation Boards at the U.S. Department of State and the U.S. Department of Commerce. Dr. Payne is one of the founders of the D.C. Chapter of the Coalition of 100 Black Women, Inc. and has received awards from the Ford Foundation, the Spencer Foundation and the U.S. Air Force.

She has traveled extensively in Africa, Asia, South America and Europe and recently conducted a fact-finding mission in Singapore; China; Malaysia; Stellenbosch, South Africa and Taiwan.

Zeta's Scholarship Principle: It Grooms the Youth as Well

Kourtni M. Turner
Zeta Archonette

The founding principles of Zeta are so profound that they cover every aspect of life. The Scholarship principle, the first principle, sets the tone with the skills and knowledge that are needed to carry out the affairs of life and business. It includes formal education and informal day to day scholarly functions that may not be academically connected. On March 12, 2011, Duwania Turner, Geraldine G. Peeples, Shawna Abner, and Rachel McDonald, members of Theta Lambda Zeta Chapter in Champaign, Illinois chartered three youth groups: Archonette Club, Amicette Club and the Pearlette Club. Demetria Candler, the graduate chapter president supported the organizing of this youth program. The late Carla Z. Peeples was also a chapter member and instrumental in helping us as the daughters of Zeta to convince the committee to organize the groups. Carla worked diligently on organizing and giving support to things for the youth program until her transition.

We had meetings and activities in our own individual clubs and we also worked together as a combined group as the Zeta Girls Youth Groups to help support the development of the younger girls and for service projects. It was during our first youth retreat that we were introduced to the four Zeta principles. We were told that scholarship means more than receiving a monetary gift. It is acquiring knowledge, learning a skill, and participating in any function that requires you to think and process information. The scholarship principle involved our academic achievements, the formal instruction we received in Zeta, and at school.

Of all the Zeta principles our youth group used, the Scholarship and Service principles are the two most action-driven principles. Finer Womanhood and Sisterhood are natural occurring principles that focus on character; they are who we are. As the president of the Archonette Club, I utilized the scholarship principle often when filling monthly requirements of preparing meeting agendas, reviewing minutes with the secretary, and writing requests and proposals for programs and projects we were interested in hosting. Zeta women are tough, they expected our best and did not rest until things were as close to perfect as possible. We perfected the art of writing letters to community organizations asking them to partner with us on projects, and to churches requesting permission to publish information on prematurity awareness in their bulletins and newsletters. Youth members also learned how to plan programs and organize events.

Scholarship activities were also present in our service to the community. Our very first community service project was handmade greeting cards for the Champaign County nursing home residents. We spent hours writing personalized messages for each person; a worthwhile act when we saw how happy they were to receive the cards. We painted messages on banners to encourage the men living in the men's shelter. The program manager thanked us and said the banners brightened the place and lifted the hope of those living there. The service efforts of the youth groups have continued through local and national partnerships, with group members committing well over 100 hours annually to service. The youth groups' level of commitment has paid off through the years with first, second and third place winnings in service, and first place winnings in scrapbook journal for three years at the Great Lakes Regional conference competitions.

Our fundraising efforts even included scholarship. In the beginning years, we sold Krispy Kreme doughnuts. Asia and I assisted with letters to parents and patrons, creating a tally form, collecting and counting money, preparing a mass order form for Krispy Kreme staff, and verifying the order with the store representative. And you know that the Big Sisters of Zeta "were not having it" if all of these materials were not top notch. These projects also improved our writing and communication skills.

Overall, the work we accomplished in Zeta through the Scholarship principle taught me a lot of life skills like communication, organization, time management, business sense, presentation skills, leadership skills and how to be a good team member. I learned so much in Zeta through this principle and the others. We had good role models in our big sisters. They spent a lot of time instructing and encouraging us. It is also important for me to mention that through my Zeta youth group experience; I have had the awesome experience of writing and publishing an article. The Vice President of our youth group, Asia Abner, and I worked together closely, so close that we are still best friends today, and we still support the girls.

When I graduated from high school, I was the recipient of the first academic scholarship that was created in honor of Carla Z. Peeples. This also taught me the value of giving back because I saw that a life of service can be honored through scholarship.

This article is dedicated to the youth advisor Duwania Turner, the late Carla Z. Peeples, the Advising Committee: Geraldine G. Peeples, Shawna Abner Price, Rachel McDonald, Barbara Gillespie, and Domesha Perkins; youth group charter members (Archonettes: Asia Abner, Kamaria Smith, Tonia Terry, Kourtni Turner; Amicettes: Mia Brown, Tierra Estes, Tequina Gordon, Mikayla Johnson, Taionna Terry, Daesha Winston; Pearlettes: Simone Gilbert, Aliya McDaniel, and Saniyah Moore), parents , and members of Theta Lambda Zeta Chapter.

Kourtni M. Turner
Zeta Archonette
First Zeta Girls Youth Group President
Theta Lambda Zeta Chapter, Sponsor

STUDENTS, SCHOLARS AND LEADERS

Introduction

Doris McAdams Stokes

Students

Lest we forget, our Founders and Past Grand Basilei were once undergraduate students who studied, took exams, wrote research papers and earned degrees just like the rest of the sisterhood has done and continues to do. Scholarship was paramount to our Founders and they not only readily agreed to share this ideal with our brothers of Phi Beta Sigma Fraternity, Incorporated, they designed portions of our name, symbols and rituals to represent scholarship. They set the requirement that to be a member of the Sorority, a woman had to be a matriculating student in a 4-year college or university. Scholarship and education were two qualities that all members were to have in common.

The first African American woman to earn a bachelor's degree in the United States did not do so until 1862. There is nothing to document her experiences as a student. This accomplishment could have not been easy just three years before the Thirteenth Amendment was passed. After its passage, earning a postgraduate degree remained a daunting task for African American women. Illiteracy, support, or lack thereof from home, finances and the general attitude at the time that women did not require education if they were just going to marry and have children, prohibited many from earning a degree. Scholarship and education however, remained a dream for many and was highly valued through generations as an opportunity for a better life and the means to assist others in the African American community.

By 1920, many, many more African American women were enrolled in colleges and universities like our Founders. Some attended historically black colleges and universities or struck out alone at white universities. Some ventured abroad to study. While it might not have been their first preference, most tended to major in subjects that were likely to result in employment after graduation such as education, social work or nursing. Outside of our Founders' efforts to establish Zeta, we know little else about them and the experiences they had on Howard University's campus nor do we know much more about the Past Grand Basilei when they were students, save what they studied and the careers they chose after graduating. At the time, there was no clear prerequisite nor established criterion for those who would be Founders or early Basilei.

Founder and Grand Basileus Arizona Clever Stemons studied at Howard University and the Pennsylvania School of Social Work, but also taught school for a year. Founder Pearl Neal excelled in music and was the first black woman in New York to earn a master's degree in music before teaching. Founder and Grand Basileus Myrtle Tyler Faithful taught mathematics and her sister, Founder Viola Tyler Goings was not only a teacher but a school administrator. Founder Fannie Pettie graduated with a degree in education and later earned a postgraduate degree in social work.

Scholars

Education was to be the predominant field of study for many of our Grand Basilei. Grand Basilei Joanna H. Ransom, Nellie Buchanan, Ruth Tappe Scruggs, Nellie B. Rogers, Edith A. Lyons, Lullelia W. Harrison, Nancy B. McGhee, Deborah C. Wolfe, Isabel M. Herson, Edith V. Francis, Eunice S. Thomas, Barbara West Carpenter, and Barbara C. Moore were all academicians or administrators at the elementary, secondary or postsecondary levels. Our current Grand Basileus Mary Breaux Wright recently retired after a 40+ year career in education. Past Grands Mildred C. Bradham and Janice G. Kissner parlayed educational backgrounds with other fields of study.

Just a few Grand Basilei branched out into non-traditional fields. Some were ahead of their time such as S. Evelyn Lewis, a physician or Blanche Thompson, a musician. Fannie R. Givens and Violette N. Anderson held positions in the legal field. Jylla M. Tearte studied mathematics before beginning a corporate career in a Fortune 500 company. Sheryl P. Underwood studied media management and mass communication before becoming a celebrity entertainer.

In a sense, being an educator is inherent in all Grand Basilei. The work of designing and implementing programs, policies and procedures for the growth of the Sorority and its members follows and utilizes the same skills as those of an educator. Developing a plan, setting objectives, identifying appropriate delivery methods, communicating effectively, integrating the new with the old, and evaluating results are time honored methods of a teacher. In general too, educators are well organized, accustomed to working with and speaking before large groups of people, adept in working with persons from diverse backgrounds and differing personalities, expert problem solvers and, most importantly, masters at encouraging others and assisting them in reaching their potential.

Leaders

We do know that in 1920, our Founders were undergraduate students who exhibited a remarkable capacity for leadership. With a shared vision, they confronted the status quo and anticipated a future for Zeta Phi Beta Sorority, Inc. They set the pace for the growing African American professional female phenomenon in 1920. Whether or not they wanted to, our Founders were thrust into leadership roles at Zeta's inception that still have an effect on the Sorority 96 years later. Black women who aspired to and were capable of leadership looked to them and professional organizations for participation and growth. Sororities offered plenty of leadership opportunities, at many different levels, as well as opportunities for networking and travel, and our Founders and Grand Basilei served as role models for many.

The position of the Grand Basileus is an unpaid one (as are all other officer positions). Our Grand Basilei, however, have been in the unique position of holding two fulltime positions, one compensated, and the other (more than likely the most demanding of the two), voluntary, while at the same time balancing their own personal goals, life, and family.

Our Founders and Grand Basilei have been students and scholars and, at the same time served as Zeta leaders who have made unique contributions to the Sorority and left their indelible mark. Each is truly an extraordinary woman who merits our admiration and praise. This chapter highlights the National Educational Foundation, a passion of some Grand Basilei; the accomplishments of others, who have an appetite for scholarship or education; or, for others, their scholarly or educational activities launched after serving.

The National Educational Foundation

Dr. Alice J. McCullough-Garrett, Dr. Kathyrn T. Malvern, and Doris McAdams Stokes, Contributors

The Grand Basilei have been the catalysts for many successful programs and services offered by by Zeta Phi Beta Sorority, Incorporated. Of the four Zeta ideals, scholarship is one that has gained significant attention from all Zeta leaders, and next to service, one that generates much activity in our chapters. The Zeta Phi Beta National Educational Foundation (Z-NEF) is an example of a program that reflects the interests and passions of our Grand Basilei.

Formally established in 1970, Z-NEF was originally envisioned as a charitable and educational trust in 1975, and was granted tax exempt status as a public charity under Section 501 (c) 3 of the Internal Revenue Code in 1976. Z-NEF is governed by a separate Board of Managers and has its own trust agreement and bylaws. In addition to individual donations and funds received from other foundations and grants, funding the foundation is provided from a percentage of the annual tax that chapters pay.

In addition to supporting higher education achievement through scholarships, the Zeta Phi Beta National Educational Foundation also conducts education programs and related research to improve individual and community living standards. In its *Articles of Incorporation,* the purposes of the Foundation are to operate exclusively as a charitable and educational organization, through its programs by:

1. Providing scholarship grants to worthy students pursuing higher education;

2. Promoting and conducting community education for improving individual and community living standards;

3. Planning and providing activities and opportunities that encourage the education and training of all women; and

4. Engaging in appropriate research related to the purposes of the Foundation.

To implement its purposes, the Foundation encourages the continuation of education in institutions of higher learning, and promotes the attainment of scholastic excellence, both in public schools and in institutions of higher learning; provides leadership grants to worthy students for the pursuit of higher education; conducts community education programs that aid and support improvement in individual and community living standards; engages in and promotes students and research in education and related matters; sponsors or supports educational programs, conferences, and seminars relating to the problems of contemporary society, and provides for the dissemination of knowledge obtained from such programs, conferences, and seminars; cooperates with other persons, organizations, trusts, funds, or foundations with purposes and activities that are similar to those of the Foundation; engages in education and other activities that will further the educational development of women; and engages in any appropriate research related to the purposes of the Foundation.

The very idea of establishing a separate foundation with a separate board of managers to distribute scholarships to young people was introduced and developed during the administration of Grand Basileus Mildred Cater Boone Bradham (1965-1970). The Foundation was formally established in 1970, during the tenure of Grand Basileus Isabel Herson (1970-1974) who served as the Foundation's first chair of the scholarship committee to screen applicants for scholarships. Under the leadership of these two Sorors, the vision of a Foundation was realized.

More Grand Basilei played pivotal roles in the Foundation. Grand Basileus Janice G. Kissner executed the Foundation's Trust Agreement in 1975 as a private charity. Grand Basileus Deborah Cannon Partridge Wolfe (1954-1965) was elected the first Chairman of the Foundation's Board of Managers. A renowned professional educator, she served in this position from 1975-1995 and was named one of three Z-NEF Founding Members Emerita. Under her leadership, scholarships were established for graduate and undergraduate study, and in certain specialty areas such as counseling, medicine and international studies. Foundation policies and procedures were developed. Soror Wolfe orchestrated the Sorority's participation in the Zora Neale Hurston Festival held annually in Eatonville, Florida.

Grand Basileus Lullelia W. Harrison (1943-1948) served as the first Vice Chair of the Foundation. Grand Basileus S. Evelyn Lewis (1925-1926) influenced the Foundation with her science and medical knowledge. Grand Basilei Edith V. Francis, (1980-1986) and Eunice S. Thomas (1986-1992) both sought to increase financial support from Sorors and chapters for the Foundation. Soror Thomas designated national fundraiser funds for the Foundation.

In 1995, Grand Basileus, Jylla Moore Tearte (1992-1996) established Regional Liaison Councils to assist the Foundation in its fundraising. Grand Basileus Barbara West Carpenter (1996-2002) named Z-NEF's Human Genome Project's Community Awareness program a signature program of the Sorority in 2001.

In 2004, Grand Basileus Barbara C. Moore (2002-2008) announced a plan for a $1,000,000 Endowment Fund campaign for the Foundation and during her tenure, the Foundation was converted from a trust to a non-profit corporation because of changes in federal tax laws.

Throughout the years, the Foundation encouraged memorial contributions and numerous named scholarships were established. I addition to the general undergraduate scholarship, available to college freshmen, sophomores, juniors, and seniors planning to enter college in the fall, a general graduate scholarship is available to graduate students working on professional, master's, or doctoral degrees, or enrolled in post-doctoral study.

Several scholarships are named for Zeta's Founder and Past Grand Basilei:

1. **Arizona Clever Stemons Scholarship** – Available to college freshmen only, enrolling in a four year college or university, for fulltime study.

2. **Deborah Partridge Wolfe International Fellowship** – Available to undergraduate or graduate United States students studying abroad and/or for graduate and undergraduate foreign students studying within the U.S.

3. **S. Evelyn Lewis Memorial Medical Health Science Scholarship** – Available to undergraduate or graduate women pursuing a degree in medicine or health sciences.

4. **Lullelia W. Harrison Scholarship in Counseling** – Available to undergraduate and graduate students enrolled in a counseling degree program.

5. **Isabel M. Herson Scholarship in Education** – Available to undergraduate and graduate students pursuing a degree in either elementary or secondary education.

6. **Nancy B. Woolridge McGee Graduate Fellowship** – Available to members of Zeta Phi Beta Sorority, Incorporated pursuing a graduate or professional degree in their chosen field.

7. **Mildred Cater Bradham Social Work Fellowship** – Available to members of Zeta Phi Beta Sorority, Incorporated pursuing a graduate or professional degree in social work.

The Foundation offers two additional scholarships. **The Zora Neale Hurston Scholarship** – Available to graduate students pursuing an advanced degree in anthropology or related social science field was and the **Mildred Spicer West Scholarship**, established in 1999 by Grand Basileus Carpenter in memory of her mother, is available to students with exceptionally high academic GPA and exemplary leadership experience and honors.

The Zeta Phi Beta Sorority National Educational Foundation continues to "promote education and community service to the highest degree."

Dr. Nancy Bullock Woolridge McGhee, 1948-1953
13th International Grand Basileus

Norma C. Dartis, National Historian; Tlynn Harrison and Doris McAdams Stokes, Contributors

Soror Nancy Bullock McGhee was a native of North Carolina. Her parents were the late Dr. Oscar S. and Mrs. Mehala C. Bullock of Raleigh. Dr. Bullock served as pastor of the First Baptist Church of Raleigh for thirty-seven years. Nancy studied at both Howard and Shaw universities and earned a Bachelor of Arts in English and a minor in music and social studies. She obtained a Master of Arts from the School of Philosophy at Columbia University New York City and a Doctorate of Philosophy from the University of Chicago, with a specialization in American Literature. Her dissertation was titled, "The Negro Preacher in American Fiction before 1900." She continued her studies at the University of London and Cambridge University both in England, while on sabbatical from Hampton Institute (University). Her study abroad was funded by a grant from the General Education Board of the Rockefeller Foundation, the Julius Rosenwald Fund and the Department of English, University of Chicago.

Dr. Nancy Bullock McGhee

After a brief assignment at the Louisville Municipal College in Kentucky and Lincoln University in Missouri, she joined the faculty of Hampton Institute (University) in 1945 as a professor in the English Department. She later became the chair of the English Department. She was featured in numerous publications including the *Journal of Negro Education* and the Midwest Journal, *Phylon*. Dr. McGhee was the Vice President of the National Council of Negro Women from 1953 to 1957. Her other professional affiliations included: the American Association of University Professors, the American Association of University Women, the College English Association, the National Council of Teachers of English, the American Council on Human Rights for which she served as the Board President from 1954 to 1958, the Virginia Foundation for Humanities and Public Policy, and, president of the Virginia Humanities Conference. Dr. McGhee was the wife of Samuel C. McGhee.

From 1942 – 1957, she held several national positions within Zeta Phi Beta Sorority Incorporated: National Antapokritis (Editor) of the ARCHON, from 1942 – 45; First Anti-Basileus from 1947 and 1948; and, 13th Grand Basileus from 1948 – 54. Dr. McGhee had the distinction too of being elected Chair of the National Executive Board from 1953 – 1958.

While Grand Basileus, the national roster exploded and chapter numbers increased tremendously. Zeta's exponential growth, resulted in the restructuring of the Sororities' regions. The Sorority concentrated more on the image of the "Zeta" woman in both the Greek and universal communities. Leadership development on all levels was implemented and became part of the new "Zeta Way" of handling business. Workshops were incorporated at both the regional and national convention levels were utilized to reinforce leadership within the sisterhood. In addition, a National Director of Workshops was appointed to emphasize national programs and projects that would impact the community interests. Other milestones included the solidifying the Sorority's Incorporation, showcasing Birch Haven as a national shrine and, a national scholarship fund was organized and employed through the newly established Office of Education Services under the leadership of the International Second Anti-Basileus. During Soror McGhee's tenure, Zeta Phi Beta chartered its first graduate chapter in Africa, Delta Iota Zeta and disseminated its song, composed by Soror Audrey B. Robinson, to the sisterhood. A new edition of the Sorority Handbook was published and plans were initiated to purchase of a building for national headquarters. The ARCHON was solidified, as the official organ of the Sorority and a budget and staff were were added to ensure its quality.

At the 1954 Boule in Louisville, KY, three honorary members were selected: Attorney Edith Sampson (Chicago, Illinois), Abby Clement Jackson (Louisville, Kentucky), and Antoinette Tubman wife of President William V.S. Tubman (Republic of Liberia, West Africa).

Additional highlights of the McGhee administration included heightened public relations and publicity related to Zeta Phi Beta sorority, Inc.'s great works. The activities and travel of the Grand Basileus throughout her term garnered more attention and became a focal point.

During her tenure as Chair of the Board, she traveled to England, Scotland, France, Italy, Switzerland, Australia, Germany, Holland, and Belgium. In 1955, she served as a member of The Crusade for Freedom Munich tour, broadcasting over Radio Free Europe. Soror

McGhee's travels included a visit behind the "Iron Curtain," and a three month stint in West Africa, Liberia (West Africa) and the Gold Coast in 1956.

Upon her retirement from Hampton University, she was named a professor emeritus and commissioned by the university's Board of Trustees to write the history of the university. *The Making of a University: The History of Hampton Institute* was published in 1991. Later, she was named the Shaw University Distinguished Alumni and honored with the position of Avalon Foundation Chair in Humanities which was the first endowed chair at Hampton. She died in February 1995 in Hampton, VA.

The Nancy B. Woolridge McGee Graduate Fellowship is available to members of Zeta Phi Beta Sorority, Inc. through the Sorority's National Education Foundation, who are pursuing a secondary or professional degree at an accredited college or university.

Editor's Note: Portions of this submission were previously published in *Zeta Phi Beta Sorority – 1920 – 1965* by Ola Adams and *Torchbearers of a Legacy – 1920 – 1997,* by Lullelia W. Harrison.

Dr. Deborah Cannon Partridge Wolfe, 1954-1965 14th International Grand Basileus

Vesta Godwin Clark

Dr. Deborah
Cannon Partridge Wolfe

A Leader In Education

I am proud to say, the 14th International Grand Basileus of Zeta Phi Beta Sorority, Incorporated, Soror Deborah Cannon was one of the reasons I joined this great sisterhood in 1980. I met Soror Wolfe when one of my soon to be "line sisters" and I, attended her church in Cranford, New Jersey, which was the next town over from my home town of Westfield. Soror Wolfe was the assistant pastor of First Baptist Church at which her father at one time was the pastor.

After church, she invited us to her home, a few doors up the street from the church. She made sure we knew the house on High Street was the house in which she was born. She also let us know she was a lifelong member of her family church. Of course, from the onset, I was immediately impressed with this woman who was short in stature, but had a booming and commanding voice.

When we entered her home, it was filled with artifacts from her trips all over the world and her library shelves were stacked with all kinds of books. Many of them were of a religious nature and it was during this first of many visits that I found out Soror Wolfe, was a Hebrew Scholar! She did her postdoctoral studies at both Union Theological Seminary and the Jewish Theological Seminary of America.

1994 – NEF members, seated: Past National Presidents Lullelia W. Harrison and Dr. Deborah C. Wolfe. Standing, l – r: Sorors Clark, Issie Jenkins, Rosalind Hale, Lorraine Clement and Kay Jones-Rosebure.

Yes, during this visit, I fell in love with this woman who talked endlessly, but kept us engaged. It was truly an honor to sit in the home of the woman who had served as the president of the organization we were about to join. We had no idea of her magnitude. Can you imagine our excitement as young women who were mere sophomores in college, nineteen or twenty years old, to have this opportunity? While at her warm and cozy home filled with a lot of stuff - nick knacks, souvenirs and books - she talked to us about: Zeta; her trips to Africa; how she was the first president of the Sorority to have an advanced degree which at her young age, was a doctorate; how she had lived in the Sorority house; and, as I would later find out she spoke about often, how she had served longer than any other Zeta president, from 1953-1965. She was proud to be a woman of Zeta Phi Beta Sorority and the way she spoke about it, we wanted to be members too, no doubt about it. She talked about her church, her family, and her parents who were educated at a time when African Americans didn't get college degrees. She talked about her brother who died young and gave us copies of a book of poems he wrote. She talked about her world travels and pointed out special souvenirs and she talked about the importance of education. Soror Wolfe was excited to learn that we were about to become charter members of Gamma Kappa Chapter at Rutgers, the state university of New Jersey which she knew was not going to be an easy feat. At that time, she was a member of the New

Jersey State Board of Higher Education and was the first African American appointed to that board and the first female to eventually chair it. She was proud to know Zeta, was finally coming to the state university in 1995. There was no question in my mind that I was going to join this organization called Zeta Phi Beta after my first encounter with Soror Wolfe.

Sorors Wolfe and Lillie Brown.

Who knew, after that first visit, that Soror Wolfe would become one of my mentors in Zeta? I was fortunate, because I lived so close to her and had easy access to a Past National President of Zeta who at one time was the Education Chief for the U.S. Department of Education.

During my journey to membership and after becoming a Zeta, I learned much about Soror Wolfe from her. In 1980, there were no personal computers or the internet. Research necessitated a visit to the library to access books, microfiche/film, and the good old encyclopedia. My line sisters and I learned Soror Wolfe received her bachelor's degree from New Jersey State Teachers College in Jersey City, New Jersey which back then cost $100 a year. She earned her master's and doctoral degrees in education from Columbia University Teachers College in New York City. Later in life, after completing divinity school, Soror Wolfe was ordained a minister in the Baptist Church becoming the first African American woman to do so. Soror Deborah Cannon Partridge Wolfe, achieved many "firsts" in her life.

As members of the Zeta Archonette Club, my sisters and I learned Soror Wolfe's contributions to education had been memorialized over the years with buildings named

1996 – Boule, Dallas, TX,
Sorors Wolfe and Clark.

after her, while she was still living which was unusual. One of our study questions that we had to answer correctly was, "What college in New Jersey had a dormitory named after Dr. Deborah Wolfe?" Answer: Trenton State College (now the College of New Jersey). In Alabama, where she was a school administrator at a young age, there are both the Deborah Cannon Wolfe High School and Deborah Cannon Wolfe Elementary School, located in Shorter and Macon counties, respectively. One of the most prestigious honors bestowed after Soror Wolfe's death in 2004 was the 2007 dedication of the Deborah Cannon Partridge Wolfe College of Education at New Jersey City University (formerly Jersey City State College and

prior to that, NJ Teachers College, her alma mater). I was privileged to attend that ceremony with her family members and Sorors. Soror Wolfe would be proud to know that her dedication to education would live forever through the schools and colleges named after her.

At our first meeting, I had no idea that I was going to form a relationship with her, a walking, talking, living legend. Soror Wolfe exemplified the Zeta ideal of scholarship to its utmost. When I was appointed New Jersey State Director by

1993 – Soror Francis, National Treasurer
Soror Marilyn Pearson, 20th International
President Jylla M. Tearte, Soror Wolfe and
NJ State Director Vesta G. Clark.

Past Grand Basileus Soror Jylla Moore Tearte, and subsequently appointed to the position of National Second Anti-Basileus, Soror Wolfe was very proud. As National Second Anti-Basileus, I served as an ex officio member of the National Educational Foundation which Soror Wolfe chaired from 1975-1995. One of my responsibilities as a Foundation member was to oversee the scholarship application process. This was no easy feat, but after updating the application, and promoting it heavily, I received more applications than the Foundation had received in the past, over 700. This was news Soror Wolfe and the Foundation members were pleased to hear. Having the opportunity to work with Soror Wolfe on the Foundation, though for a short time, was a time in my life that I will always cherish. After graduating from Rutgers, I delayed getting an advanced degree, but Soror Wolfe always encouraged me to go further. Twelve years after receiving my bachelor's degree, I went back to school and completed a master's program in 1995. Soror Wolfe was pleased and proud as education was important to her. She saw her son receive his Ph.D. and would be proud to know her grandson now has a Ph.D. and, that her two granddaughters both have advanced degrees.

Eventually, Soror Wolfe could no longer maintain her home in Cranford as she got older and moved to an adult community in Monroe Township, New Jersey. When she moved, we talked every now and then. She did not believe in answering machines or caller ID, so if you did not get her, you just had to keep trying until you did. Then, there was a time she could not speak beyond a whisper because of medical reasons, and I always wondered why God would take away the voice of this woman who used it to preach, teach, and speak. Before she passed, I had the opportunity to visit her a few times and sometimes, took her to meetings. Somewhere among my videos is a conversation between us. At our last time together, we talked about how she missed her home in Cranford, but the community she lived in was nice. Unable to attend my wedding, she asked about my husband and was happy to hear he was an ordained minister. She asked me when I was going to get my Ph.D. We talked about Zeta and "the state" of our illustrious organization.

Past National Presidents Soror Wolfe, left and Soror Francis, right, with Soror Clark, center following her appointment as National Second Vice-President.

She told me she was disappointed that I had not run for any office in Zeta since my my last one. I told her, there were other things I needed to do. We talked about the need for good leadership and the qualities of being a good leader. One thing that she said to me that has stuck with me all these years about leadership in any aspect was, "Vesta, I told you before, as a leader, not everyone is going to like you, but remember, there will always be more people who like you than those that that don't and that is all that matters." In my copy of *Torchbearers of a Legacy,* she wrote, "Dear Vesta, I'm so proud of you! Keep the faith!" Those are words to stand and live by, spoken by a true scholar. These are words of wisdom from a woman who made major contributions to the world; to the field of education; to Zeta Phi Beta, the Sorority she loved; to her family; and, to the people whose lives she touched, including mine.

The last time she touched my life, ironically was on the campus of Spelman College in August 2008. I was helping my niece move into her dorm as one of 600 incoming freshman and was on the elevator alone with a pretty young lady who noticed my Zeta tee shirt. She greeted me and told me her grandmother was a Zeta. I asked for her name and to my surprise, she responded, "Deborah Wolfe!" I felt a chill and began to tear up. I am sure, Julianna thought I was a crazy lady. What was the likelihood that out of all of the people on campus that day, that Soror Wolfe's granddaughter and I would meet on the elevator? I let her know how much I loved her grandmother and shared a little about our relationship. She was just as surprised about the entire meeting as I was, and we hugged. She was happy to meet someone out of the blue who knew her grandmother as she was embarking on her own educational journey. I introduced her to my niece and they immediately became friends. Later that day when I saw her Julianna's father, Soror Wolfe's son Roy and shared the experience, he said, "It is clear Mom orchestrated that meeting and brought us together." I agree, it was the type of thing Soror Wolfe would do and I am so glad she did. Today, her granddaughter and my niece, maintain a close relationship. That meeting will forever keep me connected to this beloved woman who had such an impact on my life, Dr. Deborah Cannon Partridge Wolfe, a leader in education.

Dr. Edith V. Francis, 1980-1986
18th International Grand Basileus

Vesta Godwin Clark

Gamma Kappa Chapter charter members at our first regional conference with Past National President Soror Francis, 4th from left.

A Trailblazer In Education

I met Dr. Edith V. Francis, the 18th International Grand Basileus of Zeta Phi Beta Sorority, Incorporated in Mount Laurel, New Jersey the day I became a Zeta. Initiation ceremonies had never been held at the State Meeting before but our ceremony was held at the New Jersey State Meeting on May 17, 1980. Our ceremony was special not only because we were new members coming in, but also because a new, long antici- pated chapter was being chartered at Rutgers, the State University of New Jersey, Gamma Kappa. Soror Francis, a resident of New Jersey, was then, the National First Anti-Basileus. What an honor it was for a National Officer, to administer to my line sisters and me, our National Oath. Yes, we were special.

That July, I was given the opportunity to travel to the Grand Boulé in Memphis, Tennessee and be the ONLY undergraduate member from the Atlantic Region to attend to attend it 1980. I literally knew no one except, Soror Katheryn T. Malvern, who was then the New Jersey State Director. No one from my sponsoring graduate chapter attended and the only other Sorors I knew were by sight because they were at the State Leadership Conference. Somewhere along the line, I bonded with a few undergraduates from California that befriended me and I was reintroduced to Soror Francis who was running for Grand Basileus. She did not have a lot of time for me, but she gave me her room number and told me if I needed anything, to not to hesitate to ask. Needless to say, she was excited to see one of the new undergraduates from Rutgers at the Boulé and that is where the relationship between Soror Francis and I began.

NJ Reception for New International 2nd Vice President May 1995 Vesta Godwin Clark and Dr. Edith V. Francis

Who was this woman whose name was on my membership certificate (even though Soror Janice Kissner was the Grand Basileus when we became members)? Soror Edith V. Francis was born in Harlem, New York and was a member of Delta Mu Zeta Chapter in there. I learned, New Jersey Sorors, also claimed her. I learned that she was married to a Sigma man, Dr. Gilbert H. Francis, and had two daughters.

At the time, she accomplished something that only six other African American women in the United States had achieved: She was the superintendent of a K-12 school district. Soror

Just Us March 1994 Vesta Godwin Clark and Dr. Edith V. Francis

Francis made history in New Jersey when she was named the superintendent of the Ewing Township Schools. Prior to her being appointed in Ewing, Soror Francis was the acting superintendent of the Princeton Regional School District. Moving on from Ewing, she also served in an acting capacity for the Irvington School District. Before retiring, Soror Francis was the Director of Community Education at the Bernie L. Edmunson Community School in East Orange, New Jersey, which offered adult education programs. During the time she spent at each school district, Soror Francis definitely left them better than they were when she got there.

She had a passion for making certain children, especially minority children, first graduated, and when they did graduate, were literate. Soror Francis was well prepared academically. She was awarded her Bachelor of Arts and Master of Arts in Childhood Education and Master of

Science in Guidance from Hunter College. She earned her doctorate in Educational Administration from New York University. Professionally, she held positions that ranged from principal to professor or from consultant to superintendent. Personally, if you ever had

the opportunity to sit and talk to her, you could learn valuable lessons that you could never learn in school. The first time I went to her home in Trenton, I was amazed at all of the academic accolades hanging on the walls and placed on the shelves that she received. Yes, this woman of grace and dignity fought for education for those who could not fight for themselves. In addition to Zeta, Soror Francis was involved in other organizations such as the Links who placed scholarship at the top of its priorities. During her time as the Links, Inc. President, she donated money towards their scholarship fund on behalf of Zeta.

My "Other" Mom Gives Me A Way May 22, 2003. Vesta Godwin Clark, Brother Reginald V. Clark, Dr. Edith V. Francis and Brother Gilbert Francis

Though there was much accomplished during her six years in office (1980-1986), Soror Francis' term as Grand Basileus was not always easy. Grand Basileus Francis focused many programs on voter education, civil rights and youth and senior citizens advocacy. She also chartered chapters in Alaska and Germany, and instituted the Golden Life Membership category. During her last year in office, I remember Sorors traveling to her home to help with a mass mailing to the sisterhood. This was a task, but we got it done. Though under attack, I never saw her "sweat." I will never forget the actions that transpired when we got to Boulé in the summer of 1986 in Anaheim, California.

Despite all that was happening, I never heard Soror Francis raise her voice or use a non-ladylike word. It was clear, she was upset, but we never saw her sweat in the privacy of her suite or in the public eye. This was the first time I really saw how we (Sorors) could treat one another. It was truly an eye opening experience and one that would forever leave a mark on me as a member of this organization. Understanding the sacrifices people make when they "chose" to seek leadership positions in Zeta and beyond. I wondered "Is it worth it?" I wondered why people make such a fuss over nonpaid positons, positions that are voluntary. This still puzzles me.

Over the years, Soror Francis became one of my "other" Moms and I considered her as someone who not only fulfilled the ideals of Scholarship, but also as the epitome of Finer Womanhood. Dr. Edith V. Francis is a woman who has both class and style. A woman who was

July 2012 Vesta Godwin Clark and Dr. Edith V. Francis

internationally known and met world leaders, but still loved me enough to send me a birthday card every year and when I got married, she participated in my wedding, and thereafter sent anniversary cards until she became ill. She's a woman who continues to hold her head high no matter what is thrown at her and moves forward. Soror Francis has been an example in my life for her belief in educational excellence and I love her for the example she set for me and others over the years.

Though she has been unable to be active in recent years, Zeta is still one of Soror Francis' first loves. She and Brother Francis currently reside in Melbourne, Florida.

Soror Dr. Edith V. Francis, was a trailblazer in Zeta and beyond.

Dr. Jylla Moore Tearte, 1992-1996
20th International Grand Basileus

The Evolution of a Scholar-Practitioner

Dr. Jylla Moore Tearte at PhD graduation from
Benedictine University, Lisle, Illinois.

Why did the Founders of Zeta Phi Beta Sorority, Inc. choose scholarship as one of the founding principles for the organization? What role did the pursuit of the principle of scholarship play in my attaining a Bachelor's, MBA and PhD Degree? How have I embellished the principle of scholarship on my life's journey as a corporate executive and an entrepreneur? What are the core elements at the intersection of scholarship and practice?

Poignant, provocative and pivotal questions have become the anchors that steady the ship of my thinking. As I wrestled at the intersection, exploring and framing the questions as a scholarly pursuit allowed me to bridge the debate. The responses to the questions evolved into a discipline of study that I have now framed as *"Encore Leadership: Transforming Time, Talent and Treasure into a Legacy that Matters."* Hopefully sharing my story will motivate others to explore the intersection of scholarship and practice to evolve to #ChangeTheArc of their lives.

If you take the time to think back on the major intersections of your life, you will often find the crossroads and turning points that were instrumental in framing the person you have become. I explored my lifeline and discovered so many memories of moments that informed or shaped my evolution as a scholar and a practitioner.

I have had an unquenchable thirst for knowledge my entire life. It all started during my elementary school days when my parents incented me with a dollar for every 'A' that I achieved on my report card. While some parenting books might dispute rewarding grades, the payout always fueled my desire to strive to bring my 'A' game to my studies to make sure that I reaped the reward. In hindsight, I also prided myself on being the "teacher's pet" because of my academic success.

It seems as though there was always something definitive that inspired my educational journey. I enjoyed writing and submitting articles to the Afro-American newspaper that was headquartered in Baltimore, simply a distant place on the map to me. I just knew that if I submitted the best article in their contest, I would receive a monetary prize. On one occasion, I did and I was in awe that it was worthy of a prize. I took advantage of an opportunity to find a "pen pal" through the newspaper but stopped the public disclosure of information when I realized that not all responders had honorable intentions. Did these early activities inspire the formation of my business, Crystal Stairs Publishing, in later years?

I remember every teacher that I had from first through eighth grade. During these years, I felt the teachers really cared about my success. That all changed when the schools integrated. I continued to navigate my educational journey and successfully participated in extracurricular activities such as the marching and concert band. I quickly used this as an outlet and a means to establish a reputation beyond the books, developing relationships that exposed me to the other side of the tracks in my hometown.

Upon graduation, I attended Livingstone College, the historically black college in my hometown, at which I was named a Samuel E. Duncan Scholar and offered a full scholarship. I knew it would be extremely difficult for my parents to afford sending a third child to college at the same time. I had not really given much thought to my college decision process so it was just a blessing during the summer prior to college that I received notification about the scholarship.

The Duncan family was a distinguished family of scholars. Samuel E. Duncan was President of Livingstone College and his sister, Elizabeth Duncan Koontz, became the U.S. Assistant Secretary of Education. She was named an Honorary Member of Zeta Phi Beta Sorority, Inc. Dr. Koontz was known to my mother and others in my hometown as "Libby." To me, she was one of the most distinguished and accomplished women I knew who had found success outside of the comfort zone of my hometown. She was an intellectual yet strikingly beautiful woman who exuded class and professionalism. I was honored, yet humbled, to have been selected a Samuel E. Duncan Scholar.

With such a prestigious scholarship, I knew I had to excel and take my work seriously. I enjoyed competing with the limited number of math majors in my class, and at an early age, I realized I could compete successfully with men. Yes, this was another incentive to learn and achieve that would be instrumental in navigating the competition that met me at the door of corporate America.

In 1976, I decided to pursue a Master in Business Administration (MBA) degree through a competitive process of selection as a Consortium for Graduate Study in Business Fellow at Indiana University in Bloomington. I didn't have a real job opportunity upon graduation, so the Consortium Fellowship was another blessing that allowed me to continue to pursue scholarship. The message was starting to become clear: Be prepared when opportunity knocks at the door and take the leap of faith to pursue the unknown. Indiana University was a definite unknown as was the pursuit of an MBA. I had never taken a business course prior to starting MBA coursework. The reality of business hit me when my Professor gave me an "F" in accounting my first year. I had to attend summer school at the University of Greensboro while interning with R.J. Reynolds in Winston-Salem, to earn the required credit to keep up with my class. Duly noted: It wasn't a dollar that incented me, it was overcoming my first major failure as a student.

It was a LONG summer, but the work was worth the "B" that I received in that accounting class. I was focused and spent more hours than most making sure I mastered the subject matter. Now I can debit and credit with the best of them. If only there had been credit cards and debit cards in the 70's, maybe the balance sheet would have made more sense! I can now delve into accounting and finance intricacies because of that "F." Lesson learned: Put the work in!

The beginning of scholar-practitioner engagement began when academic lessons were practiced through work. My first job after graduate school was with IBM. I attended so many classes in IBM, I became an expert Systems Engineer and an award winning marketing and sales leader. Translating my skills learned, to the expectations of the paycheck, was a new application of knowledge. Over the course of more than 20+ years, I learned the nuances of success to ultimately be promoted to several executive level domestic and global opportunities. I wrote *Due North! Strengthen Your Leadership Assets* to inform others about the key attributes I thought important for success based on my experience at IBM.

In 1999, I was awarded an Honorary Degree of Humane Letters from Livingstone College to acknowledge my involvement in community service, specifically my leadership as the Grand Basileus of Zeta Phi Beta Sorority, Incorporated. I immediately began using the abbreviated title of "Dr." Little did I know of the controversy in academia about use of an honorary title versus that of an "earned" doctoral degree. Past Grand Basileus Dr. Deborah Cannon Partridge Wolfe brought this to my attention, in front of the hundreds of attendees at the 2000 Boule in Philadelphia. She stated that, "Your degree was Honorary and not "earned." This was a highly personal coachable moment and I made a personal commitment to achieve an "earned" degree.

I was a speaker at the National Black MBA Conference in Philadelphia in 2003, and by coincidence or perhaps divine intervention, as I stood on the platform waiting for the train to Washington, DC, I started a conversation with a woman who was traveling to DC for the Congressional Black Caucus weekend. We sat together and I told her about the award winning, career book I had recently published: *Due North*. She asked me a poignant, provocative and pivotal question: *"What is the research basis for your theory of the 10 most important leadership assets?"* She was Dr. Ella LJ Bell, a noted professor, and she stopped me in my tracks. My continued drive for education was fueled and challenged. Another coachable moment: My leadership assets were not supported by scholarly evidence. I had substantiated their importance based on my 20 years of experience.

Dr. Bell discussed research that is fundamental to theoretical hypotheses. She introduced me to the idea of supporting my theory with research and then she introduced the concept a "scholar-practitioner." She suggested that I look into a Ph.D. program that focused on developing practitioners, corporate executives in particular, into scholars. She recommended Benedictine University's Ph.D. program at which Dr. Ram Tenkasi was a professor. She had no idea Benedictine was a fifteen-minute drive from my home in Chicago. I took her advice and applied for admission to the program.

In my application to the Ph.D. program, I wrote that I wanted to explore becoming an academic executive practitioner. I stated: *"I am a natural citizen in the world of corporations, entrepreneurs, and organizations. I am a foreigner in the world of academia. This is a life gap I commit to close through the pursuit of a doctoral degree in Organization Development at Benedictine University. Closing this gap will enable me to contribute to the field of organization development by exploring emerging trends and executing innovative solutions."* I mastered the language of academia and the rigor of research and "earned" my Ph.D. in organizational development in 2009. Dr. Tenkasi, one of the most brilliant scholars I have ever known, chaired my dissertation committee, and remains my guiding light for the pursuit of mastery of my work.

I love research. I love digging deep into literary works to uncover the patterns and scholarly experiments that generate fact-based positions. Keen exploration of a topic often opens up unimaginable opportunities. For me, keeping my eye on the prize of education opened the door for my passion, Encore Leadership. My research proposal, examination of the subject of transitioning black executives led to my current executive coaching, consulting and behavior assessment business of Crystal Stairs, Inc.

Mrs. Mattie T. Lakin, my freshman English teacher at Livingstone College, was the driver for another memory that was an impetus for my business. Through her, I grew to love black literature. She recited poetry in class and her assignments included reading books of the masters. She gave me the lifelong awareness and appreciation for the line of Langston Hughes' *Mother to Son* poem, "Life for me ain't been no crystal stair….but all the time, I'se been a-climbin." I shared the story of Crystal Stairs' evolution with Mrs. Loida Lewis during a conference, and we connected after she repeated the entire poem for me as a student of Mr. Hughes' literature. Education is a bridge and a stepping-stone for life.

In the fall of 2013, I received a call from a man who found my name on the internet. He tracked me down to share a speech that he had given to a group of teachers in North Carolina. Following a long cry after listening to the speech, I contacted him and we talked. The talk led to a request that we publish his speech in the form of a book. Having just completed my series of books on *Encore Leadership* - the textbook, the workbook and the journal - and *Book It: How to Publish a Book in 30 Days*, I saw a book in the story. Randy provided the word document and I published the story.

Vera M. Moore, seated far left, in 1948 with the staff at her first teaching job at E.E. Marten High School, Easton, Maryland.

The story is about how my Mother and Soror, Mrs. Vera M. Moore, former Eastern Director of Zeta Phi Beta Sorority, Inc., had given him an opportunity in her junior high school class that was not ordinarily given to the student who was most often disruptive or disengaged. Yet, she saw the "extraordinary" in him as he struggled with the vicissitudes of life at home and on the streets. After many ups and downs, he is now a biotechnologist focused on genomic research. *Randy: A Story of Passion, Perseverance and the Power of Unconditional Love* is a salute to teachers and mentors who often never have the opportunity to see the fruit of their faith and caring. Proceeds from the book are donated to *DonorsChoose.org,* an online repository of projects submitted by teachers to enhance the education of their students.

#ChangeTheArc is the hashtag that now inspires and informs the work of the Tearte Family Foundation. It is through the philanthropic work of the Foundation that I hope to inspire others to pursue education as an agent of change in life. For me, it has been a grand life journey to evolve as a scholar-practitioner.

It is important to connect the dots of life. The connection celebrates the past while informing present decisions and future aspirations. So often, I attribute my education as the roadmap to my life. At major inflection points, education changed the arc of my life. I hope this reflective process will assist others who are considering building a framework for their life by taking a moment to reflect on the past inflection points informed by education and scholarly pursuits.

The Founders of Zeta Phi Beta Sorority, Incorporated were truly visionary. Their understanding of the power of the scholarly pursuit of wisdom and knowledge has been the foundation of successful lives since 1920. They were astute in their declaration of scholarship as a founding principle that would, and has transcended time. They inspired me to be a scholar-practitioner.

Dr. Barbara West Carpenter, 1996-2002
21st International Grand Basileus

Rewards and Challenges of International Study

I was fortunate to grow up in a household that cherished travelling and learning about the differences in other cultures. Travel was something that we were expected to continue in our adult lives. I soon realized that many other people, particularly African American youngsters were not so fortunate. My major dream in life was to join the Peace Corps and travel the world. However, my parents thought otherwise as they felt that I too young and quite immature. When I became employed as a Professor of Education at Southern University and A&M College in Baton Rouge, Louisiana in the early 1980's, I immediately became involved with international initiatives.

Dr. Barbara West Carpenter

Currently, my title at the university as the Dean of International Affairs and University Outreach allows me the opportunity to provide international experiences for students, faculty and staff. Studies have shown that there are many challenges facing the African American population when it comes to international programs. I refer to those challenges as the "Three F's: Fear, Family and Funding."

Fear of the unknown. Just the thought of the word "foreign" takes on a whole new meaning when one speaks of international travel. Fear of not being able to communicate in another language, fear of not liking the food, and fear of being looked on as being different are just some of the concerns. Many families of minority students have never been exposed to travel abroad. Consequently, their concerns and fears are passed on to their children. Convincing families that international travel can be a valuable experience for students involves a considerable amount of time and effort. Additionally, most students at minority institutions encounter a lack of significant financial support for travel abroad. Thus, an enormous amount of time is spent securing funds to assist those students who are deserving but who cannot afford the expense of study abroad.

I tell everyone, that I have the best job in the world. It has given me the opportunity to visit countries that I have only read about. I have met incredible people who are just as curious about Americans as we are about them. However, aside from problems cited above, my real joy comes when students, faculty and staff become the beneficiaries of having traveled outside the United States and return, speaking another language, understanding another culture, looking to travel to another country the following year, and having developed an appreciation for another's quality of life

Barbara Crockett Moore, 2002-2008
22nd International Grand Basileus

The HBCU-Bane or Boon

I find questions regarding the relevance of Historically Black Colleges and Universities (HBCU) puzzling and confounding to say the least. I am further perplexed when African

Dr. Barbara Crockett Moore

Americans wonder out loud if HBCUs have outlived their mission and should be relegated to the educational junkyard. Inherent in discussions on the subject is the controversy of whether HBCUs can and should be "saved." It just seems that since HBCUs were the only place we could turn to long ago, that they deserve our respect and support.

I will admit, as a undergraduate of a striving HBCU and having worked at that institution of the past 40 years, I am biased. But that notwithstanding, I can offer unequivocal information on the importance and necessity of predominantly and historically black colleges and universities. I will not even dwell on the past glories of these institutions, except to remind that many have been in operation for close to 150 years, and that most of the people of color who are college graduates over the age of 70 graduated from one of them.

Let's talk about the current status of HBCUs. Their relevance is in the fact that the students who attend them are for the most part considered *persona non grata* or considered to not be college material by predominately white colleges and universities. Here at Benedict College, at which I serve as the Vice President for Institutional Advancement, we see countless numbers of young African American men and women come to us ill-prepared, but earn degrees, and leave as well-trained college graduates who enter the job market and compete admirably with others. What we see here at Benedict is no aberration; this same transformation happens in other HBCUs around the country.

It serves our nation well to produce contributing citizens, and it is far more economical to send a person to college for 4-5 years than to send them to prison for life. HBCUs must keep themselves on the cutting edge of educational innovations and teach students in majors that the workforce needs. Alumni and the corporate community, along with community friends, must also see that the country needs HBCUs as much as they were needed decades ago. **HBCUs are a BOON and never a BANE.**

ZETA DOVES

Introduction

Melissa J. Barnes

National Director for Zeta Doves
Diamond Life Member

Associate Degree: Secretarial Science – Paul D. Camp Community College
Bachelor of Science: Business Education, Norfolk State University
Master of Science: Urban Education, Norfolk State University
Doctoral Studies: Nova Southeastern University

As we Journey to our Centennial, our founding principles of Finer Womanhood, Sisterhood, Service, and Scholarship remind us of our rich heritage. Embedded in the heart of our principles is "Scholarship." Having the opportunity to share my vision of the Journey to Centennial through Scholarship should remind us to never waiver in scholastic and academic excellence. Throughout our childhood, we were taught the importance of maintaining good grades so that we could go to college and obtain the education that many of our forefathers were not privileged to do. While each of us was taught at an early age to foster good grades so we would have a better opportunity to a quality education, I believe our Founders believed that in the midst of the Great Depression, scholarship should be in the minds of every collegiate woman who desired to join Zeta. I also believe that our Founders wanted us to foster a legacy of scholarship by seeking women who believed that obtaining and maintaining a high scholastic average is as important today as it was during the 1920s. I believe our Founders would want each of us to provide scholarship opportunities to deserving women and men who seek Zeta as an avenue for assisting with the constant high and rising costs of a college education. As we Journey to our Centennial, let's touch the lives of those seeking our help by giving to our National Educational Foundation (NEF). Let us continue providing scholarships to honor the legacy and memory of members of our Sorority. And, let us remember that scholarship has a two-fold meaning: (1) Zetas seeking members who believe in our philosophy of maintaining high ideals of academic and scholastic achievement; and, (2) a membership that believes in giving back to support individuals seeking our assistance in achieving his or her educational endeavors. So as we "Journey to our Centennial through Scholarship," let us strive to embrace scholarship with the mindset that together we can help someone along life's journey.

As I presented this speech to Sorors during the Rededication Ceremony at the 71st Eastern Regional Leadership Conference in Charleston, West Virginia on March 5, 2016, I was grateful to our Founders who had the foresight to include "Scholarship" as one of our founding principles.

I am grateful to the National Educational Foundation for awarding me a scholarship as I began my doctoral studies. As scholars, we should all strive to uphold all principles of our organization and this includes supporting the efforts of the NEF.

Our Zeta Doves have submitted meaningful and heartfelt submissions for this Anthology. I invite you to sit in your most comfortable chair, sip some hot tea in your "royal blue and white cup" and enjoy what our Zeta Doves have to say! They discuss scholarship or answer the question, **"Why is Scholarship Important as a Principle of Zeta Phi Beta Sorority, Incorporated?"**

Marjay D. Anderson, Ph.D.

Diamond Life Member
Eastern Region
Bachelor of Science: Biology – Prairie View A. & M. University (TX)
Master of Science: Microbiology – Howard University
Doctor of Philosophy: Zoology/Physiology – Howard University

INFINITY

SCHOLARSHIP, knowledge, and wisdom form an intellectual continuum. The infinite nature of these maxims compel an interface of intelligence to prevail.

In a stanza of our national Sorority hymn, **PHI** is for scholarship . . . as **ZETA** is for zeal and **BETA** is for sisterly love. Hence, scholarship has always been a prominent precept of our Sorority. Scholarship presents a body of truth, of factual information, and empirical knowledge. Excellence in scholarship and scholastic endeavors have been hallmarks of our Sorority since its inception. Our Founders, in their eminent wisdom, recognized scholarship as a principle of innate value and as a basic fundamental cornerstone of the organization. It is scholarship that evokes the intellectual essence of being a Soror. And, their vision projected Zeta Sorors as exemplars of the highest personification of scholastic excellence. When was scholarship created? How has scholarship evolved?

Humanity, from the origins of the African ancestors, has always pursued learning as a means of enlightenment. Scholarship and intellectual prowess has represented a goal to be achieved by scholars in the ancient kingdoms. Historical analysis shows that these women and men were highly respected as they examined and recorded aspects of the natural world and explored the universe. Becoming even more sophisticated as the centuries progressed, scholastic bodies of knowledge in the creative and performing arts; the humanities; the natural, social, and technical sciences evolved and flourished. Scholars throughout time have explored the higher planes of esoteric, spiritual and philosophical thought. And, there continues to be a contemporary focus on scholarship.

Scholarship embraces the keys to excellence that include intelligence, initiative, integrity, ingenuity, innovation, and inquisitiveness. Strict, superlative academic standards provide links to pathways for success and achievement that further the cause of education. Scholarship may be accomplished on an individual level. However, scholarship is universal and transcends intercontinental, national, regional and local boundaries.

It is scholarship that empowers and energizes Sorority efforts to advance agendas that remove the obstacles that impede the improvement of the human condition. It is scholarship that launches the Sorority activism that is essential to the 21st Century involvement in leadership; cultural events; community outreach/service; economic, social, political actions; natural and health sciences strategies; corporate and government affairs; and educational progress. Missions of accomplishment continue to be documented. Scholarship, knowledge and wisdom are inextricably intertwined with infinite horizons. Strong infinite scholarship in Zeta is Strong infinite scholarship.

Marilyn A. Brooks

Diamond Life Member
Eastern Region
Bachelor of Arts Degree: French Education – Virginia Union University
Master of Arts Degree: Educational Administration and Supervision – Virginia Union University

The Preamble to the Constitution of Zeta Phi Beta Sorority, Incorporated states that one of the purposes for which we were founded is to promote the cause of education by encouraging the highest standards of scholarship through scientific, literary, cultural and educational programs.

Therefore, it is the duty of every member of this illustrious organization to try constantly to live up to the standards set before us. Grand Basileus Wolfe said that **Scholarship** implies love of knowledge and that it also indicates a **search** for truth and truth is the pathway to freedom. Therefore, Zeta's emphasis on scholarship demands:

"First, a **search** for **truth**, employing scientific methodology; second, an **objective attitude** which recognizes the ephemeral nature of man-discovered truths; third, **reflective thinking** which utilizes inductive and deductive reasoning; fourth, **flexibility** which demands acceptance of newly discovered facts; and, finally **humility** which admits that only God is omniscient."

This serves as a backdrop to better understand why after nearly one hundred years, Zeta Phi Beta Sorority has not strayed from this founding purpose. The Founders realized that there was much work that college educated women could do that would impact the entire world in perpetuating critical inquiry. It was true in 1920 and is still true today.

Critical inquiry suggests that one must reflect upon a situation, examine it and understand it. In the process, one gains wisdom. Webster defines wisdom as "The power to recognize the best ends and means to those ends." Though wisdom plays an integral part, it is not easily acquired. It is the result of hard work and a great deal of mental effort. Zeta sees the "best" ends as fulfilling our responsibility to humankind.

Clearly, obtaining and maintaining a high standard of scholastic excellence is not an easy task. It requires diligence, a quest for knowledge prompting us to want to know more and impart more to others.

Zeta Phi Beta Sorority seeks to attract women with a contagious thirst for knowledge and wisdom, and a willingness to build relationships to share information that will better all aspects of humankind.

As we approach the future with the many challenges that it brings, scholarship will continue to be prominent and necessary to for problem solving.

Beverly Cardoza

Atlantic Region
Bachelor of Science: Elementary Education – St. John's University (NY)
Master's Degree in Elementary Education – Rhode Island College (RI)
Master's in Special Education (Secondary Level) – Rhode Island College (RI)

It is a historical fact that black fraternities and sororities have inspired education and scholarship in our black children. From the beginning, the education of our black youth have been in the hands of the black community. When black colleges and universities started to spring up in American society, they took up the mantle of continuing the development of our youth's cognitive ability.

As time ticks on and we move towards a more technical and scientific future, it is imperative that the sororities, specifically Zeta Phi Beta Sorority, help women achieve a good education and secure their place in this modern society. Without education, the future will be bleak for them and opportunities will be limited. It is our duty as a sorority to help these young women reach their potential and obtain their academic goals.

Zeta Phi Beta Sorority has been mentoring women and focusing on education and scholarship since its beginning in 1920. Through visibility in the communities, it has advocated the need for learning in afterschool programs, churches, libraries and other avenues; education has been encouraged from the very young to the elderly. The Sorority has created many signature programs that are executed by the local chapters; teamed with other sororities and fraternities in sponsoring scholastic ventures; and joined other national organizations in fostering innovative methods of teaching and more modern educational facilities.

Our five Founders made it their mission to encourage young women to further their education on all scholastic levels, and the Sorority has continued that goal through scholarships on local, state, regional and national level. On a yearly basis and with fundraising efforts, local chapters have dispensed many scholarships to our female youth in different monetary denominations, from small book awards to full year tuition.

As we approach the Zeta Phi Beta Sorority Centennial in 2020, scholarship has to be one of our main focuses, pursued with vigor and diligence. This is necessary for our black youth, especially black women, to succeed in life and excel in the 21nd Century. Education is the gateway to the future and scholarship must be our mantra.

Frances Faithful

Diamond Life Member
Great Lakes Region
Bachelor's Degree: Elementary Education – Central State University

Scholarship is important as a principle of Zeta Phi Beta Sorority, Inc. because as a minority, it is a necessity to attend college to compete in the professional world. Due to financial hardships, some of us are only able to attend college on various scholarships obtained through scholastic and athletic achievements. Therefore, by taking education seriously we can receive scholarships to assist us in furthering our education, thus allowing us greater opportunities once a degree is obtained.

Jeanette W. Giles-Fleming

Southeastern Region
Bachelor of Arts Degree: English/Reading Grades 6-12 – Claflin University (1962)

From the onset, I am very proud and honored to have been a member Zeta Phi Beta Sorority, Inc. for 50 years. I am thrilled to have become a Dove! I pledged at Claflin University, Orangeburg, South Carolina in 1960.

The principle of Scholarship, the quality of knowledge and learning by a student, is the most important principle of Zeta Phi Beta Sorority because it is vital to preparing young people for living a good and wholesome life. Scholarship is an important element in obtaining a good education, which is the key to living a good life. This statement's validity today is more evident than any other era in the past. With the booming changes in the facets of education, students must be prepared to meet the challenges brought forth by these changes. **Scholarship**, along with Service, Sisterly Love, and Finer Womanhood, happens to be listed as the **first** Zeta principle. Our beloved Founders, in 1920, had an idea to reach college women in all parts of the country, including South Africa and Europe. These women had to be sorority-minded and have a desire to follow the four principles listed above.

As far as scholarship serving as a basis for our Sorority's principles, it also upholds values and goals that lead to excellence. A fine Zeta woman exemplifies such values as honesty, integrity, fairness, trustworthiness, and hard work. Zeta women have learned to treat people with respect and dignity, as well as recognize the strength of our differences, which is mandatory in the global and diverse world we live in today. As far as the Sorority goes by possessing these traits, a Zeta woman learns and practices gratitude, responsibility, and integrity, and an appreciation for her sisters, as she leads, governs, and/or interacts with them. It helps in establishing an atmosphere of mutual respect, shared caring, and professional ethics, which leads to productivity among our sisters. This surely leads to better communication and cooperation, when initiating and working on projects, services, and assignments. Zetas are always striving for excellence in whatever they do! When ZETA calls, we answer!

So, even though Service, Sisterly Love, and Finer Womanhood are important principles for Zeta women, **Scholarship**, I feel, is the most important because it serves as the catalyst for the other three.

One mandate of our Sorority is that all candidates hold a college degree or some formal educational background. This is an incentive to young women to raise their expectations for high averages, which leads to better scholarship, and reaching their goals of completing college. A good education is a "must have" in today's world. When young people strive for higher scholarship, they are better prepared to finish college, go out into the communities of the world, and make them better.

Many of the Zeta chapters around the country give scholarships to deserving graduates in our schools and universities. This service has proven to uplift students, who otherwise might not be able to attend college. Scholarship serves as a great incentive to boosting interest in higher education, and therefore, should be "first" on Zeta's list of principles!

Marian Anderson Hairston

Diamond Life Member
Eastern Region
Undergraduate Degree: Elementary Education; Bachelor of Science – Winston-Salem
State University (1964)
Graduate Degree: Early Childhood Education; Bachelor of Arts – Appalachian State
University (1986)

This country's existence since its beginning has been characterized by a thirst for knowledge. Our independence from England
was made possible through a group of Founding Fathers who
were scholars in their own right. The establishment of early
communities and cities included an educational component that
was steeped in our culture. Since the earliest colonial days, families have sacrificed to provide schools for children.

A primary mission of Zeta Phi Beta Sorority has been service
to communities. Service requires leadership; and leadership involves commitment as role
models. Scholarship is woven into the fabric of our cities and communities. It helps us work
with parents, children, teenagers, and young adults through their college years and beyond.

Levels of education are extremely important to carry out many of the Sorority's national
objectives. Exposing children at early ages to the sciences and mathematics prepares them
to be stewards in protecting the world's physical environment. A strong liberal arts education provides a sound foundation for developing leadership skills. It is, therefore extremely
important that children are exposed to technological advances by scholarly instructors.

World peace is promoted by an understanding of different cultures. One must be scholarly
to the extent that he/she is able to effectively interact with people within their particular culture. Zetas taking leadership roles in providing tutorial programs and scholarship funds will
develop this caliber of future leaders.

Dr. Lena Colquitte Harris

Southeastern Region
Bachelor's Degree: Elementary Education – Clark Atlanta
Master's Degree: Learning Disabilities – Atlanta University
Specialist: Interrelated Special Education – Clark Atlanta
Doctorate: Educational Leadership – Clark Atlanta

"A Quest for a College Education"

"I'll study and get ready and perhaps my chance will come." This quote by Johnathan Logan Seagull has been one of my guiding principles in my quest for knowledge. A good education was my primary goal in my lifetime. It did not make any difference which college I attended, I only wanted to build a good future for myself and make my mark in our society by helping others.

I was born the third child in a family of six children being raised by a single parent. My mother was a hardworking parent who struggled to support me and my siblings. However, she continued to instill in me and my siblings the value of a college education. She was never too tired to look at and check homework or ask about our school day. Therefore, I worked very hard in school to keep up my good grades, knowing that I had opportunities that my mother never had.

My life has been a struggle at time but my hard work, determination, and enthusiasm, for my education and my community landed me at Clark College in 1970, where my I pursued my dreams.

During my quest for a college education, I applied to many different historical black colleges. I already knew that I was going to become a teacher. I had practiced teaching on my younger siblings during our early years at play. Each day when I returned from school, I would teach my siblings what I had been taught in school that day. When my siblings enrolled in school, they went to school not with a blank slate but with many of the basics ingrained in their minds.

My graduation from Clark College prepared me for many teaching jobs in the Atlanta Public School District. After teaching for many years and refining methods, I decided to further my knowledge base by enrolling in the master's program at Atlanta University. Due to the severe deficits in the academic preparation of my students, I decided to study for a degree in Specific Learning Disabilities. I felt that this knowledge would help me to help the students that I taught.

My degree of Special Education Learning Disabilities was conferred May of 1982. I did not stop learning at this point. The degree of Specialist in Education was conferred in June of

1990 and the Doctor of Education in Leadership was conferred June 1997, from Clark Atlanta University. Since that time, I have added educational endorsements in Reading Instruction, Gifted Education, On-Line-Teaching Instruction, and ESOL Instruction.

I have given back to my school community forty–two years of service to the students in the Atlanta Public Schools at the elementary, middle and high school levels to ensure their school success.

I am now semi-retired. Occasionally, I do substitute teaching. I come across many of my former students who have completed college themselves. It gives me great pleasure when I am told by my former students how I motivated them to strive for an education and become successful contributing adults.

Grace Houchins

Life Member
Eastern Region
Bachelor's Degree: Education – Norfolk State College
Further studies in Education – University of Virginia
Further studies in Theology – Virginia University

Scholarship endorses and encourages young people to pursue a "higher education." Zeta Phi Beta awards such scholarships to worthy recipients regularly.

Even more mature students, gain success by awards and grants provided as scholarships. Scholarship, as financial aid or support to students according to academic merit, is one way that Zeta Phi Beta promotes personal growth and development in scholastic endeavors; but our "Fine" organization seeks more ways to define needs. We are community and "human growth" minded.

Scholarship and charity is "second nature" to Zeta Phi Beta Sorority, Incorporated. We take great pride in developing and creating the means to contribute to scholarship.

Let me take this time to applaud my Sisterhood – Zeta Phi Beta; for stepping up to the challenge.

Issie L. Jenkins, Esq.

Atlantic Region
Law and Government
Artium Baccalaureus: Indiana University
Juris Doctor: Boston University School of Law
LL.M. (Master of Laws): George Washington University Law School

All of Zeta's principles are important, but scholarship deserves particular emphasis. When Zeta was founded in 1920, its community of interest was primarily educators that focused on education and scholarship as an important means of upward mobility, and an avenue for achieving opportunities. Zeta members have a reputation as being "smart women."

Although the achievements of Zeta women have expanded to include many career paths, the avenue to this achievement has been based primarily on education and excellence in scholarship. It remains important in the 21st Century for Zeta to continue upholding and supporting its founding principle of scholarship. Now more than ever, education is necessary to achieve the standard of living most U.S. citizens wish for, and the cost of that education is increasingly becoming beyond the reach of many Americans, particularly in the minority community.

Scholarships provided by chapters help to meet the needs of students seeking higher education. Awarding scholarship support to students is an important part of community service.

In 1975, Zeta saw a need to place greater emphasis on its principle of scholarship by establishing the National Educational Foundation to carry out its national scholarship mission, and by designating a portion of annual chapter tax funds to be contributed to its National Educational Foundation to support annual scholarship awards. The support of the Sorority, chapters, states, regions, and individual sorors, has made it possible for the Zeta Phi Beta Sorority National Educational Foundation, Incorporated (NEF), to financially support students seeking higher education at the undergraduate and graduate levels.

Life members of Zeta have recognized the importance of scholarship funding. In past years, this group of dedicated Sorors have made significant contributions to the Foundation's endowment fund. I am reminded of Soror Mary Ann Tillman, who has consistently contributed to NEF scholarship funds; of Soror Dorothy Perrault's fundraising efforts in establishing a perpetual endowment fund in the Foundation; of 23rd International Grand Basileus Sheryl Underwood, contributor of valuable goods for Foundation fundraising auctions and financial contributions; of 21st International Grand Basileus Barbara West Carpenter, establishing a funded scholarship in in honor of her mother; and, of Sorors who remembered NEF in their wills, leaving funds to support Zeta scholarships.

The emphasis on scholarship has been a primary focus in Zeta regions and state organizations. Regional Directors have played a pivotal role in encouraging contributions to fund the NEF endowment fund, and initiating fund raising projects for NEF. As an example, during her tenure as the Atlantic Regional Director, Soror Jacqueline McNair, initiated a fund raising project for the endowment fund that provided significant funds.

On a personal note, I am a recipient of a Zeta scholarship, both at the undergraduate and graduate level. My commitment to and support of Zeta's principle of scholarship are based on first-hand knowledge of how scholarship funds can make the difference in successfully achieving an individual's education and professional goals. As a former Chairman of the NEF Board of Managers, I am keenly aware that Zeta serves in encouraging scholastic attainment. They represent contributions to one of the highest needs in our communities.

Geraldine Johnson

Atlantic Region
Bachelor of Arts, Virginia Union
Master of Arts, Fairleigh Dickinson University

In August 1965, I became the happiest person in the world. I was inducted in Zeta Phi Beta Sorority, Inc. I was inspired to join because Zeta was an organization composed of college women representing a variety of professions, interest, and talents. They were women who exemplified Finer Womanhood. They conducted many activities and projects within the community to improve human conditions.

At my first meeting, I was asked to say the opening prayer alone. I was proud to do the honor. The Sorors nurtured me and impressed upon us that good behavior was key to being a finer woman. They stressed that when we were in public we represented Zeta Phi Beta Sorority, Inc. This made me aware that being a Zeta was serious business and doing things in a derogatory manner was a reflection on the Sorority. Listening to the Sorors have made me a better Zeta.

In 1980, I was appointed the eighth New Jersey State Director. We had five graduate chapters and seven undergraduate chapters at the time. The chapters were only paying a minimal amount of dues and Sorors were paying nothing to the State of New Jersey. My chapter started a Career Day and partnered with South Chapter of the Continental Societies, Inc. and South Jersey Links, Inc. I was chairperson of Career Day. One day when I was in the post office to mail letters inviting the presenters to participate, the postmaster was waiting on me. She looked at the return address with Zeta Phi Beta Sorority on it and asked me what kind of organization this was. I told her about the history of Zeta. Her response to me was this, "I have never heard of this organization in my life. I only heard of the AKA and Delta sororities. Your group better put out more publicity if you want people to know what you are doing." This bothered me because I knew Zeta Phi Beta at one time was the only Sorority in southern Jersey. I pondered over what we could do to make the public aware that we were here and doing outstanding community work. As I agonized on this situation, a thought came to me. We should celebrate Founders' Day at a church of each Soror all over the State of New Jersey. I presented it to the Zeta Phi Beta New Jersey State Executive Board and they approved it. At the leadership conference we presented it and the Body approved the suggestion. During my tenure, we met at various churches and attendance was about 100 Sorors at each celebration. We donated about $500 for scholarships. After the church service, we had lunch in the fellowship hall. We continued in this manner until it was too large.

I have been an active member of Zeta Phi Beta Sorority, Inc. for over fifty years. I have attended most conferences, Boulé, Atlantic Regional and New Jersey State Leadership, and I attend all of my chapter's meetings. I was State Tamias Grammateus and Tamias, and worked on many committees, at the national level. I have worked as a recorder for workshops and debates. I love Zeta and I am proud to be one.

Dr. E. Fran Johnson

Life Member
Atlantic Region
Bachelor of Arts: Sociology and Psychology, Morgan State University
Master of Social Work: Administration and Case Work, Howard University
Doctor of Social Work: Social Psychology, Catholic University of America
Juris Doctorate: University of Maryland

My mother did not have a formal education. She went to night school. But she was streetwise and talked from her experience as a domestic worker. These are a few sayings I heard her repeat over and over that were educational and made scholarly sense to me. Although she passed years ago, sometimes I hear her speaking them to me.

- If it's a problem, it has a solution; if there's no solution, it's a fact, and you learn to live with it.
- Always have something to look forward to.
- Good manners will take you where money won't, so always say please and thank you.
- It takes less muscles to smile than it does to frown, so smile and help someone.
- Never spend more than you earn.
- Don't fight with your hands; fight with your brains. (I had a tendency to fight to make a point.)
- Being right is not always the best thing; sometimes being kind may be more victorious.
- There's nothing bad about being wrong. It is bad when you do not accept responsibility for being wrong.

Maryella Ward Leigh

Life Member
Eastern Region
Bachelor of Science: Business Education – Elizabeth City State University 1967
Certificate: Special Education – North Carolina State University 1972
Master of Science: Computer Technology – Grand Canyon University 2008
Certificate: Vocational Education Director Appalachian State University 2010

Scholarship is important as a principle of Zeta Phi Beta Sorority, Inc. because we live it. As a Sorority, we are real about being honest, about what we say and what we do. We try to expose our members to different helpful resources that will make life for them more meaningful. We actively encourage good communications among our sisters so that we can share and present our ideas to each other to develop more effective living habits.

We believe in encouraging our young Sorority sisters to acquire academics and good study achievement. We work with them closely in all areas of their lives and we try to promote healthy and wholesome thoughts. We try to make sure that they seek involvement in knowledge through merit and leadership.

Certainly goals should come into play when we pursue good scholarship. As I see it:

- Goal #1 should be SUCCESS: Success does not come fast, neither does it come cheap, but if we are committed to its pursuit and keep the faith, I believe that the door will lead us to a place of promise and real success. The journey might be rough, but the destination is what matters.
- Goal #2 should be SALVATION: Education does not equal salvation. Don't get me wrong, education is important. However without morals such as respect for others and honesty, we will not really succeed in scholarship.
- Goal #3 should be ACCOUNTABILITY: One must be accountable to something or someone. As I see it, we should be accountable to God, our family, our Sorors and mankind. One must be willing to protect the Soror's virtue and reputation. So many times we find that Sorors will join in with others who are defaming and ridiculing their sisters. I find that they don't take the time to listen or give the undergraduates a chance. They refuse to work with them on new or youthful projects.

These thoughts come from my heart and my mind as a Zeta product of 51 years. In those 50 plus years, I have seen a lot; learned a lot, experienced ups and downs and most of all, I have had the Zeta experience!

Finally, in closing, I am reminded of words I chanted over 50 years ago and they still ring loud and meaningful in my ears today.

Dr. Joanne Henry Lottie

Life Member
Doctor of French Humanities – Clark Atlanta University, Atlanta, Georgia, 1994
Master of Arts: French – Atlanta University, Atlanta, Georgia, 1968
Bachelor of Arts: French – Clark College, Atlanta, Georgia, 1966
30 quarter hours in English and Leadership, Georgia State University, Atlanta, Georgia. 1996

"If You Study and Get Ready, One Day Your Chance Will Come"

– Dr. Joanne Lottie

Growing up was not a bed of roses, but my mother would always say wonderful, encouraging words to me from age one until the day she went to be with the Lord. She would say, "Joanne, Get up! Get out there in the world. Keep a smile on your face, be nice, get an education and be the very best you can be." My mother knew the value of an education and reminded me to study daily.

At five years of age, I used to sit on my grandmother's outside steps, pass out torn sheets of paper and broken pencils and teach my cousins or whoever would listen, how to write, spell and speak correctly. I knew I wanted to be a teacher. At age six, my mother taught me how to tell time and I taught my brother, sisters, cousins and anyone else who would listen, how to tell time.

In elementary school, kids called me "Proper Talking" Joanne" because I spoke the "King's" or correct English when other kids were using slang and the neighborhood jargon. I loved speaking correctly. In high school, I observed all and listened well and became my home-room teacher's secretary. I earned A's in trigonometry, geometry and French and played the viola. My peers looked up to me; I worked so hard. After high school, off to Clark College I went with low SAT scores, yet good grades.

I was the first in my family to go to college. Some said I would only get to the college door, but not complete it. I had to prove them wrong because I could not let my mother down. My mother visited me during freshman orientation week and then wrote me a letter telling me to "If you study and get ready, one day your chance will come, baby." I excelled at Clark and when I pledged Zeta Phi Beta Sorority, I became the "smart girl" on campus. I was never late, always did my homework, and set the standard for what a college girl should be. I was in the national French Honor Society, the Top Ten, and *Who's Who* in American Colleges and Universities. I was a scholarly Zeta woman.

I completed my baccalaureate degree in French secondary education; a master's degree in French literature; and, earned a Ph.D. in French Humanities. I became the first African American woman to become principal of an International School and first African American director of the English as a Second Language Program for the DeKalb County School System.

My mother's words reverberate in my ears still and now grandchildren, nieces, nephews, cousins, neighborhood kids, newly inducted Zetas, or anyone. "If you study and get ready, one day your chance will come."

Dr. Kathryn T. Malvern

Atlantic Region
Bachelor's Degree: Howard University (DC)
Master's Degree: University of Southern California (CA)
Doctoral Degree: Rutgers University (NJ)

It is indeed my special and complete pleasure, as a Zeta Dove, to provide my perspective regarding scholarship, Zeta's awesome programmatic thrust since 1920. The Zeta Phi Beta Sorority, Inc. Constitution states: Zeta Phi Beta Sorority, Incorporated shall have as its objectives: The fostering of ideals of Service, Charity, **Scholarship**, Civic and Cultural Endeavors, Sisterhood and Finer Womanhood.

Having served in leadership at all levels including Zeta Delta Zeta Chapter Basileus, New Jersey State Director, Atlantic Regional Director, Chairman of Regional Directors, and Chairman of the National Educational Foundation, Inc., from 2000-2014, I can provide some information at those levels.

Zeta Delta Zeta Chapter has provided thousands of scholarship dollars, as well as community service throughout the Burlington County community since receiving its charter, on June 22, 1959. Zeta Delta Zeta maintains a strong presence within the Burlington County Community through outstanding scholarship awards to students attending college. The Chapter has named scholarships: the Soror Clara Bennett, the Estelle Rice and the Glenda Wilson Scholarships. Over the years Zeta Delta Zeta has provided successful fundraising programs.

A real plus was the participation of a Founder and Past Grand Basilei in our chapter's programs. Founder Arizona Cleaver Stemons lived nearby in Philadelphia and attended many of our scholarship functions. She would not allow us to pick her up at her home but took the bus, saying, "I can catch the bus right in front of my house." I would always pick her up at the bus station in Mt. Laurel and return her there after the programs were over and all pictures had been taken We also had Dr. Deborah P. Wolfe, 14th Grand Basileus, and Dr. Edith V. Francis, 18th Grand Basileus, who lived nearby and attended and participated in many of our scholarship programs and celebrations. These are just a very few of the attributes of Zeta Delta Zeta Chapter, all because of Strong Leadership, with Sorors who believe in their leaders and have the same visions for successfully reaching the Zeta Mission in general, and building Scholarship in particular.

Yes, Zeta Delta Zeta's scholarship awarding has grown tremendously over the 57 years of existence, due to its "High Energy" Scholarship Programmatic Thrust that the community looked forward to and supported.

Myrthe Francois McClain

Pacific Region
Bachelor's Degree in Education: Dillard University (1958)
Master's Degree in Education Psychology: University of Southern California (1975)
Worked as an Elementary School Teacher - 1958 -1976
Worked as a School psychologist 1976 -1996
Retired in June 1996

I was reared in New Orleans, LA during segregation. My parents had ten children and money to attend college did not come easily. I am one of four sisters and three of us earned our degrees from Dillard University. My family has always placed a premium on education. One of my brothers earned his degree in Santa Barbara, CA. The others worked hard and earned their education while doing military service.

Scholarship is the most important principle of Zeta Phi Beta Sorority. When I think about Scholarship, I think of such statements as, "Once you get your education, no one can take it from you," and "It's not how you look on the outside, but what's on the inside, your character and knowledge."

I also think about how fortunate it is to use education as a key to follow one's dreams and succeed in life. There are many who are not allowed to study or have no opportunity to do so. I am so very proud of my Sorority, Zeta Phi Beta. We have so many highly educated and capable members in all professions. I am also very proud that we give to help others to continue in their education. I thank God for our Founders and our Sorority.

Edna Metoyer

Life Member
Great Lakes Region
Bachelor of Science: Biology (Minor: Chemistry and Psychology) – Virginia
Commonwealth University
Post Graduate Studies: University of Saint Francis

Scholarship is very important to Zeta Phi Beta Sorority, Inc. Scholarships are awards for a student to further his or her education and are usually based upon various criteria. Scholarships are usually awarded and do not have to be repaid. The student usually receives a scholarship based on academic or athletic ability, or for agreeing to follow a particular career path. Scholarships are not only given for financial need alone.

We need to encourage young ladies about the importance of learning and what the future holds for them when they can excel. Let them know when their learning and grades can qualify them for a scholarships no matter what their area of choice is. Zeta Phi Beta Sorority, Inc. offers scholarships to those young ladies who apply and meet the criteria of the organization on the local, state, regional and national levels. These scholarships typically are less competitive and can be another means for young ladies who are interested in becoming a member of Zeta Phi Beta Sorority, Inc.

I received a scholarship my entire four years at Virginia Union University in Richmond, Virginia and majored in biology with a minor in chemistry and psychology. I became a medical technologist and certified (ASCP) after attending the Medical College of Virginia. I am also an alumnus of Virginia Commonwealth University. I did postgraduate studies at the University of Saint Francis. I retired after thirty years as a medical technologist. Getting good grades and receiving a scholarship relieves the need for having to repay too much in loans if the scholarship doesn't meet your total need. Always strive for a scholarship.

Lizzie Gilliam Miller

Great Lakes Region
Bachelor's Degree: Education – Louisville Municipal College
Further Education at Simmons Bible College – Bible Studies

To my beloved Sorors of Zeta Phi Beta Sorority, I am proud to be a member of Zeta Phi Beta Sorority for more than seventy years. I began as an undergraduate student at the Louisville Municipal College (the University of Louisville) and earned a Bachelor's degree in education. I later attended the Simmons Bible College in Kentucky and completed one year as a student of the Bible. I was reared in a very religious family of teachers and ministers in Mississippi, a prejudiced state, not only from the white population, but from some of the black successful teachers and upper-class community leaders, who felt that they were a part of an "upper class of society" community. I encourage those Sorors who have been the recipients of a Zeta Phi Beta Sorority scholarships to be forever blessed to be a part of an organization that will assist those who have the attributes of a virtuous woman. Scholarship is a principle on which our beloved Founders stood for. It was not the color of your skin, or who your parents were, or where you lived that defined you, but what your commitment to an organization exemplified.

It is important when applying for employment after completing your educational goals, to have an organization such as Zeta Phi Beta Sorority, to be on your resume as an active and supportive member of a worldwide organization that is recognized for its generosity to all mankind regardless of race, color, creed or culture.

I sincerely believe that Scholarship is the most important principle of Zeta Phi Beta Sorority. It is important because I am from a very proud family and I can remember that when I needed help because of the illness of my father, and my older brother was in the Army, my second brother saw the need to withdraw from high school in the 11th grade to get a job to support our family. My mother was unhappy, but grateful. I would have quit college to go to work also, but one of our church members Frances Halsell was a Zeta and she asked the graduate chapter to give me a scholarship of $25.00 so that I could complete my senior year and become gainfully employed.

I am from a very proud independent family, and no one but the members of the graduate chapter knew the state that I was in. The scholarship afforded me the opportunity to graduate with dignity and honor from the University of Louisville. It was an honor to be a member of the last segregated class at that university.

I am still a very, very personal person who is grateful for the doors and opportunities that were opened to me from the members of the graduate chapter, Eta Zeta Chapter. The Great Lakes Region and the national leaders saw my potential and appointed me to positions in which I could "reach out and touch those who were less fortunate than me" through Scholarship and Sisterly Love. My favorite song is "May the work that I have done speak for me. May the life I live speak for me. For when I am resting in my grave, there is nothing more that can be said. May the work I have done speak for me." And for this, I remain eternally grateful to Zeta for giving me the opportunity to complete my education and represent my organization with dignity and admiration for our beloved Founders.

Dr. Bettina M. Scott

Atlantic Region
Associate of Arts Degree: Baltimore Community College
Bachelor of Science Degree in Education: Towson State University
Master of Arts Degree in History: Morgan State University
Doctor of Philosophy Degree in Education: University of Maryland - College Park
Master of Divinity Degree: Howard University School of Divinity
Master of Arts in Pastoral Care: Loyola University Maryland

Scholarship is the most important principle of Zeta Phi Beta Sorority, Inc. because scholarship is the foundation of who we are as a sisterhood and an organization. Scholarship as defined by the dictionary means learning, acquiring knowledge through academic pursuit but to Zeta it is that and more. Through the years on campuses across the country, Zetas were known to be scholars, young women serious about studying to show themselves approved. Many campuses gave awards to the Greek-letter organizations whose members attained the highest academic average and Zeta Phi Beta Sorority won these awards more often than any other Pan-Hellenic organization. But that was just the beginning.

What our Founders knew was that scholarship was not just a school or university attribute but training for a life of scholarship and the pursuit of knowledge. College and university educational experiences prepare students with the basics and life provides the long-term experiences of learning. Zeta Phi Beta Sorority has been able to grow and evolve in its other principles because we are in constant pursuit of knowledge that will assist us in understanding more about human nature and how we can know, understand, and work more harmoniously with our members to achieve greater success. The constant pursuit of knowledge has led us to the understanding that we can be finer as we look to stand out as smart, competent, well dressed, beautiful (inside and out) women of service to our various communities.

This pursuit of knowledge has allowed us to progress to more involved and more complicated service to the community through our partnerships with AARP and Elder Care, St. Jude Hospital, the National Park Service, and the service quests that speak to the many facets and intricacies of modern society. There are many aspects that could not have even been conceived of by our Founders 96 years ago but their understanding of scholarship and the need for our Sorors to be perpetual scholars has served the sisterhood well and catapulted us into the 21st Century on top of our game.

Brenda R. (Gibson) Reed

Life Member
Great Lakes Region
Bachelor of Science, Business Administration, Detroit College of Business
Master of Arts, Guidance and Counseling, University of Detroit

Scholarship is important because of our focus on education. Our National Educational Foundation has numerous scholarships named for influential Zetas.

The Great Lakes Region has the Soror Ione Hartley Gibson Scholarship and the Soror Ida B. King Scholarship. The State of Michigan awards scholarships in the name of Past Michigan State Directors. Kappa Rho Zeta Chapter awards scholarships in the name of Ione H. Gibson, organizer and Basileus Emeritus of KPZ; a book award in the name of Soror Barbara Warren, a teacher in the Detroit Public Schools; and, Soror Thelma Everett, a teacher in the Highland Park Public Schools and graduate of Wiley College.

In the State of Wisconsin, Kappa Beta Zeta Chapter awards a scholarships in the name of Soror Bernice Bynum who taught in the Milwaukee Public Schools.

Sigma Alpha Zeta Chapter in Wisconsin, the chapter I organized and chartered at Boulé 2000, awards a scholarship in the name of Soror Yolanda Jones one of the charter members who lived in Sturtevant, WI where our chapter was chartered. I served as Basileus of SAZ for 10 years and the title of Basileus Emeritus was bestowed upon me by my Sorors in 2007.

Mary S. Simpson

Great Lakes Region
Bachelor of Arts Degree: Hunter College

The word scholarship is most important because it means the character, qualities, activities or attainments of a scholar. This word or principle encompasses the other three principles or objectives of Zeta Phi Beta Sorority, Inc. which are Finer Womanhood (good character and qualities), Service (activities in the community) and Sisterhood (a solidarity of women based on shared conditions, experiences or concerns).

When one is a scholar, oftentimes one is blessed to get scholarships to help pay for one's education. However, if one does not get scholarships, she can work to help pay for courses and/or her parent(s) can pay or she can apply for grants or loans.

To be a person who is scholarly is a blessing as she is serious about obtaining a quality college education.

Laura M.A. Smith

Great Lakes Region
Bachelor's Degree: Jackson State University (formerly Jackson College)
Master of Science in Education: Indiana University
Vocational License: Home Economics – Alcorn College

Thank God that Zeta Phi Beta is still giving scholarship awards. I won a $100 scholarship award in 1948 from Lambda Beta Chapter of Zeta Phi Beta. This scholarship was very helpful to me because it paid for my tuition for one year at Jackson College (Jackson, Mississippi). Keep up the good work up because every scholarship given is a blessing for the student who receives it.

Patricia K. Thomas

Atlantic Region
Bachelor of Science: Home Economics/General Science – Virginia State College
(Virginia State University)
Certification: Elementary Education – Kean University

Through the years, the criteria for receiving a scholarship has changed. Scholarships once implied a form of financial aid based highly on economics and ethnicity. However, that precedence is no longer the protocol. Most scholarships today are based on merit, talent and sports ability. Additionally, the persons giving the award establish the value, purpose and the recipient of the award. Today's scholarships use a small competitive field that does not include those who do not meet the redesigned guidelines.

Where does that leave the student who is not a Rhodes Scholar, talented student, or the star on the team? It leaves independent non-profit organization offering scholarship assistance, namely, one of the Divine Nine, Zeta Phi Beta Sorority. If not us whom? We still are the pathway to educational pursuit, achievement and success.

The Library Card

Pearl W. Thompson
as told to Doris McAdams Stokes

A library card is such a small thing, but receiving one in July 2015 made a big difference in the life of Soror Pearl Wortham Thompson. Born in 1923 in North Carolina, Pearl's father died eight days after her sixth birthday and her mother struggled to support her four children. Pearl, the oldest child, was an intelligent, outgoing and determined student who graduated from Washington High School in Raleigh, a school that had been established for black students only. Like so many other African Americans at the time, she was subjected to Jim Crow era laws which meant segregation reigned and determined where people of color could live, attend school and access public facilities.

In 1942, Pearl enrolled in Shaw University in Raleigh and studied to become a teacher. The university, chartered in 1865, was established specifically for African American students. Many attended it believing that education was the foundation of a better life. Becoming a teacher was a logical path to being an employed professional woman as only black teachers could work in black schools.

Assigned to write a paper for one of her classes, Pearl began her research at Raleigh's sole library for blacks that had just been established in 1935. It was located in a dilapidated white wood house on Hargett Street. Shelves had been added for the used, castoff books they held yet the black community treasured them all and visited the library regularly. Unable to find the book she needed for her paper, Pearl decided to visit the Olivia Raney Public Library, for whites.

At almost 6 feet tall, Pearl Thompson was always the tallest Soror in a photograph.
She is standing, in the center during Omicron Zeta's (Raleigh, NC) Finer Womanhood program in
1950. Soror Gwendolyn Larkin Holloway is seated first on the left and
Soror Doris Larkin McAdams is standing, last on the right.

From behind the behind the counter, the librarian wasted no time in telling her, "You are in the wrong place. This is a white library." She further informed Pearl that could not check out books because she would not be issued a card. Undeterred, Pearl told her she was writing a paper and she just needed to read a specific book that was not at the black library. Sent back outside, Pearl had to re-enter the library through the basement. After waiting for hours, in the dusty basement used for storage and sitting on a box, she was finally brought the book which she read in near darkness. Determined to complete her research, Pearl took notes. She finished her paper and put the entire incident behind her.

After graduating from Shaw, Pearl taught school in Raleigh's segregated schools for 12 years. She married and moved to Cincinnati, Ohio in 1957. She integrated an all-white staff at Hyde Park Elementary School and successfully taught there for over 30 years. But, she never could forget that incident and the denied library card, even after retirement.

In 2015, Pearl returned to Raleigh with her daughter and granddaughter, to visit and reminiscence "at home." There were just five places she wanted to visit and one of them was the library. At 92 years old, she still remembered the incident and the library card that had been denied to her decades ago. Although the both libraries, the one for blacks and the Olivia Raney Library had been demolished many years earlier, she stopped by the Cameron Village Regional Library and could not resist telling the staff there her story. Determined to make amends, the deputy director of the Wake County libraries issued a card to her on the spot, albeit 73 years later. Pearl became an instant celebrity appearing on the front page of newspapers across the U.S. and featured in television news stories around the world. Her telephone rang for weeks with requests for interviews.

Pearl Wortham Thompson became a member of Zeta Phi Beta Sorority, Inc. at Shaw University's Omicron Chapter. She was active with Omicron Zeta Chapter (Raleigh) and Beta Zeta Zeta Chapter (Cincinnati). Soror Thompson currently resides in a retirement facility and recounts her story to all who will listen.

UPHOLDING THE LEGACY

Scholarship,
My "KEY" to Success

Ramona Collins

Clara Tolliver Taylor, my grandmother, the sixteenth of eighteen children born to slaves, worked in the cotton fields to take care of her ten children until she became a cook at the local middle school. At the age of 54 she decided to complete her education and obtain her GED.   She loved the outdoors and could identify every type of tree, leaf, insect, bird and animal. She was a natural teacher, counselor, and healer and was always willing to share her knowledge with others. In 2004 she received a Legacy of Achievement Award from the State of Louisiana recognizing her as the oldest working employee in the state. At age 93, she continued to work until February 2007, one month before she passed. SCHOLARSHIP!

Ruby James Fields, my aunt/2nd mother, was a lover of nature who enjoyed all the beauty that nature had to offer. She loved education and knew that "a mind was a terrible thing to waste." She was devoted to teaching and inspired young people to open their minds and be flooded with knowledge. She graduated valedictorian from her high school and was the first female to receive a bachelor's degree in chemistry at Grambling State University.   She went on to receive a Master of Science degree, and Educational Specialist certification while teaching high school biology and chemistry until her death. SCHOLARSHIP!

Courtne S. Collins, my daughter, though extremely shy, was always a very smart and bright student. After high school, she continued her education at the University of Central

Oklahoma obtaining a bachelor's degree in marketing with a minor in business law. She later decided to further her education by seeking a master's degree in hospital management from Texas Southern University. Upon completion of her degree with honors, she decided to join the United States Navy as an officer. Stationed in Okinawa, Japan, she is now a Medical Regulating and Control Officer for Fleet Surgical Team 7 where she supervises 14 people. SCHOLARSHIP!

Jourdan S. Brown, my daughter, learned to read before the age of three. Jourdan has always excelled in her education. Graduating a year ahead of her peers, she was in the top 1% of her senior class. With a 4.58 GPA, her near perfect score on the ACT and high SAT score qualified her as a national merit finalist and African American Achievement Scholar. Jourdan was admitted to thirteen colleges with eight full scholarships. She also received numerous other national and local scholarships. She is currently a junior at Rice University where she received a full academic scholarship. Majoring in biological sciences, she will continue her education through medical school in hopes of becoming a pediatrician. SCHOLARSHIP!

Scholarship is a concept that is dear and near to me. I have had several positive influences in my life which all encouraged me to excel in education. My grandmother always encouraged me to go to school and get an education because "Education is the key and without the key, you can't get into the door." Growing up with a family of educators (my mom was an elementary school teacher for 38 years and most of my aunts and uncles were educators), I often found myself focusing on education more than the average person. During my early years, I participated in high ability and math and science programs each summer at Grambling State University. After completing high school, I enrolled at Southern University and A&M College on a Naval ROTC scholarship, hoping to become a naval officer. During the course of my studies, I sometimes found myself wanting to change my path and not continue school, but I always thought back to the words of my grandmother. I knew I wanted and needed my key. I wanted what was inside that door. That was my driving force in obtaining my degree: Being the best that I could be and encouraging my children to do the same. SCHOLARSHIP! Finally, to that end, I personally fund an annual scholarship as evidence of my commitment to our Zeta ideal, Scholarship!

Education: The Journey Is More Important Than the Diploma

Iana J. Daniels, M.S., M.A.

"Why are you in school again?" was a common question when I was working toward my second master's degree. When I shared my intention to pursue a doctorate, the question was "Don't you have enough degrees? Why do you want another?" My response was simple, "Why not?" In Guyana, I was limited not only by the availability of local institutions of higher learning, but also by the programs of study. More importantly, my mother sacrificed living away from her family for five years for my sisters and me to have the opportunity for education and options to become professional women and productive members of society. Why should I not seek as much education as possible? However, for me it is not about accumulating degrees or credentials, it is about the journey to the degree that I find fulfilling and exhilarating. It is about the relationships with classmates, professors and staff that are important. It is about the education gained outside the classroom during study groups and projects. It is about the discussions and intellectual arguments both outside of and within the classroom that add context to the assigned texts.

I now know that everything my mother did was in preparation for our lives as professional women and leaders. Education was not up for negotiation, it was not a matter of "if," but "what" and "when." As soon as I learned to read, my mom took me to the library to get my library card. It was not enough to check out a book, I had to read a book or two before my mom picked me up. I also had to take at least one book home with me and talk to my mom about the books I read. Most importantly, I could not stick to only one genre. I was encouraged to explore numerous categories before deciding which I liked best. From this experience, I came to appreciate the sanctuary of a library or bookstore, and all that is sitting on a shelf waiting for my eyes to view and hands to caress within the pages. Today I have my preferred reading genres, but I am open to reading anything that is written because just as I have a story, everyone has a story. Everyone also has a voice, and it is by exploring other points of view that we are able to understand the other side of any argument or negotiation.

Iana J. Daniels
Graduation from GA Tech

My mom also developed our speaking and writing skills from an early age, supplementing and reinforcing our classroom education. Again, this was non-negotiable. I was called a "Yankee" before I knew what the term meant. In Guyana, it meant I was "proper" or too good to speak Creole. Within the walls of our home, we prac-ticed proper English usage and diction only. No Creole. When it came to spelling and phonetics, I was taught to break words into syllables, spell them phonetically, and then consult the dictionary before asking my parents for help. I absolutely dreaded it at the time, but in retrospect, it prepared me for adulthood and being a professional. I now realize I was developing the skills needed for public speaking, and can now truly appreciate what I thought was punishment at the time.

Iana J. Daniels,
GA Tech Graduation with
Margaret Daniels (mother)

When it came to writing, like most Guyanese children, I began with a pencil and a double lined notebook to learn how to write letters and numbers with few errors. I was elated when I was finally able to write with ink on regular lined paper. This meant I knew how to write in cursive with few mistakes, and still do. I entered high school on September 9, 1985 and it was the last time I saw my mom until December 1990. The lack of her physical presence did not end her mentorship. This was before the internet and therefore email. Phone calls were monthly at best, so we wrote letters. If one of my letters contained spelling or grammar errors, my mom would return a copy of the letter with corrections. It annoyed me and I truly dreaded it.

As an adult and a professional, I can now appreciate what my parents, what my mother did for us. As a result I cannot seem to stay away from school either formal (degree seeking) or informal (professional development classes). I love books and have a library of my own, both physical and digital.

My parents were strong influences in my life, and I will be forever grateful for the lessons they taught and the sacrifices they made

Iana J. Daniels, GA Tech Graduation
with sisters (L-R)Iana Daniels, Yetunde Rubinstein, Omo-Bisi Daniels

Scholarship, Sacrifice and Self-Worth: Lessons Learned From My Grandmother

Stephanie LaQuinta Dukes

Graduation
Photograph,
1938,
Mrs. Essie M.N.
Helper-Morgan

"You did what!?" The words could be heard four houses down the block. Screaming at the top of her lungs was the young lady's "mama" who was really her cousin. When the young lady was only three years old, her mother passed away; so her cousin stepped in to complete what her mother could not. "Essie Marie Nelson, have you lost your mind?" her mama continued. Her father came rushing around the side of the house to see what was going on, and after looking around, in a calm voice he asked, "Fannie, what's going on?"

Shaking her head in disbelief, opening and closing her eyes as if to see more clearly, and at the same time, biting on her bottom lip, Essie Marie's mom clenched her hand as if to make a fist. She spun around saying, "Essie Marie done lost her mind!" Then she let out a scream and placed her hands on her hips.

"Essie Marie, what seems to be the problem?" Without moving his head, his eyes rolled over to her, conveying the message, "You have one chance and one chance only to get it right, so choose carefully the words which come out of your mouth."

"Daddy, all I did was try to stop Estelle from crying."

Her father looked deeper into her eyes to deliver the next question, "Why did you feel you had to stop Estelle's crying?"

Stephanie L. Dukes;
Granddaughter of
Mrs. Essie M.N. Helper-Morgan,
1986

"That's just it Daddy, it was because of me. Today when they announced the class rankings, she started crying, saying her parents wouldn't understand. She kept on crying. So, I told Principal Morley that, if it would stop her from crying, Estelle could deliver the commencement speech."

Essie Marie's mama, still perturbed, spoke again, "Lord, Lord, child did you not think about your parents, and how they would feel?"

"Yes, Mama," she replied. "You and Daddy always said you would love brother and me no matter what." Slowly, Essie Marie moved closer to her daddy and gazed intently at her mama as she continued talking. "Estelle's speaking, as salutatorian, does not change that I am the class valedictorian. I will lead Union Academy's Class of 1938 on graduation day. You and everyone else will know that your daughter is number one and no speech will change who and what I am."

The Quest: Stories of Remarkable Scholarship and Service

Alice J. McCullough-Garrett, Ed.D.;
Annie McCullough-Chavis, Ed.D. and
Nashett Chaunté Garrett, Ed.D.

The Quest is a compilation short biographies from three outstanding female educators describing their unyielding desire and determination to overcome barriers, obstacles and personal tragedies to reach what they believe to be, their God given destinies. Alice J. McCullough-Garrett, Ed.D., Annie McCullough-Chavis, Ed.D. and Nashett Chaunte' Garrett, Ed.D., all legacies, are not only linked through scholarship, but also through their genetic makeup and, as Sorors of Zeta Phi Beta Sorority. Let the Quest begin as you read the inspiring stories of these three extraordinary women, who have obtained the pinnacle of scholastic achievement and service, to their community and to others.

A Legacy of Scholarship — Alice J. McCullough-Garrett, Ed.D.

I always desired to attend college. My father always said he wanted one of his five daughters to be a teacher, and since I was the first to go off to college, I chose this career path. Preparing

to go away to college was not easy for a poor country girl from rural North Carolina with a single parent, four sisters and my brother. The oldest of my siblings was 12 when my mother died; I was seven; and the youngest, my brother, who is now a Sigma, was only four years old. Although I have only a vague memory of my mother, I do remember hearing her pray to live until her children were grown. Unfortunately, that did not happen.

Once I realized that a college education was possible, I was mindful that study and scholarship were important and served as a ticket for me to dream of a career beyond working on the farm, picking, harvesting and barning tobacco, or raising hogs and chickens as a hired hand. From the $5.00 fee to take the SAT as a senior in high school to the completion of my doctorate degree in 1995, I received my education with the support of full scholarships and work study programs. Not having money to take the SAT resulted in my attending a small African Methodist Episcopal Church junior college in Kittrell, North Carolina, and when I presented my high school transcript there, I was awarded a full scholarship and a work study position.

Graduating summa cum laude from Kittrell Junior College guaranteed me a scholarship to Allen University, in Columbia, South Carolina, yet another African Methodist Episcopal Church school. At Allen I met and admired the ladies of Zeta Phi Beta Sorority, Inc. who were known as the scholars on campus. I joined those scholars in spring 1968 and at the end of that term, with all of my family in attendance and as a first generation college student, I graduated summa cum laude.

In 1972 I was accepted into a scholarship program for a Master of Arts in teaching at Fordham University in New York with all expenses paid and a weekly stipend. I graduated cum laude in 1974 and received a teaching position in the New York City Public Schools.

I moved back to North Carolina in 1977 and taught in the Wake County Public School System. I became the first teacher to serve on the Board of Trustees of the North Carolina Center for the Advancement of Teaching. In this capacity I learned of an opportunity to earn a doctorate degree in educational leadership at the University of North Carolina at Chapel Hill through a program that offered tuition and a one-year sabbatical, with a stipend. I joined a group of eight doctoral students in 1990 and in 1995, I graduated. I did it with full family support.

The process of studying and pursuing scholarships presented many challenges as well as rewards, including U.S. Congressional Recognition in 1991 for Teaching Excellence and the Order of the Long Leaf Pine in 2002, the highest honor given to a citizen of the state of North Carolina. My motto in life has always been, "Regardless of your circumstances, find your space and occupy it." In many ways, scholarship was my space.

A Legacy of Academic Excellence and Scholarship — Annie McCullough-Chavis, Ed.D.

I always believed that God had a distinctive purpose and plan for me and that I had special potential as a child, or so I was told by several elders in my church and in my community.

This concept of being special resonated with me throughout my formative years and motivated me to seek out knowledge and learning with great passion, and to contemplate a teaching career, as teachers were highly respected in our rural community. My sister and I both believed that Daddy had chosen us to be his college graduates and teachers, so I was eager to start school to fulfill that calling.

I began school in 1953 and was happy to be taught by a family friend who had loved my mother and had taught each of my four older siblings. This teacher provided more than just an education; she took a keen interest in me and treated me like a daughter. Throughout first grade, I recall this revered mother figure said, "Anne, you are smart, just like your mama." I believed her, so I worked extremely hard in school to excel, despite my grief. For me, reading and learning provided solitude and a conduit to grieve the loss of my dear mother, who passed just prior to my starting first grade. My teachers showed an extraordinary interest in me and my desire to excel increased. Throughout elementary school I was one of the best students in my classes. My academic excellence continued in high school and I graduated near the top of my class (#4) while also participating in many extracurricular activities. I then turned my focus to attending college.

I encountered several barriers: I did not have the money to take the college entrance exam (SAT); I had not applied to any schools; and, I did not have the funding or scholarships to cover tuition. The first barrier was removed when my guidance counselor noticed that I had not taken the SAT and approached me about it. I informed her that I did not have the $5.00 to take the SAT. She scolded me, saying, "You are too smart not to go to college." Then she registered me for the SAT and paid the fee herself.

I applied to North Carolina A&T and Johnson C. Smith Colleges. With my high grade point average, SAT score, and, excellent transcript, I was immediately accepted by both colleges. One offered a partial scholarship and the other assured me that after attending first semester, I would be offered a scholarship for the second semester if my grades were good. Both college offers were significant, but at this point my mentor, a graduate of Fayetteville State University (FSU), offered me an opportunity that I could not refuse especially since I yearned to further my education. She avowed, "If you go to New York to stay with your dad for the summer, work, and save your money for books and tuition, I will find you a place to stay in Fayetteville so you can attend FSU." I was elated. I applied to FSU, worked as a maid in a New Jersey hospital during the summer, and saved my meager wages.

In September 1965, I began my studies at FSU as a thankful and proud first-generation college freshman, and immediately noticed the sororities and fraternities on campus. The ladies of Zeta Phi Beta Sorority, Inc. captured my interest and admiration because of the way they conducted themselves and their extensive involvement in campus life. Chapter members became Miss FSU or other campus queens, leaders, and scholars. I joined this select group of ladies on April 2, 1967, and became the first in my family to become a Zeta. This involvement further increased my thirst for knowledge and my need to succeed at FSU. I graduated cum laude (#5) as Miss FSU.

My progression and career in education was not a typical path as both of my graduate degrees were earned after marriage and while traveling with a military husband, having children, and working fulltime as a social worker. During this time, I learned of a part-time Master's of Social Work program at the University of North Carolina at Chapel Hill. I applied and, once again, my excellent transcripts, work history, and recommendations afforded me entry into this stellar graduate program. I was also awarded a fellowship by the North Carolina Department of Human Resources, and my work ethic, continuing thirst for knowledge, and support from my family resulted in my earning an Master's of Social Work degree in 1987, and being honored as the recipient of the prestigious Kizer Bost Social Work Award.

After graduation I became a school social worker and part-time college instructor and, four years later, a fulltime college instructor. After teaching and functioning in higher education and realizing the importance of strengthening my scholarship and credentials, I began working on my doctorate degree in higher education leadership at North Carolina State University. However, after a year in the program, I knew that my passion lay in teaching as opposed to administration. I entered an educational leadership program at FSU with other fourteen students. Working and attending school fulltime was a challenge, but I continued teaching and attending school, and I strived for excellence. I then earned my doctorate in 2002 through the opportunities God had given me.

I have always believed that the measure of an individual is the totality of the parts of his or her life. Two elements that have driven me throughout my life are scholarship and taking advantage of opportunities God presents to me. I am a Zeta of 48 years and a college professor of 28 years, and both are momentous parts of my life.

Me Too — Nashett Chaunté Garrett, Ed.D.

I am fond of hearing my mother tell the story of how she dressed me, at two weeks old, in a blue and white dress, and took me to my first Zeta meeting. I have been a Zeta ever since. My mother, my aunt, and my godmother have always been hard-working Zeta role models for me. Once I represented my mother at a Zeta conference, introduced my aunt as a Zeta youth presenter, and served as the youth speaker at an Eastern Regional Conference. I was entered in many Zeta contests and usually with a contingent of Zetas behind me, I won. I also earned a full scholarship to attend North Carolina Agricultural & Technical State University (NCA&TSU) in 2003.

The Zeta experience for me included seeing my mother and my aunt, both educators, pursue education and service in their communities. Inspired by their example, I wanted to be an educator and a Zeta too. I joined Zeta Phi Beta Sorority, Inc., during the second semester of my freshman year in college. At NCA&TSU, I had the opportunity to bring in other ladies and served as president of the National Pan Hellenic Council and the student government association. A scholarship at NCA&TSU is named in my honor for my work and service.

Like my mother, I, too, received scholarships for my education. By the time I graduated from high school in 1999, I had received nearly $300,000 in scholarship offers and had been accepted to all my chosen schools. After graduating from NCA&TSU, I accepted a full fellowship to the University of Georgia at Athens and graduated in 2005 with a master's degree in mathematics education. With that degree I became a teacher at my alma mater. Shortly afterwards, I was accepted in the educational leadership doctoral program at North Carolina State University. My life was not without its challenges. During this time my dad was terminally ill, so I divided my time between studying and helping to care for him. He always encouraged me to never stop pursuing my goals. Dad passed away before I graduated with a doctorate in educational leadership in 2012.

Further following in my mom's footsteps, I became a principal, and now I am the Director of Accountability for the Rowan Salisbury School System. I speak to and encourage students to be scholars and pursue their goals. I often share my favorite scripture (Luke 12:48) with students: "To whom much is given, much is required."

My mother, my aunt, my godmother and I are Zeta legacies committed to Scholarship, Service, Sisterly Love, and Finer Womanhood. From our experiences we can attest that scholarship matters.

Scholarship = Determination

Miranda Griffin, FL Area I Coordinator

"Scholarship is determination to change your economic potential in a competitive and ever changing world."

– Miranda Griffin

My mother, who had an eighth grade education and my father, who had a sixth grade education were determined to instill the pursuit of education in all fourteen of their children. They knew that education was a key to job opportunities and financial stability for their children and they were determined that we all finished a high school. Even though we lived in a small economically underdeveloped town in Mississippi, they trained us to dream big, work hard and never give up no matter how difficult the circumstances.

Soror
Miranda Griffin

This "can do, must do" attitude was in me as I was determined to receive an electrical engineering degree from Mississippi State University. My parents did not have the finances to send me to college. My scores on the ACT test indicated that I did not have the aptitude to complete an engineering degree. I became one praying young teenager because God was going to have to make a way for me. I applied for financial aid, but because I was a first generation college applicant, I made mistakes that caused the funds to be delayed. By July of 1985, I had not received approval for financial aid. I had won a local scholarship that provided $500 per semester for four years. August arrived with still no approval for financial aid. My parents were concerned that I would not be able to attend college that fall and they thought that it would crush me. Instead of being crushed, I became more determined. I asked my father and oldest sister to just take me to Mississippi State and I would find a way to stay until my financial aid come through. I used my $500 scholarship to pay for a meal plan so I wouldn't be hungry. I borrowed other students' books to study and do my homework. I got a parttime job on campus to pay for all other basic necessities. My parents called each week to check on me and my financial aid status. Mississippi State, at the time, allowed you to attend class for three-quarters of the semester without payment before the professor would have to drop you from the roll, and you would have move out of the dormitory. October came and it was time to pay up or get out. I made my weekly long, agonizing walk up the hill from the freshmen dormitory to the financial aid office to find out my fate. The financial aid counselor told me that I was still missing one item from my file before my financial aid could be released: The proof that my parents were still financially responsible for eight children as their tax forms only indicated five.

Soror Miranda Griffin

I told the female financial aid counselor my story of how I had come to Mississippi State with only $500; that I was first generation college attendee; that my parents were poor and counting on me to figure out how to pay for my education; that I was doing well in all my engineering classes despite the fact that my ACT test scores indicated that I would not be successful; and, that I was a black female engineering student, a rarity. I told her that I was determined in spite of all the odds that are against me in achieving an electrical engineering degree. She looked at me, marked my financial aid package complete and told me, "You make your parents and me proud by getting that degree."

Soror Miranda Griffin

Five years later I graduated with an electrical engineering degree from Mississippi State University. I used my story of determination to inspire my younger brothers and sisters to pursue a college education. Two of my brothers subsequently attended Jackson State University and graduated with bachelor's degrees. Whenever things got tough for them and they needed funds, I provided them because achieving my degree allowed me to economically help them, and they were determined to finish their degrees too.

My Journey with The National Educational Foundation

Dr. Rosalind Pijeaux Hale

Soror Rosalind Pijeaux –
December, 1967
Newly Inducted Member of Alpha
Beta Chapter
Dillard University–New Orleans, LA

As a member of Zeta Phi Beta Sorority, Incorporated, it is natural to value scholarship as it is one of the four founding principles. However, my journey with the National Educational Foundation, the Sorority's scholarship arm, is a unique one. I value my experiences tremendously and am happy to share them with others.

I would not have been able to attend college without the scholarship I received from Alpha Gamma Zeta Chapter, in New Orleans. I attended and graduated from Xavier University of Louisiana, a historically black college (HBCU). I was impressed that this Sorority had established a foundation specifically focused on scholarship.

Part One - My journey began in 1967...

I researched the history of the National Educational Foundation and was pleased that my journey in Zeta Phi Beta Sorority, Incorporated coincided with the beginning of the National Educational Foundation (NEF). I became a member of Zeta Phi Beta Sorority, Incorporated in Alpha Beta Chapter on December 15, 1967 at Dillard University. Soror Mildred Cater Bradham, 15th Grand Basileus, proposed the idea of a scholarship foundation during that same time.

Part Two – My journey continued 1992 – 2002....

In 1992, I was appointed by the 20th International Grand Basileus Jylla Moore Tearte, Ph.D.

Soror Rosalind Pijeaux Hale, Ed.D., Diamond Life Member
Alpha Gamma Zeta Chapter - New Orleans, LA
13th South Central Regional Director, 1992-1994
National Educational Foundation, 1994-2002
National Trustee, 2002-2006
National Educational Foundation, 2014-2018

to be the 13th Director of the South Central Region. Her theme, "World Class Service" exemplified the professionalism and quality espoused under her administration. The "Unconquerable" South Central Region is comprised of the states of Alabama, Arkansas, Mississippi and Tennessee. As a resident of Mobile, Alabama, I was very active at the local and state levels, but never envisioned myself in a national position. From 1992-1994 I served in this capacity with the theme "The Zeta Link: A Network of Professional Women." This theme followed the national one and invigorated the Sorors in the region to network.

The Zeta Link encouraged undergraduate and graduate Sorors to work together and learn from each other to be the best they could be in their educational aspirations, careers, and in service in the communities. Through the development of this professional network, the area of scholarship was highlighted. Undergraduates were shown first-hand that obtaining a good education could lead to wonderful career opportunities. Excellence in scholarship provides options that are not available without it. Conversations were shared between undergraduate Zetas aspiring to such careers as medical doctors, nurses, public health professionals, pharmacists, lawyers, accountants, teachers, school administrators, college professors, and a variety of other careers. An important result of this network was providing undergraduate Zetas with information about advancing their education beyond an undergraduate degree and ways to fund those aspirations.

Serving as the 13th South Central Regional Director was a wonderful experience and allowed me to work with Sorors not just within the South Central Region, but all over the United States. I attended other regional conferences, conducted workshops, and served on various national committees. As a former mathematics and science educator, I was very involved with the "Challenger Kids project" launched by the International Grand Basileus in cooperation with the U.S. Space Camp located in Huntsville, AL. I participated in the Space Camp and conducted a workshop at the 1994 Boule about my experiences and the benefits of attending. All chapters were encouraged to send at least one student to the Space Camp as part of this initiative. Promoting science and mathematics education, especially for African American youth, continues to be an ongoing challenge.

In addition, as a member of the Sorority's National Executive Board (NEB), I worked with the three immediate past Grand Basilei, Sorors Janice G. Kissner, Ph.D., 17th Grand Basileus; Edith V. Francis, Ph.D. 18th Grand Basileus; and, Eunice S. Thomas, Ph.D., 19th Grand Basileus who were NEB members too and my memories of them will linger forever. However, some of my most memorable moments were listening to three past Grand Basilei discuss the National Educational Foundation. These three, Soror Lullelia W. Harrison, 12th Grand Basileus, Soror Deborah Cannon Wolfe, Ph.D., 14th Grand Basileus, and, Soror Isabel M. Herson, 16th Grand Basileus, were already serving on the NEF. I remember being amazed at the seriousness of their reports and the manner in which they described the procedure for distributing the scholarships. Little did I know that I would be able to work side-by-side with them on this initiative.

During this time, I held the position of assistant professor at the University of South Alabama. Ultimately, I felt the need to pursue other career options. In the summer of 1994, I accepted a position at the University of South Carolina in Columbia, South Carolina. This new position afforded me the opportunity to concentrate on only teaching graduate and doctoral courses, and serving on dissertation committees in the doctoral program. I also collaborated with other African American professors in educational leadership. Yet, this move to the Southeastern Region also meant I would have to relinquish my position as South Central Regional Director.

My experiences during my two years as the South Central Regional Director had ignited a flame of national service within the Sorority in me. Thus, at the Boule in 1994 I looked for ways I could still serve at the national level. The National Educational Foundation, was a natural choice. Since serving on the NEF is not a National Executive Board position, I could seek this office without consideration of my regional location. I remember I ran for office with no campaign materials. I created a flyer with my driver's license photo on it that read, "Vote for Hale. She will not fail!"

I knew I was taking a chance, just being nominated from the floor. I had to get my application finished within the time allowed and go to the regional caucuses to explain why I was seeking the position, but many Sorors already knew me because of the initiatives I had worked on as a Regional Director. They knew my passion for Zeta and my passion for serving. I will always remember the 12th South Central Regional Director, Soror Johnnye Witcher, Ed.D., from Montgomery Alabama, who had been elected as Chair of the National Executive Board in 1992 thus paving the way for me to be appointed as the 13th South Central Regional Director, going to the microphone and nominating me by saying my full name, Dr. Rosalind Pijeaux Hale. Of course she had to spell it. She has served as my mentor and colleague for many years and I have learned a lot about life and Zeta through our relationship over the years. I appreciated her support as I attempted to serve Zeta in another capacity.

At the 1994 Boule, as I was exiting my position as 13th South Central Regional Director, I was elected to the first of my two terms as a member of the Board of Managers for the NEF. I served from 1994-1998 and was re-elected in 1998 to serve until 2002. Serving two consecutive terms on the Board of Managers is the maximum allowed. The structure of the Board of Managers for the NEF is unique in that four members are elected in staggered terms by the Sorority membership (2 at each Boule), and three members are appointed by the Grand Basileus, also in staggered terms.

I was very excited as I was sworn in because I also realized that I would be working with three past Grand Basilei who had a passion for the NEF and had worked with it since its inception. Soror Lullelia W. Harrison, 12th Grand Basileus; Soror Deborah Cannon Wolfe, Ph.D., 14th Grand Basileus; and, Soror Isabel M. Herson, 16th Grand Basileus, were still serving on the NEF. Additionally, the Soror who served as the legal counsel for the NEF, Soror Issie L. Jenkins, Esq., was still assisting with legal matters. My journey continued as I learned from them. I saw their untiring efforts to pursue additional funding to maintain the mission of the NEF which is "to support higher education achievement through scholarships and conduct community education programs and related research to improve individual and community living standards."

A major initiative during my initial term on the Board of Managers was the *Human Genome Project (HGP)*. The *HGP* was a genetics research project to map and determine the genes of an individual. The National Education Foundation's *HGP* was funded through the Department of Energy and provided education and information through workshops and conferences for urban and suburban minority communities across the country, abroad, and at the United Nations. National researchers in this field provided information about how this research could impact the minorities. With this partnership, Zeta Phi Beta Sorority, Incorporated became the only Greek-lettered organization to partner with the Department of Energy with the *Human Genome Project.*

The first NEF *HGP* conference was held in 1998 on the campus of Xavier University of Louisiana which continues to be recognized as the top university that produces African American graduates who are accepted into and go on to complete medical school. This was the most logical place to conduct a conference on this topic. Since I had moved from Columbia, South Carolina back home to New Orleans to serve as chair of the Division of Education at Xavier University of Louisiana, my alma mater, I coordinated this effort as a member of the NEF Board of Managers. The mayor of New Orleans proclaimed the weekend of the conference as Zeta Phi Beta Sorority, Incorporated Human Genome Project weekend and recognized my chapter, Alpha Gamma Zeta Chapter, for coordinating this effort.

My second term included a shift in the dynamics of the governing the Board of Managers. Under the leadership of the three past Grand Basilei, the Bylaws were revised to ensure that leadership would transition smoothly from them to the elected and appointed members. I continued to be in awe of the leadership of these three past Grand Basilei. They had the foresight to make sure the leadership of the Foundation would continue running smoothly, even after they could no longer serve. An addition to the bylaws, was the creation of the Regional

Liaison Councils (RLC). Each regional director was asked to designate Sorors to serve as the regional liaison and to establish a Council within the region. The role of the Regional Liaison Council was to assist the Board of Managers in implementing NEF programs and to obtain funds to support it. I was pleased that I was assigned to coordinate this effort. One of the first initiatives developed utilizing the RLC was the Silent Auction held at the Boule. This was a fun way to obtain funds for the Foundation. RLC members contacted Sorors within their regions to obtain items. Sorors donated items from all over the world for the auction.

Part Three – My journey continues 2014 and beyond...

To my surprise, I was asked by the 24th Grand Basileus, Soror Mary Breaux Wright, to serve on the National Educational Foundation Board of Managers in 2014. Of course, I was honored and responded affirmatively. Soror Issie L. Jenkins, the remaining Honorary Member Emerita, and Soror Kathryn Malvern Ph.D., the immediate past NEF chair, had both been on the Board of Managers when I was initially elected in 1994, the other Board members were all newly elected. I saw this as an opportunity to provide the history from my past term and to learn from those newly elected and appointed members. (Note: Honorary Members Emerita are members who were serving on the Board at the time of its incorporation. They hold this title on the Board of Managers until resignation, incapacitation or death. The other three Honorary Members Emerita were Sorors Harrison, Wolfe and Herson.)

Upon my return to the NEF Board of Managers I was immediately thrust back into serving on the scholarship acceptance committee. This brought back many memories of late night meetings and review of applications. Serving with the current National Second-Anti Basileus, Soror Bibliana Bovery, has really been a wonderful experience. Luckily, the process is more streamlined now that there is more technology available. Still, having the opportunity to read the essays makes me realize the continued need for the NEF and the financial support to sustain it.

I also serve on the fundraising committee. The NEF Board of Managers works diligently to acquire funds for its ongoing scholarships, initiatives, and community projects via this committee. Members of Zeta Phi Beta Sorority, Incorporated are encouraged to make yearly tax-deductible donations as well as bequests in their wills. Foundations and organizations are approached and grant sources are researched and applications are submitted for support. Finally, future fundraising activities are planned which include a return of the Boule Silent Auction, a new NEF pin/pendant, and a one-of-a kind art project. All of these efforts will maintain the caliber of NEF programs and increase the number of scholarships and community education programs that can be offered.

An initiative coordinated by the NEF to support the community that I look forward to getting more involved with in the near future is the "Healthy Choices for a Brighter Future" program. It is designed for youth and encourages them to maintain healthy lifestyles and positive social interactions. Workshop topics include healthy living topics and, the importance of education and leadership development. Although the youth auxiliary members were the initial target audience, the workshops have been free and open to other youth in the community.

The NEF is making a concerted effort to inform the sisterhood about available scholarships and how to apply. Although quite a few scholarship applications are received, not many are from members of Zeta Phi Beta Sorority, Incorporated. It is hoped that the revised website (www.zphibnef1975.org) and online application process, along with workshops conducted at the regional and state meetings, more members who qualify for the scholarships will apply.

The purposes of the National Educational Foundation coincide with the Sorority's founding principle of scholarship. I know that my journey will continue through ongoing support of the initiatives of the National Educational Foundation even when I am not an official member of its Board of Managers.

My Experiences with Zeta Phi Beta Sorority's Ideal of Scholarship

Dawn Young Johns, M.Ed.

In 1971, Rosa Fortson, my Sunday School teacher at Greater Bethel A.M.E. Church in Miami, Florida, told me about Beta Tau Zeta Chapter's scholarship. Of course, I had an interest. At that time, my parents were assisting two other children with their studies at Howard University. I knew Mrs. Fortson was a member of Zeta Phi Beta Sorority, and I also knew Dorothy Lee, my high school physical education teacher at Miami Killian, was a member of the Sorority. They both assisted me with completing my application. As a result of my academic achievement and community service, I was awarded $500.00.

My sister, Pamela Young, was initiated into the Sorority at Howard University in 1969. However, when I began at Howard, my focus was solely on my studies. In my junior year, when approached by Algenita Scott, my dormitory counselor, about the "Zeta Rush," I was curious, but I hesitated because I had some concerns about the pledge period and its effect on my studies. When I shared my thoughts, the Zeta members emphasized that study sessions were integral parts of the pledge period. That proved to be true and I became a member of Alpha Chapter, Zeta Phi Beta Sorority on April 14, 1974, and that same semester my GPA was 4.0. I graduated summa cum laude the following year.

Zeta invested in me by selecting me as an award recipient. I knew at that moment in high school that if I ever chose a sorority, it would be the illustrious Zeta Phi Beta Sorority, Incorporated, with its lofty ideals of SCHOLARSHIP, Service, Sisterhood and Finer Womanhood.

As a side note, my mother, Estella M. Young, who completed her bachelor's and master's degrees once her youngest (me) was in high school, also became a Zeta through Beta Tau Zeta Chapter in 1975. What a pleasure it is for me to remind her that I was her "Big Sister" for a few weeks. We have a wonderful legacy in Zeta.

Letters from My Daughters

Janice M.T. Johnson, M.Ed.

My husband and I have been blessed beyond measure with four beautiful daughters: Christina who is twenty-four, Monica, twenty-three, and a set of twins Alicia and Angela who are twenty. We spent their childhoods teaching them about concepts like the golden rule, honesty, and the of value education. Growing up they knew that college was not an option but a necessity. Christina and Monica graduated from college and are currently obtaining secondary degrees. Alicia and Angela are currently in their junior year of college. All four of our daughters were recipients of academic scholarships from Zeta Phi Beta Sorority, Incorporated. One day, I asked them about their reflections on scholarship, service and life lessons on what education allowed them to learn. Below are their reflections.

Christina:

When I was a little girl, I wanted to be a teacher when I grew up. Even at a young age I knew that in order to be a teacher I had to go to college. So college was where I was going to go. I attended Salem College, the oldest women's college in the nation. During my time at Salem I began to understand that education had a greater level of value than I associated it with. At the time, I did not think learning could be any more important than my parents already stressed to me. But I learned that education is everywhere and one can find oneself and purpose through education.

While at Salem I had the opportunity to study the management of luxury fashion brands at Bocconi University in Milan, Italy. During this time I started to understand that education

 131

was all around me. Education occurred during my conversations with my professors and classmates about the different customer experiences that occurred at various high end fashion stores. Education occurred during my trip to Cremona, Italy where I listened to a song played on the world's second oldest violin. Learning occurred when I went to Venice and listened to the tour guide explain that the pictures on the walls in Saint Mark's Basilica cathedral told stories from the Bible since most people could not read at that time. One of my favorite learning moments occurred during a lecture when I had to dissect advertisements from Dolce & Gabbana. While dissecting print advertisements against the core ideology of the brand, I realized I was talented at this type of work. Not only was I good at dissecting themes of advertisements but I enjoyed it as well. From this lecture, this moment of learning and understanding, my passion for marketing of luxury brands was born. This newfound interest led me to a topic for my senior thesis toward my degree in business administration. I identified the competitive advantages of companies in the athletic apparel industry.

Currently I am continuing my education at Seton Hall University at which I am obtaining a Master of Business Administration with a concentration in Marketing. After I graduate from Seton Hall, I plan to join the workforce as a luxury fashion brand marketer. Although I no longer want to be a teacher, the understanding that education is the key that will unlock the door to achieve my goals remains the same.

Monica:

When I was a child, school was not easy for me. I struggled with reading, spelling, and attentiveness. Needless to say, I did not like school. In retrospect, I have come a long way from child I used to be. Despite my early academic setbacks, my parents did not allow me to become discouraged. Being an African American female, my parents knew that it was imperative that I strive for excellence and develop a good work ethic. It was understood in my family that it was necessary for me and my siblings to work twice as hard, for fear that our race would in some way take away from our accomplishments. College was not a suggestion in our house, it was a requirement.

When I acquired better study skills and became a better student, I took pride in my academics. I became insatiably curious about science, math, and psychology. I participated in numerous extracurricular enrichment programs and youth leadership symposiums. I even had the opportunity to spend two summers shadowing doctors and researching biological and dermatological processes at a Minority Science Initiative program based in Philadelphia, Pennsylvania. This program increased my academic self-efficacy and prepared me for college. This program also ignited my passion for research.

With the support of my family, I went to High Point University in High Point, North Carolina on an academic scholarship. I majored in psychology and minored in communication. I graduated summa cum laude in three and a half years. At High Point, I was able to conduct research on the interrelationship between transgression severity, friendship, and forgiveness. This research article has since been published and increased my academic achievements which made me a better candidate for graduate school.

Currently, I am pursing a dual Ph.D. in Counseling Psychology and School Psychology at the State University of New York at Buffalo in New York. I am proud of how far I have come and am excited for all that I have yet to accomplish. Since my passion for research was ignited in high school it has not died. Currently, my research interests include African American acculturation, multicultural psychology, and minority mental health. I ultimately plan to become a clinician, college professor and researcher. I am dedicated to making a positive impact and difference in the world and I have my parents to thank for that due to their unwavering support of me despite my difficulties with school. I also thank Zeta Phi Beta Sorority, Inc. for the scholarships that provided much needed financial assistance and inspiration.

Alicia:

I attend Mary Baldwin College in Staunton, Virginia and I am majoring in business administration with an emphasis in marketing and management with a concentration in communication. Since moving to Virginia, I have found opportunities to further my education in ways that I never thought about before. While taking tax accounting to satisfy a requirement for my degree I learned that I was gifted at tax accounting. While other people see an array of numbers and dollar signs, tax accounting makes perfect sense to me. After taking the final exam for my tax accounting course, my professor emailed me and let me know that I was the only person in the class to get a perfect score.

After the semester was over, I figured that would be the end of my tax accounting career. When I told my father about my success with tax accounting he heavily encouraged me to become Volunteer Income Tax Assistance certified to help people by filing their taxes. At first I did not see the importance of becoming certified but when he explained it as a way to continue my education and use the gifts God blessed me with to help others, I knew it was something that I had to do. Currently I am IRS and VITA certified and I volunteer every Thursday at a community center where I file taxes for low income Virginians.

In my opinion, education is not only a process but can be full of surprises. When I came to Mary Baldwin I had no idea that I would uncover new personal talents. I especially did not expect to be able to provide valuable services to others with my new talents. I am thankful to my father for not only pushing me to become certified so that I can help others but for also instilling a helpful spirit and the importance of education in me and my sisters. Although accounting is not my end goal, using my education to help others along the way will always be one of my career goals.

Angela:

I attend Mary Baldwin and am majoring in psychology. When I think about education I think about applying learning. I currently have an internship at a physical therapy and rehabilitation facility in Stanton, Virginia. While doing my internship, I applied the concepts I learned in class to the real world. I had a client, Matt, who I worked with worked after knee replacement surgery. A week before Matt came into the office, my professor had lectured on the healing process of bones in class. I learned that it is easier for bones to heal than muscles because of the amount of blood supply available. By the time I met Matt, I was knee it would take about six to eight weeks for his knee to heal.

I knew what to expect as Matt went through many weeks of therapy. I was able to encourage him during the times he felt defeated by a lack of results. I would remind him that Rome was not built in a day nor would his knee recover instantaneously. I would often remind him that although he did not see immediate results, he was right on track for recovery.

After spending time at the rehabilitation facility, I am confident that after I graduate from college I want to attend a physical therapy school to help others like Matt. To me learning is encouraging and uplifting others. Although I am only an intern, I am able to use my knowledge of the body to encourage and uplift Matt in doing his exercises and gaining strength in his knee and leg again. I know that I will become a physical therapist one day and I will enjoy passing on my education to my clients by helping them understand their bodies and healing.

* * *

As parents, my husband and I are truly grateful for the lessons that our daughters have learned and applied to their lives. We are thankful to God for blessing them along the way and enabling them to overcome various obstacles such as learning challenges, indecisions about next steps in their educational and life journeys, financing higher education, and other bumps in the road. Fortunately, our daughters understand that high academic achievement has intrinsic as well as financial value. For that, my family is thankful for organizations such as our awesome Sorority, Zeta Phi Beta Sorority, Incorporated, which awarded financial scholarships for each of our daughters. In addition, Zeta Phi Beta Sorority, Incorporated also offered all of our daughters various opportunities to grow and develop through the youth affiliates.

After reading my daughters' thoughts and reflections in their letters, I am reminded of the African Proverb that states, "It takes a village to raise a child." My husband and I are truly thankful for the people along the way, grandparents, aunts, uncles, church youth group leaders, school teachers, college professors, Archonette advisors, and others who are a part of our village. They enhanced what we taught our daughters by reinforcing their understanding that learning is a lifelong experience and that education is the key to success.

An Education Beyond the Mind – Priceless

Claudia DuBois Jones

My parents were products of the 1920's and 1930's, respectively. Neither graduated high school. After completing eighth grade, my father left school to help care for his younger siblings following the death of his mother. Shortly after completing ninth grade, my mother also left school. Despite that, both of my parents were literate and had already acquired the "soft skills" that eventually molded them into productive members of society. Ten children were born of their union and, as with most parents, their greatest desire was that their off-spring climb higher on the rungs of the educational ladder than they had. My mother was so persistent about us achieving this goal that it became an eleventh commandment in our household, "Thou shalt graduate from high school." Although challenging for a few, all of us graduated high school; eight pursued postsecondary education ranging from state licensure to a doctoral degree; and six entered "helping fields." The life lessons instilled by my parents have served us best.

Educational institutions don't offer what my father possessed. He had a Ph.D. in common sense. He was a pragmatist recognizing that the whole was made up of little parts that just needed piecing together. By his actions, my father taught us altruism, tolerance and compassion. He was kind to everyone and would help anyone in need, encouraging the same from us. This was an all but inevitable outcome, since, with ten children living under the same roof, we had no choice but to learn how to deal with multiple personalities. His legacy as a quiet giant lives on through each of us as we now demonstrate for our offspring the hard work, tact, and diplomacy needed to succeed in the world.

As a homemaker, the responsibility of taking care of ten kids was a daunting task. However, my mother welcomed her role of child rearing. During the week, chores dominated our time, but on Sunday we were in church for ten hours. Looking back, she deserved a Nobel Peace prize just for keeping us under control. In fact, we affectionately nicknamed her the, "Judge" because she ran her household like a courtroom. She was a strict disciplinarian with non-traditional devices to whip us into conformity while praying for us. One of her favorite devices was a prominently displayed wall plaque bearing the words "Give Us This Day Our Daily Bread." If ever the plaque was missing when we got home from school, it meant "hot water" for one or more of us. According to my mother's mindset, obedience and discipline were the staples necessary to succeed. And throwing ourselves on the mercy of her court was *not* a viable option.

Although not highly educated, both my parents were able to impart the skills and knowledge to give us a competitive advantage in the workforce. Both developed in us a strong work ethic, emphasizing that, whatever the job, we do it well. Most of all, they taught us to follow our dreams and never give up. The sum of the skills taught by my parents produced two teachers (who both became administrators), one minister, one social worker, two police officers, two truck/delivery drivers, and two factory workers.

My master's degree in educational administration cannot compete with the practical education I received at home. While an advanced degree was required to pursue my career, my parents' teachings are responsible for the person I am today. Those "soft skills" my mother and father taught mean so much more and took me so much further than the signed and sealed certificate stored in my file cabinet.

As I share these thoughts, my heart is full to overflowing with gratitude and humility, two more lessons from my parents. The value of postsecondary education over a lifetime may easily exceed hundreds of thousands of dollars, but the value of lessons learned from my parents is priceless!

The Quest to be a Soldier and a Scholar

Rhonda M. Lawson

"Why am I putting myself through this?"

I ask myself this question every time I sit staring at my computer screen, struggling to find new information to add to my dissertation proposal. The question pops up each time I have to reach for my credit card to make a tuition payment. It echoes in my mind each time I remind myself that this doctorate is an optional degree.

Yet, whenever I ask myself that question, I remember that I began this journey in pursuit of something greater. Yes, I could have been happy with having achieved a master's degree, but I knew I wanted more. I had always dreamt of having "Doctor" in front of my name, and I would never feel comfortable knowing that I never pursued that dream.

More importantly, I think of the people who are watching me, many of whom had been inspired to achieve their own degrees because of my efforts. To stop would not be only letting myself down, but all of them as well. There's no motivator like knowing you have your own cheering section composed of those who love you most.

You see, I have been a big proponent of education ever since joining the United States Army in 1994. I had come upon financial difficulties at the end of my sophomore year at Loyola

University in New Orleans, and could no longer afford to go to college. My financial aid had run out, and my family didn't have the money to keep me in school. I had made the decision to sit out of school until I could make the money to pay my debt and return later. Unbeknownst to me, while I was making that decision, an Army recruiter, possibly trying to make his quota for the month, was going through his records and ran across my old Armed Services Vocational Aptitude Battery scores from high school. For those not familiar with the military, this is the entrance test that helps determine what jobs future recruits could get once they joined the service. I had only taken the test to get out of class that day! Apparently I'd scored pretty high, so he gave me a call and asked if I'd still like to join the Army. I had no better options at the time, so I jumped at the chance to start a career while earning much needed college money with the GI Bill and Army College Fund. Both my parents were active duty Air Force airmen, and I had four years of Army Junior Reserve Officer Training Corps experience, so I was already familiar with military life. It sounded like a win-win to me.

However, some of my instructors and administrators at Loyola weren't having that. When they found out that I would be leaving college to join the Army, I was told that the Army was no place for me, and that my place was in school. They'd arranged for me to sign a promissory note to defer my debt and stay in school one more semester. Well, that semester came and went. And although I made good grades and joined my beloved Zeta Phi Beta Sorority, Inc., becoming a charter member of Iota Omicron chapter, on top of working a part-time job and work study, I still could not earn all of the needed money I would need to continue my college career.

I had placed myself into a situation where I not only owed Loyola money, but because I had left school, I had to begin paying my student loans. So on the morning of February 16, 1994, the day after Mardi Gras, my recruiter picked me up from home and drove me to the Military Entrance Processing Center, where I raised my right hand and joined the U.S. Army as a private first class, thanks to a recommendation from my Senior Group Leader at John F. Kennedy Senior High School's JROTC program.

Some thought I had given up on my college dreams, but that was far from the case. I had promised my family that I would finish school, and I aimed to keep that promise. Because I had been an English major in college, I knew I wanted a job where I could use my education and build a career that I could use when I left the Army. I had no idea military journalists existed, but because my ASVAB scores were so high, the Army journalist was offered, and I quickly took it. Additionally, immediately after joining the Army, I began sending $100 a month to Loyola to pay down my debt. After receiving guidance from the Army Education Center at my first duty station, Fort Knox, Kentucky, I contacted Sallie Mae and signed a forbearance deferring all of my student loans for three years.

I was then delighted to find that a number of colleges offered classes at the education center, so I began taking one class at a time with Elizabethtown Community College until I was able to pay off my debt to Loyola and request my transcript. That opportunity came during my deployment to Afghanistan in 2001 in support of Operation Enduring Freedom. This would be my first time leading soldiers into a combat zone, which was stressful enough, but it turned out to be a blessing. Thank God we all came back safe and did great things to tell the Army's story, but the deployment also gave me the opportunity to pay off all of my education debt, including my student loans!

I restarted my education journey shortly after being reassigned to the Sinai Peninsula in Egypt. By this time, I had been married and divorced, had a child, and had just been promoted to sergeant first class after nine years in the Army. During a lunchtime conversation, a fellow soldier had asked me if I planned to sign up for any of the classes that the University of Maryland University College office at the education center offered. I remembered that I no longer had any education debt, so I was able to order my transcripts from both Loyola and ECC, apply for a degree plan with UMUC, and use the Army's tuition assistance program to pay for it.

Going to school was now practically free! The U.S. military has a program that basically pays for an active duty soldier's undergraduate degree. Tuition assistance allows a soldier to receive up to $750 per class for up to three classes per semester as long as the soldier remains in good standing in the military. Because of the price of the school I attended, I only had to pay for books, but some soldiers chose to attend more affordable schools where books cost were covered.

I graduated from UMUC in 2006 with a Bachelor of Arts in Communication Studies after taking both in-person and online classes. I was now stationed at Fort Meade, Maryland and able to participate in my graduation. Wearing my cap and gown with my Zeta stole was one of my proudest moments. And having my mother, sister, and daughter there to witness the ceremony made it all the better. It had taken me longer than I'd planned to get there, but I had finally fulfilled my promise. I'd received my college degree while maintaining a successful Army career, raising a little girl on my own, and serving my community with Tau Eta Zeta chapter in Baltimore! I even had the honor of leading the chapter's efforts in establishing the first Soror Sharon K. Harvey Memorial Scholarship, named after our beloved chapter member whose life had tragically been cut short. I was proud of my work as a soldier, student and Zeta, but my thirst for knowledge had not been satiated.

Shortly after leaving Maryland and stationed in Korea, I found out about a program that the University of Oklahoma offered for which the school would actually fly the instructor to various military installations in Asia and Europe and teach the entire semester in one week. It would take five hours a night for five nights and all day on Saturday and Sunday. It would also require an assignment that would be due before the class met, and another one after the week of instruction. It was hard work, but I was ready for the challenge, so in 2007, I applied for OU's Master of Public Administration program.

I was stationed at a remote base near Northern Korea and taking the class would require an hour-long bus ride or 45-minute train ride each night to Yongsan Air Base, where the classes were held. We had a curfew, so I often had to leave class early in order to make it back to my base on time. And had I mentioned that I was active with Pi Eta Zeta chapter all this time?

Eventually, I realized that Public Administration wasn't what I wanted. I needed something more in line with my communications background. The only other degree plan offered in Korea that wouldn't require me to change schools was Human Relations. I took it, even though taking classes in person would require me to travel to Osan Air Base, which was even further away. I laugh as I think back to the bus, train, and taxi rides I had to take each night to travel back and forth to class. It was a haul, and it wasn't easy, but I enjoyed the classes, and was proud to be working on my master's degree. It was a slow process however, because military exercises and other obligations would often cause me to drop a class or sit them out altogether. Although I loved the in-person classes, I began taking online classes whenever I was unable to travel. I'll always be thankful to my military leadership who supported me leaving work early to get to class. Not every soldier had such support.

By the time I was reassigned to Fort Stewart, Georgia in 2009, I was four classes away from finishing my degree. By this time, I was still a single parent, taking care of not only my daughter, but also my 6-year-old nephew who had moved to Georgia with us. I had chartered Chi Pi Zeta Chapter and become the chapter's first president, and had just been informed that my brigade, of which I'd just become the Public Affairs Officer, would be deploying to Iraq the following year. Determined to not have to take classes while deployed, I decided on a move that I would never suggest to anyone: I took three classes at once! I was now taking three master's level classes while preparing for a deployment and leading a chapter of five Sorors on top of being a single parent of two. I was not the nicest person at that time, nor was I the most available. No time to date, and less time to party! Thank God my mother moved in with me a few months before my deployment to ensure the kids could stay in their school while I was in Iraq. Her help was truly a blessing, and I thank God for her every day.

I'm not sure how I did it, but I passed all three of those classes with at least a grade of B, and began looking for a way to complete the last class before having to deploy. I found the perfect option: an instructor would be travelling to an Air Force base in Florida to teach a class for a week. I'd been through this in Korea, so I knew what to do. Since my mother took care of the kids, I hopped in my car, drove to Destin, Florida, and used my timeshare so I would have a place to stay for a week.

By the time I deployed, I had completed all requirements for my degree. I was unable to participate in the graduation ceremony, but I was blessed to have tuition assistance to pay for my education. Of course a master's degree is more expensive than a bachelor's degree, so tuition assistance couldn't cover everything. What was left came from my pocket. Although I could have used my GI Bill or Sallie Mae to cover the overage, I chose to pay for it myself. This allowed me to transfer my GI Bill and Army College Fund to my daughter to help cover her education, and I wouldn't have to worry about student loans. God always has a plan!

Armed with both degrees that the Army paid for, I constantly encouraged every soldier I could to pursue an education. The military has so many programs to help service members achieve their degrees, which in turn can help them get promoted faster, but it's a shame that many of them don't use these opportunities. While in Iraq, I was approved to teach Human Resource Management at night at the education center—yes, there are education centers on some deployed bases—to help other service members receive their degrees. Many took advantage of the opportunity, but many didn't. Some classes would be cancelled due to not having the minimum enrollment.

I experienced the same thing when I came to Belgium. After teaching two HR classes, I had to stop because my classes were cancelled due to a lack of enrollment and soon, the center had to stop offering them. I admit that I sometimes grow impatient with some of my colleagues when they tell me they don't have the time. Do they realize to whom they're speaking? If only they knew the nights I stayed up all night working on papers for my doctoral course at Northcentral University, finishing in just enough time to get an hour of sleep before having to get ready for work. If only they were there when I had to take leave from work to finish my comprehensive exams. But then, I have to remind myself that I don't know everyone's story or situation. I wasn't blessed to judge, but to encourage and support.

So today, I continue to encourage those whom I'm charged to lead to pursue their educations. I don't mind sharing my story. Although it may sound extraordinary to some looking from the outside, I know the average grades I made in high school, having not made straight A's until the middle of my junior year. I remember the struggle of having to work my way from academic probation in my first semester of college to having a 3.0 GPA by the time I left to join the Army. So far, nearly all of the service members who work directly for me are enrolled in college, with one of them only a comprehensive exam away from his master's degree. I like to think that we are adding to the number of noncommissioned officers with advanced degrees, an accomplishment only thought to be reserved for commissioned officers. Admittedly, the number of military service members, whether commissioned or noncommissioned, possessing a doctorate is minimal, but that number is growing.

So as I sit staring at my computer, pulling myself together after yet another round of dissertation proposal rewrites, or another fit of being overwhelmed with too many responsibilities while leading yet another small, newly chartered Zeta chapter, I think of those who I have encouraged over the years:

My daughter, who has had her own struggles in high school. She needs to see that I haven't given up, so she can't either!

My soldiers and airmen, some of whom I have counseled because of their lack of civilian education, and others I have applauded for achieving theirs. I will continue to push them long after I leave the Army.

The students to whom I have awarded scholarships throughout the years.

The community members who look to me with pride and awe as they watch me juggle education, Army, motherhood, and Zeta. If only they knew how tedious that juggling act can get!

My chapter, full of women who have made their own educational achievements. I take pride in the fact that one of our first initiatives as a chapter was to start a scholarship program, and we successfully awarded two $1,000 scholarships in 2015, our first year of existence, and are on track to repeat that success in our second year.

The women who I hope to help with my completed dissertation on African American female leaders in the corporate sector.

Yes, I get discouraged sometimes. Yes, I get tired a lot. However, when I need encouragement, I turn to my Sorors and fellow soldiers who are working toward the same goal. I share my successes and frustrations with my Doctoral Divas Sisterhood Circle and the Doctoral Doves Facebook Group. Their encouragement, coupled with my quest to remain an example to my daughter, have talked me off of the proverbial ledge many a night.

My educational journey is no longer only about me. Someone needs to see that where there is a will, there is a way, and that if we remain focused, we can achieve what is meant to be ours. That story will never be told through giving up. Today, I take pride in the fact that the young woman who joined the Army at 20 years old, swearing up and down that she was going back to college after her initial five-year enlistment, has stuck it out and will be retiring next year after 23 years of successful military service with not one, but three degrees. Now that's a story worth telling! To God be the glory!

Scholarly Actions Yield Opportunities and Blessings

Bobbie Nell Crudup Qualls

Scholarship... What a worthy objective the Founders of Zeta Phi Beta Sorority visualized over ninety six years ago! I am confident our Founders envisioned "scholarship" with the term SCHOLAR in mind...women with traits of integrity, faith, perseverance, vision, determination and wisdom. At a young tender age, they prayed for wisdom as they sought knowledge. "Blessed are those who find wisdom –those who gain understanding." (Proverbs 3:13) Our studious Founders were learners and they wanted each prospective Zeta to be "a learner." They envisioned each lady entering college with a profound desire to gain a high degree of mastery in at least one academic discipline. This learning goal would be achieved only by "long systematic study and application of this knowledge." They fulfilled this goal understanding that Scholarly Actions Yield Opportunities and Blessings.

Reflecting on my childhood background as a scholar, I was a learned student of academic subjects and values (conduct). My parents would echo throughout the house, "Be sure to close your mouth and (obey) and, listen to the teacher; you may not get all A's but you will get A's in conduct." Yearly, I learned to simultaneously excel in both. I graduated as salutatorian of my class and, I dared not have anything less than a B+ in conduct on my report card. Happily, my high school scholarly actions granted me the opportunity to further my education by attending Alcorn State University in Lorman, Mississippi.

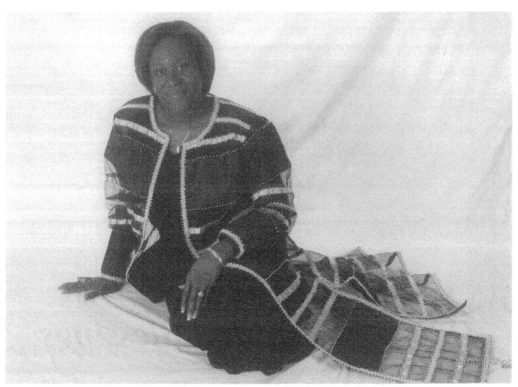

GLR 2005 State Director of Year Award
Soror Bobbie Crudup Qualls – Regional Director Soror Ira Ebbs

My knowledge about "Greekdom" was very limited when I entered Alcorn in August 1968. It remained that way throughout my freshman year as I concentrated on my academic studies and my 'work study obligation" (my job on campus). In my sophomore year (1970), I became curious and excited about Greek Life. I started saving my earnings as a mentor for the Upward Bound program just in case I decided to pledge. I started observing sorority members in general, bonding together, worshipping together, studying together, stepping together, and serving together. Zeta Phi Beta Sorority held my attention. I wondered who these young ladies were. I kept watching and studying them and looked the group up in the yearbook to read their objectives. Wow! Zeta Phi Beta Sorority exemplified Sisterly Love, Scholarship, Finer Womanhood and Service. I decided that sorority was for me and the the rest is history

Earning a college degree with honors and membership to Zeta Phi Beta Sorority granted me the opportunity to travel to Louisville, Kentucky, with my teaching credential and a job offering in the Jefferson County Public School System.

I came to Kentucky with less than two hundred dollars in my purse. When my parents sent me a $34 check a week after I arrived in Kentucky, I refused to cash it because I knew my parents had eight other children at home to provide for and yes, I was blessed: "Bobbie you will start teaching in less than two weeks," I proclaimed to myself. I recalled that although money was a rarity during my childhood, my parents put a few dollars away to share with their children and others. Most sharing came in the form of food from the garden. No one came to my parents' home without leaving with a "care package." They loved living the scripture, "He who is generous will be blessed, for he gives some of his food to the poor." Proverbs 22:9.

The following days were rewarding ones as I reflected on receiving a $700 scholastic award from a Caucasian sorority and a $500 scholarship from Great Lakes Region. I was thankful for these scholarships that enabled me to use my Master's Degree in Guidance and Counseling to assist students, the schools and community.

I vowed then, as I had in Mississippi, that I would lend a helping hand and serve others as my parents, teacher, home and church community had with me. "They are to do good, to be rich in good works, to be generous and ready to share" (1 Timothy 6:18)

Z-HOPE Chapter Incentive Scholarship: A grand opportunity to award and reward others

The Kentucky State Association had no "line item for scholarships" when I entered office as Kentucky State Director in 2002. It was imperative for me as State Director to align my State's goals and objectives and the Grand's programmatic thrusts. I wanted my state to be recognized more uniformly on the state, regional and national levels for their contributions and service to our Sorority and the community.

In 2002-2003, I began visualizing **Chapter Incentive Scholarships**. I visualized that when chapters were recognized at the regional or Boule level, I would personally provide that chapter an incentive scholarship of $100-200, My thoughts became a reality (Serve + Recognition = Reward).

The Basilei of Eta Zeta Chapter, left to right: Sorors Vivian Landrum-Clayton, Brunhilda Williams-Curington, Toni Thomas, Joyce B. Holliman, Bobbie Crudup Qualls, Ira J. Ebbs, Margie F. Artis and Lizzie G. Miller.

In 2005, I started dreaming regularly about state scholarships, while Sorors N. Akande and T. Wilson were at my home assisting me with Zeta work. I started talking about scholarships and asked Soror Akande to record my thoughts and thus, an unofficial draft was formulated for the State of Kentucky, the **Z-HOPE Chapter Incentive Scholarship**. The requirements:

- The scholarship focus must be in conjunction with Grand Basileus' Programmatic thrust.
- Each chapter recognized on the regional and/or national level would be awarded a chapter Incentive of $100.00 - $200.00.
- One fourth (¼) of the state auction monies would be placed in a scholarship fund.
- The 2005 scholarship would be based on the national program Z-HOPE and entitled Z-HOPE Incentive Scholarship.

I officially opened a scholarship account and personally contributed $1,000.00. At the Kentucky Leadership Conference in November 2005, ten chapters received $100.00 each and I donated another $1,000 to the Kentucky chapters that had implemented Z-HOPE projects and were recognized on the regional level. In 2009, at the Kentucky State Association, as the immediate past State Director, I presented seven hundred dollars ($100 each to seven chapters) that had been recognized as Z-HOPE winners during the 2008 Boule. At the 2012 Kentucky Leadership Conference, I gave the scholarship committee chair a $1,000 check to present with the scholarship committee report. When it was reported to the body, I received a grand surprise: The Kentucky State Association Scholarship was named in honor of me!

Kentucky State Association
Bobbie Crudup Qualls
Book Scholarship
Recipient: Soror M. Samuels
An Elated Scholarship Recipient

One of the undergraduate sorors stated with a welcoming smile, "Soror Qualls, this is an honor and a special recognition for you." I quietly reflected, God has blessed me, and I am blessed to bless someone else as I serve God and humanity. With humility, I thanked God: Thank you God for my parents who modeled the power of integrity and the importance of having a generous heart. Thank you Almighty Father for fulfilling my scholarship vision, and providing me the opportunity to make a difference in the lives of others.

The recipients of the Kentucky State Association Bobbie Nell Crudup Qualls Book Scholarship: 2013, Soror DeShawn Burrell; 2014, Soror Tiffany Brannon; and in 2015, Sorors Bria Staten and Mercedes Samuels.

Moving Zeta and Me Forward

Shirley Ruth Stansberry, Ph.D.

In 1951, as a 5 year old little girl filled with sadness, watching the men lower my father into his grave, I was filled with curiosity and yearning for understanding. My mother said, "Your dad would want you to get an education and to go on to college." I looked up at my mommy and said, "I do not understand." She said, "Keep living." This was when my desire to learn and understand began.

We moved to Michigan but it was too late for me to start school. I would cry a lot because I watched my older siblings leave every morning to go to school, but I was left at home. The following fall, I entered kindergarten. I was one happy child. The teachers could not give me enough knowledge. I was like a sponge. I soaked up everything. I never understood why kids did not like school.

While in high school, I had a geometry teacher who gave me a purpose and challenge. He had me explaining problems to the kids in my class that did not understand and who did not do well in class. Once I explained the problems to them, they did better. I told my teacher that I was going to be a geometry and algebra teacher when I grew up.

I was my mom's eleventh child. I knew she was not financially able to send me to college. I knew then that God and I had to work that financial piece out. I won a 4-year full scholarship to Michigan State University in 1965 and majored in mathematics. While attending Michigan State I made the Dean's list. After graduating in 1971, I taught at Benton Harbor High School for six years. While teaching, I continued my studies at Michigan State University in the evening and summer. I completed the requirements for my master's degree in 1977.

I married and relocated to Littleton, Colorado after my husband obtained a new position in Denver, Colorado. I obtained a math teaching position at Smoky Hill High School in Cherry Creek School District. During my second year there, I became a member of Zeta Zeta Zeta Chapter of Zeta Phi Beta Sorority, Inc., (1979). I taught math at Smoky Hill High School for twenty six years.

While I was teaching, I won a scholarship to Colorado School of Mines for the summer to study energy sources. Upon completion, I received the Mable Miller Scholarship to study at the University of Denver and received my Ph.D. Also, while teaching at Smoky Hill, I received several principal's awards and the Channel Six "Outstanding Teacher's Award" and I wrote lesson plans for the station. I held every position as a member of Zeta Zeta Zeta Chapter, and served as Colorado State Director under Grand Basilei Tearte, Carpenter and Moore.

As I continued to teach, I attended H & R Block tax courses and received their tax certificate. That was not enough. I attended real estate classes and became licensed. I worked hard at getting people qualified to purchase homes and I worked part-time for H & R Block. Both part-time positions involved helping people.

Upon retiring from teaching in 2002, I worked part time for Metropolitan State University of Denver from 2003-2007, supervising student teachers, and teaching math and education classes.

When my husband retired in 2008, we relocated back to Benton Harbor, Michigan. As a National Trustee, serving from 2008-2012, I needed to be a financial member of a chapter. I became one of the chartering members of Chi Kappa Zeta Chapter during my tenure as the National Graduate Member of the Executive Committee (2012-2014). For my love of Zeta, I became a Diamond Life Member and continue to do what is right and I continue to try to move Zeta forward.

I continue to be like a sponge learning all I can. I was a member of the first Zeta Organizational Leadership (ZOL) cohort (2005), and three advanced ZOL groups. I was in the first certified group for the Amicae Sponsor training. I enjoy being kept up to date with new knowledge. I am a Centennial visionary and I am looking forward to 2020 and what I learn on the journey.

My Golden Ticket:
From Homeless to Scholar

Cierra L. Sterling

I would like to think my story started off like the ones in many of the novels: My parents were so happy to have me and bring me home from the hospital. In reality, I know that was far from the case for me as my mother was only twenty and having her second child. She was not even sure who my father was. It could've been her fiancé and high school sweetheart or the married man she fell in love with. My mother being so young with two children under the age of three and with very little education, fell into a trap that many people did during the late '80s and early '90s. Her beauty and intelligence could not save her from being just another victim of the cocaine crack epidemic.

Graduation Day May 2011

When I was three, my mother's addiction had become even too out of control for her. One day she left my brother and me on the front stoop of her apartment building. Fortunately our great aunt worked as the assistant manager of the building and was notified by a neighbor that we were roaming around and they could not find our mother. Our aunt left work to find our apartment a mess, and that we had been consuming raw ground beef because we were hungry. She took the day off to clean us up. At that moment my life would just never be the same.

Growing up was an extreme test. My mother was in and out of prison for most of my childhood. We were being raised by our great grandmother who really did her best to make sure we had everything we needed. She was the nicest woman I have ever known, and worked as a lunch lady because she too had very little education. She always stressed the importance of education, and that it was up to us to make sure we made something out of ourselves. She always told me I was too amazing to not to make all of my dreams come true.

Growing up, school just came naturally to me. I was always the smartest kid in the class, but I had so many emotional issues I found it hard to really connect with others around me and really excel. I had so many behavior issues, teachers often gave up on me before I ever hit my fullest potential. I was not like the other kids in the class who just had to worry about being a child. I had real adult issues to worry about, and it hindered me from just being a child.

My childhood was an endless cycle of craziness and dysfunction. My mother would get out of prison, have more kids, and demand we live with her. Our happy family being all together never lasted very long since we would never stay in the same place more than a year. I always found myself taking care of her and my siblings. I was only a child myself having to raise my other siblings. It was my responsibility to make sure they were fed and looked cleaned. I was always in fear someone would come and take us away, so it was my job at ten years old to make sure that did not happen. I was the first to wake up, get the younger ones dressed and off to school. I often found myself lost, and not really sure how to handle all the pressure my life came with. Many nights, I sat and watched my mother smoking crack, and being so high she would pass out. I would clean her up and do my best to hide her from my younger siblings.

When we were not living with our mother, we were shuttled from one family member to another. The four of us were often times split up because no one wanted the hassle of taking care of four children that were not their own. Our family tried to do their best, but many of them were struggling themselves with a lack of money and education. I was not always treated the way you would think family would treat you. I was put into many homes where I was abused mentally and physically. Education was never the focus, and often I did not make it to school. As a child I was not exactly sure, but I knew my life had to be different. I knew I had to make something of myself.

High school was the turning point in my life. I was living with my great aunt who was one of the meanest people I knew. She always had great intentions for us, but had a horrible way of executing them. She was verbally and physically abusive. She felt that if she was tough, we would rise to the occasion. There was no dating, hanging with friends, or anything social. I was not even allowed to participate in school activities because she did not want me hanging out. School was my solace from my rage and the constant destruction of my self-esteem. She used every chance she got to let me know I would never be anything, and I was going to be just like my mother. I hated being in that house, but only stayed to protect my younger sister from her destruction. I was strong enough to take the beatings, so I did so because I wanted my younger sister to know she was amazing. I did not want her to believe the lies about her being ugly and stupid. One day in the middle of one of the many attacks on me, I fought back. I stood up for myself, and was thrown out of the house.

My aunt packed up some of my things and sent me to my mother's house. Once I got to the local crack house I knew I could not stay there. My mother looked me in the face and asked me where I was going to go because I could not stay with her. Her boyfriend who was a drug dealer and a pimp would not allow me to live there for free so I had to find somewhere to go. I was lucky to find two friends from the neighborhood who would sneak me in their houses at night so I wouldn't have to sleep on the street. I was able to get a job at a local fast food place that kept me busy during the day, and allowed me to eat. Being on the street was the first time I felt free. It was far from the perfect situation, but allowed me to feel in control of my life. It was the driving force to my success.

I always knew I was smart, but never really felt I could be anything special. It was my high school home economics teacher, Ms. Sherry Logan, who saw something in me I never even saw in myself. She took every chance she got to tell me how amazing I was. My first day in her class she told me God put me in her class to save me and she would help me in any way. During my time with her, she would help me wash my clothes and make sure I had food to eat. She always kept me motivated and lifted me up in prayer. My junior year of high school she asked me if I was considering college. Before that moment I never thought about college; it did not seem like something that was doable for me. I still was not convinced about going to college until she told me it would get me away from San Antonio and I could live in a dorm. I only applied to college to have a place to live. I was still sneaking in my friends' houses to sleep. My aunt would report me as a runaway to continue to get government benefits and would make me come home, and then kick me out soon after. I had to make major changes. I went to summer school, and graduated after my junior year.

I packed my stuff in a suitcase and headed to Texas Woman's University (TWU) in Denton, Texas. On that Greyhound bus, I was not sure what would happen to me. I just knew it had to be better than being on the street. When I got to TWU, I had an acceptance letter and no financial aid. All I knew was I was going to school, and I was not going back to San Antonio. I went to the registrar's office with a piece of paper about a tuition discount and my suitcase. I told him what I had been through and that I just wanted to go to school. He asked me to sit in the lobby and an hour later he walked out with a piece of paper, and told me I would not have to pay tuition for the four years at TWU. All I could do was cry.

I was then escorted to the advising office to get registered and then shown to my dorm to get all settled in. My roommate asked where all my stuff was, and I let her know everything I had was in my suitcase. Hours later she came back from Walmart with stuff for me and made me promise to graduate. My time at TWU was amazing. I started to make friends and finally was able to participate in on-campus activities. I was attending a local church where I met a young lady who was always so nice to me. She would later tell me all about Zeta Phi Beta Sorority, Incorporated. The next year, I joined her as a soror.

After graduation from TWU it became my life's work to help others who were in situations just like me. I wanted to share my story, and inspire those around me. I always say I went to college and never wanted to leave. I have been blessed to have a successful career in higher education. I spend my days helping others achieve their goals when it comes to the higher education systems. When I went to TWU I had no idea how it worked, and I made mistakes along the way. Now my life's work has been to help young people get accurate and up-to-date information about higher education. Being a Zeta taught me all about the importance of serving those in my community. I volunteer my time and talents to make sure students in underserved communities have access to information in order to be successful. I want them to know they really can be whatever they want to be, and just how powerful education can be.

As I look back, my life may have started out rocky, but I was really able to make something of myself. I learned my success is not determined by my genetics, but by my choices. I was able to be an example to those around me. I dedicate my time and talents to assisting people who have all the potential in the world, but don't know how amazing they really are. I love to use my story to motivate. I want our youth to keep their heads up because there is so much out there, and all we have to do is go after it. My education was my golden ticket and unlocked a world I never knew existed. My education allowed me to go from the daughter of a drug addict to being a scholar. I will begin my Ph.D. coursework next year.

Three Generations of Zeta Scholars

Helen Townsend-Beteet, R.Ph., M.H.A.

One of my proudest days in my life was in May of 2011 when three generations of Zeta Master's level scholars came together to celebrate. My daughter, Soror Alexandria Beteet received her bachelor's and master's degrees simultaneously from St. Louis University's school of Business in Accounting with her grandmother and I present. She had continued the linage of Zeta women in my family valuing and excelling in academics. The journey began with a determined father. It was understood from the beginning that my grandfather James Sansing wanted his girls to be college educated women. So in the 1944, his eldest daughter Helen Sansing left Indianola, Mississippi to enter Alcorn Agricultural and Mechanical College (now University) after completing high school in West Point, Mississippi at Holmes Seminary. During her first year in college the matriarch of the family, Dora Godbold Sansing died. My Aunt Helen was able to continue her education and create a path for her little sister Evelyn Sansing to enter the same school three years later. Aunt Helen became a charter member of Zeta Chapter at Alcorn A&M. While in college she was a majorette in the band. She graduate with a degree in home economics in 1947. A former classmate describe her as the prefect blend of beauty and brains. Her sister, Evelyn (my mother) also became a member of Zeta Phi Beta Sorority, Inc. at Alcorn and likewise graduated with a degree in home economics. Their Dad believed in higher education, but he also selected majors he felt suitable for women.

These Zeta young women excelled in their careers in the Delta of Mississippi during the 1950's. Soror Evelyn took a position at the new Gentry High School back in her hometown of Indianola. She assisted in the selection of the school colors and co-wrote the high school song, the Gentry Ode. Soror Helen became an instructor for 39 years at the Ruleville Central High School. She received a 40 year service award from the State of Mississippi for her contributions to schools and the community. Soror Evelyn Sansing, after marrying her high school sweetheart, move to Kansas City, Kansas in the mid- 1950's. She became an assistant principal of the historic Vernon school for African American middle school students. She was involved in their preparation for integration into high schools in Kansas City, Kansas. She became the mother to three sons and two daughters. She took years off teaching for her children, but became the "go to" seamstress in the Brentwood community of Kansas City.

Soror Evelyn and Soror Helen as college students at Alcorn, circa late 1940s

She also became a braille instructor for her cousin who became disabled while in the armed forces. Even in the 60's the military had no integrated schools for the blind. When the army was looking for a "private" instructor, she applied. His classroom was paid for by the Veterans Affairs and was housed in our family's basement. Her cousin became a successful court reporter. She returned to teaching in the late 1960's. She became the only African American lay teacher at Bishop Ward Catholic High School, in Kansas City, Kansas. She not only taught clothing and foods, but designed the majority of costumes for the high school musicals. She belonged to a fashion designer women's club and even had her own model to display her designs at fashion shows. As the kids became more independent, she continued her education and earned a Master's Degree in Counseling and Guidance from the University of Missouri, Kansas City. With her new degree she transitioned to become the lead Guidance Counselor for Bishop Ward. She also returned to active membership in Zeta Phi Beta Sorority, Inc. serving in many offices on the local and regional level. She served 6 years as the Kansas State Director for Zeta Phi Beta Sorority, Inc. (1980 – 1986). She was also very involved in politics. She would host "coffees" at her home for African American candidates as well as in retirement she became a silver-haired legislator. Many elected officials still recognize her role in winning elections and appointments in Wyandotte County.

Continuing the tradition, my mother encouraged her children to advance in education. And in the tradition of my Aunt, I (known as little Helen) became a charter member of the Omega Theta Chapter of Zeta Phi Beta Sorority, Inc. on the campus of Kansas University. The Zetas became known for their scholarship on the campus with all charter members graduating in degrees that included mathematics, English, microbiology, psychology, business, theatre, speech pathology and pharmacy. While at Kansas University, I became the 1st known African American female to graduate from the University's school of pharmacy.

After practicing in managed care for many years I decided to continue my education in health care. My first semester in the graduate program I learned that my husband and would soon be parents. Before completing my master's degree I had two small children and served as the sorority State Director for Kansas (just like my mother). It was with the help my husband, Mike Beteet, parents, and Sorors that I was able to remain in school while also managing one of the largest managed care pharmacies greater Kansas City. In 1995, I attained my Master's in Health Care Management (now known as Master's of Health Policy) from the University of Kansas. I was invited back to speak to the Kansas University Minority graduating classes and received recognition from the Chancellor Bernadette Gray-Little. I have continued to be involved in healthcare focusing on Specialty Pharmacy and consulting.

Through those years, my daughter Alexandria became a Pearlette, Amicette, and Archonette. She also became a Girl Scout and a top student in school. She attended her first Zeta Leadership conference in Washington, DC when she was six months with her Zeta mom and Zeta Grandmother in 1989. She and my mother were my consistent companions during these years to Zeta conferences on the local, state, regional and national level. Alexandria often won oratorical awards at her youth conferences, placing 3rd in at the Boule in Hollywood, CA. She also was an active member in Jack and Jill of America. She had numerous university offers by her senior year, but St. Louis University's Business and Accounting school won her heart. She became third generation in her family to become a member of Zeta Phi Beta Sorority, Inc. while an accounting student at St. Louis University. She received her Bachelor's degree and Master's degree within four years of study at the University. (I later learned my mother earned her undergraduate degree in three years).

On the campus of Alcorn, late 1940s, Soror Sansing, seated center. Fellow student Medgar Evers, last on right.

Ironically a few years back, I found that we were actually the "4th generation" of Blue and White. I had the opportunity to visit my great Aunt Albertine Reid in Clarksdale, Mississippi while she was still living. She was in her 90's then, but was still very active. While looking at the photos, awards and certificates on the decorated family walls, I noticed one resembling a Zeta membership certificate. At closer inspection I noted it was not a Zeta certificate, but a Phi Beta Sigma Fraternity, Inc. certificate granted to my great Uncle Marion Reid in 1927. He was a farmer, business man, and a faculty member at Coahoma Community College in Clarksdale, MS. The Marion M. Reid Gymnasium stands as a legacy to his leadership at the college and his community. I asked my mom if she knew her Uncle was a Sigma, she smiled and said she knew. He would keep an eye on the young Sansing girls when their paves would cross at various Zeta and Sigma events in Mississippi.

Our family now has three generations of Zetas, all attaining Master's Degrees in varied professions. I believe my grandfather would be proud that he blazed the trail for the Sansing girls, the Townsend granddaughter and the Beteet great granddaughter to pursue professional fields of study. My Aunt Helen Sansing Stephens passed away in February of 2009 was not able to witness of emergence of the third generation, but I knew she would be so proud. I believe my great uncle, Marion Reid is smiling down on us as well. Education has been valued and expected in our family. Zeta Phi Beta Sorority, Inc. was the right vehicle for us to flourish educationally. My mother always believed in continuous learning. When she retired, she went back to teaching quilting at the neighborhood senior center and became the church librarian for her church. There would always be something new to learn and always an opportunity to share what one has learned for the benefit of others.

Zeta Chapter, Alcorn, 1940s. Soror Helen stands, 3rd from right.

In spite of...

Carolyn C. Wadlington, Ed.D.

Dr. Carolyn C. Wadlington,
Doctorate Degree
November 17, 2013

My experience dates back to the mid-1980s. As a student eager to learn, but having a difficult time in a class, I reached out to my professor for assistance and guidance. After my initial contact with the professor, I was faced with this personal attack, "Let us face it; you are from a predominately black high school, a suburb with a declining economy, and an increasing crime rate. I really do not see you making it here at this institution of higher learning." It was at that moment, I began to feel anxiety and the pressure about the possibly of failing. I felt the personal attack was aimed at the quality of my prior academic achievement, the socioeconomic status of my community, and that the professor made an assumption about my upbringing. However, I did not let his negative comments deter me from reaching my goal. In-spite of, I pressed on and graduated in four years. I was overwhelmed with joy when I received the official notification of graduation and my graduation announcements. As luck would have it on the day I received the wonderful news I saw the same professor who had made the negative comments. I greeted him and invited him to my graduation. In spite of the professor's comments I succeeded and realized that someone's opinion of me doesn't define me. His words didn't kill me; they made me stronger.

Dr. Carolyn C. Wadlington with my aunts.

After graduation, I was even more determined to help others and I began my career in education. I still had a ringing in my head of the harsh negative comments that were spoken to me as an undergraduate. I pressed on and began working toward my master's degree. In-spite of, I graduated with a master's degree in Instructional Leadership.

I continued to work in the field of education and as a teacher in an elementary school setting. Some years later I began to listen to the conversations about No Child Left Behind (NCLB) and the Achievement Gap. As an elementary school teacher in an African American school, both topics directly affected me as an educator and the students I was charged to educate. As an African American educator and alumnus of a public school system, I understood the importance of a quality education and appreciated the spirit behind NCLB. It typically only takes one poor academic year for a school to be stigmatized by declining test scores. The test scores at my school were not declining, but, according to NCLB it would only take one year for a decline in standardized test scores and student achievement to begin.

Focusing on my job as an educator, I wanted to take steps to prevent this and become proactive instead of

Dr. Carolyn C. Wadlington
Master's Degree May 2000

Dr. Carolyn C. Wadlington Proud Daddy moment
Undergrad Degree December 1988

reactive. There has always been a possibility of a decline in test scores and student achievement, but I felt it was not necessary to wait until the decline occurred to identify strategies for student success. I wanted to attack the problem before it began to invade our school community. However, the implementation of any intervention would be counterproductive if children didn't learn to relax and refocus their nervous energy. Once I noticed students beginning to exhibit signs of anxiety when any form of the word "test" was mentioned, I decided on a plan of action that could be put into place. So, in-spite of, I enrolled in graduate school to further my education and prove I could make a difference. I used prior knowledge and the hot topic of NCLB, the Achievement Gap and a class that changed my life, Methods of Relaxation, to make a difference. Having learned several methods of relaxation techniques and having students practice them in everyday life, I believed the techniques were beneficial to students in relieving the anxiety associated with test taking. Upon completion of my research it was shown that the students increased their test scores by 14% in reading and 10% in math. In-spite of being told I wouldn't make it, I made it and helped students gain confidence in their ability by becoming better test takers. In spite of, I'm Dr. Carolyn C. Wadlington.

Dr. Carolyn C. Wadlington
The handshake of completion
from the president of NIU

UNDERGRADUATE SCHOLARS: OUR FUTURE... OUR DREAMS...OUR HOPES

Introduction

Anjylla Y. Foster

Undergraduates on Howard University Campus tour during
Zeta Organizational Leadership Conference in 2015

Undergraduate Sorors are as diverse as the universe. Since 1920, members of the sisterhood have explored unchartered territory and recorded many firsts. The current undergraduates are trailblazers who are achieving goals that are both challenging and engaging.

They were inspired to become members of Zeta by individuals and by chapters through examples of community service and a host of other reasons. They applaud their role models and those who have inspired their dreams. They hope for a future fulfilled by career aspirations that will make them global citizens who will change the world.

I am extremely proud of these young ladies whose determination to accomplish scholastic goals resonates as the primary driver of success. It is a privilege to present my phenomenal undergraduate Sorors of Zeta.

Scholarship Reflections of the Alpha Chapter Basileus

Arayna Spratley

Scholarship has always meant a lot to me. I come from a family where A's and B's were the only acceptable grades, and B's were stretching it, honestly. I spent my weekdays inside doing homework or playing educational games while I watched my friends play outside through the windows, and my summers consisted of educational prep for the next school year. My friends used to make fun of me, but I always felt great when I came home with that award-winning report card making my whole family proud. I learned at a young age that although I had to sacrifice for it, scholarship was something worthwhile. Whether it was the six hours I spent reading a book going to a different time period, or the time I spent doing extra educational games that helped me get into advanced classes (which were more fun than the normal ones), or the countless essays and speeches I wrote that helped me get into Howard without paying anything, scholarship was valued.

Scholarship and your great execution of it will take you to places that you never dreamed. It opens perspectives and opportunities that were once just dreams or visions. Scholarship represents a world of endless possibilities to me. Now a graduate of Howard University, my last five years of sacrifice was completely worth it. Nothing has felt more amazing than walking across the stage to get my degree and hearing my Sorors "Z Phi" me as encouragement and as a sign of pride.

When I first came to Howard. I remember a speaker telling us how we could not have it all. We couldn't have a social life, great grades and an adequate amount of sleep. The drive that comes from being dedicated to scholarship proved that speaker to be wrong. Not only was I able to have great grades and keep up friendships, but I was able to run a chapter successfully for two years and obtain a regional and state position, all while having impeccable beauty sleep. Scholarship is not just your grades at school, but it is the drive and dedication you have to yourself and your community to be the best 'you' that you can be. Scholarship is all encompassing because as Triumphant Soror Zora Neale Hurston said, "No matter how far a person can go, the horizon is still beyond you." The ideal of scholarship continues to encourage me to keep striving for my horizon.

First in My Family to Complete College

Taeana Stephens

Scholarship has always and will always be important to me. As the oldest among my siblings, I shouldered the responsibility to do well in school so my siblings could look up to me as a role model. Throughout grade school and high school, I had high academic achievement. I knew the next step was to go off to college. There were many obstacles in the way, but the support from my family helped me get through.

From my first year in college until now, I've learned a lot about myself and gained skills that contributed to my academic success. Being the first person in my family to graduate from college is a huge accomplishment, and my family is super proud of me.

Since my parents went to college for a short amount of time and did not finish, I was not sure what college was going to be like. I went in excited, nervous, and anxious all at the same time. Throughout the years, not only did I excel academically, but I was also learning life skills that I could take with me for the rest of my life.

A critical skill was time management. I learned how to juggle lots of different things at once. I always had jobs throughout college, but I never let that interfere with school. I never overbooked my work schedule to conflict with my school schedule. I am glad that during high school, I constantly used a planner to help me stay on track because that spilled over to college. I have to write everything down, like homework, events, work, meetings, etc. Keeping a planner was another skill that contributed to my school success by helping me to prioritize my time, especially with several commitments. A third skill I learned was self-care. Even though school is stressful, you still have to make time to practice self-care. Self-care is important, especially for college students because it helps you reboot if you are feeling stressed or overwhelmed.

I am ecstatic to be a member of a sorority that honors the importance of Scholarship. Being a part of Zeta Phi Beta Sorority, Inc., it is amazing to be surrounded by educated, strong women who are concerned about their education and bettering their community. It makes you even strive more to do well because your Sorors around you are there to support and encourage you as you are to them. The support and encouragement from my Sorors is another contributor to my academic success in college.

It is my intent to make sure that others will achieve the goal of completing college so that first generation will become all generations.

Determination Drives Scholarship

Jasmine Branch

Scholarship is one of the four principles that Zeta Phi Beta Sorority, Inc. was founded upon. However, no one said that staying on the path of scholarship for personal growth was the easiest to travel. Your personal search for so much knowledge and wisdom is what I believe helps you determine not just who you are as a person, but how you react to life's strife and hardships. One thing to realize is not all teachers want to see you succeed and not all teachers want to give you that "easy A." Thus, I believe that in order to achieve, succeed, and to be prosperous today, you must have determination more than ever.

My favorite quote comes from Michael Jordan: "If you're trying to achieve, there will be roadblocks. I've had them; everybody has had them. But obstacles don't have to stop you. If you run into a wall don't turn around and give up. Figure out how to climb it, go through it, or work around it." I feel like this describes my journey perfectly.

I haven't always had the ideal collegiate experience. There have been many roadblocks such as transferring from one school to another, and numerous teachers who didn't think that I was smart enough to pass their class and said that I was lazy. Determination is a trait much stronger than pride. There have been times when I just wanted to give up, but those were the times that I looked to God for strength. One thing that I can suggest to my fellow Sorors is that strength comes from your determination, support from your parents and sisters, and God's good will to help you keep going. Determination has helped me overcome numerous roadblocks and obstacles, making the wisdom that I can share with others so much greater.

While attending numerous leadership conferences, I have been afforded the opportunity to meet and develop personal relationships with several leaders in our organization who are great scholars. This has helped me see the potential of my educational journey and my personal growth for the near future. I am determined to be an exceptional scholar.

Profiles of
Undergraduate Sorors

KEELAYE JAMES
Florida A&M University
Tallahassee, Florida
MAJOR: Broadcast Journalism
EXPECTED GRADUATION DATE: 4/5/2018
CURRENT CHAPTER: Gamma Alpha
REGION: Southeastern
YEAR JOINED ZETA: 2016

WHO OR WHAT INSPIRED YOU TO BE A ZETA? The Gamma Alpha Chapter.

CAREER ASPIRATIONS: I want to be a news reporter. I enjoy being in front of a camera. If I do not get that career, I would not mind having a job in the communication field.

ARIEL POSTLE
Elizabeth City State University
Elizabeth City, North Carolina
MAJOR: Physical Education Sport Science
EXPECTED GRADUATION DATE: 5/14/2016
CURRENT CHAPTER: Alpha Gamma
REGION: Eastern
YEAR JOINED ZETA: 2014

WHO OR WHAT INSPIRED YOU TO BE A ZETA? I was inspired by Zeta's unwavering efforts to see others succeed.

CAREER ASPIRATIONS: I aspire to be a military athletic trainer and one day become the head trainer for a professional team.

NNEKA OKEREKE

Seton Hall University
South Orange, New Jersey
MAJOR: Biology
EXPECTED GRADUATION DATE: 5/16/2016
CURRENT CHAPTER: Psi Pi
REGION: Atlantic
YEAR JOINED ZETA: 2015

WHO OR WHAT INSPIRED YOU TO BE A ZETA? My curiosity inspired me to join Zeta. I saw the past and present members from my chapter on our campus. They held themselves to a standard that everyone who saw them wanted to emulate. The strength of their bond was evident. I always wondered why they were so close. They were ambitious leaders and always embraced their femininity. Now that I am a member, I understand everything I admired about them. I have been able to come out of my comfort zone and strive for those things I was always afraid to attempt. It makes me work harder to continue the work they have done for our chapter and for Zeta. Zeta continues to take me on a journey of self-discovery, and I am excited to experience everything to the fullest.

ROLE MODEL: My grandmother is my role model because she never let financial or societal barriers of living in a third world country prevent her from living her life. She always stressed the importance of getting an education despite the fact that she never attended college. She always remained a respected woman in our community, and those who knew her could attest to her good works. Even though she is no longer with us, she has left a legacy that all of her children and grandchildren continue to sustain.

CAREER ASPIRATIONS: In Nigeria, people die from illnesses that could be treated with simple medication. But because of a lack of resources and a corrupt government, there are restricted and limited access to health facilities. This is why I study biology and social work. I took several social work classes to remain informed on available resources and assistance programs. I want to open a clinic that will help.

ALANAH CROWDER

University of North Carolina, Greensboro
Raleigh, North Carolina
MAJOR: Nursing
EXPECTED GRADUATION DATE: 5/11/2018
CURRENT CHAPTER: Omega Nu
REGION: Eastern
YEAR JOINED ZETA: 2016

WHO OR WHAT INSPIRED YOU TO BE A ZETA? The people I knew who were involved and their presence and service on campus.

CAREER ASPIRATIONS: Ultimately, after I graduate with my Bachelor of Science in Nursing, I would like to gain experience in the nursing field in CNA and RN work to see how nurses are treated in the field, and ensure they are adequately trained and prepared for the work. I would like to help organize and facilitate a clinic, and address health racism and food deserts from a nurse's perspective.

NICHELLE COBB

Florida A&M University
Tallahasse, Florida
MAJOR: Broadcast Journalism
EXPECTED GRADUATION DATE: 5/1/2018
CURRENT CHAPTER: Gamma Alpha
REGION: Southeastern
YEAR JOINED ZETA: 2016

WHO OR WHAT INSPIRED YOU TO BE A ZETA? My mother initially inspired me to join Zeta, but once I went to college, I began to become inspired by the sisterhood and positive role models the Zetas on my campus displayed.

CAREER ASPIRATIONS: I want to become an entertainment reporter. I would also like to publish my own magazine, geared toward young African American teenage girls, that would focus on building self-esteem and positive self-image.

ALAINNAH WHITE

Florida A&M University
Tallahassee, Florida
MAJOR: Political Science
EXPECTED GRADUATION DATE: 5/4/2018
CURRENT CHAPTER: Gamma Alpha
REGION: Southeastern
YEAR JOINED ZETA: 2016

WHO OR WHAT INSPIRED YOU TO BE A ZETA? The passion of the Gamma Alpha Chapter is what inspired me to join Zeta Phi Beta Sorority, Inc. All ot the members in the chapter exemplified many of the same morals, so I was immediately inspired to join Zeta.

ROLE MODEL: My role model is my mother. I aspire to be like her every day. She's balanced life well career wise and keeping my family together.

CAREER ASPIRATIONS: Becoming a criminal defense attorney is my career aspiration. I plan to own my own law firm, and continue to service individuals even with a criminal charge and/or background.

MARICA BRYSON

University of Pennsylvania
Philadelphia, Pennsylvania
MAJOR: Management and Marketing & Operations Management
EXPECTED GRADUATION DATE: 5/15/2017
CURRENT CHAPTER: Mu Iota
REGION: Atlantic
YEAR JOINED ZETA: 2016

WHO OR WHAT INSPIRED YOU TO BE A ZETA? The community service aspect of the Sorority and the physical sisterhood that I saw the ladies within the Sorority share with one another on a daily basis inspired me to join Zeta.

CAREER ASPIRATIONS: I strive to become a consultant after graduation and later pursue my goal of becoming a successful entrepreneur.

INDIGO FERDINAND

Florida Agricultural and Mechanical University
Tallahassee, Florida
MAJOR: Molecular and Cellular Biology
EXPECTED GRADUATION DATE: 5/1/2019
CURRENT CHAPTER: Gamma Alpha
REGION: Southeastern
YEAR JOINED ZETA: 2016

WHO OR WHAT INSPIRED YOU TO BE A ZETA? My mother and many of the women in her graduate chapter are great examples to me. I spent my life in the youth auxiliaries, which fostered my love and zeal even more.

CAREER ASPIRATIONS: To earn my PhD in Pharmacology and to research new therapies for Type 1 diabetes.

DESTINY HOUSTON-JORDAN
University of Illinois at Springfield
Springfield, Illinois
MAJOR: Psychology and Elementary
Education
EXPECTED GRADUATION DATE: 5/17/2017
CURRENT CHAPTER: Alpha Phi
REGION: Great Lakes
YEAR JOINED ZETA: 2016

WHO OR WHAT INSPIRED YOU TO BE A ZETA? My cousin and the work that her chapter does inspired me to join Zeta.

CAREER ASPIRATIONS: I want to work in the schools, so I can inspire students, whether it be through teaching or counseling.

QUANIQUAL FORBES
Florida A&M University
Tallahassee, Florida
MAJOR: Pre-nursing
EXPECTED GRADUATION DATE: 4/30/2018
CURRENT CHAPTER: Gamma Alpha
REGION: Southeastern
YEAR JOINED ZETA: 2016

WHO OR WHAT INSPIRED YOU TO BE A ZETA? The Zetas on my campus who actually exemplify their principles on and off campus

CAREER ASPIRATIONS: I want to become a nurse practitioner specializing in neo-natal care. I hope to one day open my own practice and hire women straight out of college to give them an opportunity.

HONORA CARLSON-STROM
Hampton University
Hampton, Virginia
MAJOR: Kinesiology
EXPECTED GRADUATION DATE: 5/8/2017
CURRENT CHAPTER: Rho Alpha
REGION: Eastern
YEAR JOINED ZETA: 2016

WHO OR WHAT INSPIRED YOU TO BE A ZETA? The Rho Alpha Chapter of Zeta Phi Beta Sorority, Incorporated.

CAREER ASPIRATIONS: I want to work with physically disabled children in adaptive sports. Sports have proven to be a positive impact and can build the confidence to believe that one can achieve anything. Although one may have a physical difference, it doesn't mean that anything needs to be different. They are as capable as any able-bodied individual.

DESIREE JONES
Hampton University
Hampton, Virginia
MAJOR: 5 Year MBA (Business
Administration)
EXPECTED GRADUATION DATE: 5/13/2018
CURRENT CHAPTER: Rho Alpha
REGION: Eastern
YEAR JOINED ZETA: 2016

WHO OR WHAT INSPIRED YOU TO BE A ZETA? Their principles and the Rho Alpha Chapter's determination to do great things and be committed to their community service.

CAREER ASPIRATIONS: Create a mentoring program for college freshmen to help keep them on track academically in their freshman year.

TRIA'LE THOMAS
Florida A&M University
Tallahassee, Florida
MAJOR: Psychology
EXPECTED GRADUATION DATE: 12/10/2017
CURRENT CHAPTER: Gamma Alpha
REGION: Southeastern
YEAR JOINED ZETA: 2016

WHO OR WHAT INSPIRED YOU TO BE A ZETA? Soror Shaakira White served as a major inspiration for me joining the Gorgeous Gamma Alpha Chapter at FAMU. I began to watch the Zetas on campus and fell in love with the humbleness, beauty and sophistication of Zeta Women. I aspired to be like them and to be surrounded by women that were more like me. My junior year I finally took the step to becoming a Finer Woman.

CAREER ASPIRATIONS: I aspire to graduate from Florida A&M, and go straight into graduate school. Then after obtaining my master's degree, I'd like to join the Peace Corps and help children in under-developed countries. After I come back from two years abroad, I'd like to begin working on my doctorate while working as a practicing therapist and/or counselor.

LEXA GARRETT
Florida A&M University
Tallahassee, Florida
MAJOR: Elementary Education
EXPECTED GRADUATION DATE: 4/30/2018
CURRENT CHAPTER: Gamma Alpha
REGION: Southeastern
YEAR JOINED ZETA: 2016

WHO OR WHAT INSPIRED YOU TO BE A ZETA? I was inspired to join Zeta when I saw how hardworking, dedicated, loving, strong, and how real the Zetas on the campus of FAMU were. I had no idea about Greeks prior to coming to FAMU. I am the first one from my entire family to ever go to college. When I started to do my research on the organization, I fell in love with what Zeta stood for and what they do for the community. All of these factors inspired me to join this organization and because of that, I am here today proudly wearing my royal blue and white.

CAREER ASPIRATIONS: When I finally become a teacher, I will strive to bridge the gap within education. I want all students—no matter their SES, religion, race, or learning styles/methods—to be successful. I want all students to receive the same opportunity when it comes to public education no matter the school or environment they are in. I am not only wanting to do this, I am determined to make this happen!

GERIAN SUMMERS
Northern Kentucky University
Highland Heights, Kentucky
MAJOR: Accounting and Finance
EXPECTED GRADUATION DATE: 5/9/2017
CURRENT CHAPTER: Alpha Rho
REGION: Great Lakes
YEAR JOINED ZETA: 2014

WHO OR WHAT INSPIRED YOU TO BE A ZETA? My mother, who is also a Zeta.

ROLE MODEL: Toi Jones, Cincinnati native, who is also owner and operator of Onyx Solutions. She is a leader in her community and always strives for excellence. She is a woman who also majored in accounting and serves as a mentor for me.

CAREER ASPIRATIONS: After I receive a B.A. in Accounting and Finance, I plan to attend Chase Law school and pursue my J.D. Once I have completed my degrees I aspire to start a career with the IRS in their fraudulent audit department and try these cases in a court of law.

AYANNA BOZEMAN
Hampton University
Hampton, Virginia
MAJOR: Strategic Communications
EXPECTED GRADUATION DATE: 5/12/2018
CURRENT CHAPTER: Rho Alpha
REGION: Eastern
YEAR JOINED ZETA: 2016

WHO OR WHAT INSPIRED YOU TO BE A ZETA? My wonderful mother and sister who are both Zetas. They are both women of great impact, and I look up to them as they have done great things with Zeta and the community.

CAREER ASPIRATIONS: My aspiration is to be happy and to become a reporter for a high end news station like CNN or become a reporter for entertainment news. I would also love to be an entrepreneur and put my creativity to the test.

ABIGALE GODWIN
University of North Carolina at Charlotte
Charlotte, North Carolina
MAJOR: Pre-Nursing
EXPECTED GRADUATION DATE: 5/5/2018
CURRENT CHAPTER: Upsilon Xi
REGION: Eastern
YEAR JOINED ZETA: 2016

WHO OR WHAT INSPIRED YOU TO BE A ZETA? Anita Joseph

CAREER ASPIRATIONS: I aspire to be a nurse in the U.S. Army Nurse Corp, with the hopes of continuing my education to become a nurse practitioner.

PATRICE ELLESTON
Hampton University
Hampton, Virginia
MAJOR: Kinesiology
EXPECTED GRADUATION DATE: 5/14/2017
CURRENT CHAPTER: Rho Alpha
REGION: Eastern
YEAR JOINED ZETA: 2016

WHO OR WHAT INSPIRED YOU TO BE A ZETA? The chapter and organization itself as well as previous life experiences.

CAREER ASPIRATIONS: I plan to receive my doctorate in physical therapy. Furthermore, to expand my practice I also plan to become a professional sports trainer, either with an NFL team or with individual athletes.

KALEI SHAW
University of Illinois at Springfield
Springfield, Illinois
MAJOR: Business Administration and Communications
EXPECTED GRADUATION DATE: 5/17/2017
CURRENT CHAPTER: Alpha Phi
REGION: Great Lakes
YEAR JOINED ZETA: 2016

WHO OR WHAT INSPIRED YOU TO BE A ZETA? The principles that Zeta Phi Beta were founded upon are what inspired me. Being a great student, a finer woman, and being able to give back to the community are all things that I am and will continue to magnify and represent.

CAREER ASPIRATIONS: I plan on graduating with a double major in Communications and Business Administration with a concentration in sports management. I plan on getting an internship with Disney because they own ESPN. And, later I want to further my knowledge in the sports management field and become a manger for a college sports team and then move on to the NBA.

ALEXANDRIA MORELAND
Hampton University
Hampton, Virginia
MAJOR: Journalism
EXPECTED GRADUATION DATE: 5/8/2017
CURRENT CHAPTER: Rho Alpha
REGION: Eastern
YEAR JOINED ZETA: 2016

WHO OR WHAT INSPIRED YOU TO BE A ZETA? Fall 2014 Rho Alpha

CAREER ASPIRATIONS: My ultimate goal is to become a television personality and an actress in film. I want to inspire others to chase after their dreams and lead by example in the media.

CYDAISHA DUPREE
Rider University
Lawrenceville, New Jersey
MAJOR: Psychology
EXPECTED GRADUATION DATE: 12/20/2016
CURRENT CHAPTER: Chi Alpha
REGION: Atlantic
YEAR JOINED ZETA: 2015

WHO OR WHAT INSPIRED YOU TO BE A ZETA? Zeta's principles, service history, and current work in bonding communities

CAREER ASPIRATIONS: To obtain my master's degree in clinical counseling and rehabilitation and become a clinical counselor or psychologist

DAMAYA ROBERTS
Texas State University
San Marcos, Texas
MAJOR: Business Management
EXPECTED GRADUATION DATE: 8/12/2016
CURRENT CHAPTER: Omicron Xi
REGION: Southern
YEAR JOINED ZETA: 2015

WHO OR WHAT INSPIRED YOU TO BE A ZETA? I wanted to be a part of something great, and my definition of great is Zeta Phi Beta Sorority, Incorporated.

CAREER ASPIRATIONS: I will graduate from Texas State University almost a year early this upcoming summer, August 2016. I am majoring in business management with a concentration in HR. I will continue my studies at Abeline Christian University, where I will work on obtaining my MBA in Organizational Development. I hope to become a Human Resource supervisor on the corporate level.

KEN'NITA AGEE
Western Michigan University
Kalamazoo, Michigan
MAJOR: Nursing
EXPECTED GRADUATION DATE: 4/30/2018
CURRENT CHAPTER: Tau Delta
REGION: Great Lakes
YEAR JOINED ZETA: 2016

WHO OR WHAT INSPIRED YOU TO BE A ZETA? Niquoya Brown.

CAREER ASPIRATIONS: Surgical Nurse.

LACHELLE HARRIS
Texas State University
Houston, Texas
MAJOR: Nursing
EXPECTED GRADUATION DATE: 5/14/2016
CURRENT CHAPTER: Omicron Xi
REGION: Southern
YEAR JOINED ZETA: 2016

WHO OR WHAT INSPIRED YOU TO BE A ZETA? The passing of my brother.

CAREER ASPIRATIONS: Pediatric Nurse Practitioner

CENE HARRIS
Louisiana State University
Baton Rouge, Louisiana
MAJOR: Psychology
EXPECTED GRADUATION DATE: 5/13/2016
CURRENT CHAPTER: Rho Epsilon
REGION: Southern
YEAR JOINED ZETA: 2014

WHO OR WHAT INSPIRED YOU TO BE A ZETA? The women of the undergrad chapter at my university.

CAREER ASPIRATIONS: Become a licensed clinical psychologist and open my own practice.

RENEE' HALL
Youngstown State University
Youngstown, Ohio
MAJOR: Psychology
EXPECTED GRADUATION DATE: 5/6/2017
CURRENT CHAPTER: Eta Eta
REGION: Great Lakes
YEAR JOINED ZETA: 2016

WHO OR WHAT INSPIRED YOU TO BE A ZETA? The sisterhood.

CAREER ASPIRATIONS: I want to become a school psychologist and help create educational programs for inner city school kids. I want to provide programs for children who may not have the same opportunities as children in suburban areas. After years of experience I want to open my own practice.

KYSA PHILLIPS
Texas State University
San Marcos, Texas
MAJOR: CIS
EXPECTED GRADUATION DATE: 5/14/2017
CURRENT CHAPTER: Omicron Xi
REGION: Southern
YEAR JOINED ZETA: 2015

WHO OR WHAT INSPIRED YOU TO BE A ZETA? Sisterhood.

CAREER ASPIRATIONS: Professional artist and program builder.

NAOMI LOCKETT
Rider University
Lawrenceville, New Jersey
MAJOR: Psychology
EXPECTED GRADUATION DATE: 5/13/2016
CURRENT CHAPTER: Chi Alpha
REGION: Atlantic
YEAR JOINED ZETA: 2015

WHO OR WHAT INSPIRED YOU TO BE A ZETA? I grew up in Zeta youth groups and have been groomed all my life to become a Zeta.

CAREER ASPIRATIONS: I want to obtain my doctorate in psychology and work with children to improve their lives

BRIA STATEN-FAVORS
University of Louisville
Louisville, Kentucky
MAJOR: Communication
EXPECTED GRADUATION DATE: 5/14/2016
CURRENT CHAPTER: Delta Theta
REGION: Great Lakes
YEAR JOINED ZETA: 2014

WHO OR WHAT INSPIRED YOU TO BE A ZETA? I was inspired by both a mentor I had in high school as well as the Zetas who were on campus when I was a freshman.

CAREER ASPIRATIONS: I hope to continue my education by receiving a master's degree in Higher Education Administration. I want to work in the Office of Communications and Marketing at a college or university and one day rise to Director of Marketing.

SHIRLEY HEADEN
High Point University
High Point, North Carolina
MAJOR: Elementary Education
EXPECTED GRADUATION DATE: 5/7/2016
CURRENT CHAPTER: Epsilon Tau
REGION: Eastern
YEAR JOINED ZETA: 2013

WHO OR WHAT INSPIRED YOU TO BE A ZETA? The desire to join a sisterhood in which I can be myself and grow at the same time.

CAREER ASPIRATIONS: Teacher and school counselor.

KE'SWANIS BRISCOE
The University of Louisiana at Monroe
Monroe, Louisiana
MAJOR: Pre-Medical Laboratory Science
EXPECTED GRADUATION DATE: 5/14/2019
CURRENT CHAPTER: Beta Theta
CHAPTER STATE: Alabama
REGION: Southern
YEAR JOINED ZETA: 2015

WHO OR WHAT INSPIRED YOU TO BE A ZETA? A member of this great Sorority inspired me to become a member because of her love for the Sorority and the way she exemplified the principles of Zeta.

CAREER ASPIRATIONS: My career aspiration is to become a research scientist for St.Jude Children's Research Hospital.

TYLER HOLLIMAN
Bowling Green State Universty
Bowling Green, Ohio
MAJOR: Public Health
EXPECTED GRADUATION DATE: 12/18/2016
CURRENT CHAPTER: Psi Epsilon
REGION: Great Lakes
YEAR JOINED ZETA: 2013

WHO OR WHAT INSPIRED YOU TO BE A ZETA? When I was 12 years old, I participated in Girls to Pearls, which was created by Zeta Phi Beta Sorority, Inc.- Gamma Zeta Zeta Chapter, located in Columbus, OH. I was mentored by my aunt Mel Causey, my cousin Paige Fields-Rodgers and one of my charter members, Cathy I. Copeland Mock. They guided me and helped all along the way before joining Zeta, and they stil do until this day. I appreciate them. The current chapter members during the time on Bowling Greens campus were approachable, kind and always willing to help. They held themselves to a higher standard and always carried themselves in a positive light. I will never forget that.

CAREER ASPIRATIONS: I would like to be sexual health educator for African Americans in urban areas and inner cities to promote health education and wellness. Ultimately, I want to start my own non-profit organization centered in helping others to help themselves to the best of their abilities.

ASHANTI HOYLES
University of the District of Columbia
Washington, DC
MAJOR: Business Management
EXPECTED GRADUATION DATE: 12/20/2016
CURRENT CHAPTER: Kappa Alpha
REGION: Eastern
YEAR JOINED ZETA: 2016

WHO OR WHAT INSPIRED YOU TO BE A ZETA? I was inspired to join Zeta Phi Beta Sorority, Incorporated because the Zetas I encountered were hard working and exceeded my expectations. I was encouraged by these women because they represented the definition of Finer Womanhood on campus, on the job and in the community.

ROLE MODEL: One of my role models is Ruby Dee/Ruby Ann Wallace. She helped pave the way for African American women in the arts and was a well-known civil rights activist. She was also a good friend of Dr. Martin Luther King Jr.

CAREER ASPIRATIONS: My career aspiration is to enhance my current leadership skills in the public health care sector so I may positively impact the lives of others.

AMBER MARTIN
Rutgers University
Camden, New Jersey
MAJOR: Biology
EXPECTED GRADUATION DATE: 5/19/2017
CURRENT CHAPTER: Theta Omicron
REGION: Atlantic
YEAR JOINED ZETA: 2015

WHO OR WHAT INSPIRED YOU TO BE A ZETA? My mentor inspired me to be Greek; Zeta just captured my heart.

CAREER ASPIRATIONS: I have not decided on a major for graduate school yet, but I aspire to work in health care with kids.

DEANNA-KAYE DALEY
Xavier University of Louisiana
New Orleans, Louisiana
MAJOR: Chemistry
EXPECTED GRADUATION DATE: 5/6/2017
CURRENT CHAPTER: Beta Delta
REGION: Southern
YEAR JOINED ZETA: 2015

WHO OR WHAT INSPIRED YOU TO BE A ZETA? I became a member of this organization because I wanted to be involved with the sisterhood and brotherly love I see and hear about so often. I also wanted to become a Zeta, so I can play a part in upholding the traditions, guidelines and history many individuals abide by that were set by the Five Pearls.

CAREER ASPIRATIONS: I inspire to become a forensic scientist.

ROSE TUSA

Northwestern state University
Natchitoches, Louisiana
MAJOR: Liberal arts with concentration in
Scientific Inquiry
EXPECTED GRADUATION DATE: 5/6/2016
CURRENT CHAPTER: Xi Epsilon
REGION: Southern
YEAR JOINED ZETA: 2014

WHO OR WHAT INSPIRED YOU
TO BE A ZETA? The Sorors of
Xi Epsilon.

CAREER ASPIRATIONS:
Primary Care Physician.

MARYAM LAIYEMO

Howard University
Washington, DC
MAJOR: Administration of Justice
EXPECTED GRADUATION DATE: 5/7/2016
CURRENT CHAPTER: Alpha
REGION: Eastern
YEAR JOINED ZETA: 2016

WHO OR WHAT INSPIRED YOU
TO BE A ZETA? "There is a
Zeta in every girl regardless
of race, creed or color, who
has high standards and principles, a good scholarly average, and an active interest in
all things that she undertakes to accomplish."
Reading this quote by Founder Viola Tyler
Goings was the main inspiration for my interest
in Zeta Phi Beta Sorority, Inc. This exemplifies
the true inclusive nature of Zeta Phi Beta Sorority,
Inc., and the commitment to quality, over quan-
tity when selecting members. This statement truly
moved me and indicated that superficial aspects
are not looked at; rather it is the character, scholarship, and passion of a person that are analyzed.
These are the true characteristics a member of
Zeta Phi Beta Sorority, Inc. should exhibit.

CAREER ASPIRATIONS: To obtain a Doctorate of
Medicine, which will enable me to achieve my
career goal of improving the health of the general
population, with emphasis on the segment of the
population that suffers disproportionally higher
burdens of preventable diseases.

CHRISTINA HICKS

Southeastern Louisiana University
Hammond, Louisiana
MAJOR: Social Work
EXPECTED GRADUATION DATE: 5/13/2017
CURRENT CHAPTER: Eta Lambda
REGION: Southern
YEAR JOINED ZETA: 2015

WHO OR WHAT INSPIRED YOU
TO BE A ZETA? Seeing the
strong sisterly bond and
encouragement to excel that
is shared among the ladies
who make up this Sorority.

CAREER ASPIRATIONS: To continue to be a hardworking, dedicated, and a strong minded individual seeking to utilize my knowledge and skills
that have been gained as a way to help others
within the community, while motivated towards
continuing to excel and advance on various levels.

D'ANA SIMMONS

Cleveland State university
Cleveland, Ohio
MAJOR: Organizational Leadership focused in
management
EXPECTED GRADUATION DATE: 12/12/2016
CURRENT CHAPTER: Psi Theta
REGION: Great Lakes
YEAR JOINED ZETA: 2014

WHO OR WHAT INSPIRED YOU
TO BE A ZETA? Paris Jones

CAREER ASPIRATIONS: My
career aspiration is to start
my own company in a spe-
cific industry. This would
put me at the top of the chain and would make
me my own boss. This can be a big motivating
factor and a crowning achievement to my career
aspirations. To a lot of people if they start a successful business, they view themselves as successful, but just the thought of having that type

of opportunity would put a checkmark on my list of goals.

DESTINY RAWLS
Florida Gulf Coast University
Fort Myers, Florida
MAJOR: Criminal Justice and Legal Studies
EXPECTED GRADUATION DATE: 7/31/2017
CURRENT CHAPTER: Gamma Tau
REGION: Southeastern
YEAR JOINED ZETA: 2014

WHO OR WHAT INSPIRED YOU TO BE A ZETA? When I first came to college as a freshman in 2013, I had aspirations of being involved on campus, specifically in Greek life. I had already done my research and decided that if I was going to join a sorority it would be Zeta Phi Beta Sorority, Incorporated. The Zetas on campus at the time made themselves approachable, making it easier to express interest by attending events and having normal conversations with the members, whether it was about Zeta or just life in general. The fact that these women did not act like they are better than others just because of their letters exemplified Finer Womanhood in my eyes, and was one of the biggest inspirations for me to join. Being a Zeta has had a huge influence on my growth as an individual by presenting me with opportunities to step out of my comfort zone.

CAREER ASPIRATIONS: After graduating from Florida Gulf Coast University in 2017, I plan to attend law school. Since I was younger, it has been my dream to become a lawyer. I am still debating on which specific field of law I plan to pursue, but I am leaning towards family matters such as divorce, probate/estate, and custody. Eventually, I plan to become a judge.

NIQUOYA BROWN
Western Michigan University
Kalamazoo, Michigan
MAJOR: English
EXPECTED GRADUATION DATE: 4/30/2016
CURRENT CHAPTER: Tau Delta
REGION: Great Lakes
YEAR JOINED ZETA: 2014

WHO OR WHAT INSPIRED YOU TO BE A ZETA? My mother

CAREER ASPIRATIONS: I want to have my own counseling practice specializing in marriage, couple and family counseling.

ANTOINETTE CAREY SPRIGGS
University of North Texas at Dallas
Dallas, Texas
MAJOR: Biology
EXPECTED GRADUATION DATE: 5/19/2017
CURRENT CHAPTER: Chi Upsilon
REGION: Southern
YEAR JOINED ZETA: 2015

WHO OR WHAT INSPIRED YOU TO BE A ZETA? There were so many women who supported me, helped me, and loved me unconditionally. When I found out that they were members of Zeta Phi Beta Sorority, Inc., I knew this was the path for me!

CAREER ASPIRATIONS: It is my goal to pursue a Doctorate in Veterinary Medicine. I will then open my own practice, offering services to those experiencing homelessness while advocating for better housing, education, and life skills training.

KENDAL BROWN

James Madison University
Harrisonburg, Virginia
MAJOR: Psychology
EXPECTED GRADUATION DATE: 5/7/2016
CURRENT CHAPTER: Theta Nu
REGION: Eastern
YEAR JOINED ZETA: 2015

WHO OR WHAT INSPIRED YOU TO BE A ZETA? I was inspired to join Zeta by the bond of sisterhood between like-minded, educated, and strong women.

CAREER ASPIRATIONS: This fall, I will be pursuing my Master of Science in Student Affairs and Higher Education at Indiana State University. After earning my master's, I aspire to work in the field of Student Affairs at a university and eventually become Vice President of Student Affairs. I would like use my education and passions to help college level students achieve their goals and reach their full potential.

KEISHANA WASHINGTON

Clark Atlanta University
Atlanta, Georgia
MAJOR: Criminal Justice
EXPECTED GRADUATION DATE: 5/22/2017
CURRENT CHAPTER: Psi Chapter
REGION: Southeastern
YEAR JOINED ZETA: 2016

WHO OR WHAT INSPIRED YOU TO BE A ZETA? The community service aspect of the organization and the love they have what they do.

CAREER ASPIRATIONS: To join the military (Air Force) and to be a future FBI or CIA agent.

JASMINE CARPENTER

The Ohio State University
Columbus, Ohio
MAJOR: Human Developement and Family Science
EXPECTED GRADUATION DATE: 12/18/2017
CURRENT CHAPTER: Xi Gamma
REGION: Great Lakes
YEAR JOINED ZETA: 2015

WHO OR WHAT INSPIRED YOU TO BE A ZETA? Being around a group of females who want to serve the community while also representing the organization through the finer principles that we stand for. Also being around females who are super personable, not making me feel like I have to change myself around them. They never made me feel like that. They asked me to join their organization because they wanted me to add to the chapter.

CAREER ASPIRATIONS: I want to become a child life specialist somewhere in Ohio, so I can give back to my community by helping kids going through tragic times in their lives.

TE-NIA MACFARLANE

High Point University
Winston-Salem, North Carolina
MAJOR: Psychology, Sociology & Anthropology
EXPECTED GRADUATION DATE: 5/8/2018
CURRENT CHAPTER: Epsilon Tau
REGION: Eastern
YEAR JOINED ZETA: 2015

WHO OR WHAT INSPIRED YOU TO BE A ZETA? Shirley Headen.

CAREER ASPIRATIONS: I would like to become a child psychologist and work with juvenile delinquents.

LELA THOMPSON
James Madison University
Harrisonburg, Virginia
MAJOR: Social Work
EXPECTED GRADUATION DATE: 5/4/2017
CURRENT CHAPTER: Theta Nu
REGION: Eastern
YEAR JOINED ZETA: 2016

WHO OR WHAT INSPIRED YOU TO BE A ZETA? I wanted to be a part of an organization of women who are college educated and interested in aspiring to do all they can to further themselves and the world.

CAREER ASPIRATIONS: After earning my Bachelor's of Social Work degree, I plan on attending graduate school to earn my MSW. I hope to enroll in a graduate school that offers a dual degree program for both Social Work and Public Health. I also plan on becoming a Licensed Clinical Social Worker. I hope to work in the mental health field as a school social worker.

CIMONE CUMMINGS
Youngstown State University
Youngstown, Ohio
MAJOR: Criminal justice
EXPECTED GRADUATION DATE: 5/7/2019
CURRENT CHAPTER: Eta Eta
REGION: Great Lakes
YEAR JOINED ZETA: 2016

WHO OR WHAT INSPIRED YOU TO BE A ZETA? A good friend.

CAREER ASPIRATIONS: Working in broken societies by studying criminology to prevent/predict crimes from occurring.

PATRICIA LOTT
University of New Mexico
Albuquerque, New Mexico
MAJOR: Liberal Arts
EXPECTED GRADUATION DATE: 12/7/2016
CURRENT CHAPTER: Nu Tau
REGION: Pacific
YEAR JOINED ZETA: 2015

WHO OR WHAT INSPIRED YOU TO BE A ZETA? Christina Foster

CAREER ASPIRATIONS: I want to work in Student Affairs and ultimately become a director of an ethnic resource center. I want provide proper advisement to underrepresented minorities to get in careers that are not easily accessible to them.

TOMESHIA SPRIGGS
High Point University
High Point, North Carolina
MAJOR: Human Relations
EXPECTED GRADUATION DATE: 5/7/2016
CURRENT CHAPTER: Epsilon Tau
REGION: Eastern
YEAR JOINED ZETA: 2013

WHO OR WHAT INSPIRED YOU TO BE A ZETA? The Zeta on campus my freshmen year

CAREER ASPIRATIONS: Possibly to work for a non-profit organization that helps minority women

LEIGH-ANN WILLIAMS
University of Louisiana at Monroe
Monroe, Louisiana
MAJOR: Toxicology
EXPECTED GRADUATION DATE: 5/14/2016
CURRENT CHAPTER: Beta Theta
REGION: Southern
YEAR JOINED ZETA: 2011

WHO OR WHAT INSPIRED YOU TO BE A ZETA? Meeting sorors who lived the principles

CAREER ASPIRATIONS: My career goal is to be a clinician in a hospital or health care setting. I would also like to work in academia teaching on the collegiate level.

TYLER KING
Alabama State University
Montgomery, Alabama
MAJOR: Forensic Chemistry
EXPECTED GRADUATION DATE: 5/7/2016
CURRENT CHAPTER: Epsilon Beta
REGION: South Central
YEAR JOINED ZETA: 2013

WHO OR WHAT INSPIRED YOU TO BE A ZETA? All I have ever known is Zeta Phi Beta. My mother is Zeta; my sister is a Zeta. They helped to become the woman I am today.

CAREER ASPIRATIONS: I want to become a forensic toxicologist, which will eventually lead to me becoming a drug chemist, thus obtaining my very own private lab.

ANGELE DOSSOUS
Florida Gulf Coast University
Fort Myers, Florida
MAJOR: Child and youth studies
EXPECTED GRADUATION DATE: 5/1/2017
CURRENT CHAPTER: Gamma Tau
REGION: Southeastern
YEAR JOINED ZETA: 2016

WHO OR WHAT INSPIRED YOU TO BE A ZETA? I love what Zeta stands for with their principles, and I wanted to have that sisterhood and connection of other ladies in my life.

CAREER ASPIRATIONS: I would love to be a future educator to inspire children all over.

AFUA ASANTE
Seton Hall University
South Orange, New Jersey
MAJOR: Nursing
EXPECTED GRADUATION DATE: 5/16/2016
CURRENT CHAPTER: Psi Pi
REGION: Atlantic
YEAR JOINED ZETA: 2015

WHO OR WHAT INSPIRED YOU TO BE A ZETA? My current chapter sisters' work ethic and love for Zeta inspired me.

CAREER ASPIRATIONS: I aspire to be a Pediatric Nurse Practitioner. From a very young age, I have been interested in medicine solely because my mother and father are health professionals. The anatomy and physiology of the human body has always intrigued me. I admire the compassion that nurses give to their patients every day. In the future I will use the knowledge I have attained to heal our future children.

FATIMA GUNN
Indiana University-Purdue University Indianapolis
Indianapolis, Indiana
MAJOR: Health Sciences
EXPECTED GRADUATION DATE: 5/6/2017
CURRENT CHAPTER: Omicron Pi
REGION: Great Lakes
YEAR JOINED ZETA: 2015

WHO OR WHAT INSPIRED YOU TO BE A ZETA? The Zetas who were on my campus at the time showed a sisterly bond that was so real and genuine. The relationsip they all had was strong, and I wanted to grow that same sisterhood. These women showed great confidence and were very down to earth, open, honest, and warm hearted.

CAREER ASPIRATIONS: My ultimate career goal is to become an occupational therapist that specializes in pediatrics and helping young children.

NAILAH RIMMER
Sacramento State
Sacramento, California
MAJOR: Communications
EXPECTED GRADUATION DATE: 5/20/2017
CURRENT CHAPTER: Nu Upsilon
REGION: Pacific
Year Joined Zeta: 2015

WHO OR WHAT INSPIRED YOU TO BE A ZETA? The demeanor of the gracious women who came before me. How they carried themselves and treated others inspired me to pursue my Zeta walk.

CAREER ASPIRATIONS: I wish to be either on radio or television inspiring many to be better, do better, and most of all, think better. I would like to be a motivational speaker who will speak upon the neglected topics like mental health and racism within the collegic and grade school system. I want to show those who feel like they are by themselves that there is a rainbow after the storm.

KIRSTYN MINER
North Carolina A&T State University
Greensboro, North Carolina
MAJOR: Social Work
EXPECTED GRADUATION DATE: 5/13/2017
CURRENT CHAPTER: Zeta Alpha
REGION: Eastern
YEAR JOINED ZETA: 2016

WHO OR WHAT INSPIRED YOU TO BE A ZETA? The women of Zeta Alpha Chapter of Zeta Phi Beta Sorority, Inc. are who inspired me to join Zeta. Seeing them around campus and how they carry themselves with class, they exemplify the true definition of Finer Womanhood. As an interested person, I was made to feel very comfortable by these ladies. They were very welcoming. They made me feel like joining this Sorority would feel like home, and it does. I currently hold a 3.94 GPA and I have had several courses with my sorors who have upheld our principle of Scholarship.

CAREER ASPIRATIONS: I aspire to be a social worker for families and at-risk youth. I want to be a support system and a role model for the people in my community. I want to have a positive impact on every person I encounter to give them courage to make it through life.

BRIANA HOLMES
Trinity Washington University
Washington, DC
MAJOR: Social Psychology
EXPECTED GRADUATION DATE: 5/7/2017
CURRENT CHAPTER: Sigma Pi
REGION: Eastern
YEAR JOINED ZETA: 2015

WHO OR WHAT INSPIRED YOU TO BE A ZETA? I joined Zeta because of the strong sisterly bond.

CAREER ASPIRATIONS: I want to work on research in the psychology field.

JALISA HEYWARD
California State University Sacramento
Sacramento, California
MAJOR: Criminal Justice
EXPECTED GRADUATION DATE: 12/17/2016
CURRENT CHAPTER: Nu Upsilon
REGION: Pacific
YEAR JOINED ZETA: 2015

WHO OR WHAT INSPIRED YOU TO BE A ZETA? My best friend and now soror, Nailah Rimmer, sisterhood, and finner womanhood

CAREER ASPIRATIONS: To become the State Prosecutor of California.

KIASIA ANDERSON
Trinity Washington University
Washington, DC
MAJOR: Human Relations
EXPECTED GRADUATION DATE: 7/22/1995
CURRENT CHAPTER: Sigma Pi
REGION: Eastern
YEAR JOINED ZETA: 2015

WHO OR WHAT INSPIRED YOU TO BE A ZETA? My Aunt Vanessa.

CAREER ASPIRATIONS: I would love to become a social worker or counselor for troubled teens.

ANEISHA ROBINSON
American University
Washington, DC
MAJOR: International Studies
EXPECTED GRADUATION DATE: 5/8/2018
CURRENT CHAPTER: Sigma Pi
REGION: Eastern
YEAR JOINED ZETA: 2016

WHO OR WHAT INSPIRED YOU TO BE A ZETA? The principles of the organization and the women who were members inspired me to join Zeta.

CAREER ASPIRATIONS: I aspire to help uplift and empower Black people in the United States and other marginalized people across the globe through community outreach and education.

SHATESHA MORRIS
California State University, Sacramento
Sacramento, California
MAJOR: Criminal Justice & Social Work
EXPECTED GRADUATION DATE: 5/19/2018
CURRENT CHAPTER: Nu Upsilon
REGION: Pacific
YEAR JOINED ZETA: 2015

WHO OR WHAT INSPIRED YOU TO BE A ZETA? Soror Shannon Johnson (Aunt).

CAREER ASPIRATIONS: To graduate college with a degree in both criminal justice and social work as a Summa Cum Laude scholar. Apply to attend a law school, obtain a J.D and become a family court lawyer. Eventually become a family court judge. Publish a book about the adversity I have faced throughout life. Hold a national position in Zeta Phi Beta Sorority, Inc.!

KADESHA MITCHELL
Trinity Washington University
Washington, DC
MAJOR: Human Relations
EXPECTED GRADUATION DATE: 5/7/2017
CURRENT CHAPTER: Sigma Pi
REGION: Eastern
YEAR JOINED ZETA: 2015

WHO OR WHAT INSPIRED YOU TO BE A ZETA? My Sisters inspired me to join Zeta. I wanted to be their Role Model and I wanted them to know you can do anything that you love as long as you put your mind to it.

CAREER ASPIRATIONS: Career counselor for children.

T'KEYAH JOHNSON
High Point University
High Point, North Carolina
MAJOR: Criminal Justice
EXPECTED GRADUATION DATE: 5/7/2018
CURRENT CHAPTER: Epsilon Tau
REGION: Eastern
YEAR JOINED ZETA: 2015

WHO OR WHAT INSPIRED YOU TO BE A ZETA? Shirley Headen, current Basileus of Epsilon Tau Chapter, inspired me to join by her exhibition of Finer Womanhood.

CAREER ASPIRATIONS: My career aspiration is to make a difference in a rural community by becoming a physician, specializing in gastroenterology. I would like to establish my own private practice, but assist at the local ER in my spare time.

BEATRICE BONNER
University of Illinois at Springfield
Springfield, Illinois
MAJOR: Communication
EXPECTED GRADUATION DATE: 5/17/2018
CURRENT CHAPTER: Alpha Phi
REGION: Great Lakes
YEAR JOINED ZETA: 2016

WHO OR WHAT INSPIRED YOU TO BE A ZETA? My family values and my desire to do service for the community through the Sorority inspired me to join Zeta.

ROLE MODEL: My mother is my role model. No matter what life has thrown at her, whether it be illness or financial issues, she has overcome the odds to succeed in life.

CAREER ASPIRATIONS: I plan to graduate with a degree in Communications with a focus in radio and television broadcast. I plan to use my degree to be a news anchor. I would also like to promote for politicians. One day I hope to have my own radio or television show that would inspire not only my generation but future generations to make positive decisions.

MAXINE DAVIS
American University
Washington, DC
MAJOR: International Studies and Public Health
EXPECTED GRADUATION DATE: 5/7/2016
CURRENT CHAPTER: Sigma Pi
REGION: Eastern
YEAR JOINED ZETA: 2015

WHO OR WHAT INSPIRED YOU TO BE A ZETA? I took a moment to reflect on the most inspirational women in my life. I noticed that the one thing they all had in common was that they were all leaders, destined for greatness and were all Zetas. I aspired to be like them and they inspired me to join Zeta.

CAREER ASPIRATIONS: I would like to bridge the gap between health outcomes and cultural traditions/practices on an international scale.

KALIYAH JAYNES
University of New Mexico
Albuquerque, New Mexico
MAJOR: Psychology, pre-nursing
EXPECTED GRADUATION DATE: 5/12/2018
CURRENT CHAPTER: Nu Tau
REGION: Pacific
YEAR JOINED ZETA: 2015

WHO OR WHAT INSPIRED YOU TO BE A ZETA? I was inspired to join Zeta because of the action and presence that the Nu Tau Chapter had on the UNM campus. Because of their actions, kindness, and positive attitudes, I was driven to explore the history and purpose behind this organization. I love the principles of Zeta and hold them close to my heart. It is for these reasons that I was inspired to become a member of Zeta Phi Beta Sorority, Incorporated.

CAREER ASPIRATIONS: My career aspirations are in healthcare and medicine. I have a strong passion for mental health. I am currently attending school as a psychology major and am applying to the nursing program at the University of New Mexico. I am pursuing a career as a psychiatric nurse practitioner in the hopes of treating those with mental disorders as well as removing the stigma that surrounds mental health.

ARAYNA SPRATLEY
Howard University
Washington, DC
MAJOR: Psychology
EXPECTED GRADUATION DATE: 5/7/2016
CURRENT CHAPTER: Alpha
REGION: Eastern
YEAR JOINED ZETA: 2013

WHO OR WHAT INSPIRED YOU TO BE A ZETA? My mother, Cleo Spratley.

CAREER ASPIRATIONS: My aspiration is to develop curriculum for schools to provide a better education for students. Ultimately, I'd like to become the President of Howard University.

DESTINIE STATUM
North Carolina State University
Raleigh, North Carolina
MAJOR: Social Work and Africana Studies
EXPECTED GRADUATION DATE: 6/6/2017
CURRENT CHAPTER: Mu Xi
REGION: Eastern
YEAR JOINED ZETA: 2014

WHO OR WHAT INSPIRED YOU TO BE A ZETA? The organization's principles and my amazing Big Sisters.

CAREER ASPIRATIONS: To become a social worker who focuses on the mental and physical health of people of color.

JOHNIA MURRAY
North Carolina State University
Raleigh, North Carolina
MAJOR: Psychology
EXPECTED GRADUATION DATE: 5/8/2018
CURRENT CHAPTER: Mu Xi
REGION: Eastern
YEAR JOINED ZETA: 2016

WHO OR WHAT INSPIRED YOU TO BE A ZETA? The open and kind hearts that were extended to me upon my arrival at this university

CAREER ASPIRATIONS: To work in the public and private sector to help people from an individual and collective perspective through daily actions and big situations

ELIZABETH OGUNSUYI
American University
Washington, DC
MAJOR: Political Science
EXPECTED GRADUATION DATE: 5/1/2019
CURRENT CHAPTER: Sigma Pi
REGION: Eastern
YEAR JOINED ZETA: 2016

WHO OR WHAT INSPIRED YOU TO BE A ZETA? Zeta's founding principles.

CAREER ASPIRATIONS: To attend law school after my undergraduate studies so that I may later become a prosecuting attorney and then eventually the next U.S. Attorney General.

KAYLA OVERDIEP
NC State University
Raleigh, North Carolina
MAJOR: Sociology; Business Administration
EXPECTED GRADUATION DATE: 5/6/2017
CURRENT CHAPTER: Mu Xi
REGION: Eastern
YEAR JOINED ZETA: 2016

WHO OR WHAT INSPIRED YOU TO BE A ZETA? Cynthia Sharpe, Destinie Statum.

CAREER ASPIRATIONS: To become a college counselor/advisor for high school students, specifically for students of color and other underrepresented groups.

TAYLOR JANUARY
Alabama A&M University
Huntsville, Alabama
MAJOR: Computer Science
EXPECTED GRADUATION DATE: 12/9/2016
CURRENT CHAPTER: Sigma Beta
REGION: South Central
YEAR JOINED ZETA: 2014

WHO OR WHAT INSPIRED YOU TO BE A ZETA? My mother

CAREER ASPIRATIONS: To become a software engineer for an innovative company that can help me grow in my field.

KIMOY TAYLOR
American University
Washington, DC
MAJOR: International Relations & Economics
EXPECTED GRADUATION DATE: 3/7/2018
CURRENT CHAPTER: Sigma Pi
REGION: Eastern
YEAR JOINED ZETA: 2016

WHO OR WHAT INSPIRED YOU TO BE A ZETA? I love what the organization stands for. A group of women who want to impact their community instead focusing on their inner circle. I want to spread that message across my college campus. Also, I love the ideal of Finer Womanhood. I recognize that I have a long way to go to become the woman I want to be, and I believe Zeta can help me get there.

CAREER ASPIRATIONS: I aspire to work for a consulting firm or be an analyst for the United States government in the Asian Pacific Region.

QUINCI LEGARDYE
University of New Mexico
Albuquerque, New Mexico
MAJOR: English - Creative Writing;
Psychology
EXPECTED GRADUATION DATE: 5/14/2016
CURRENT CHAPTER: Nu Tau
REGION: Pacific
YEAR JOINED ZETA: 2014

WHO OR WHAT INSPIRED YOU TO BE A ZETA? The principles of service and Finer Womanhood

CAREER ASPIRATIONS: I will be continuing my education after undergrad in a Master of Fine Arts program in Creative Writing. My dream is to publish my own novel one day. I am also pursuing a career in the publishing industry either as an editor or book agent.

IMANI WHITBY
Western Michigan University
Kalamazoo, Michigan
MAJOR: Elementary Education
EXPECTED GRADUATION DATE: 4/29/2016
CURRENT CHAPTER: Tau Delta
REGION: Great Lakes
YEAR JOINED ZETA: 2016

WHO OR WHAT INSPIRED YOU TO BE A ZETA? I was inspired by the diversity of the organization

CAREER ASPIRATIONS: To become a superintendent of an urban school district.

AMANDA MBATA
North Carolina A&T State University
Greensboro, North Carolina
MAJOR: Social Work
EXPECTED GRADUATION DATE: 5/13/2017
CURRENT CHAPTER: Zeta Alpha
REGION: Eastern
YEAR JOINED ZETA: 2016

WHO OR WHAT INSPIRED YOU TO BE A ZETA? The character, attitudes, and support rendered by the current chapter members to me prior to my interest is what led me to pursue Zeta.

CAREER ASPIRATIONS: Upon graduation, I desire to attend graduate school and receive my Master's in Social Work. After receiving my degree, I will receive the continued necessary education and training so that I can become a licensed clinical social worker and work in couples and family therapy as well as help those living with mental illnesses. I am a pageant girl so I desire to work in the arts also.

ARLENA JOHNSON
Trinity Washington University
Washington, DC
MAJOR: Human Resource Management
EXPECTED GRADUATION DATE: 12/10/2017
CURRENT CHAPTER: Sigma Pi
REGION: Eastern
YEAR JOINED ZETA: 2016

WHO OR WHAT INSPIRED YOU TO BE A ZETA? Zeta Phi Beta Sorority, Inc. is the only NPHC organization with high standards, a belief in education, sisterhood, and service for the community.

CAREER ASPIRATIONS: To become a Human Resource Manger for the VA or become a Naval Officer. I would like to become the first African American officer assigned to a submarine.

MARISSA LOTT
University of New Mexico
Albuquerque, New Mexico
MAJOR: Business Administration
EXPECTED GRADUATION DATE: 5/14/2018
CURRENT CHAPTER: Nu Tau
REGION: Pacific
YEAR JOINED ZETA: 2015

WHO OR WHAT INSPIRED YOU TO BE A ZETA? The people who were in the chapter at my school were very inviting. They were very informative about the organization and what they believe in.

ROLE MODEL: My father is my role model. He has inspired me to push through any situation, whether it was easy or not.

CAREER ASPIRATIONS: Open my own business. I want to open a nail and hair salon. I've always liked doing nails. I took a cosmetology class during a senior year of high school that gave me 55 hours towards a license. I've wanted to continue to go down this road, but I want to have the education so I can understand how to start my own business more efficiently and economically.

ANNDRELL MCDONALD
University of the District of Columbia
Washington, DC
MAJOR: Political Science
EXPECTED GRADUATION DATE: 5/10/2018
CURRENT CHAPTER: Kappa Alpha
REGION: Eastern
YEAR JOINED ZETA: 2016

WHO OR WHAT INSPIRED YOU TO BE A ZETA? I loved how welcoming their spirits were, and what the founding principles are.

CAREER ASPIRATIONS: To become a radio/TV personality.

TUEREI WILLIAMS
The Ohio State University
Columbus, Ohio
MAJOR: Public Affairs
EXPECTED GRADUATION DATE: 5/8/2016
CURRENT CHAPTER: Xi Gamma
REGION: Great Lakes
YEAR JOINED ZETA: 2015

WHO OR WHAT INSPIRED YOU TO BE A ZETA? My scholarship advisor who mentored me and the women in Xi Gamma Chapter at the time.

CAREER ASPIRATIONS: My current career aspirations include eventually working as a diversity provost at a university. In the fall I will attend Ohio University to obtain my Master's in Higher Education and Student Affairs. I plan to work towards increasing access to higher education for minority students and students of low socioeconomic status.

JHYRE POSTON
University of New Mexico
Albuquerque, New Mexico
MAJOR: Psychology
EXPECTED GRADUATION DATE: 5/1/1996
CURRENT CHAPTER: Nu Tau
REGION: Pacific
YEAR JOINED ZETA: 2014

WHO OR WHAT INSPIRED YOU TO BE A ZETA? The finer women on my campus who were doing great things.

CAREER ASPIRATIONS: Giving back to my community has always been an important factor of my life and I would like to see that done through my career. Becoming a children's psychiatrist would benefit me in a way that I know I would be helping the future generation thrive. Taking time to leave behind a legacy for the next generation to be their best selves is the key to the future and I would like to play a part in that.

SUYENT RODRIGUEZ
University of New Mexico
Albuquerque, New Mexico
MAJOR: Psychology and Spanish
EXPECTED GRADUATION DATE: 5/15/2017
CURRENT CHAPTER: Nu Tau
REGION: Pacific
YEAR JOINED ZETA: 2015

WHO OR WHAT INSPIRED YOU TO BE A ZETA? Brandi Wells, Z-HOPE, and Finer Womanhood

CAREER ASPIRATIONS: To become a psychology professor with an Afrocentric approach to the course material and research.

JENAY WALKER
Western Michigan University
Kalamazoo, Michigan
MAJOR: Social Work
EXPECTED GRADUATION DATE: 6/25/2016
CURRENT CHAPTER: Tau Delta
REGION: Great Lakes
YEAR JOINED ZETA: 2016

WHO OR WHAT INSPIRED YOU TO BE A ZETA? A friend of my family who is a Zeta, and my high school teacher.

CAREER ASPIRATIONS: I would like to work in the school system as a school worker. I also want to start a non-profit for children who age out of the foster care system. The program would help them get resources they need to transition from a child to an adult. It would teach them life skills needed to be successful in life.

KIPLYN TAYLOR
University of Southern Mississippi
Hattiesburg, Mississippi
MAJOR: Spanish
EXPECTED GRADUATION DATE: 12/15/2017
CURRENT CHAPTER: Lambda Theta
REGION: South Central
YEAR JOINED ZETA: 2014

WHO OR WHAT INSPIRED YOU TO BE A ZETA? My mom and the massive amount of community service for Eldercare, March of Dimes, and Stork's Nest inspired me to join Zeta. I also looked around my campus and saw that the members of Zeta were the kind of women I wanted to surround myself with.

CAREER ASPIRATIONS: I plan to start off my career as an interpreter in hospitals or law offices. As time goes on, my ultimate goal is to achieve a position as an interpreter for political leaders at the United Nations. I want to help bridge the gap between language barriers and meet some of everyone!!

DEMONDREA STARNES
Northern Kentucky University
Highland Heights, Kentucky
MAJOR: Exercise Science
EXPECTED GRADUATION DATE: 5/13/2017
CURRENT CHAPTER: Alpha Rho
REGION: Midwestern
YEAR JOINED ZETA: 2014

WHO OR WHAT INSPIRED YOU TO BE A ZETA? Mother

CAREER ASPIRATIONS: Sport and performance coach

KYA SIMMONS

DePauw University
Greencastle, Indiana
MAJOR: Communications
EXPECTED GRADUATION DATE: 5/22/2016
CURRENT CHAPTER: Lambda Tau
REGION: Great Lakes
YEAR JOINED ZETA: 2014

WHO OR WHAT INSPIRED YOU TO BE A ZETA? I was inspired to join Zeta when I saw the members on my campus living the principles described on the website. They demonstrated the essence of Finer Womanhood and gave me a place where I could feel welcomed on campus. I was further inspired when I discovered that the chapter was only three years old and they were winning awards and doing other things that other Greeks on campus were not. I saw them blazing new paths and that was something I wanted to be a part of.

CAREER ASPIRATIONS: My career aspirations are to first get my master's degree in Higher Education and Student Affairs, then work in an office that focuses on the success of underrepresented students such as first generation students, students of color and those who identify on the LGBTQ spectrum and ultimately be named dean of a college or university.

JAANA RANDLE

University of Illinois at Springfield
Chicago, Illinois
MAJOR: English; Creative Writing
EXPECTED GRADUATION DATE: 5/14/2018
CURRENT CHAPTER: Alpha Phi Chapter
REGION: Great Lakes
YEAR JOINED ZETA: 2016

WHO OR WHAT INSPIRED YOU TO BE A ZETA? The dedication to their community and the others around them is what inspired me to join Zeta.

CAREER ASPIRATIONS: After graduating from college, I would like to have my on fiction novel on the stands. I would like to be developed enough as a writer that I can create a series for the public to read and enjoy. Also, further down the line, my ultimate goal, I would love to star, direct, and produce a film based on my own work.

AYSIA EVANS

University of North Carolina at Greensboro
Greensboro, North Carolina
MAJOR: Political Science and Sociology
EXPECTED GRADUATION DATE: 5/12/2017
CURRENT CHAPTER: Omega Nu
REGION: Eastern
YEAR JOINED ZETA: 2016

WHO OR WHAT INSPIRED YOU TO BE A ZETA? I wanted to gain more self-discipline and reliance to be able to conquer any hardships I may face in the future.

CAREER ASPIRATIONS: I would like to be a politician and use my knowledge and assumed political power to uplift the Black community.

SHANITA FORT

Augusta University
Augusta, Georgia
MAJOR: Business Management
EXPECTED GRADUATION DATE: 5/13/2016
CURRENT CHAPTER: Sigma Rho
REGION: Southeastern
YEAR JOINED ZETA: 2012

WHO OR WHAT INSPIRED YOU TO BE A ZETA? My father

CAREER ASPIRATIONS: I would like to continue to grow my custom work business, Twizted Works. I would like to be able to also start a school for African, African American, West Indian, and Native American children. With my school, I want to emphasize our culture and our history. I want to groom young kids to be more than stereotypes and to make a great name for themselves.

VIRGINIA MCKEE
Morehead State University
Morehead, Kentucky
MAJOR: Spanish
EXPECTED GRADUATION DATE: 5/13/2016
CURRENT CHAPTER: Delta Pi
REGION: Great Lakes
YEAR JOINED ZETA: 2015

WHO OR WHAT INSPIRED YOU TO BE A ZETA? My fellow Soror and legacy Rian Penman inspired me to do my own research and I saw that my values really align with the Zeta way of life.

CAREER ASPIRATIONS: I'd like to be a nurse, but I want to move up the ranks and eventually be the head nurse in charge of all others, just like my grandmother was.

TARA THURUTHUVELIL
Seton Hall University
South Orange, New Jersey
MAJOR: Biology
EXPECTED GRADUATION DATE: 5/20/2017
CURRENT CHAPTER: Psi Pi Chapter
REGION: Atlantic
YEAR JOINED ZETA: 2016

WHO OR WHAT INSPIRED YOU TO BE A ZETA? I wanted to get more involved on campus and did a lot of research about the different Greek sororities. I found the sisters of Zeta Phi Beta and the organization itself to be the most humble and comforting organization that I could relate to the most.

CAREER ASPIRATIONS: I hope to graduate with a Bachelor's in Biology and later attend graduate school to become a physician's assistant.

LAURA BURKE
University of Alabama Huntsville
Huntsville, Alabama
MAJOR: Psychology
EXPECTED GRADUATION DATE: 12/5/2016
CURRENT CHAPTER: Omega Tau
REGION: South Central
YEAR JOINED ZETA: 2014

WHO OR WHAT INSPIRED YOU TO BE A ZETA? I was inspired by seeing the Zetas on my campus work so hard and do so much while looking so cool

CAREER ASPIRATIONS: I want to work with special needs children

SHAKAJA MCDANIEL
University of Southern Misssissippi
Hattiesburg, Mississippi
MAJOR: Psychology, Minor Child and Family Studies
EXPECTED GRADUATION DATE: 5/12/2017
CURRENT CHAPTER: Lambda Theta
REGION: South Central
YEAR JOINED ZETA: 2014

WHO OR WHAT INSPIRED YOU TO BE A ZETA? I was influenced by numerous strong women of Zeta Psi Zeta Chapter of Zeta Phi Beta Sorority, Incorporated. My mother, Darlene Page, and my mentor, Shirley Catchings, were major influences. When I was younger, I thought that a Zeta woman is what every young girl was supposed to be. As I matured, I saw there were other options out in life, but Zeta still stuck near and dear to my heart. Zeta has raised me from my youth. I was a Pearlette, Amicette, Archonette and, in 2014, I became a Zeta woman. The people who influenced me taught me that you do not have to fit a specific idea or social standard of what others want you to be. They also taught me it is not all about the praise you get for doing service, but it is all about actually lending a helping hand to your fellow man.

CAREER ASPIRATIONS: In May 2016, I will be graduating from the University of Southern Mississippi with a Bachelor of Science in Psychology and a minor in Child and Family Studies. After graduation I will be enrolling in graduate school to earn my Master's in Social Work. I either want to work as a drug and alcohol abuse counselor, high school counselor, or a hospice care social worker.

EUGENIA JOHNSON
University of North Carolina at Greensboro
Greensboro, North Carolina
MAJOR: Human Development and Family Studies / Pre-Med
EXPECTED GRADUATION DATE: 5/12/2018
CURRENT CHAPTER: Omega Nu
REGION: Eastern
YEAR JOINED ZETA: 2016

WHO OR WHAT INSPIRED YOU TO BE A ZETA? The idea of Finer Womanhood really inspired me to join Zeta, and the chapter on my campus was very open and welcoming.

CAREER ASPIRATIONS: I love working with children so my dream is to become a Pediatrician. After I get my degree, I would like to travel to countries who are not medically developed and dedicate my time and services. One day, I hope to open my own practice.

DORETHA BENN
East Tennessee State University
Johnson City, Tennessee
MAJOR: Communication Studies
EXPECTED GRADUATION DATE: 5/7/2016
CURRENT CHAPTER: Sigma Xi
REGION: South Central
YEAR JOINED ZETA: 2015

WHO OR WHAT INSPIRED YOU TO BE A ZETA? I was inspired to join Zeta because of the value of Finer Womanhood. It is one thing to speak about scholarship, service and sisterhood, but it is something completely different to put those values into practice and make them a way of life. For me, Zeta was the only sorority that decided to set itself apart and hold itself to the highest standards. Being a Finer Woman is an honor and a privilege not awarded to all.

ROLE MODEL: My role model is my grandmother, Elizabeth Ann Mebane. Although she is no longer living, she is still my inspiration to be the woman I am today. The most important lesson she ever taught me was to never stop learning. She said that, "Once we think we know it all is the moment we truly start to die. Knowledge is power and with this power you have the chance to change the world." She is one of the reasons that I continuously pursue knowledge to be able to help make this world a better place for those to come.

CAREER ASPIRATIONS: I was recently accepted into the master's program for Higher Education Student Affairs Administration at the University of Vermont. I believe that the years spent at a college or university are the most transformative in someone's life. By working at a university, I will be able to help shape and inspire the leaders of tomorrow.

NAOMI SHORT
Tougaloo College
Jackson, Mississippi
MAJOR: Music Performance
EXPECTED GRADUATION DATE: 5/7/2017
CURRENT CHAPTER: Nu Beta
REGION: South Central
YEAR JOINED ZETA: 2014

WHO OR WHAT INSPIRED YOU TO BE A ZETA? I was inspired by my cousin, Halima, who became a Zeta during Fall '96 - Epsilon Theta.

CAREER ASPIRATIONS: My career aspirations include but are not limited to teaching music history and performance (K-12 and the collegiate level). During my lifetime I would like to teach/counsel abroad, preferably in Germany.

LATRICE SMITH
Northwestern State University
Natchitoches, Louisiana
MAJOR: Nursing
EXPECTED GRADUATION DATE: 5/16/2019
CURRENT CHAPTER: Xi Epsilon
REGION: Southern
YEAR JOINED ZETA: 2016

WHO OR WHAT INSPIRED YOU TO BE A ZETA? I admired how dedicated this Sorority is to service and wanted to have the sisterly bond that was consistent with any Zeta I meet.

CAREER ASPIRATIONS: I would like to be a travel nurse for a year then continue my studies to become a Geriactric Nurse Practitioner with a doctorate degree.

RAVEN GATES
Miami University
Oxford, Ohio
MAJOR: Strategic Communications
EXPECTED GRADUATION DATE: 5/14/2018
CURRENT CHAPTER: Xi Rho
REGION: Great Lakes
YEAR JOINED ZETA: 2016

WHO OR WHAT INSPIRED YOU TO BE A ZETA? The amount of service Zeta does for the community

CAREER ASPIRATIONS: I want to work for a public relations firm or possibly work for a nonprofit organization. I want to help control the relationships built with the community as well as with other organizations. Also, I would like to work with the media department for an organization and control what content is put out there for people to see.

GILLIAN AGYEMANG
Virginia Commonwealth University
Richmond, Virginia
MAJOR: Clinical Laboratory Science
EXPECTED GRADUATION DATE: 5/14/2016
CURRENT CHAPTER: Eta Theta
REGION: Eastern
YEAR JOINED ZETA: 2015

WHO OR WHAT INSPIRED YOU TO BE A ZETA? I was born premature as part of a set of quadruplets so the association with the March of Dimes drew me to Zeta. I was also inspired by the Zeta women on my campus and saw that they really embodied sisterhood. I had a craving to be around women that support and uplift each other and have a strong bond. When I interacted with them it solidified the fact that Zeta was for me.

CAREER ASPIRATIONS: After graduation I will be working in a clinical laboratory performing blood typing, providing blood products to patients and ensuring that they are safe for transfusions. I hope to become a laboratory manager after I gain bench experience. I would also like to become an athletic trainer because I enjoy athletics and have a passion for the health care sector.

TYNEKIA ABNEY
South Carolina State University
Orangeburg, South Carolina
MAJOR: Business Management
EXPECTED GRADUATION DATE: 5/5/2017
CURRENT CHAPTER: Psi Alpha
REGION: Southeastern
YEAR JOINED ZETA: 2016

WHO OR WHAT INSPIRED YOU TO BE A ZETA? Mary White

CAREER ASPIRATIONS: First, I want to work within the Human Resources department of a company to ensure all employees are treated equally and fairly. Afterwards, I want to be a music producer and have my own music recording studio and my own record label. I too would like to make and create Hip-Hop, R&B, and Rap beats for recording artists. Lastly, I would like to get involved in architecture and design.

DOMINIQUE ROBINSON
American University
Washington, DC
MAJOR: Justice and Law
EXPECTED GRADUATION DATE: 12/21/2016
CURRENT CHAPTER: Sigma Pi
REGION: Eastern
YEAR JOINED ZETA: 2015

WHO OR WHAT INSPIRED YOU TO BE A ZETA? The continuous zeal and hard work I saw Zeta women put into this organization and their community inspired me to want to join the bond of sisterhood within this amazing organization.

CAREER ASPIRATIONS: I would like to be a corporate attorney.

NADINE GEORGE
University at Albany
Albany, New York
MAJOR: Sociology
EXPECTED GRADUATION DATE: 5/14/2016
CURRENT CHAPTER: Epsilon Nu
REGION: Atlantic
YEAR JOINED ZETA: 2015

WHO OR WHAT INSPIRED YOU TO BE A ZETA? My inspiration for joining was seeing my Sorors make strides on our campus and within the community, portraying strong leadership skills and sisterhood. They were very engaging and passionate about supporting each other and promoting change for women and black communities. That's something that I am also passionate about and wanted to be a part of.

CAREER ASPIRATIONS: Social Worker, Activist, Legal Advocate against Violence Against Women

JASMINE NIXON
Elizabeth City State University
Elizabeth City, North Carolina
MAJOR: PE Teaching
EXPECTED GRADUATION DATE: 12/10/2016
CURRENT CHAPTER: Alpha Gamma
REGION: Eastern
YEAR JOINED ZETA: 2016

WHO OR WHAT INSPIRED YOU TO BE A ZETA? My two aunts that are second mothers and are Zetas as well inspired me to join this Sorority. I saw no other sorority that would help me better myself as a person & making me a better woman.

CAREER ASPIRATIONS: My career aspirations is to become a physical education teacher and to also become a basketball coach.

EBONY JOHNSON
Drexel University
Philadelphia, Pennsylvania
MAJOR: Nursing
EXPECTED GRADUATION DATE: 6/10/2019
CURRENT CHAPTER: Kappa Sigma
REGION: Atlantic
YEAR JOINED ZETA: 2016

WHO OR WHAT INSPIRED YOU TO BE A ZETA? The sisterhood

CAREER ASPIRATIONS: Nurse Practitioner

NELKEYA WOOD
Florida A&M University
Tallahassee, Florida
MAJOR: Health Science: Pre-Occupational Therapy
EXPECTED GRADUATION DATE: 8/5/2016
CURRENT CHAPTER: Gamma Alpha
REGION: Southeastern
YEAR JOINED ZETA: 2016

WHO OR WHAT INSPIRED YOU TO BE A ZETA? I was inspired to join Zeta Phi Beta after witnessing the grace with which the ladies of the Gamma Alpha chapter carried themselves. They were fun-loving, personable, and always providing service to the community. I am proud to now belong to that lineage.

CAREER ASPIRATIONS: Although my major and degree will be Health Science with a concentration in Pre-Occupational Therapy, I am furthering my education to pursue a career in nursing. My ultimate objective is to become a nurse anesthetist.

NAIYA SMITH
North Carolina Agriculture and Technical State University
Greensboro, North Carolina
MAJOR: Journalism and Mass Communications
EXPECTED GRADUATION DATE: 5/16/2019
CURRENT CHAPTER: Zeta Alpha
REGION: Eastern
YEAR JOINED ZETA: 2016

WHO OR WHAT INSPIRED YOU TO BE A ZETA? Zora Neal Hurston

CAREER ASPIRATIONS: I want to own a publishing company for children who want to publish books. Being a person who published books as a child, I noticed that many people enjoy receiving money from aspiring authors and do not care about their dreams. I want to be different and help people achieve their dreams.

TRENICIA GERALD
University of the District of Columbia
Washington, DC
MAJOR: Psychology
EXPECTED GRADUATION DATE: 5/14/2016
CURRENT CHAPTER: Kappa Alpha
REGION: Eastern
YEAR JOINED ZETA: 2016

WHO OR WHAT INSPIRED YOU TO BE A ZETA? The principles that Zeta stands on and the women who I've meet over the years that are apart of the Zeta family.

CAREER ASPIRATIONS: Upon graduating in May with a Bachelor's in Psychology, I plan to attend graduate school to study mental health counseling. I want to be a therapist in a juvenile detention center. Also, would like to open an group home for mothers ages 15-24.

JENNIFER DELAHOUSSAYE
East Tennessee State University
Johnson City, Tennessee
MAJOR: Psychology
EXPECTED GRADUATION DATE: 5/7/2016
CURRENT CHAPTER: Sigma Xi
REGION: South Central
YEAR JOINED ZETA: 2015

WHO OR WHAT INSPIRED YOU TO BE A ZETA? I joined Zeta because I wanted to make lifelong friends and set an example for young ladies to follow.

CAREER ASPIRATIONS: I hope to be a School Counselor in the near future so that I can inspire children in this generation to continue to strive in their education and to be the best that they can be.

DEANNA MCMILLAN
Spalding University
Louisville, Kentucky
MAJOR: Natural Science
EXPECTED GRADUATION DATE: 6/4/2016
CURRENT CHAPTER: Tau Rho
REGION: Great Lakes
YEAR JOINED ZETA: 2015

WHO OR WHAT INSPIRED YOU TO BE A ZETA? Friends

CAREER ASPIRATIONS: After completing my Bachelor's Degree, I plan on continuing my education and gaining my MSAT (Master of Science in Athletic Training). Thereafter, I plan to obtain my EDE so I can teach athletic training. I would like to become an entrepreneur, rendering my services as an ATC to little league programs. Ultimately, I want to work where my gifts will prove useful and someone will be touched.

ALLISON MELVILLE
Florida Gulf Coast University
Fort Myers, Florida
MAJOR: Dual Major in Legal Studies and Criminal Justice with a minor in Political Science
EXPECTED GRADUATION DATE: 5/1/2018
CURRENT CHAPTER: "Glamorous" Gamma Tau
REGION: Southeastern
YEAR JOINED ZETA: 2016

WHO OR WHAT INSPIRED YOU TO BE A ZETA? What inspired me to join Zeta is the way they presented themselves on my campus. The Gamma Tau chapter constantly was putting in work, supporting others, and lending a helping hand. Certain members got very close with me and were vitall in helping me get through my freshman year of college and I looked up to them because they truly represented the principles of zeta in living form. After getting to know them I did my research and realized Zeta was the only way for me.

CAREER ASPIRATIONS: I have aspirations of becoming a paralegal as soon as I leave college, then attending l;aw school, and soon after becoming a Corporate Attorney in Atlanta, Georgia.

ANGELLIC ROSS
Northwestern University
Evanston, Illinois
MAJOR: Performance Studies, Film/Media Studies Minor, Civic Engagement Certificate
EXPECTED GRADUATION DATE: 6/18/2016
CURRENT CHAPTER: Nu Sigma
REGION: Great Lakes
YEAR JOINED ZETA: 2013

WHO OR WHAT INSPIRED YOU TO BE A ZETA? The women on my campus

CAREER ASPIRATIONS: I hope to own my film company that produces film for and by youth and young adults in underprivileged communities.

CRYSTAL THOMPSON
Georgia Southwestern State University
Americus, Georgia
MAJOR: Business Management
EXPECTED GRADUATION DATE: 12/6/2016
CURRENT CHAPTER: MU MU
REGION: Southeastern
YEAR JOINED ZETA: 2015

WHO OR WHAT INSPIRED YOU TO BE A ZETA? My Mother who is a Finer Woman herself

CAREER ASPIRATIONS: My life has really been one of a kind, but making sure I do all I can do my best at for my dad. Because I know he would want me to succeed in life. Being a member of the GREATEST Sorority of all kind has definitely help me gain true sisters/friends. My goals are to finish college strong and go back for my master's in IT or IFS and partner with my brother at LT Consulting in Washington, DC.

BONISHIA THOMAS
University of Southern Mississippi
Hattiesburg, Mississippi
MAJOR: Criminal Justice
EXPECTED GRADUATION DATE: 5/13/2016
CURRENT CHAPTER: Lambda Theta
REGION: South Central
YEAR JOINED ZETA: 2014

WHO OR WHAT INSPIRED YOU TO BE A ZETA? As a young lady, I knew the physical, mental, and professional skills I learned would better prepare me for adulthood. When I read the history of Zeta on www.zphib1920.org, it confirmed my decision to join. I not only wanted to be a Zeta, I needed to be a Zeta.

CAREER ASPIRATIONS: I aspire to become a mental health professional, restoring family systems and improving human conditions through prevention and intervention as well as mentoring at-risk youth and delinquents as a Licensed Marriage and Family Therapist.

GAYLEN RIVERS
Illinois State University
Normal, Illinois
MAJOR: History / Social Sciences Education
EXPECTED GRADUATION DATE: 5/12/2018
CURRENT CHAPTER: Lambda Epsilon
REGION: Great Lakes
YEAR JOINED ZETA: 2015

WHO OR WHAT INSPIRED YOU TO BE A ZETA? My sister. She became a Zeta in 2013 and her experience made me want to join Zeta.

CAREER ASPIRATIONS: I would like to start out teaching in a high school. After that I would like to work at either the DuSable Museum of African American History or the National Museum of African American History and Culture.

KHEILAH SHORT
Trinity Washington University
Washington, DC
MAJOR: Communications
EXPECTED GRADUATION DATE: 5/19/2018
CURRENT CHAPTER: Sigma Pi
REGION: Eastern
YEAR JOINED ZETA: 2016

WHO OR WHAT INSPIRED YOU TO BE A ZETA? The spirit and sisterhood of this great organization. The calling to serve others and make changes to this world.

CAREER ASPIRATIONS: To first, be a radio broadcaster. Then, I want to eventually host my own talk show and discuss global issues with fellow women. I would also love to be a public relations specialist.

ALEZAIHVIA MELENDEZ
Bennett College
Los Angeles, California
MAJOR: Social Work
EXPECTED GRADUATION DATE: 5/7/2018
CURRENT CHAPTER: Chi Gamma
CHAPTER STATE: North Carolina
REGION: Eastern
YEAR JOINED ZETA: 2016

WHO OR WHAT INSPIRED YOU TO BE A ZETA? Spring 2013

CAREER ASPIRATIONS: After grade school, I plan to work with domestic violence, sex trafficking and torture survivors at a law firm. I would like to support these victims as they are going through their various traumatic experiences in and out of the courtroom.

BRIELLE BENNETT
Illinois State University
Normal, Illinois
MAJOR: Social Work
EXPECTED GRADUATION DATE: 6/9/2017
CURRENT CHAPTER: Lambda Epsilon
REGION: Great Lakes
YEAR JOINED ZETA: 2015

WHO OR WHAT INSPIRED YOU TO BE A ZETA? I was inspired to join Zeta Phi Beta Sorority, Incorporated when I learned of the many contributions the organization made to Black History. From fighting for the rights of women, to marching with leaders during the civil rights movement, women of Zeta were at the forefront of the path to equality. Even though we have these rights now, I learned that Zeta is still actively involved in the community, which really stood out me. As a woman passionate about social justice, I knew that it would be amazing to join an organization of women that was built on such rich foundation of equality for all.

ROLE MODEL: My role model is a lovely Soror, which I have had the privilege of knowing long before my journey to Zeta Phi Beta Sorority Incorporated. She is a woman who will give the clothes off her back to a stranger on the street. Her goals and ambitions are bigger than this world and with these she can move anyone she comes in contact with. I aspire to be like the woman she is because women like her are rare to find. Not only does she motivate and encourage me to strive to give my best to Zeta, she inspires me to be a better woman in life and to never believe that any dream I have is too big.

CAREER ASPIRATIONS: Upon graduation in May of 2017, I would like to serve as an intern at the Illinois State Capitol, working under legislators to gain experience in the area of state and government policy. Upon completion of this internship I would like to take the skills I've learned and work in an administrative position at an agency that serves at risk youth.

BRIANNA TAYLOR
East Tennessee State University
Johnson City, Tennessee
MAJOR: Marketing
EXPECTED GRADUATION DATE: 5/7/2017
CURRENT CHAPTER: Sigma Xi
REGION: South Central
YEAR JOINED ZETA: 2015

WHO OR WHAT INSPIRED YOU TO BE A ZETA? Faith Vaughn

CAREER ASPIRATIONS: I want to live comfortably while I follow my dreams under my degree. I want to be travel and see the world while having the opportunity to do what I love

AMBROSIA JIMMERSON
University of North Texas at Dallas
Dallas, Texas
MAJOR: Applied Arts and Science
EXPECTED GRADUATION DATE: 6/19/2017
CURRENT CHAPTER: Chi Upsilon
REGION: Southern
YEAR JOINED ZETA: 2015

WHO OR WHAT INSPIRED YOU TO BE A ZETA? the sisterhood.

CAREER ASPIRATIONS: I aspire to one day own a successful business.

JORIE GOINS
Northwestern University
Evanston, Illinois
MAJOR: Journalism
EXPECTED GRADUATION DATE: 6/17/2016
CURRENT CHAPTER: Nu Sigma
REGION: Great Lakes
YEAR JOINED ZETA: 2014

WHO OR WHAT INSPIRED YOU TO BE A ZETA? The ladies of the Nu Sigma Chapter, who are now my chapter Sorors were so incredibly kind and welcoming to me, even before I was a member. They were (and still are) all involved in a myriad of activities at NU and beyond. Most importantly, I saw a bit of myself in each of them and felt that when I was around them I had finally found kindred spirits, with whom I truly identified. This and the fact that they actually demonstrated all of the principles of Zeta led me to make the decision to pursue membership in Zeta Phi Beta Sorority, Inc. It is easily one of the best decisions I made in my college career.

CAREER ASPIRATIONS: I hope to write for a magazine, on various subjects including arts, politics, career and issues affecting women, especially women of color. It is my dream to one day have my own publication that serves young career oriented women of color. I am also a dancer and would like to continue dancing and choreographing. Trying to balance my two loves has been an adventure, and it's not over yet!

BRITTANY JOHNSON
College of Charleston
Charleston, South Carolina
MAJOR: Psychology
EXPECTED GRADUATION DATE: 5/7/2016
CURRENT CHAPTER: Chi Iota
REGION: Southeastern
YEAR JOINED ZETA: 2014

WHO OR WHAT INSPIRED YOU TO BE A ZETA? Violette N. Anderson and the Sisterhood

CAREER ASPIRATIONS: I would like to become a prosecutor. I currently intern at the Solicitor's Office as well as work at a law firm. Violette N. Anderson is my role model because she was the first black woman to practice before the U.S. Supreme Court. Her actions then inspire me to continue to blaze new paths in the legal field.

KIANA LEVERITTE
Tuskegee University
Tuskegee, Alabama
MAJOR: Environmental Science Natural Resource Management
EXPECTED GRADUATION DATE: 5/7/2017
CURRENT CHAPTER: Theta Beta
REGION: South Central
YEAR JOINED ZETA: 2015

WHO OR WHAT INSPIRED YOU TO BE A ZETA? I was inspired by the ideal of being a finer woman.

CAREER ASPIRATIONS: I hope to one day work on a wildlife conservation refuge or work for a eco-logical conservation agency or medium such as National Geographic or the World Wildlife Federation. I'll be in a fulfilling career as long as it is in direct correlation with endangered wildlife.

DEION DORNAL
Morehead State University
Morehead, Kentucky
MAJOR: Business Management
EXPECTED GRADUATION DATE: 5/13/2017
CURRENT CHAPTER: Delta Pi
REGION: Great Lakes
YEAR JOINED ZETA: 2015

WHO OR WHAT INSPIRED YOU TO BE A ZETA? The principles of Zeta.

CAREER ASPIRATIONS: I plan to go into human resources as a recruiter or payroll manager. Another route I would like to take is retail management and work my way up in a corporation.

KEVYN ALLEN
Morehead State University
Morehead, Kentucky
MAJOR: Communications
EXPECTED GRADUATION DATE: 5/14/2018
CURRENT CHAPTER: Delta Pi
REGION: Great Lakes
YEAR JOINED ZETA: 2015

WHO OR WHAT INSPIRED YOU TO BE A ZETA? The sisterhood.

CAREER ASPIRATIONS: To have a job with n event planning firm or my own event planning service.

RIAN PENMAN
Morehead State University
Morehead, Kentucky
MAJOR: Art
EXPECTED GRADUATION DATE: 5/14/2017
CURRENT CHAPTER: Delta Pi
REGION: Great Lakes
YEAR JOINED ZETA: 2016

WHO OR WHAT INSPIRED YOU TO BE A ZETA? My mom.

CAREER ASPIRATIONS: Work at a Museum.

MONE'T GRADY
Morehead State University
Morehead, Kentucky
MAJOR: Special and Elementary Education
EXPECTED GRADUATION DATE: 4/12/2018
CURRENT CHAPTER: Delta Pi
REGION: Great Lakes
YEAR JOINED ZETA: 2015

WHO OR WHAT INSPIRED YOU TO BE A ZETA? Everyone who is Greek in my family is a part of the blue and white family.

CAREER ASPIRATIONS: My career aspiration as of now is to work in the education field as a middle school counselor.

COURTNEY SIMS
Tougaloo College
Tougaloo, Mississippi
MAJOR: Chemistry
EXPECTED GRADUATION DATE: 5/1/2016
CURRENT CHAPTER: Nu Beta
REGION: South Central
YEAR JOINED ZETA: 2013

WHO OR WHAT INSPIRED YOU TO BE A ZETA? I was inspired to join Zeta by the young ladies on my campus; I was further inspired to join Zeta because it has been established since day one that this organization was more than an average social club. Our Five Pearls created this organization to become aware, stay aware, make a difference, and challenege the injustices of our time. Women of Zeta also have a certain way about themsevles - a walk, a stance, a stare, and a light - that only Zeta women can possess. These are the things that inspired me to become a woman of Zeta.

CAREER ASPIRATIONS: After graduating from Tougaloo College, I will be working with the University of Mississippi Medical Center in conjunction with University of Kentucky in the area of Infectious Diseases and Behavioral Research. Next year, I plan to enroll as a Microbiology/ Immunology graduate (PhD) student at the University of Mississippi Medical Center. My ultimate career goal is to practice bench research.

ARIA REAL
High Point University
High Point, North Carolina
MAJOR: Interior Design
EXPECTED GRADUATION DATE: 5/6/2017
CURRENT CHAPTER: Epsilon Tau
REGION: Eastern
YEAR JOINED ZETA: 2015

WHO OR WHAT INSPIRED YOU TO BE A ZETA? After researching all of the Divine 9 sororities I connected with Zeta Phi Beta Sorority, Inc. the most. I was inspired by the priority put on scholarship and service and the humble manner in which Zetas accomplished both. I loved the Zetas I met. All of them were sisterly even before I was finally a part of the best sisterhood in the world.

CAREER ASPIRATIONS: My loftiest goal with my degree is to create low-income homes with high capacity for growth, preservation, and the makings of a greater society. I will get to that goal by experiencing many different fields of Interior Design and working with firms to serve various clients from the rich to the poor, private to commercial.

BLAKE BASS
Michigan State University
East Lansing, Michigan
MAJOR: Anthropology
EXPECTED GRADUATION DATE: 5/7/2016
CURRENT CHAPTER: Phi Gamma
REGION: Great Lakes
YEAR JOINED ZETA: 2014

WHO OR WHAT INSPIRED YOU TO BE A ZETA? I wanted a family because I was an out-of-state student; the chapter at Michigan State provided me that family, along with the Sigmas.

CAREER ASPIRATIONS: I plan to join the United States Marine Corps and be a functioning Forensic Anthropologist.

IREISHA VAUGHN
Seton Hall University
South Orange, New Jersey
MAJOR: Sociology
EXPECTED GRADUATION DATE: 5/25/2017
CURRENT CHAPTER: Psi Pi
REGION: Atlantic
YEAR JOINED ZETA: 2014

WHO OR WHAT INSPIRED YOU TO BE A ZETA? What inspired me is the fact Zetas did not care about receiving recognition on campus. It was evident they put on programs, performances, and fundraisers because of their love for Zeta.

CAREER ASPIRATIONS: To become a human resources manager.

IMANI HENDERSON
University of North Texas
Denton, Texas
MAJOR: Kinesiology
EXPECTED GRADUATION DATE: 5/14/2018
CURRENT CHAPTER: Rho Delta
REGION: Southern
YEAR JOINED ZETA: 2016

WHO OR WHAT INSPIRED YOU TO BE A ZETA? I admired the principle of Finer Womanhood and how active Rho Delta was on campus.

CAREER ASPIRATIONS: Once I graduate, I would like to become a Physical Therapy Assistant to gain experience in the field and then go to Physical Therapy school and potentially work with a professional sports team.

DE ANGELA WEAKLEY
Miami University
Oxford, Ohio
MAJOR: Architecture
EXPECTED GRADUATION DATE: 5/15/2019
CURRENT CHAPTER: Xi Rho
REGION: Atlantic
YEAR JOINED ZETA: 2016

WHO OR WHAT INSPIRED YOU TO BE A ZETA? The way the ladies in my chapter carried themselves. They where so nice and professional.

CAREER ASPIRATIONS: I'm getting my master's in architecture, and I plan to get my bachelor's in entrepreneurship. I plan to start my own firm and save all my money and buy a lot of land and build my own community and give poor people an education, jobs, and homes. I then plan to eventually go into politics.

HAYLEY DALE
University of North Carolina at Greensboro
Greensboro, North Carolina
MAJOR: Therapeutic Recreation
EXPECTED GRADUATION DATE: 5/6/2017
CURRENT CHAPTER: Omega Nu
REGION: Eastern
YEAR JOINED ZETA: 2016

WHO OR WHAT INSPIRED YOU TO BE A ZETA? Leshaia Davis-Johnson inspired me. She was the first face I saw on campus, and she gave me a warm welcome. By being kind and representing Zeta, she left a great first impression. In addition to the principles of Zeta, I was also attracted to Zeta because its principles and values are parallel with my own, and I value that.

CAREER ASPIRATIONS: I'm currently an undergraduate studying Recreation and Parks Management with a concentration in Therapeutic Recreation. Once I graduate I plan on attending graduate school and studying Occupational Therapy. My dream is to create a special non-profit organization to serve and practice Occupational Therapy and serve those individuals in the community who may need OT but have been poverty stricken.

FEDERICA STATON
Morris College
Sumter, South Carolina
MAJOR: Mass Communications
EXPECTED GRADUATION DATE: 5/7/2016
CURRENT CHAPTER: Pi Theta
REGION: Southeastern
YEAR JOINED ZETA: 2015

WHO OR WHAT INSPIRED YOU TO BE A ZETA? My God-sister's work ethic and drive to better her organization. The principles on which Zeta was founded are the same principles and standards to which I hold myself.

CAREER ASPIRATIONS: Public Relations specialist

TAMEIKA RAMSEUR

University of North Carolina at Greensboro
Greensboro, North Carolina
MAJOR: Dance Education
EXPECTED GRADUATION DATE: 12/15/2016
CURRENT CHAPTER: Omega Nu
REGION: Eastern
YEAR JOINED ZETA: 2015

WHO OR WHAT INSPIRED YOU TO BE A ZETA? My mother who is a role model in my life.

CAREER ASPIRATIONS: I would like to teach high school dance to children who are not able to afford to take lessons outside of a public setting. After teaching in the public school system, I would like to open my own dance studio where I will prepare students to have professional dance careers.

KELLEE HARVEY

Morehead State University
Morehead, Kentucky
MAJOR: Business
EXPECTED GRADUATION DATE: 5/15/2018
CURRENT CHAPTER: Delta Pi
REGION: Great Lakes
YEAR JOINED ZETA: 2015

WHO OR WHAT INSPIRED YOU TO BE A ZETA? An older Soror.

CAREER ASPIRATIONS: Business Owner

SHIANN TALMADGE

University of North Carolina at Greensboro
Greensboro, North Carolina
MAJOR: Pre-Law
EXPECTED GRADUATION DATE: 5/6/2019
CURRENT CHAPTER: Omega Nu
REGION: Eastern
YEAR JOINED ZETA: 2016

WHO OR WHAT INSPIRED YOU TO BE A ZETA? My mother inspired me in many ways.

CAREER ASPIRATIONS: I aspire to be an advocate defense attorney for underprivileged adolescents

JANAE WILLIAMS

Elon University
Elon, North Carolina
MAJOR: Pure Mathematics
EXPECTED GRADUATION DATE: 5/19/2018
CURRENT CHAPTER: Xi Omicron
REGION: Eastern
YEAR JOINED ZETA: 2015

WHO OR WHAT INSPIRED YOU TO BE A ZETA? The principle of Finer Womanhood and wanting to be a better version of myself than the day before.

CAREER ASPIRATIONS: My sole career aspiration is to graduate from Elon University with my B.A. in Pure Mathematics. This is my only goal because I believe that my career and future success story will eventually fall into place the way it is meant to.

MARI'ONNA BAILEY

Jackson State University
Jackson, Mississippi
MAJOR: Childcare and Family Education
EXPECTED GRADUATION DATE: 4/23/2016
CURRENT CHAPTER: Lambda Beta
REGION: South Central
YEAR JOINED ZETA: 2016

WHO OR WHAT INSPIRED YOU TO BE A ZETA? I wanted to be a part of a sisterhood that was committed to serving the community.

CAREER ASPIRATIONS: My future goals are to open my own childcare center after I obtain my Master of Business

Administration. I also have plans to become a professional photographer as well as a motivational speaker.

NICOLE PALMER
Coppin State University
Baltimore, Maryland
MAJOR: Nursing/Psychology Minor
EXPECTED GRADUATION DATE: 5/21/2018
CURRENT CHAPTER: Nu Gamma
REGION: Atlantic
YEAR JOINED ZETA: 2012

WHO OR WHAT INSPIRED YOU TO BE A ZETA? Service

CAREER ASPIRATIONS: To become a Registered Nurse and to open up a Health and Wellness Clinic.

DENISHA THOMAS
Louisiana State University
Baton Rouge, Louisiana
MAJOR: Kinesiology; Pre-Medical Concentration
EXPECTED GRADUATION DATE: 5/12/2017
CURRENT CHAPTER: Rho Epsilon
REGION: Southern
YEAR JOINED ZETA: 2014

WHO OR WHAT INSPIRED YOU TO BE A ZETA? The opportunities to grow as both a woman and a leader on my campus and in my community inspired me to join Zeta.

CAREER ASPIRATIONS: I aspire to become a neurosurgeon who will blaze new trails in biomedical research regarding the nervous system.

CARISMA COLLIER
Georgia Southwestern State University
Americus, Georgia
MAJOR: Human resource management
EXPECTED GRADUATION DATE: 5/6/2016
CURRENT CHAPTER: Mu Mu
REGION: Southeastern
YEAR JOINED ZETA: 2011

WHO OR WHAT INSPIRED YOU TO BE A ZETA? Another Zeta.

CAREER ASPIRATIONS: Doing what's right for the employee.

RHONDA BALDWIN
Miami University
Oxford, Ohio
MAJOR: Media and Culture
EXPECTED GRADUATION DATE: 5/27/2017
CURRENT CHAPTER: Xi Rho
REGION: Great Lakes
YEAR JOINED ZETA: 2016

WHO OR WHAT INSPIRED YOU TO BE A ZETA? I always feel the need to learn and grow as a person. Zeta Phi Beta Sorority, Incorporated is an organization that allows me to grow as a person and as a woman.

CAREER ASPIRATIONS: I personally want to become a scriptwriter and produce my own television show that deals with real life issues that today's youth face. I also want to open my own non-profit organization for special needs children, so they can have a place of their own along with all the resources they need to live life to its fullest.

CHELSEA APPIAH
Miami University
Oxford, Ohio
MAJOR: English and Women's Studies
EXPECTED GRADUATION DATE: 12/16/2016
CURRENT CHAPTER: Xi Rho
REGION: Great Lakes
YEAR JOINED ZETA: 2014

WHO OR WHAT INSPIRED YOU TO BE A ZETA? The Zetas on my campus at the time were the most admirable, academically-driven, and genuine women I encountered. They embodied the definition of Finer Womanhood and I had a great desire to become part of the sisterhood.

CAREER ASPIRATIONS: Upon early graduation in Fall of 2016, I will be working as an Au Pair in Spain for 3 months. Afterwords, I will be pursuing my Master's degree in Student Affairs and Higher Education. I will be undergoing the application process in the Fall. However, I chose to graduate early so I could travel to Spain for a few months. I hope to be enrolled in a Master's program and begin in Fall 2017.

SHANICE DOWDY
University of Southern Mississippi
Hattiesburg, Mississippi
MAJOR: Forensic Science (Criminal Justice)
EXPECTED GRADUATION DATE: 5/13/2018
CURRENT CHAPTER: Lambda Theta
REGION: South Central
YEAR JOINED ZETA: 2015

WHO OR WHAT INSPIRED YOU TO BE A ZETA? Santricia Dowdy and because I saw the good that the organization brought to the community.

CAREER ASPIRATIONS: My aspiration is to take the time to graduate the university and work in the police department. I would like to be a criminal investigator to help solve crimes as well as decrease common crime in cities. I would like to

get my mortician's certificate and help my community at home with low budget funeral costs. I want to give back to the community while making it safer for future generations.

SHAQUANTA MERAND
Morris College
Sumter, South Carolina
MAJOR: Sociology
EXPECTED GRADUATION DATE: 5/7/2016
CURRENT CHAPTER: Phi Theta
REGION: Southeastern
YEAR JOINED ZETA: 2016

WHO OR WHAT INSPIRED YOU TO BE A ZETA? The history and standards.

CAREER ASPIRATIONS: I want to become a case worker. Then go to graduate school and get my master's in social work to become a social worker.

ARKITTA KNOX
Rust College
Holly Springs, Mississippi
MAJOR: Sociology
EXPECTED GRADUATION DATE: 4/26/2017
CURRENT CHAPTER: Iota Gamma
REGION: South Central
YEAR JOINED ZETA: 2014

WHO OR WHAT INSPIRED YOU TO BE A ZETA? A Zeta named Tamika from the undergraduate chapter at Rust.

CAREER ASPIRATIONS: My career aspirations are to graduate Rust College in 2017 and start working with Teach for America. I also plan to attend graduate school and work with my CNA license in a nursing home.

AUTONEA EVANS
Rust College
Holly Springs, Mississippi
MAJOR: Math Education
EXPECTED GRADUATION DATE: 4/26/2018
CURRENT CHAPTER: Iota Gamma
REGION: South Central
YEAR JOINED ZETA: 2014

WHO OR WHAT INSPIRED YOU TO BE A ZETA? My great aunt.

CAREER ASPIRATIONS: After graduation I plan to be a 7th grade math teacher.

SHAYNA SCOTT
North Carolina State University
Raleigh, North Carolina
MAJOR: Fashion And Textile Management: Concentration in Fashion Development And Product Management
EXPECTED GRADUATION DATE: 5/7/2016
CURRENT CHAPTER: Mu Xi
REGION: Eastern
YEAR JOINED ZETA: 2014

WHO OR WHAT INSPIRED YOU TO BE A ZETA? My mentor from freshman year, Soror Rameika Jones!

CAREER ASPIRATIONS: I will eagerly seek employment as an assistant designer in the fashion design field. It is imperative that I am able to blend theory with hands on experience. My ultimate goal is to create garments that invite clients to be comfortable in the skin they are in. My passion has and will always be for people, encouraging and building up the youth in surrounding communities!

TYE'RESHINA TAYLOR
Jackson State Univetsity
Jackson, Mississippi
MAJOR: History
EXPECTED GRADUATION DATE: 5/5/2017
CURRENT CHAPTER: Lambda Beta
REGION: South Central
YEAR JOINED ZETA: 2015

WHO OR WHAT INSPIRED YOU TO BE A ZETA? Chuconna Anderson was my inspiration to become a Finer Woman. I was also an Archonette under the TPZ Chapter.

CAREER ASPIRATIONS: I am a B.S. history major at Jackson State University. After receiving my Bachelor's degree, I plan to earn my Master's degree and then teaching. I aspire to empower young adults about life and the numerous opportunities they have. While in the education system, I plan to mold young ladies into what we know as Finer Women, by going back home and directing the Archonettes.

ROXIE CARROLL
UNC Charlotte
Winston-Salem, North Carolina
MAJOR: Kinesiology Exercise Science
EXPECTED GRADUATION DATE: 12/17/2017
CURRENT CHAPTER: Upsilon Xi
REGION: Eastern
YEAR JOINED ZETA: 2016

WHO OR WHAT INSPIRED YOU TO BE A ZETA? The founding principles, Scholarship, Service, Sisterhood and Finer Womanhood.

CAREER ASPIRATIONS: To provide affordable healthcare to the urban communities.

MCKAYLA STOKES
Virginia Commonwealth University
Richmond, Virginia
MAJOR: Criminal Justice
EXPECTED GRADUATION DATE: 5/15/2017
CURRENT CHAPTER: Eta Theta
REGION: Eastern
YEAR JOINED ZETA: 2015

WHO OR WHAT INSPIRED YOU TO BE A ZETA? The opportunity to serve my community while gaining a sisterhood of godly women who allow me to grow inspired me join Zeta.

CAREER ASPIRATIONS: Following graduating with my Bachelor of Science in May of 2017, I will be pursuing law school to study social justice. I have hopes of one day founding a non-profit organization with my twin sisters that offers legal representation and counseling to underrepresented teen women.

MALIKATAH LANE
Benedict college
Columbia, South Carolina
MAJOR: Psychology
EXPECTED GRADUATION DATE: 12/7/2016
CURRENT CHAPTER: Kappa Beta
REGION: Southeastern
YEAR JOINED ZETA: 2015

WHO OR WHAT INSPIRED YOU TO BE A ZETA? To give back and become a woman of change.

CAREER ASPIRATIONS: Become a social activist, also a psychologist in urban communities.

TONI WHITE
North Carolina Central University
Durham, North Carolina
MAJOR: Nursing
EXPECTED GRADUATION DATE: 6/1/2018
CURRENT CHAPTER: Gamma Gamma
REGION: Eastern
YEAR JOINED ZETA: 2015

WHO OR WHAT INSPIRED YOU TO BE A ZETA? I have a strong passion for women's empowerment and I saw just that when I observed the Gamma Gamma Chapter of Zeta Phi Beta Sorority, Incorporated. I admired their unwavering humble attitude even while accomplishing multiple achievements. Anytime service was being held on campus, the Zetas were always visible with a welcoming spirit.

CAREER ASPIRATIONS: I will be attending Watts School of Nursing at Duke University Health System to finish my education to become a Registered Nurse this June. After receiving my Registered Nurse license, I plan to be a traveling nurse, serving underserved communities. While travel nursing, I will be working towards my Doctorate of Nursing, which will lead to opening up my own clinic in an undeserved community.

MAYA JORDAN
Virginia Union University
Richmond, Virginia
MAJOR: History/ Political Science
EXPECTED GRADUATION DATE: 5/7/2016
CURRENT CHAPTER: Nu
REGION: Eastern
YEAR JOINED ZETA: 2015

WHO OR WHAT INSPIRED YOU TO BE A ZETA? I was inspired to join Zeta Phi Beta Sorority, Incorporated through a very influential woman by the name of Reverend Dr. Carolyn D. Clark. She introduced and exposed me to Zeta. From there, I knew I had to be a part of a sisterhood that is so empowering!

CAREER ASPIRATIONS: My career aspirations are to attend law school, pass the bar and become a defense attorney!

KHADIJAH DENNIS
University of South Carolina
Columbia, South Carolina
MAJOR: Broadcast Journalism
EXPECTED GRADUATION DATE: 5/6/2016
CURRENT CHAPTER: Psi Eta
REGION: Southeastern
YEAR JOINED ZETA: 2015

WHO OR WHAT INSPIRED YOU TO BE A ZETA? Latronda McCoy. She is the epitome of what it means to be a member of Zeta Phi Beta.

CAREER ASPIRATIONS: I aspire to have a career in broadcast media as a producer or reporter for a news agency in a city that never sleeps and will always inspire me to do great things outside of my job. I also want to continue building upon the platform God has blessed me with, The Conqueror Movement, a communications platform that informs, educates and inspires millenials to be involved in local and national news.

DEJANIA EVANS
Indiana University - Bloomington
Bloomington, Indiana
MAJOR: Exercise Science
EXPECTED GRADUATION DATE: 5/8/2018
CURRENT CHAPTER: Delta Epsilon
REGION: Great Lakes
YEAR JOINED ZETA: 2015

WHO OR WHAT INSPIRED YOU TO BE A ZETA? My inspiration to join Zeta came from me realizing that Zeta wasn't an organization that wanted to change who I was but an organization that would enhance who I am personally and professionally.

CAREER ASPIRATIONS: After I finish my undergraduate degree in Exercise Science I hope to recruit for multiple men's basketball teams at various HBCUs to first help enhance the reputation of HBCU athletics and to also bring in talented young African American males to strengthen the culture of athletics at HBCUs. Then, I hope to go on to coach men's basketball at a HBCU.

ONIKA WOODLEY
Arkansas Baptist College
Little Rock, Arkansas
MAJOR: Human Services
EXPECTED GRADUATION DATE: 5/1/2016
CURRENT CHAPTER: Psi Rho
REGION: South Central
YEAR JOINED ZETA: 2015

WHO OR WHAT INSPIRED YOU TO BE A ZETA? My Cousin Wanda Jones.

ROLE MODEL: I would have to say my mom. She raised three kids. After the last one graduated high school, she went back to college and got her Bachelor's degree and then her Master's. She was my inspiration to return and finish college, and my age didn't matter.

CAREER ASPIRATIONS: Once I graduate college in May 2016, I plan to attend graduate school at UAPB and receive a Master of Rehab Counseling. I want to work with juveniles and adults who are dealing with substance abuse.

CELESTE SMITH
The University of North Carolina at Greensboro
Greensboro, North Carolina
MAJOR: Media Studies
EXPECTED GRADUATION DATE: 5/11/2019
CURRENT CHAPTER: Omega Nu
REGION: Eastern
YEAR JOINED ZETA: 2016

WHO OR WHAT INSPIRED YOU TO BE A ZETA? My mother, Soror Shannon Chavis-Smith, and my grandmother, Soror Brenda Joyce Harris.

ROLE MODEL: My mother and grandmother are my role models for introducing Zeta to me and demonstrating daily what it means to live "Finer." Robin Roberts is also my role model. She has had an amazing career as a television journalist, even as she endured multiple personal challenges with grace and with which she continued to navigate a successful career and personal brand.

CAREER ASPIRATIONS: I aspire to be a television journalist and deliver accurate and reliable news to society. My dream is to provide the news through entertainment.

LALAH WARE
Morehead State University
Morehead, Kentucky
MAJOR: Vocal Music Education
EXPECTED GRADUATION DATE: 5/14/2018
CURRENT CHAPTER: Delta Pi
REGION: Great Lakes
YEAR JOINED ZETA: 2015

WHO OR WHAT INSPIRED YOU TO BE A ZETA? My mother.

CAREER ASPIRATIONS: I aspire to teach choir and color guard at the high school level. I would also like to teach dance at all scholastic levels.

LATORIA VICK
North Carolina State University
Raleigh, North Carolina
MAJOR: Architecture
EXPECTED GRADUATION DATE: 5/7/2020
CURRENT CHAPTER: Mu Xi
REGION: Eastern
YEAR JOINED ZETA: 2016

WHO OR WHAT INSPIRED YOU TO BE A ZETA? My mother, LaVerne Vick, who is a Zeta, inspired me to join Zeta.

CAREER ASPIRATIONS: I hope to work in government to redesign project housing. I believe if housing developments are better designed, they will create a better environment for those who live in them. Then, the people who come from them will have a better foundation. I believe home plays an essential part in how people go on in life to conquer the world.

AYANA SMITH
Lenoir-Rhyne University
Hickory, North Carolina
MAJOR: Psychology and Human Community Services
EXPECTED GRADUATION DATE: 5/13/2016
CURRENT CHAPTER: Theta Tau
REGION: Eastern
YEAR JOINED ZETA: 2015

WHO OR WHAT INSPIRED YOU TO BE A ZETA? My choir director in my freshman year was a member of Zeta Phi Beta Sorority, Inc. She encouraged and helped me throughout my whole freshman year. She was very sweet and carried herself with dignity. I want to be just like her.

ROLE MODEL: My grandmother is my role model because she raised me and my brothers. She made sure we had whatever it was we needed, even if she had to go without. She also pushed me to complete my educational goals and to strive for whatever I want in life.

CAREER ASPIRATIONS: My career aspirations are to work with "bad" teenagers. I want to work with these teenagers because I want to push them to accomplish whatever goals they have in life. I also want to be an example to them and let them know that even though they may come from an unprivileged background, they can still accomplish every goal they want to accomplish in life.

JHONE' EGERTON
The University of North Carolina at Greensboro
Greensboro, North Carolina
MAJOR: Dual MAJOR: Special Elementary/ Education Elementary
EXPECTED GRADUATION DATE: 5/12/2017
CURRENT CHAPTER: Omega Nu
REGION: Eastern
YEAR JOINED ZETA: 2015

WHO OR WHAT INSPIRED YOU TO BE A ZETA? The principles set forth by our Founders and the members on my campus inspired me to join Zeta Phi Beta Sorority, Incorporated.

CAREER ASPIRATIONS: I aspire to be a high school special education classroom teacher while working towards obtaining my Master of Science in Special Education and PhD in Educational Leadership and Administration. As a classroom teacher, I aspire to create and implement a program that will increase the chances of attending and completing a two- or four-year degree by students with disabilities.

CHERRELL WINFIELD
Henderson State University
Arkdelphia, Arkansas
MAJOR: Elementray Education K-6
EXPECTED GRADUATION DATE: 5/13/2017
CURRENT CHAPTER: Xi Eta
REGION: South Central
YEAR JOINED ZETA: 2014

WHO OR WHAT INSPIRED YOU TO BE A ZETA? The undergraduate members of Zeta Phi Beta Sorority, Inc. inspired me to be a Zeta when I first met them. They were just regular, nice people who were funny and nice to be around. As time went on during my freshman year, they were friendly, invited me out to events, and asked how my classes were going while they talked and cretaed a relationship with me. I did not know they were Greek until I went to events to see them do work for the Sorority they loved. I became intrested in Greek life, so I asked questions and attended their meetings. I made up my mind from there. Zeta was the perfect choice for me.

ROLE MODEL: My role model is my mother, Carolyn Winfield. She is my twin, and we share the same soul. We are the same person in diffrent bodies. She inspires me to be me and not worry about what other peopole think of me. She advises me to pray about things and listen to God. She understands me without me having to talk. My mother has been through a lot in life, and she is a successful spiritual woman of God. She is the most positive person in my life, and she inspires me to be me.

CAREER ASPIRATIONS: My career aspirations are to graduate with an undergraduate degree in Elementary Education K-6 and an English as a Second Language certificate. After that, I want to pursue my career with a master's in counseling and join a graduate chapter where I can continue my volunteer work and scholarship achievements. I want to work in the public school system, inspiring young minds at an early, so they can be the best they can be.

TIANA WATKINS
Murray State University
Murray, Kentucky
MAJOR: Accounting
EXPECTED GRADUATION DATE: 5/13/2017
CURRENT CHAPTER: Nu Rho
REGION: Great Lakes
YEAR JOINED ZETA: 2015

WHO OR WHAT INSPIRED YOU TO BE A ZETA? Former members of Nu Rho inspired me to become a Zeta by how open and welcoming they were to me when I first started college, by how they exemplified the five Zeta principles, and by staying true to themselves.

CAREER ASPIRATIONS: I plan on becoming a Certified Public Accountant in the next five to eight years working for a non-profit organization that help and gives back to the community.

ALEXIS CARSON
North Carolina State University
Raleigh, North Carolina
MAJOR: Science, Technology, & Society
EXPECTED GRADUATION DATE: 12/16/2016
CURRENT CHAPTER: Mu Xi
REGION: Eastern
YEAR JOINED ZETA: 2016

WHO OR WHAT INSPIRED YOU TO BE A ZETA? The loving spirit of the Mu Xi chapter here at NC State.

CAREER ASPIRATIONS: One of my career aspirations is to be a leader, a CEO, or someone in a position of power, for a well-known technical company in Information Technology. Once I have done this and have established myself, I would like to pursue my passion for music and nourishing my talents in this area of my life.

TIANA JACKSON
Tennessee Technological University
Cookeville, Tennessee
MAJOR: Exercise Science and Psychology
EXPECTED GRADUATION DATE: 5/7/2016
CURRENT CHAPTER: Mu Sigma
REGION: South Central
YEAR JOINED ZETA: 2014

WHO OR WHAT INSPIRED YOU TO BE A ZETA? Ivy Prophete.

CAREER ASPIRATIONS: In whatever career path I take, I want to remain loyal and humble. I want to remember that what God has for me is for me and no one else.

KELLI LACY
Tuskegee University
Tuskegee, Alabama
MAJOR: Mechanical Engineering
EXPECTED GRADUATION DATE: 5/5/2017
CURRENT CHAPTER: Theta Beta
REGION: South Central
YEAR JOINED ZETA: 2015

WHO OR WHAT INSPIRED YOU TO BE A ZETA? My inspiration to join Zeta stems from the image and personalities that the ladies of the Theta Beta Chapter of Zeta Phi Beta Inc. displayed to me. There was not a hint of superficiality or a sense of hierarchy that would make an individual feel inferior. There was and still is a sense of welcome and love exuding from the chapter, and it truly stuck to me and inspired me to join.

ROLE MODEL: My current role model is Shonda Rhimes, the writer and executive producer of the show Scandal. This woman utilizes her power and her airspace to bring up current issues occurring around the world and specifically in the United States. She is a firm believer in women's rights, the choice of a woman to do as she chooses with her body, and a powerhouse of intellect, skill and keen insight into the emotions and turmoil faced by black families.

CAREER ASPIRATIONS: I see myself working at a research facility improving the efficiency and performance of automobiles and simple mobility vehicles such as bikes. Furthermore, I will be certified as a personal trainer and make a competitive salary from owning my own business and website targeted towards women as a whole.

ALEXANDRIA PANKEY
University of Tennessee Knoxville
Knoxville, Tennessee
MAJOR: Interior Design
EXPECTED GRADUATION DATE: 5/13/2017
CURRENT CHAPTER: Pi Epsilon
REGION: South Central
YEAR JOINED ZETA: 2015

WHO OR WHAT INSPIRED YOU TO BE A ZETA? Zeta's principles and the chapter's involvement on campus. My father is member of Phi Beta Sigma Fraternity.

CAREER ASPIRATIONS: After graduation, I desire to work in Atlanta, GA at an architecture/interior design firm that specializes in education, cultural, and worship design.

KEYONA WATKINS
University of North Carolina at Greensboro
Greensboro, North Carolina
MAJOR: Elementary Education
EXPECTED GRADUATION DATE: 5/15/2018
CURRENT CHAPTER: Omega Nu
REGION: Eastern
YEAR JOINED ZETA: 1995

WHO OR WHAT INSPIRED YOU TO BE A ZETA? My Aunt, Meshon Watkins inspired me to be a Zeta at first. When I started to come to programs and see who the lovely ladies were, they inspired me to join.

CAREER ASPIRATIONS: Elementary Education Teacher; Math Teacher

JIMIA STURDIVANT
University of Alabama at Birmingham
Birmingham, Alabama
MAJOR: Biomedical Sciences (Pre-Med)
EXPECTED GRADUATION DATE: 12/16/2017
CURRENT CHAPTER: Gamma Theta
REGION: South Central
YEAR JOINED ZETA: 2015

WHO OR WHAT INSPIRED YOU TO BE A ZETA? I was inspired to join Zeta by the opportu¬nity to make a change for the better good.

CAREER ASPIRATIONS: I greatly aspire to become a successful Obstetrician Gynecologist because it is my passion and I know this because I was granted the opportunity to discover that myself upon real life medical observations. I also want to create a foundation for younger girls to excel and become aware of their physical, mental and spiritual well-being and power to do any and everything they absolutely can do

SYLMONEYVESTA HALL

Florida Gulf Coast University
Fort Myers, Florida
MAJOR: Communication-Public Relations/Pre-Medical Studies
EXPECTED GRADUATION DATE: 8/1/2017
CURRENT CHAPTER: Gamma Tau
REGION: Southeastern
YEAR JOINED ZETA: 2014

WHO OR WHAT INSPIRED YOU TO BE A ZETA? I was inspired to join Zeta based on the principles it was founded on, and by the older members of my undergraduate chapter. All the women of the chapter were very welcoming and inclusive when I came to Florida Gulf Coast University as a freshman, and they took the time to get to know me personally.

CAREER ASPIRATIONS: Upon graduation, I aspire to attend medical school, where I would like to prepare for a career as a joint-certified Anesthesiologist-Pediatrician. I eventually want to practice medicine in an underserved and under-represented location.

THE SISTERHOOD SPEAKS

What I Have Learned About Scholarship

Scarlet H. Black

Soror Scarlet H. Black
in office as school principal

The Founders of Zeta Phi Beta Sorority were coeds during a time that higher education for African Americans and women was rare. From this beginning and throughout our ninety-six year history, entering and graduating from college is still a rarity for some. Many of today's millennials and beyond, continue to be the first in their families to achieve this American dream. For me, the principle of scholarship began in the home my grandfather built. He had one of the few black businesses in the community and owned a barber shop and several properties.

Every Thursday night, my family and members of the neighborhood would convene at his home for Bible study, or small group discussions on the latest articles found in *Ebony, Jet,* or the Afro-American newspaper that came in the mail religiously each week. Summers were spent reading an established list and number of books, each requiring a book report for my grandmother. Trips to museums in Washington, D.C. and Philadelphia, Pennsylvania were planned to understand our history, as well as that of America's. From this upbringing, my brother and I learned that the pursuit of scholarship was more than having a high GPA. While a high GPA was an expectation without deviation, the principle of scholarship went well beyond pure academics. Scholarship also meant intellectual freedom and an appreciation for learning all that you could about many different things. This was a principle I learned early in life and hold on to even now. It is a principle that has taken me far in my personal life and career.

I was very blessed to be offered two academic scholarships. The first was for four years at a respected historically black college and university, and the second was for four years of study at the college of my choice, from my mother's local Zeta chapter. I chose the latter and never regretted my decision. I used that scholarship wisely and went on to become a member of the best Sorority for me, Zeta Phi Beta Sorority, Incorporated, because of its zeal and belief in me. I haven't looked back!

I went on to earn two master's degrees and complete graduate courses at the doctoral level. My professional career has been spent in education, as a teacher, licensed school counselor and subsequently, a school principal. I will always be an educator as I will always be a Zeta. To have the honor and privilege of affecting the growth of children and instilling in them the joy of learning, has been one of the most precious gifts God has granted me in my life. For me, this gift solidifies what I learned about scholarship long ago and it is my responsibility to pass it on. As my Zeta mother would often say, "To God be the glory!"

The Learned Zeta

Marsha R. Brookins, M.Ed.

"The capacity to learn is a gift; the ability learn is a skill; the willingness to learn is a choice."

– Brian Herbert, Author

When I first read this quote, I was taking a graduate class, the Art of Teaching, which focused more on how a student learns and not so much how to teach. Throughout the course, I continued to ponder this quote, and I was struck deep in my cerebrum cortex on how I could apply this to anything I set out to master, including Zeta Phi Beta Sorority, Incorporated.

I am forever a student. On November 20, 2013, I was inducted into Zeta Phi Beta Sorority, Inc., and I remember the advice I received from the Maryland State Director during her remarks, "Learn Zeta and enjoy the journey along the way," a modest statement laden with perspective. I set out to learn as much as I could about the organization, its history and leaders, all the while enjoying time with my Sorors. From my previous experience, I knew the best way to learn is to find a good teacher, so I sought out seasoned, well-learned Zetas who demonstrated a depth of knowledge about the Sorority's history and business. I met some for dinner, went for coffee with others, and chatted for hours with many who I considered to be in my "learning circle." They didn't know they were a part of my "circle," but they didn't seem to mind the countless hours of talking and sharing their wisdom and knowledge with me. I immediately jumped head first into the business of Zeta by working tirelessly in my chapter, holding positions, chairing committees, volunteering time, and giving money. Talk about on the job training; I was now full speed on this path and from my horizon, I visualized myself continuing to grow at all levels along the way.

It was a fast first year. By December, I had attended my first State Executive Board meeting and by March 2014, the State Leadership Conference. By June, I had received MIP, undergraduate, youth and Amicae training certificates. I attended my first Boule in July in our founding city, Washington, D.C. as a delegate. I was determined to go hard or go home. All done in year one, I didn't slow down, didn't burn out, nor did I show signs of decline. I realized that I was a high energy person who required intellectual stimulation in the form of learning and new experiences. Stagnation and complacency would not be problems for me.

In year two, I attended the Atlantic Regional Executive Board Meeting, joined the 2015 ZOL cohort and that fall, the Atlantic State Leadership Conference. I attended the 2016 National Executive Board meeting in Orlando, Florida and am registered for Boule in July. I consider this level of engagement impressive and am proud to have two of my intake sisters with me going with me. I have met many Sorors across the country, with decades of membership who haven't accomplished what I've done in my first three years.

What have I learned? I know that the principles that our five Founders founded this Sorority on are the values that I pledged to uphold. The principle of scholarship doesn't just mean raising funds for students. My personal responsibility is to learn and expand personally and professionally, to seek information to lead and transform the lives of those I serve. The second lesson: don't allow the bumps in the road nor the impatience or misdirection of others, impede your progress. Everyone has a journey to take. All will go on one and many will enjoy it, but only a few will receive the rewards from it. My journey begins with the belief that I cannot lead with what I don't know, so I continue without wavering to gather as much information as I can, to become a well learned Zeta.

Developing Scholars

Peggy A. Brown-Harris

Dedicated Teacher
Soror Peggy A. Brown-Harris

There are many ways in which the concept of scholarship is exemplified and the best way for me is through my years of teaching. Children should be motivated to learn, and I am encouraged to do my best. Developing scholars for lifelong learning is important to me and teaching has been a very rewarding profession. I seek to challenge the youth I teach to think, explore and succeed in their formative years within the education system, and apply this knowledge to real-life situations. The greatest reward of all is when former students visit, some bringing a friend or two, and through their reflections, discovering how much of an influence and inspiration my teaching, my caring and dedication made in their lives. Their words of appreciation are far more meaningful than any plaque, certificate or trophy I could receive for achieving my mission.

I have been recognized by my colleagues as Teacher of the Year not once but twice. Then, I was honored twice as an Outstanding Minority Teacher. Each recognition has elevated my devotion to teaching and has served me in my quest to develop scholars.

Paying It Forward:
Mentoring Through STEM

Kalilah Wilkinson Catlett

As a child, my parents ensured that I understood the importance of a great education. They always encouraged my sister and me to be the best. While most young girls my age wanted to become doctors, lawyers, or teachers; I wanted to become an engineer. I remember saying this one day in class and my teacher gave me this strange look. She said, "Kalilah you know that men are engineers, not women. You should pick a more realistic career path when you grow up." Thankfully, my parents raised me to follow my mind, and I told her with confidence, "My daddy told me I can be anything I want to be, and I WILL BE an engineer. You just wait and see."

I'm extremely grateful my parents took the time to build my confidence at a young age. They made sure I knew, with hard work and determination, I could accomplish any goal I set in my mind. That I could achieve any goal I set my mind to became an ongoing theme in my life. I always pushed forward despite the possible roadblocks ahead. Years later, I have a bachelor's degree in Computer Science from Morgan State University, a master's degree in Systems Engineering from Johns Hopkins University and yes, I became an engineer! Just like I said I would when I was a little girl. I achieved my goal, but what do I do now? That was an easy decision: I want to pay it forward and be a living example for young women. I want to let them know that the power to achieve one's dreams is within themselves; all you have to do is believe.

Now, it's easy to say the phrase pay it forward, but without action, the words are meaningless. I wanted to give the words meaning by seeing how I could make an impact on young women interested in **S**cience, **T**echnology, **E**ngineering and **M**athematics (STEM). STEM has become the single most talked about acronym, with increasing appeal, among young people within the nation's educational system. Growing up, I was heavily involved in STEM programs even before the acronym became trendy. My father is an avid reader. I can remember him spending countless hours in the library researching various topics to deepen his knowledge. He would give my sister and me homework assignments to challenge our minds. My parents believed in continued learning, and even during the summer months, our learning process did not stop. Once my father discovered I had an interest in science, he researched various science and leadership development programs for minority students. My parents

"My leadership and mentoring abilities will encourage women to not only pursue, but achieve the goals that they set for themselves."
Soror Kalilah Wilkinson Catlett

often spoke to my guidance counselors to locate the right summer program that aligned with my interests. One summer, I attended the Upward Bound program at the University of Maryland, Baltimore County (UMBC). Upward Bound is a program designed to promote the development and enhancement of students' academic and leadership skills, and it allowed me to network with other students from various economic and cultural backgrounds. Surrounded by other young women who shared my love for science, helped boost my confidence further, and I knew I wasn't alone in my interest for STEM. Attending this program and many others shaped my young mind and prepared me for my future self, but unfortunately, many of the counselors in these programs didn't look like me. Most often, they were males of a variety of races and rarely did I see an African American female. Not seeing many African American women was troubling as I wanted to understand the woman's perspective in the male-dominated STEM fields. Thankfully, I addressed these concerns when I attended Morgan State University and met Soror Sheila Wiggins.

Soror Wiggins was a professor in the Computer Science Department. Although soft spoken, when she did speak, she had a commanding presence that made me take notice and listen. Students often came to Professor Wiggins' office to discuss their plans because she was easy to talk to and she always gave great advice. I loved her story of how she worked as a professional software engineer for several years, but the pull to educate and prepare young people for the challenges ahead in the industry called her to become a professor. I learned so much from her: how to conduct myself in a professional environment; the possible challenges I would face as a woman in a male-dominated field; and, most importantly, how to be a role model. She is my living example of scholarship. I worked hard in her computer systems course to learn about computer architecture and assembly language. Soror Wiggins demanded excellence, and nothing less than 110% would do. I felt the impact of an African American woman that I admired and respected sharing her knowledge and personal experiences with me. Soror Wiggins always told me to have integrity, to lead by example, and that professional achievement would mean nothing if I did not take the time to teach and share my experiences with other women who aspired to STEM careers. I took that message to heart and once I graduated from Morgan State University, armed with my bachelor's degree, I set out to make my impact on the world.

I have spoken at numerous events and workshops about my journey in STEM. The best part is watching the look of awe on the faces of young women when I articulate my accomplishments, both personally and professionally. I remember that amazed expression because I had the same look when I was a girl listening, hoping and dreaming, "One day that will be me!" Sadly, I've had various young women say to me, they have never seen a female engineer, much less an African American female engineer. I see the positive impact I have as a young African American woman breaking the stereotypical image of an engineer. I'm passionate about STEM and encouraging young women to challenge themselves to explore STEM-related careers. Don't let anyone tell you what you can't do. I'm living proof that with the right support system, determination and faith, you can achieve limitless goals. As my mom always said, "Kalilah, all it takes is a mustard seed of faith. You have faith, baby that's all you need to make it through this life. Never give up, and always keep moving forward." My mother's words continue to guide me today. They help fuel my goal to encourage and mentor as many young women as I can while continuing to move forward no matter the possible challenges and obstacles ahead. In mentoring young women interested in STEM, I always provide the following words of advice:

•   **Get a Mentor:** The road ahead can be challenging. When I was in college I kept repeating Philippians 4:13; *"I can do all things through Christ who strengthens me."* Being a STEM major was difficult at times; however I surrounded myself with mentors that provided leadership, guidance and words of encouragement when I needed them the most. I have mentors in my professional, personal and sorority life. Having these relationships has strengthened my character and increased my growth. Always remember that being a mentor or mentee is a two-way relationship. Both parties need to work together to bring out the best in each other. Everyone needs a helping hand. *Don't go on this journey of discovery alone; allow someone to help you.*

•   **Do Community Service:** As a Zeta woman, service is what I do within my local, state and national communities. Lending a helping hand to my fellow man is as important as excelling academically. Once I graduated from college, I got a job working as a systems engineer for a Fortune 500 company. I was so excited to showcase the knowledge I learned in college. On my first day of orientation, I learned that the project I was supporting would affect millions of lives traveling through our air traffic system within the United States. I was blown away when I heard the stories from former air traffic controllers on the impact the current system had on their jobs and what our new project could do to help improve the air traffic control system and keep many lives safe. This knowledge transfer and interaction made me look at my job differently. I had the opportunity to serve my country by improving how the Federal Aviation Administration (FAA) manages U.S. air traffic. Understanding the bigger picture placed a greater importance on my work. I take great pride that when I fly; I was one of the engineers that kept passengers safe. *Always remember the bigger picture and that you are connected to a greater purpose to serve your fellow man in any way you can.*

•   **Learn the latest trends within STEM:** STEM is ever changing and adapting with each generation. The demand for newer and smarter technology is growing faster than we have scientists or engineers to develop those new and innovative ideas. I encourage young women who want to become engineers to do their research. Take the time to understand fully what an engineer actually does versus what you think an engineer does. Network with different types of engineers to gain a better understanding of whether that field is something you would like to pursue. Take some time to research in-state or out-of-state colleges and universities that offer the type of engineering studies in which you're interested. Look at their current research grants. This information should be available on websites or you call the school directly for more information. The key is to do your research and stay current on the latest trends for the career path of your interest. Think of your research like the evolution of telephone; from rotary phones, to push button phones, to portable phones and now, cellphones. That development took time, dedication and research by talented scientists and engineers. *It is a journey to discover your career path.*

•   **Participate in STEM Programs:** I was in middle and high school during the pre-Google days and my parents had to rely on flyers or word of mouth to hear about STEM programs. Now, at the click of a button, one can research and find local and national STEM programs that will allow young women to network with like-minded students. These programs are designed to expose students to various STEM disciplines and working professionals. Many tech companies hold STEM competitions to promote STEM and award scholarships. These programs are not only a tremendous opportunity for students but parents as well. Parents will get a chance to network and share ideas. Having that support system for both students and parents is extremely important. If you are a parent that doesn't have a technical background, this network will expand your knowledge and provide opportunities to learn different ways of to engaging your child. A list of national STEM programs for young women and their parents:

- First Lego League: http://www.firstlegoleague.org/
- Girls Inc.: http://www.girlsinc.org/
- Girls Who Code: http://girlswhocode.com/
- TechBridge: http://www.techbridgegirls.org/
- Viva TechnologyTM: http://www.greatmindsinstem.org/

My final thought: *Live for the moment and have fun along the way!* STEM is exciting, and I look forward to seeing the next generation of young women that will lead the STEM movement forward. We have come a long way as women interested and working in STEM careers. It's amazing to see the growth; however there is still much work to do. I continue my promise to encourage, educate and promote STEM because I have a responsibility to Pay It Forward!

Time Waits for No One

Amber Hendrick, Esq.

Give them their roses while they're here. Paw-paw's voice begins to trail off as he concludes the story of one of his final visits to see his mother toward the end of her life. I honestly cannot remember exactly how the story ends after that, but it's the sort of cautionary tale that stands on its own. It doesn't need a conclusory statement to drive the point home. I can hear the regret in his voice. I can feel the message in the weight of the silence that lingers in the air after he finishes. I can see it on his face. The heaviness of a regret that gnaws at you, that sits in your bones that creeps up on you and chokes you with its memory when you are trying to have a moment of peace. It is the sort of feeling that you do not want to remember while simultaneously hoping to never forget.

I have always had a close relationship with my Mal-maw and Paw-paw. Though I have no recollection of it, I lived with them for a few years as a young child. I know that I have spent the majority of my holidays over the past 26 years with them—Thanksgivings, Christmases, Easters, Mother's Days, Mardi Gras, and even quite a few birthdays (my Paw-paw's birthday is the day before mine) were spent with them. They were there for graduations, baptisms, and even dance recitals where I performed dances my body has long since forgotten how to do. I spent summers with them, random weekends with them, and when my brother and I came down with the chicken pox around the same time, we both recovered at their house. The beauty in being so familiar with your grandparents is that they start to feel like a second set of parents.

That is also the danger.

In general, we take our parents for granted. We go through the usual tug of war with our parents: needing them, but wanting to grow independently from them and their watchful eye, their annoyingly accurate advice and admonishments, their unsolicited opinions, and their rules. Even though they tell us to enjoy being a child, we try to speed through to adulthood when we can have our own money and be away from them. We spend a lot of time longing to get away, and to be able to spend time with other people. We just assume that our parents will be there. We believe that there will always be another time to enjoy some quality time. Therein lies another danger.

Certainly, there will be more time. Time is the indefinite continued progress of existence and events in the past, present, and future regarded as a whole. Although we do not know when our time here will end, we know that an end will eventually come.

They say that youth is wasted on the young. We spend our youth wishing to speed up time so that we can be old enough to do all the "cool" things we want to do, then time eventually starts to pass us by and we live long enough to wish we had done things differently. We sit and listen to our grandfathers recount the story of a dying mother telling her son that she would have sacrificed all the money he sent her over the years in exchange for some of his time, but the tale does not move us to the point of action because we assume we have more time. We get annoyed when our mothers urge us to get off of our phones and go talk to our grandparents, to sit and take in the history they can impart, to write it down. We go sit and hear the stories, but we do not listen because we assume there will be a time for a retelling, and then we will write it down.

A few years ago, Paw-paw was diagnosed with Alzheimer's disease. It did not seem so bad at first. Every once in a while, he would ramble on about getting a skateboard from Uncle Bill, who had long since passed on, but for the most part Paw-paw could still function and have a normal conversation. It seemed like there would be plenty of time before the disease really started to ravage his brain, before his memory became less reliable, before his behavior changed. It seemed like there would be more time to gather his stories.

This past year, when I realized that time had started to pass us by, I decided to sit down with my Paw-paw and gather his life story. He told a lot of jokes. He was like the class clown who causes a scene when called upon by the teacher because he cannot provide an answer. I could tell he was trying to reach for memories that escaped him. Thankfully, Mal-maw was there to fill the holes in the story, but that still leaves at least a quarter of his life unaccounted for.

Now, I am just left with lingering questions about the man my Paw-paw was before he became my Paw-paw, the answers to which might have already faded from the readily dissolving remnants of his memory. There is no insight into how being born a black male to a single mother in a small town in rural Virginia during the Great Depression shaped the man he is today. Nothing to explain why a childhood skateboard from an uncle was so significant that it was one of the first memories he attempted to hold onto before Alzheimer's took it away. Nothing about his relationship with his sister. No stories about his motivations, of what he wanted to be when he grew up, or if he felt he accomplished the goals he set for himself. No personal stories of his mother. No deeper understanding about why he thought it would be more valuable to spend his time working to provide his mother financial assistance than to spend his time visiting with her. Perhaps, he just assumed he would have more time.

Maybe Paw-paw no longer feels the twinge of regret he once felt when discussing not spending enough time with his mother before she passed. Perhaps he has made peace with that memory, or he has lived long enough to forget it. One day, I too might make peace with the fact that I waited too long to become curious about Paw-paw's story. One day, the heaviness will no longer creep up on me, I will no longer feel the twinge of regret for not asking more questions, for not writing things down, for assuming that there would always be another time. I know now that there is always more time, but it does not wait for us to seize it. It just keeps ticking. This is one of life's ultimate lessons that we will all learn.

Lessons Learned While Pursuing a Doctorate Degree

Nell Williams Ingram, Ph.D.

In 1976, while working on my master's degree, I met with current doctoral candidates. We discussed the pros and cons of that university and pursuing further degrees. For some reason, my interest was heightened and I started research on what was involved in earning a doctorate degree. One of my discoveries was that the Ph.D. (Doctor of Philosophy) was considered a "more prestigious" degree than the Ed.D. (Doctor of Education). I did not fully understand why this was, but many professors and students told me this and advised that I work toward a Ph.D. I decided to take the high road and pursue a Ph.D. The next advice I was given was to not get a third degree from the same university but to enroll in a different university, and to choose my doctoral committee members carefully. These three pieces of advice served me well during the next four years.

My spouse and I moved to a small town north of Dallas to teach prior to deciding on a university. The Gainesville ISD was the one school system that we could both find teaching positions in. There, I chose North Texas State University (now the University of North Texas) to pursue my doctoral degree as it was only 30 miles from Gainesville. One of the first hurdles I faced was determining my major emphasis of study and a schedule. Teaching fulltime as a first-year teacher was already a challenge yet I researched my North Texas State University department's schedule far out into the future to determine the availability of classes I would need to meet my degree plan. This was my first real lesson in time management and strategic planning.

I found that pursuing a doctorate degree is attainable for anyone. Here are my tips and lessons learned:

1. Discuss your plans fully with your spouse or significant other and ask about their level of support for your endeavor. Make sure they are "on board." You cannot implement your plan without family support. It is definitely doable to have a family and go to school but working out a plan for the simplest things (meals, extracurricular activities, job responsibilities) makes your plan workable. I really utilized my time management skills.

2. Do your strategic planning. Work with the university to review future semester offerings. Don't want to find you are unable to take a specific class because of the time it is offered. This is especially important if you work a fulltime job. My job as a first-year teacher was demanding.

3. Stay resolute and determined. Perseverance is the key! About 80% of your degree pursuit experience will be how you jump hurdles and not let anything sidetrack you. Oftentimes, I believe, professors set up those hurdles just to see how you react. Don't give up! Jump those hurdles and move forward.

4. Complete an exhaustive review of the appropriate major you wish to seek. Don't choose the "easiest" major to complete. What will you do with that degree when you finish? How will it pay off? I majored in Adult and Continuing Education. Years later, I wish I had done more research into the job market and majored in Higher Education OR at least minored in it. I allowed the courses I had for my master's degree to guide my minor so I would not have to complete additional coursework. Choose your major and your minor wisely.

5. Research the job market and its predictions for the future in your field of study.

6. Share your educational career plans with your immediate supervisor if you are working. Some bosses will be very impressed and will show their support. Realistically, some might not care for or feel that your plans are a worthy effort. With support, life will be easier. My principal was very supportive. If I needed to be excused from Parent-Teacher Conferences because of a class, he understood. I made sure I was the first one to volunteer for other projects. Always show appreciation for support at any level.

7. Choose your doctoral committee wisely. This was advice I followed. The department assigned me a professor in my major but I had a choice in naming the other two. (My university required three.) One of the first things I observed was the attitude of my major professor. He appeared indifferent and I felt like an insignificant graduate student. I inquired around campus and it was known that he had some pre-determined ideas about African American students. I knew I would have to handle him "with a long-handled spoon." With this in mind, I set out to find the "right fit" of professors for my other two committee positions. I received a tip about placing a statistician on my committee. The second tip was to select someone that would be partial to and respect me, someone who would not be afraid to speak up for me and protect my interests. I chose well. Both of the two advisors I selected helped me through the process.

8. Network with other students in your major department. Get to know them; especially those who have gone through comprehensive examinations. Discover what they are like and talk to more than one person to get a variety of opinions. This is not "cheating." This is reality and life.

9. Determine your dissertation title. This is a big decision and you must choose wisely. Be prepared to get some push back if it is not a title that your major professor (or the committee) agrees with you. Choose something that you have a passion about so it won't seem like a chore. It took me a few months to figure this out: don't argue with the major professor if you want to get over this hoop. Make the suggested changes and remember, he or she must sign off on that document eventually. Choosing the right dissertation topic and completing the best research possible can lead to future articles and speaking engagements.

10. Hire a reputable typist who knows the guidelines of your university. While you might be skilled in this area, this will take a lot of stress off your shoulders. Many graduate school offices have a list of recommended typists. As I completed each section for review, I typed my own drafts to save money and solicited the assistance of an English teacher to proofread. When it came to the final copy, I hired someone else to type.

11. Work closely with your doctoral committee as you prepare for oral exams and the dissertation defense. I followed some of the testing strategies we taught in public school. I did not study the night before; I relaxed. My philosophy was "If I don't know it now, one more night would not make a difference." I did consult with other graduate students who had recently completed their orals and their defense. It is your dissertation so no one knows it better. Be passionate as you describe your research; be confident. Sounding unsure about the research leads to additional questions from the team.

To finish your study, research and dissertation, and then complete the graduation "hooding ceremony" is a monumental experience, one that will be one of the proudest times in your life. There will be many hurdles and often you will wonder "Why am I doing this?" or you will think "This is not worth the headache!" but you will find it is a worthy investment in your career and future.

Then, wear your title proudly. The first time someone says your name with the title, "Dr. Ingram" will become the sweetest sound you have heard next to the first time someone calls you by your married name or the first time your child says "mama," A terminal degree will be yours forever and will result in respect from the public and your peers. It will open doors. For example: two years ago I had to go to the emergency room. One of my teachers was in the waiting room and called me "Dr. Ingram." The nurses moved me up on the waiting list. This is a true story. In addition to the title, there is the prestige, the credibility of being an authority in your field, the opportunities to develop a career in many different levels, secondary or postsecondary and the opportunities and choices of what to do career wise, research, writing, teaching, administration, or consulting.

I hope my Lessons Learned help will incent you to stick with your mission and persevere!

Journey

Johanna Jerome

When I was just a little girl, after my father passed, my mother became a single parent of four. I remember she had such a hard time dealing with the "race of life," as she used to call it. This quote always stayed with me. I put it in my mind that life was always a race. A race to get somewhere first, a race to finish something first, a race to let everyone know you were the first.

I applied myself to be the best, to be the first in everything I did. My mother was a "Sugar Cane Kid" from the Caribbean islands who came to America in search of a better life and a need to accomplish something.

My perspective about life as a race changed during my college years. I met so many people who were older than than me, enrolled in undergraduate classes, and I thought, "Life is not a race but indeed a journey." It is a journey that many of us take and never realize all the steps we took to get somewhere. The journey makes us, not the race to finish first.

Wisdom: The Principle Thing

Janice M.T. Johnson, M.Ed.

I grew up in a middle class Christian home and was encouraged to do something positive with the blessings God gave us. My mother was a stay-at-home mom until all of her children were in school full time. She then began a fulltime job. At that time, my father, a military veteran, worked a traditional 9 to 5 job and neither of my parents had a college degree. From an early age my siblings and I were taught to respect and appreciate education for the doors it could open for us. We grew up knowing that the statement was not "if I go to college" but "when I go to college." My parents grew up during a time when Jim Crow and segregation was the norm, even in northern states. A college education for African Americans, or blacks as my parents would say, was not common at that time. My parents were so convinced that a college education would open many doors for us that they did all they could to make sure that we had the opportunities that were not readily available to them.

When my siblings and I were approaching high school age, as if leading by example, my father began taking college courses. He also took his skills as an electrician and became a public school teacher of industrial arts, often referred to as shop class. My mother worked as a school secretary. Even though there were five children in my family my parents were determined to make college an attainable option for all of us. My dad took on a second fulltime job at night to ensure that college would be possible for us. He continued to work two jobs and attend school in the evenings. Of my parents' five children, all of us attended college and three of us have advanced degrees. My father and my third oldest sister graduated from college the same year. Most of us received partial scholarships for undergraduate and graduate school which helped defray the rising cost of college. My siblings and I were blessed with the opportunities that my parents worked so hard for us to have. We attended the colleges of our choosing, were able to pursue our chosen careers and live the American Dream. Keeping the lessons my parents taught us in mind and applying that wisdom, allowed us to go to college, do well, and take time to help those less fortunate than us.

I am proud and grateful to be a fulfillment of the dreams my parents had for their children; dreams that my husband and I continue for our children. My parents' philosophy of working hard, taking advantage of opportunities, never stop learning, using what God gave you to do something positive, and paying it forward has made a lasting impression on me. Even though my parents have transitioned to heaven, I still hear them reciting the scripture in Proverbs 4:7, "Wisdom is the principal thing. Therefore get wisdom. And in all your getting, get understanding." For me the message was clear, people can learn and increase their knowledge but wisdom comes from understanding what to do with the acquired knowledge, recognizing our blessings, helping and encouraging others to do the same.

Part of the wisdom I gained from college and my upbringing is to help others achieve their academic goals. My husband and I have been able to support our four daughters in achieving their dreams. But it is equally as important to support other young girls. I am able to do this through my work with Zeta Phi Beta Sorority, Incorporated. By raising money for scholarships as a Sorority, we are assisting young women of color to be able to achieve their career goals. In a world where reality TV stars and YouTube sensations are seen as successful, I believe now more than ever programs such as our youth affiliates are imperative in creating a solid foundation for our young. This will help girls to understand the value of an education as well as take their education seriously so that they are able to apply for our Sorority's scholarships when the time comes for them to further their education. The importance of an education has been instilled in me and my siblings from our youth. I instilled the same values in my daughters. I am proud to be able to work with an amazing Sorority to instill Finer Womanhood and Scholarship in the daughters of our communities as we collectively build foundations, encourage and teach our future leaders of the world.

Scholarship: We All Have a Bit

Monica M. Leak, M.A., CCC-SLP, M.L.S.

As a socially conscious, action-oriented organization, the principles established by our beloved Founders serve as markers of identity and articulate our core beliefs and values. To attain success requires some level of scholarship. Scholarship is defined as knowledge achieved through study or academic achievement.

Scholarship, yes we all have a bit. We have scholarship as acquired through book knowledge. We have scholarship as obtained through dialogue and interactions with others. We gain knowledge through experience. The means through which we achieve scholarship are as varied as our personalities, our socioeconomic status or our place of residence. We learn through our senses. We are visual learners, tactile learners, auditory learners, and kinesthetic learners. Our styles may have one of these qualities in single focus or may function in combination, but no matter the style or the means of learning and achieving scholarship, we all have a bit.

It is that bit of scholarship that positions us in spheres of influence. Just a bit of scholarship made you college and career ready. With a bit of scholarship, you have become a finer woman phenomenon, a mover, a shaker, deal maker, and negotiator with endless possibilities.

A common saying found on bookmarks and classroom bulletin board borders is, "Readers are Leaders." While true in our efforts to plant the seeds of learning in the young, it continues to hold true throughout our lifetime. Do you remember the first book you read by yourself? Do you remember your excitement of being able to read that book to your parent, a teacher, a younger sibling or neighbor? It was a moment of pride and accomplishment. That first book became foundational for developing your concepts of print, understanding characters, settings and plots, responding to questions, inferencing, and critical thinking. Just think: you got all of that from a book!

So what happens when we continue to apply ourselves to learning through books, whether it is related to our professions, academic pursuits or areas of interests, or not? Reading reduces stress, strengthens analytical thinking skills, expands the vocabulary, improves writing, and increases knowledge. Every time you read, your mind obtains new information. This information may apply to a current life situation, or it may be for pure enjoyment, but once that bit of knowledge has entered the mind, it can prove useful at a time of need. How often have you been in a conversation when something you recently read in a newspaper, magazine article, or a book provided an example or a situation relevant to the topic of discussion?

Most recently, one of my book clubs selected a work by a local author. This particular book was a murder mystery set in a soul food restaurant in Prince George's County. The book had recipes for breakfast, main courses, desserts and special drinks, so we took the recipes and had a fun soul food-themed meeting filled with discussion and fellowship. That work of fiction added several new recipes to my cooking arsenal! The added bonus to this particular meeting was arranging a Skype discussion with the author, who was impressed by our soul food spread.

Many undergraduates spend countless hours in the library or with study groups preparing for projects, presentations, research papers, and midterm or final exams. Who can remember the professors who assigned nearly half a text for the week's reading assignment? By graduation, you may have become so tired of academic reading that you said you did not want to see another text book ever, but here you are crossing the stage to shake the hand of the university chancellor.

Despite the sometimes dread of tackling another academic text, the more knowledge you have, the better equipped you become to face any challenge that may come your way. Knowledge through information attained through the reading of books opened the door to college preparedness, career readiness and to a discovery of self, new places, and interests. Just remember that knowledge attained is something that can never be taken away from you, so keep reading.

The first few lyrics of the song, *Love Under New Management* by Miki Howard, are "Experience is a good teacher. It takes someone like me to know." Those words remind us of the lessons learned about love and life through our experiences. We learned what it meant when Mama said hold your ear when she hot combed your hair on a Saturday night. You learned through sometimes painful experience what happens when you were disobedient to your parent(s) or teacher(s). You learned through experience how to avoid drama and strategies for maneuvering out of the middle of someone's dramatic episode (not my circus, not my show).

Through experience we learn a lot about ourselves. We are reflective. We take inventory. We gauge what we know that can be applied to a particular situation, or what may have no relevance whatsoever to our current goals and visions. We map out our next steps. We are intentional. We have a purpose.

We have a forward-moving drive as a result of all of the lessons learned from our experiences. We learned to self-advocate when we saw that a professor was grading differently. We discovered our voice in efforts to establish a branch of the NAACP on campus. We recognize the stop-and-reevaluate moments through the experience of trying to juggle too many things at one time or having too much on our plates. That little word "no" is a powerful tool. We learn to use it.

Not only through my experiences have I gained knowledge, but also through the experiences of those who came before me. From my mother, who participated in many student-led protests during the Civil Rights Movement as a student at North Carolina A&T State University, I learned the value of taking a stand and having the courage to do so. From my father, I learned that movement is never ending. You are always moving forward in efforts to engage the community, effect change and address the issues of the day. From my grandmother, I learned, "get all you can, and can all you get." This quote references that process of preserving foods that seemed to take all day, but resulted in a beautiful quart-sized jar that she could keep for a long time. My grandmother worked for many years as a domestic and then as a dorm mother at North Carolina Central University. She encouraged her grandchildren to keep going in their educational pursuits and not stop learning.

From my great aunties who taught in segregated, multi-grade one-room school houses, I knew that sometimes you had to get up early in the morning, put coal in a pot belly stove to heat the school building, use out-of-date, hand-me-down books, and I learned that effective teaching produced great learning even with limited resources. These are lessons I have learned well, and I'm able to share those lessons with others.

In prekindergarten classes, we discuss our five senses: touch, sight, taste, smell, and hearing. Much can be learned through our senses. Through touch, I feel differences in textures and quality of fabric. Through touch, I express affection and concern. When I travel to visit my sister, I experience touch through the best hug ever from my nephew, Kenneth (almost a teenager who still gives hugs). Through touch, my younger students let me know they need their shoes tied or draw my attention to who is supposed to be the line leader. For some of my students with more bounce in their steps, holding my hand is a necessity to keep them and the rest of the group together.

I can assess a need through sight that may cause me to rise to action without knowledge of a student's reading or math test scores, to provide tutoring assistance after school or to partner with a local organization to provide books for students or participate with Communities in Schools to provide early literacy training for parents. That responsive action came from seeing a need and doing something about it.

Snack time in a pre-k class is filled with lessons about taste. There are the squinted eyes, the hand-squeezed noses, the chipmunk cheeks (a snack stuffed in one cheek and moved to the other), and the "I'm just going to let this sit on my tongue before I swallow it move." The initial taste of something influences your decision to continue eating or to consider it something for which you have yet to acquire the taste for and as such, will not likely try again.

The sense of smell can alert all the other senses. The scent of a nice cologne can alert you to a nearby masculine presence. If that fragrance is attached to a smart, clean-cut brother, well that's when you say a silent thank you for the senses of sight and smell!

The sense of hearing is quite valuable because through hearing, you receive messages. The "She said he said stuff" you should most likely ignore and resolve in your mind that in the mess there is truth and that truth at some point will be revealed. We hear good news. We hear bad news. Through this sense of hearing, we process all of the messages and then make decisions.

Knowledge through academic sources, knowledge through experience and knowledge attained through our senses contributes to our ongoing legacy as individuals and to the corporate body of our Sorority as we continue to build on the principles of Zeta while blazing new paths. We have taken different paths to arrive at the knowledge we presently hold, and that which we strive to gain all speaks to that one principle, scholarship, we all have a bit.

Living Life Is Scholarship

Lynéa N. Laws, Ph.D.

The word scholarship in the form of a noun pertains to acquiring knowledge by the acts of studying and learning. It is commonplace for the learning and studying to be performed under the watchful eye at an educational institution. Yet, many negate the best opportunities for scholarship: through life's experiences.

Deciding to step out on faith and doing something that is rarely done can cause you to find yourself in unfamiliar territory; however, all things have a reason and a season.

On the day I received my first contract for international work, I could have easily dismissed it and allowed fear to enslave me and continued with my familiar job as a special education advocate. But, I desired liberation. I sought liberation from my own fear because I wanted my light to shine.

During my time abroad I began to blog, sharing my life experiences and a minute portion of the thousands of thoughts that crossed my mind continuously. As I began to explore the world and share those moments with others, I realized my light was shining bright and I was "unconsciously giving other people permission to do the same." Had I played small and listened to my negative inner self and the naysayers who said to me, "Don't do it. Those people are crazy over there!" or "Why do you want to go there? What's wrong with your life here?" or, "Girl, you crazy. You need to stay home with your own kind," I would not be where I am today nor would I have had the many wonderful experiences I encountered. Most importantly, others may not have been motivated to follow their own dreams.

I am a scholar practitioner who has educated others via life experiences – both great and indifferent – on how to obtain the most out of life by choosing to allow my light to shine. These lessons have taught me: selflessness is better than entitlement; it's always better to give than to receive; what you see on the outside is not a definitive indicator of what takes place behind closed doors; receiving an education particularly at the collegiate level, is a great opportunity to take advantage of and not be squandered away; and being female actually has numerous bonuses. Moreover, time is priceless and you must carve a portion out at least monthly to reflect and share with friends and family. And, ultimately, life doesn't require a plethora of belongings to live well.

Each of us has a purpose in life. It is our duty to pursue and fulfill that purpose so that our light can shine thus, igniting the light of someone else. Often times, we are our own worst enemy and critic. Instead of going forth and fulfilling our dreams we allow self-doubt to derail our potential achievements. We are all equipped with the tools to be scholars. The difference is in how you choose to utilize the tools. Will you use them to destroy your barriers and create a pathway or, will you use your tools to simply clean up the debris left behind? The choice is yours.

The Scholarship of Research, Discovery and Interaction

Marian Martin

Scholarship can be learning or knowledge acquired by studying and/or research. Scholarship, knowledge acquired by learning and instruction, could have been one point that our founding sisters had in mind when they outlined the principles of the Sorority. In 1920, teaching and nursing were the primary fields available for women, in particular African American women, seeking to complete a college degree in further pursuit of a career path. This might have come to mind as they sought to come up with a principle.

Getting the 501(c)3 status for the Stork's Nest of Oklahoma City, Inc had boosted my self-confidence so that a few years later when another cousin who had been trying to get that status for a family cemetery in Texas said she was having trouble getting someone to help her, I volunteered. Again, I sent off for the IRS packet and read to see what I would need for the various stages. The cousin had indicated she would like to apply for historic designation and a historic marker too. The requirements for documentation for both were slightly similar. I had to carefully read instructions for each of the three activities and make notes indicating what was needed for each; what I could readily access; what I would need help with; and, what I would need county records or genealogy data for.

I recalled that old saying, "There is no I in teamwork," so I thought I would get several people in the community and in the family involved in the various aspects of getting the cemetery ready. Yes, we moved forward confident that we would receive the historic designation and the historic marker. We were publishing a quarterly family newsletter so we told the family what we planned and how much money would be needed. They responded favorably and were enthusiastic.

My cousin and I met during her lunch hour one day and checked the "to do" list as we compiled documents. We submitted the application, fee and documentation for the 501(c)3 status and thankfully after a short time, it was approved.

I had never visited the cemetery so asked my cousin to once again describe in detail the layout and provide information about the history of the cemetery as she remembered it. And, I read what I could find on the history of that cemetery and those who had owned the land. My list for my cousin involved: getting a woman from the area to get me the names of those who were buried in the cemetery; finding the land and deed records on the property on which the cemetery was located; obtaining information on the current owner(s) of the land; and, determining if the land was sold or given to the family. Genealogy research was next on my list in finding out who had been a veteran, or a minister, or a person of a different ethnic background, or just something interesting about their lives or how they died. There were two cemeteries, one for the Caucasian members of the community and one for the African American members, although there were some Hispanic, Indian and Asian inhabitants in the African American cemetery. Our work was for the African American cemetery.

Once again I interviewed my cousin and had her describe the layout of the cemetery. All the information was accumulated and when Oklahoma was snowed in that winter, I remained in Texas and began writing the history of the cemetery. Using my cousin's verbal description, I drew the layout of the cemetery and we asked one of the women who lived in the area to take the necessary photographs. The Texas instructions for historical designation stated that if one error was found in the application, the documentation would be returned and we would have to wait until the next year in order to resubmit. My two cousins plus my son proofread everything very carefully. One cousin was an attorney and both cousins were familiar with the cemetery and many of the inhabitants. When I was satisfied the proofer's questions and notations were answered and corrected, we carefully went down the instruction pages and put the photos, land records, history and other documentation in order and to be submitted. We were excited when we received notice that the historical designation had been approved. The shorter history containing additional facts and the additional documents were compiled with the new photos, deeds, and pictures of the cemetery layout, and this was submitted to the group responsible for granting the historical marker. They, too, stated that if there was one error the documents would be returned and we would have to wait a year to resubmit. We were again thrilled to receive notice that we were approved for the historical marker.

In 1990, Ernest Boyer introduced an academic model advocating expansion of the traditional definition of scholarship and research into four types of scholarship in order to provide a broader meaning to the *teaching versus research* debate. He wanted the traditional research, or the scholarship of discovery to be broadened to include new social and environmental challenges beyond the campus as well as the reality of contemporary life. Boyer wanted the definition of scholarship to include: discovery; integration – summarizing information and giving it personal meaning or application; engagement which involves the application of disciplinary expertise and sharing with peers; and, teaching and learning – allowing public sharing and the opportunity for application and evaluation by others.

After hours of research, discussion, and writing; getting people in the county involved so they helped clear brush and mow the lawn, take photos, and provide land records and deeds; getting family members involved and interested so they donated money to pay for repair and raising of some of the headstones; and, purchase of the historical marker, all culminated into a truly worthwhile project. Also, we needed to get family and community members excited enough to attend a ceremony and fellowship during Memorial Day weekend. This two year period was not only a journey of learning, discovery and interaction but was a period of excitement and exhilaration, and was a revival of an age-old tradition for Memorial Day. I often thought of something my grandmother always quoted, "If you are going to do a job, do it right." It helped me give that necessary attention to detail as we assembled the documentation needed. In this instance, scholarship was indeed a learning adventure into research, discovery and interaction and clearly met the definitions outlined by Boyer.

Cultivating Graduate Student Scholar Success: An Insider's View

Leslie L. Perkins

Leslie Perkins

This message is for undergraduate Sorors who plan to pursue a master's or doctoral degree program. I am an academic support specialist, who, until recently, worked for over 20 years with undergraduate students at a variety of colleges and universities. For the past two years, I have worked at an institution that only offers graduate programs and while here, I have noted striking similarities regarding students and their readiness to take on advanced levels of academic pursuit. Despite the name of the program or the institution, when you enroll in postgraduate study, you should expect the level of academic rigor to significantly increase. And in order to remain successful, you will need to step up your game as well. Many undergraduate Sorors are admitted into graduate programs, but only those with a strong commitment, sharp focus and effective time management skills will succeed.

Just as college is *not* like being in high school or the 13th grade, graduate school is *not* like being in college as an undergraduate. That first year of graduate study involves an emotional, psychological, and academic transition to the world of graduate education. Self-motivation, self-discipline, and a realistic assessment of your own physical and mental energy become "must have" abilities since graduate study always entails a narrower focus and more thorough consideration of key concepts and ideas, many that may not even have been introduced during your undergraduate study. The time required to complete reading assignments, do research, and participate in various workshops, class projects and discussion groups, etc. can quickly overwhelm an unsuspecting or marginally prepared student. Unfortunately, it's usually not until well after they are doused with gasoline and engulfed in flames that most graduate students even consider seeking out academic support services, but by then it's often too late. Be honest with yourself and assess your study habits *prior* to beginning your graduate program, perhaps as soon as you learn you've been given the opportunity to continue your education.

What is academic support and how can specialists help? The term refers to the integration of a unique set of assessments, strategies, and services, along with university resources all provided to help students study smarter, boost their potential and meet or exceed progress benchmarks. Requested services include goal setting, time management and organization strategies, test preparation and test taking strategies, note-taking strategies, assessing and using learning styles to adapt study techniques, learning to use a syllabus effectively, and active reading/learning techniques. During undergraduate study, these services would usually have been available in a single office with a name like the Student Success Center. However, for graduate students, these services, if available at all, are often accessed only through special "new graduate student' programming or select faculty members or mentors who offer academic coaching or counseling, or similar assistance to their students and protégés. Academic support specialists help students learn more about themselves as learners. They help students analyze their study skills and suggest ways to optimize those skills so that students become confident, effective and independent scholars. They individualize their work with each student based on the student's needs, so you should always expect to talk about your past and current academic habits. Together, you'll identify and refine specific academic goals and the behaviors required for you to achieve them.

Lastly, academic support specialists often serve as formal or informal mentors, role models, and ultimate challengers to nurture students to their fullest capabilities.

Of the services most often requested, organization or planning is the most essential for students attempting to balance multiple life roles and responsibilities. Here then, are a few quick pointers about planning to help you on your way...

- Create and maintain one master calendar that includes *all* of your commitments – self, family, academic, social, etc. Post all special occasions, event dates, deadlines and due dates in your calendar system and then plan backwards from those dates, including sufficient prep time and automatic reminders.
- Regardless of the type of Learning Management System (LMS) your institution uses, there are usually calendar feed options to sync with electronic calendar systems. The most popular options are Google Calendar, Outlook, and I-calendar.

- Periodically review your email and other correspondence to make sure all activities have been logged and are current. Include as much information as possible in the sections that will be visible on the "face" of your calendar. For example, in addition to the start and end times (including travel), include contact phone numbers, the purpose of the activity or event, your areas of responsibility and materials.

- Use your calendar's color-coding system to easily identify those tasks and activities that are non-negotiable, i.e., family and graduate school. This additional information will help you prioritize, when necessary. Prioritizing and scheduling go hand in hand, but prioritizing will rank the activities and commitments you posted on your master calendar to assure you have time for what matters most.

- Once everything is posted, there are a few questions to address. How does your course load fit in with your workload and life commitments? Will you be a full or part time student? Will you work *and* go to school? Where and when will you study? Do you live on, near on or off campus? Travel and parking take more time. Have arrangements been made for husband, children or elderly parents? What social or civic commitments are likely to make demands on your time and energy this term? Take time to answer or address each one of these questions or concerns. Are revisions in order? If so, make them.

- Now, you can use that calendar to see at a glance not only what you've already committed to but also what level of importance you've assigned to those commitments. And when you do, you can say with confidence, "I'm not available until 4pm that day;" or simply, "Sorry, I'm booked." Note that you will benefit from going through this same process before the start of each term. Do it early enough to make changes.

- Break down larger and more difficult tasks or activities into smaller, more manageable chunks.

- If possible, schedule tiresome and less interesting activities for periods when you have the most energy.

- When you complete your graduate degree program, pay it forward!

The Journey Begins Now!

Sandra E. Phipps, B.S., M.Div.

Sandra E. Phipps, May 2013
Graduation from
Payne Theological Seminary

A "Journey" is how I have come to look at my life in the midst of all of my ups and downs and twists and turns. This journey, that I thought I started so long ago, is only just a beginning.

When I graduated from high school in 1985, I had high hopes of attending the University of Cincinnati and graduating. That dream soon ended and I found myself at home. Life has a way of waking you up, and showing you who is truly in control. My mother passed away in 1991 from cancer and at the age of 23, I wondered what I was going to do without my mom. I can still hear her saying "You are not a twin and you can make it on your own."

Her statement has carried me through the hurdles in my life. I got back in school and eventually ended up in the CLIMB program at Wilberforce University, an alternative learning program for adult learners. I am proud to say I am a WILBERFORCEAN! My first earned degree was done for my parents. Although my mother wasn't there with me in person, she was there in spirit.

My only sister passed in 2005 yet this did not stop me. In 2009, I wrote my first book *Behind the Mask.* My father, diagnosed with Alzheimer's disease, drove away and was lost for a few days in 2010, yet in 2011, I released my first gospel CD "For your Glory." I began working on an associate degree in early childhood development and my story shifted once again. I felt led by the Lord to contact Payne Theological Seminary and eventually, pursued my master's degree. By now, my educational goals were centered on my children (by marriage), to let them know that if I could study and learn at my age, so could they. Once again, I am proud to say that I obtained my Master of Divinity Degree from Payne Theological Seminary in 2013. Not only did I graduate from Payne, but my thesis, *Blending Traditional and Contemporary Worship Styles in the American Baptist Church, USA in Columbus, Ohio,* was selected for publication in *The A.M.E. Church Review,* a national publication. It was a great honor to be published in an A.M.E. journal as a Baptist preacher. Also in February 2013, I became a member of the most prestigious Sorority, Zeta Phi Beta, in Gamma Zeta Zeta Chapter.

My educational journey continued in October 2013 when I began coursework towards a doctorate degree in organizational leadership with an emphasis in Christian ministry at the Grand Canyon University. My expected graduation year is 2017.

Although I've been blessed to have a few accomplishments, my journey is beginning now! Walking across the stage next year will be another accomplishment marking a journey I began over 30 years ago. I finally know who I am, and the woman I have become. My favorite scripture, Philippians 3:14, *"I can do all things through Christ which strengthens me"* inspires me to keep going, and I pray that it inspires you, my sisters of the Royal Blue and White family will continue to do the same. The Journey begins now!

Immerse Yourself

Connie V. Pugh, M.B.A., M.H.R.M., M.A.

I am a strong advocate for exploring educational experiences outside of brick and mortar institutions. Studying abroad deepened my appreciation and understanding of cultural context, as well as, trends in multicultural and diverse societies.

After weeks of preparing for my trip to Guatemala and the hour ride from the airport, I finally reached the university that I would call home for the semester. Four heavily armed guards greeted our bus at the gate prior to entering the sprawling campus. My initial excitement turned to a bit of anxiety as my classmates and I discussed our safety as Americans on foreign soil after seeing the armed guards.

One by one, our credentials were checked prior to proceeding on campus. Approximately 2-3 minutes later, our driver stopped and shouted, "Enjoy the accommodations." I sprang from my seat and raced into the dormitory, eager to begin my journey and an experience of a lifetime.

During our time there, my classmates and I took a series of trips (Solola, San Marcos, Santa Cruz, Jaibalito, San Lucas Tolimán, and Santiago) to experience the contextual reality of the locals and to analyze the differences in cultures between the United States and Guatemala. The course encouraged respect toward others who differ in ethnicity, religion, race, political views, beliefs, ideology, and worldviews.

The experience fostered self-exploration and challenged my personal, social, and cultural filters. Being immersed in another culture deepened my appreciation of the many freedoms and opportunities that we, as Americans, take for granted such as libraries filled with books; inside plumbing and running water; and, the right to receive a free public education.

As I traveled from city to city, I noticed the townspeople's pride. They worked in various humble professions to provide for their families yet, they lived rich lives; many of them had very little in terms of personal possessions but appeared extremely happy. Upon reflecting further on their lives and initially thinking they were oppressed, I decided that Americans have misplaced value systems. We have so much, but rarely demonstrate the happiness of the people that I witnessed during my studies abroad.

Speaking to the townspeople, visiting local churches, witnessing a funeral in progress, zip lining through the jungle, and sharing a ride with 30-35 other people in the back of a pick up truck were definitely noteworthy highlights of my travels. I strongly encourage students to study abroad. Inasmuch as some countries might experience civil unrest, educational institutions generally ensure that students studying abroad follow safety protocols and remain safe.

My experience was like none other in that every day was filled with learning and exploring the culture, the language, and the cuisine. That will last a lifetime. I am grateful to Zeta Phi Beta Sorority, Incorporated for providing a portion of my trip's expenses through a scholarship I received.

The 4th "R"

Pamelia W. Readus

My third grade teacher was new to the school system and I was excited to be going into her class, ready for the 3 R's – Reading, "Riting," and "Rithmetic." The new teacher was sweet, kind and given her strong religious beliefs, she taught a 4th "R" called Religion. There were days when I would ask myself did we read or write today? I wanted to get to the "time tables;" I had spent all summer memorizing the table.

Some would argue there should not be a separation of church and state. Some parents want prayer in schools. However, it is my opinion that if your beliefs are rooted and grounded in a child by the family, the child, will not stray from morals that makes them good citizens.

My sweet teacher had other ideas for us as her students. She was from the city and we lived in the country. She was going to enlighten us about life. She was going to teach us that our parents were incorrect on which day of the week was the Sabbath.

This dear sweet teacher could not just boldly tell us that we go to church on a wrong day. How would she change the minds of parents? Businesses use children to get

Pamelia W. Readus
Delta Omega Zeta Chapter
Huntsville, Alabama

parents to buy their products all the time and she planned her next steps accordingly. Her first move was to invite six females one weekend to her home, and the next month, six males. How exciting was that? We were going to our teacher's home for the weekend.

We arrived at her home on a Friday afternoon. The first thing we did was play in her yard, rolling down a hill. As the evening sun set, playtime ended. Then, it was time for dinner and Bible study. We were to review Exodus 20 and Matthew 5, chapters we had studied for a month in school. The class we attended on Saturday worship was studying the Beatitudes. Now, guess who knew those chapters? Being the leader that I am, I quickly raised my hand and said that we knew the Beatitudes. I motioned for the other student to stand as we recited those scriptures. Our teacher was proud of us. She was excited to hear the good news from her students.

My teacher did not know that the visit to her home changed my life but not my religious beliefs or practices. I continue to worship on Sunday. At her home, I met her oldest daughter and thought she was the most well put together young lady I had ever met. She was meek, mild, and very smart. She was a computer programmer and worked for IBM. When I left my teacher's house, all I could think about was her amazing daughter and how I wanted to be just like her when I grew up. As soon as I returned home, I wrote in my journal that I would go to college, get a degree in computer science, and work for IBM. This was the first time I had entertained the thought of going to college. I renewed my vision year after year and researched everything I could about computer science and IBM. Eight years later I went to college, majored in computer science yet because of a geographical reasons, I turned down a job offer with IBM and took a job with Boeing instead.

My third grade teacher's plan of teaching religion started me on a journey of scholastic achievement for which I am forever grateful. All adults should realize that they are role models, and that they have no idea of their impact on a child's life even when you do not know that child is watching you.

Along the Way

Nicole Saunders

Life is what you make it. That is probably one of the most overused terms of the millennium. I, on the other hand, like to believe that life is what you make it from the lessons it teaches you…*if* you pay attention.

I got this revelation about three minutes ago when I was attempting to pull my binder out of a drawer while soothing the itch in my right ear with a Q-tip. If that seems minimal to you then you have never had anybody explain how delicate the inside of your ears are or how fatal it can be for your nerves if you dig too deep. So please, spare me the look of confusion during these next paragraphs as I explain to you what I mean.

The revelation: "You cannot concentrate on what needs to be done if you have something in your ear." As I stood there trying to satisfy my ear *and* pull the binder out of a half open drawer at the same time I had to ask myself, "Okay Cole, what is more important? The risk of hurting yourself because you are being careless and impatient or being able to write with a clear mind with no pain pulsating through the entire right side of your face?"

I exaggerated the level of pain but you get my point. You cannot be productive when you constantly have people in your ear telling you what to or what *not* to do. You have to get to a point where you are able to receive opinions and constructive criticism from others without it interfering with what you know God has called you to do. One of my favorite authors and preachers, Joyce Meyer said it this way, *"Hear what others have to say, but listen to God."* Follow your heart. God will always give you the instructions.

In Genesis, God told Abraham to leave the only home he had ever known. He did not tell Abraham where to go, how to get there, or when he might arrive but Abraham still obeyed. Obedience defined is "following commands or guidance; conforming to or complying with requested behaviors." Sometimes things do not happen because we are not in the right place and have not met the right people. It is like expecting it to snow in the summer. Unless a major climate change occurs, there will never be snow in the summer. Snow is a result of being in the season of winter.

You will not ever get what you want until you are where God needs you to be, until you are where you are supposed to be. However, what you want may not always be what is best for you and God *will* make a way for you to realize that. That is one of the magnificent things about God; even when it seems like God is not listening or showing you "the way," He always and forever will have your best interests at heart. In the midst of the discomfort, confusion and at times the silence…God will still make sure you get where you *need* to be.

I have heard people quote this phrase many times, "The teacher is always quiet during the test." That said; God never tries to make you feel alone. I honestly believe that He is patiently waiting for you to show Him what you have learned. Regardless of everything, God means you well and it is all for a reason. What you are going through is not a setup for failure. What you are going through is a setup for triumph and victory.

So never quit, and stop blaming God for something you did not have the patience to finish. You have to keep pushing. God is still setting things up, rearranging and even removing what and who needs to be out of the way. I hope God never takes away the things you love most, but if He does or if He has, just know it is for your own good. Even if you do not know how or why, just keep trusting the process. That is one thing about God…He will teach you what you need to know. You just have to be willing to sit through the lesson.

As we continue to grow and move forward in life, let us learn to appreciate God for the times and situations that we cannot figure out on our own. Let us learn to appreciate God for the unchanging repetitious moments in our lives that He uses as tools to help us see the truth in order to get free and move forward. Let us thank God for His ways, learn to be less anxious about things we want and surrender to God everything we want for what He wants.

Not long ago, I felt like all hell had broken loose in my life and then somehow, a week later, God fixed everything I *thought* was wrong. You know, it is a dangerous thing trying to fix what is not broken. Sometimes we can be our worst enemy. Our thoughts, anxieties and feelings can be our worst enemy. Take a moment and look around where you are right now. You could be at a diner, in a classroom, in your car, or in your bedroom but understand this one thing; God has already given you everything you need to feel peace everywhere you go. If I told you to imagine yourself in your favorite place, I am sure a smile would make a sanctuary out of your face and a certain level of warmth would invade your heart. Now you know the power of your thoughts. I encourage you to think about the people in your life that can make you laugh so hard your stomach starts to hurt. Choose to think about that one thing, that one aspiration or that one dream that keeps you looking forward to tomorrow. Choose to think about your favorite people, places and things every day. Keeping your peace is but only a thought away.

I thank God for the good experiences in my life and the not so good experiences in my life that have allowed me to share these words of wisdom with you. I am thanking God for allowing me to think about all the goodness He has done for me even when I thought He was punishing me when I forgot how faithful He truly is. I am exactly where I need to be and it is a blessing to have it be more than just a thought. So forever and always, I will encourage each of us to enjoy these moments. After all, these moments are preparing us for the next. Remember it is all a process.

Frame of Reference

Natasha Nicole Smith, M.L.I.S.

Frame of reference.

It was a dark fall afternoon when I first heard that phrase during my Introduction to Mass Communication course at Howard University. The Thanksgiving holiday was quickly approaching and many of my classmates and I were gearing up for our first visit home since we became students. Our professor hit us with a very timely awakening.

With only a few months since college opened, our professor told us that that we would return home changed; our perspectives would be broader and our way of thinking challenged. Most of us were about to face the reality that we would be returning to our homes with new eyes.

As a young adult who spent the first 18 years of her life in one house on the same block that her mother and aunts and uncles grew up in, this would prove to be significant. Upon returning to my hometown of Detroit, I found the discussions about the happenings of the neighborhood I grew up in, or the people I attended high school with, quickly bored me. With my newfound knowledge, I wanted to talk with anyone who would listen about my encounters with various members of the "diaspora," a subject that immediately became my favorite one at Howard. I wanted to ask family members why no one had ever told me about black Greek letter organizations. For the first time in my life, I wanted to discuss not only the societal ills that fell upon my city, but also across the United States, in Africa, and the Caribbean. I wanted to tell my family and friends about the music and food that I was exposed to. I was excited to share this with my family. My world had changed, and whenever I sat down and discussed it with friends and family from home, I learned that for some, their worlds had also changed yet for others, their lives appeared stagnant.

Little did I know, this would only be my first encounter with the phrase, "Frame of reference." Five states, two degrees and many travels later, I find myself applying my continually broadening view of the world to every decision and situation I face. And, while doing that, I aim to understand that not everyone is coming from a similar place and, therefore, may not have the same point of reference.

From a three-word phrase a professor taught me when I was just an optimistic 18 year old student, every situation has been viewed through the lens of all of my experiences prior. Every decision made is an opportunity to ensure that I am viewing it with the broadest scope possible.

Reflections on Scholarship: The Door Is Open

Kathleen Turner Thomas

Kathleen Turner Thomas
Diamond Life Member
Beta Zeta Chapter–Washington, DC

Our minds can travel in myriad directions when reflecting on "Scholarship." This founding tenet of Zeta Phi Beta Sorority is closely linked to "Sisterhood" and "Service," with all three lovingly bound together as a foundation for "Finer Womanhood." As I think of scholarship, I like to visualize an open door.

The simple dictionary definition for "schol/ar/ship" (n.) is "learning." To consider only this one word in its simplicity is to ignore all that lies on either side of the open door. When we "open the door to learning," we must consider what may be on both sides. Much went into getting to the door marked "learning," and even more may emerge on the other side. We are often reminded to be lifelong learners because, "learning never ends." So as we learn, the thirst for knowledge increases, and we jump aboard a path to continuous progress and success. Any study of black history and/or women's history quickly reveals the struggle to gain the right to read and attend schools. It has been a hard-fought battle that continues to this day. The beauty imbedded here is that once you have learned something, it can never be taken away.

To look again at the visual of the door, let us gaze down the road to see what leads up to the "Door of Learning." That road is long and often difficult, but we can summon travel tools that include perseverance, effort, attitude, conscientiousness, and tenacity. Successful travel here means applying oneself to the tasks and the subject matter at hand, taking the time to attack difficult material, and producing an end-product commensurate with the diligence necessary to achieve a goal. Angela Duckworth has labeled it "grit" in her book of the same name. The subtitle reads, "The Power and Passion of Perseverance."

I consider myself fortunate that "effort" and the concept of "doing one's best" were always paramount qualities espoused in my family home. "Effort" was even given a letter grade on my report card, and I think my parents looked there first when reviewing the quarterly report of my progress. It has certainly been my foundation in reaching for Scholarship. When we set high expectations, we can develop learning habits where we expect excellence. I think this expectation follows when the effort has been expended and the results are being viewed. Effort is one of the few components in the teaching/learning process that we can actually control ourselves. Let us make the most of this essential element in our lives.

When we return to a consideration of Scholarship and to the "Door of Learning," we can look on the other side now and glimpse the rewards for the work we have done. Of course, learning is intended to be a reward in and of itself, the personal gratification received for the time on task. Often though, we can and should see true benefits for what has come from this concentrated work ethic. When true Scholarship is reviewed and revealed, hopefully we can see what Oprah Winfrey calls "our best selves." We have a foundation that includes achievement, wisdom, and understanding—it is not only knowledge, but "know-how," as well. Book learning and competence are joined with common sense and practical applications. With effort transcending both sides of the door, we know how to take what we have learned, continue to build upon it, share it, and make it useful to ourselves and others. We can amass a never-ending repertoire of what we know and what we are able to do.

With this idea of sharing and spreading, extending and expanding, we find that learning or knowledge and the Scholarship attained will form the perfect setting and climate to move forward into the areas of Sisterhood and Service as we strive to become Finer Women. The physical randomness of the X and Y chromosomes makes us "women." The intangible gifts such as love, intelligence, compassion, maturity, and empathy make us "finer." It is when we are strong women, finer women, comfortable within ourselves, continually striving to reach our highest potential, that we can form and strengthen the bonds of sisterhood and extend the charitable outreach of service to others.

With gratitude to our Founders for this vision for our Sorority, we can form international links with individual Sorors, chapters, states, and regions through Sisterhood, Scholarship, and Service in our continuing quest toward Finer Womanhood.

Only We Can Tell Our Story

Denese Wolff-Hilliard, Ed.D.

So many Zetas are educators. In this vital public service position, we play a dynamic role in the development of the next generation. As black female educators, we harbor a unique set of skills that continue to go untapped because our distinctive perspective on teaching black children is rarely surveyed. So, we are obligated to tell our own stories. From Gloria Ladson-Billings, Geneva Gay, and Gail Thompson, for instance, we learn that culturally relevant teaching strategies are not only a good way to teach black children, but they are also just solid teaching strategies. Those researchers validate the good work we black educators produce in our urban classrooms every day. Zetas who work with black urban children have amassed a host of strategies that help children achieve academic success.

During my 36 years in public education, I have worked primarily with black impoverished children and learned firsthand about the stressors these children coped with on a daily basis. Witnessing the many shortcomings these children face, lack of basic fundamental resources, lack of medical care and lack of understanding, I became an advocate for helping teachers work more proactively with that population. In order to work with children who come from highly-stressed environments, teachers must have a basic understanding of who their students are and how their living experiences shape the students' ability to learn.

Teachers are inundated with data, demographic, test, schoolwide, district-level, special and population data. Typically absent from most data collection is information about the students' life experiences. Of all the data sets that teachers have to manage, life experiences data may be the most important piece teachers need at their disposal. Without that vital link, teachers may continue to expect black children from poverty "to leave their family and cultural backgrounds at the school house door and live in a kind of 'hybrid' culture composed of the community of fellow learners" (Cole, 1995, p. 10).

Realizing that the one-size-fits-all approach to teaching is not beneficial to any student, I encouraged teachers at my former elementary school to take a long, hard look at their teaching styles and reflect on those strategies that really worked for their students. As a result of a close examination of their philosophy and strategies, many of the teachers gave some thought to the new ideas.

What did the teachers do differently? When children found a concept challenging, they provided help on the spot, instead of referring them to a tutorial session which was the district's recommendation. The grade level leaders added a variety of supplemental resources, classroom libraries, science lab rotations per grade level, and a school garden, to the schedule. Some drew on the human resources in the community, such as partnering with senior citizens in the neighborhood to serve as gardening mentors. The kindergarten teachers added story time to morning announcements so that children were exposed to more literature. The pre-kindergarten teachers created what they called calendar lessons which included study about each holiday into the daily routine. Hallway bulletin boards reflected black history lessons throughout the year, not just in February. However, one of the most important changes was the teachers' insistence on discovering community examples and role models to serve as real-world additions to the curriculum.

Collective wisdom brings several perspectives to the forefront. Teachers shared ideas and strategies, visited one another's classrooms, and even reached across grade levels for new methods. They learned about their own strengths and weaknesses as teachers. They mulled over which strategies worked best to help our children reach their full potential. Realizing that everything is connected, the teachers no longer viewed students only through the lens of test scores and demographic data because such a myopic view did not allow them to truly see the little people sitting in the classroom.

The next step, however, was to share this knowledge with other teachers of black children. At my urging, some of the teachers served as school-level presenters. Others took on the task as district-level workshop contributors. A few more brave souls showcased their knowledge at state level conferences. This is how the sharing begins, and those of us who teach impoverished black children must share our knowledge so that the public gets it right.

Black teachers are walking storehouses of knowledge unique to the black student. We validate one another when we document our teaching experiences, advertising how we invest in our children so that they are creative, resilient, and empowered. Too many of us have been silent about teaching this exclusive group of students. As an organization of college-educated women, as teachers of black children, and as Zetas, we have a duty to share our exceptional teaching expertise with academia. No one can tell our story better than we can.

Reference

Cole R. W. (1995). *Educating everybody's children: Diverse teaching strategies for diverse learners.* Alexandria, VA: ASDC.

THE VOICES OF ZETA

How My Military Experience Prepared Me to be a Zeta Scholar

Lawander (Lloyd) Bradley-Bey

Lawander, the Zeta Scholar

As a senior in high school, I always knew that I was going to college. For me it was a matter of figuring out how to pay for it. I've always considered myself a gifted scholar. I never really had to study to get good grades, and I finished seventh in my class of 115 in a small town in the Mississippi, Delta. I received a few scholarships to some colleges out of state but I knew my parents weren't going to allow me to take advantage of those. I was the middle daughter of three girls and my proud Mississippi father kept a close, tight leash on "his girls and his dogs." I remember all the boys in the town made fun of my dad, who built a fence around our house to "keep the boys out, but not the dogs in." I had to figure out how to get to the one school close enough to home to gain my parents approval. It would be the same one my older sister attended.

Unfortunately I didn't get a scholarship to that school like my sister did, so I had to find another way to pay for college. When the Army recruiter showed up and offered me the avenue I needed, the GI Bill, I jumped on it. Since I had relatives in military service already and it was not a new concept to my family, this was an easier "sell" to my parents than going out of state to school. My dad knew the drill sergeant would be far stricter than him and would "keeping an eye on his girl."

Lawander's Army Medals Earned

Off I went to the Army with the sole objective of getting money for college. Unbeknownst to me, I was to get so much more. Along with learning to be an ammunition specialist, my military training taught me: the poise of a finer woman; how to be a servant and help others; the importance of family and sisterhood; and, most significantly, the value of continued learning through scholarship.

Lawander with Mom and Sister

My military experiences impressed and inspired me to become more educated than I had initially set out to be. I learned the hard way that only one person was responsible for me and my career: me. To progress in the military, I had to improve my skills and knowledge and not become stagnant and complacent.

Military service promotes continued studies and rewards those who follow its leadership programs, thus encouraging everyone to excel. While serving in Saudi Arabia during Operation Desert Storm and Operation Desert Shield, I employed my leadership skills, and during my idle time, I continued to study and learn. After leaving the military and moving into civilian life and to college, I carried the embedded principle of scholarship with me. I earned my first degree (and became a member of Zeta Phi Beta Sorority), thirsting for more knowledge. To this day, I still participate in continued education courses, certification classes, Zeta leadership academies, and have earned my MBA. The learning never stops.

DESERT SHIELD - SAUDI ARABIA

Postcard I sent home in 1990 during Desert Shield – Saudi Arabia

Scholarship:
An Instrument of Change

Shirley Chopp-Chevalier

As college educated women, we band together sharing a common goal of making the world a better place for our having been here. Education has not only allowed me to be an instrument of change, but it has also facilitated wondrous changes in my life. Let me share with you the journey and life experiences that have brought me to this point.

Humble Beginnings. I come from a long line of sharecroppers. My maternal great-grand-parents were slaves from Johnston County, North Carolina. They came to Brazos County, Texas around 1890. None of my maternal family members could read or write until the mid-1930s when their children were allowed to attend school if it did not interfere with crop harvest time. My parents met in the early 1940s when my paternal grandfather and two men from the Barton Farm (Robertson County, Texas) took two wagons to the neighboring farm, loaded what they could onto the wagons and, under cover of the dark of night, stole away to the Barton Farm. According to the landowner's records, the sharecropper's harvest was never good enough to cover what was owed. However, there was an unwritten rule that, if one were able to make it to another farm, the previous landowner would not come after you. Once I told my oldest brother that I had read in a section of a book on the history of Robertson County that the people who lived on the Barton Farm were considered ignorant and still treated as slaves. They were known as the "Brazos Bottom N____s." He acknowl-edged this to be true, and the term was used by blacks and whites for many years. So you and my oldest sister would have been considered "Brazos Bottom N____s," I remarked, and he responded that indeed they were – and so was I!

Public Education.   I graduated from W. D. Spigner High School at 17 years of age and was salutatorian of my graduating class of 42 students in Calvert, Texas, an agrarian community with a population of 2,073. I chopped and picked cotton from six years of age until leaving for college at 17. No, I was not so advanced that I skipped a grade. My birthday is in December, and in Texas, a child must be six years old by September 1st or until the next school year. My mother sent me to school at five years with a note explaining that she had applied for my birth certificate but noted that I was born on August 13th. By the time the principal threatened to put me out of school if she did not send the required birth certificate, I had almost completed second grade and was at the top of my class. Our principal, Professor Spigner, prided himself on remembering every students' birthdate. During my senior year, one day as we stood outside waiting for him to ring the lunch bell (yes, he had a hand-bell), he congratulated me on graduating. He spoke fondly of my mother, and challenged me saying, "I can tell you on what date you were born - August 13th." I was smart enough not to tell him any differently.

Undergraduate Experience.   Coming from a small farming town, the descendant of slaves and sharecroppers, how did I end up with a degree in electrical engineering? There were two answers: parental expectations and a community in which the village "raised the child." As teenagers growing up on the banks of the Brazos River, my parents saw only a life of servitude as sharecroppers. My father had only a sixth grade education. Professor Spigner often talked about how "smart" my mother was. She had dropped out of school her senior year when my father asked her to marry him. They were the proud parents of 10 children. They had high expectations for their children. I remember every six weeks when grades were sent home, my father's ritual was to sit in his recliner with my mother sitting next to him on the sofa. My parents would call our names one at a time. My father would review our grades and pronounce, "C is for crazy and D is for dumb. F is for a fool and B is for better. A is for alright." My mother would then address what each child needed to do to improve. Our teachers were on first-name basis with our parents and did not hesitate to put us in their cars at the end of the day, take us home, and tell our parents everything we did or did not do in school. There were no notes sent home.

Our teachers also served as the gatekeepers to our education. They doled out their encouragement and support based on their expectations for our future success. My oldest brother was lousy in sports and band, but he was very brilliant, hardworking, and was the graduating valedictorian of his class.   The new young basketball coach encouraged him to major in civil engineering. Mr. Grimes had started in civil engineering at Prairie View A&M, but washed out his freshman year. He gave my brother his drafting instruments and guided him in enrolling in college. Two years later, I was graduating from high school and naturally, was expected to attend college. My brother asked me, "What are you planning on doing after you graduate?" Of course, my reply was, "Go to Prairie View." The next question was, "What are you going to major in?" We had no school counselors, so nobody had talked to me about what was available, and I did not know what to say. Not wanting him to know that I was totally ignorant, I said, "Maybe I'll major in engineering." I was now wading into quicksand because he knew I did not know anything about engineering. His next question was, "What kind?" Uh-oh. I was now in quicksand up to my neck. I asked, "What kinds are there?" He then explained that at Prairie View there were civil, electrical, architectural, and mechanical, and gave an overview of what each one entailed. Having to save face, I asked, "Which one is the hardest?" He said, "Electrical engineering." At that point I told him, "That's the one I am going to major in then, electrical engineering."

Since my small, rural school only taught math up to geometry, I had to start remedial math in trigonometry. We were supposed to have had chemistry in high school but our science teacher spent her time offering those bound for college an introduction to physics. To teach the chemistry, she had to travel to the white school, check out lab equipment, and return after each class. On a college level, I was deficient in math, physics, and chemistry, major courses for engineering.

By mid-term my grades were three B's, two C's, a D, and an F. I was so embarrassed that I did not go home for Thanksgiving. After the holiday, my brother returned to campus with a plate of food and new underwear for me from my mother. He also said, "Daddy said to tell you, C stands for crazy, D stands for dumb, and F stands for fool." He really found that hilarious. At the end of the semester, my grades were four A's, two B's, and a C (the best I could do to recover from an F). I was finally able to go home for Christmas and face my parents. In four years, I graduated "magna cum laude" with a major in electrical engineering and a minor in mathematics. My brother tells people that he graduated in civil engineering.

"Z-Phi." As an engineering student, my associations were mostly with male students. My freshman year I met the first male in my life for whom my interest extended beyond shooting marbles and BB-guns. It was love at first sight. The Texas A&M University system, of which Prairie View was a member, did not initially permit Greek letter organizations on campus but during our sophomore year, they were permitted. The man with whom I was smitten pledged Phi Beta Sigma Fraternity and naturally, I decided to pledge Zeta Phi Beta Sorority. I became a Zeta in January 1970. That following fall I served as the third Basileus of Omega Gamma Chapter at Prairie View. Through educational endeavors, I was able to engage in a life-long association with the finest group of men and women I have ever known, and with whom I am still close. Among them was the love-of-my-life, a fellow electrical engineering student, who has been my first and only love for over 45 years and the father of my two daughters, who are also Zetas.

Non-Traditional Role. In the 1970s as a black, female electrical engineer, I was considered a dual-minority. As the descendant of slaves and sharecroppers, a girl reared in a rural, segregated, southern town, and a graduate of a historically black college, it was a culture shock for me to become suddenly immersed in the white male world of technology. During this time, America was struggling with civil rights and affirmative action. (My brother, who worked at Texaco Oil, was called their "civil rights" engineer). I did not receive any assistance in transitioning from academia to the workforce. I was treated by my co-workers as either a novelty or a "token" (hired to fill a quota). To my supervisors, I was hard working, intelligent, and an over-achiever. I soon learned the difference between knowledge and wisdom – *knowledge is a storehouse of facts; wisdom is knowing how to use it.* This was an advantage I had over my white male counterparts. And, with the work ethic instilled in me by being black – I had both. By reading books, observing others, putting in long hours, and trial-and-error, whether it be teaching myself to program in computer languages, design in digital logic, or perform systems engineering, I never said "no" to any job and I always figured out how to make it work. I never let them "see me sweat." I have worked as a facility engineer, aerospace engineer, systems engineer, and computer performance analyst. I have worked for the U.S. Army Corps of Engineers, Lockheed Aerospace, the NASA Space Shuttle Program, and IBM Corporation. Throughout my career I was satisfactorily rewarded by my supervisors with high pay and bonuses.

Changing the World. If the pay and life were so good, why did the descendant of slaves, a country girl of humble beginnings and an over-achiever, decide to leave it all behind? I thought with my background and experiences, I had a story to tell that could make a difference in the lives of young black Americans. With the times facing the black community, teen pregnancy, drugs, incarceration, and the black male crisis, by all indicators, black students were "at-risk." To make a difference, I taught Sunday school to the adolescent class. In December 1990, as president, and with eight other inactive Zetas, Omicron Gamma Zeta Chapter was chartered in the Clear City/Houston, Texas area. After serving as chapter president, I was elected chapter youth coordinator. My plan was to quit my job with IBM and pursue a career as a school counselor, which would have required me to teach in the public schools. However, one of our chapter members noted that, if she were not a single parent, she would have pursued a career in a newly state-approved program for school psychologists. Hearing my objectives, she noted that what I was discussing was more associated with a school psychologist job. As it turned out, one of the two universities in the state offering the program was a few blocks from where I lived, the University of Houston at Clear Lake, which only accepted six applicants per year. On my application, I noted my experience as a youth coordinator for the Zeta youth auxiliary, and was accepted on the first attempt. I received a Master of Arts in Behavioral Science, School Psychology in May 1995.

My internship was very intense and challenging. I was supposed to work only six hours per week; however, I was given a full caseload of the most difficult cases in the district, and was putting in over 50 hours per week to meet federally mandated deadlines. I never complained or thought of quitting; only did my best to learn and grow and advocate on behalf of the children. I must say that, although challenging, my experiences and training during this internship prepared me to approach any case or situation with confidence and with knowledge and wisdom, be able to make decisions in the best interests of the children.

During my experiences as an intern, I realized that the master's level was an entry level to the profession and, in order to be the best that I could be in order to serve a diverse population, I needed to pursue additional coursework and training. My internship supervisor advised me to apply to the Texas A&M University doctoral program in educational psychology that would not only lead to a doctorate in educational psychology, but also child clinical psychology. I applied to the Texas A&M program and was accepted. My extensive training in the

University of Houston's master's program allowed me to be waived from several classes, and I could pursue additional hours in coursework specific to minority populations. I also had the opportunity to work with the Head Start program and as a case manager in a multi-million dollar grant program involving undergraduate students serving as mentors to at-risk students. All of my experiences and training have been stepping stones in my plan to make the world a better place for my having been here.

The Pièce de Résistance. After receiving my doctoral degree from Texas A&M, I was sitting in my apartment in College Station, Texas when I received a call from the President of Zeta Phi Beta Sorority, Barbara C. Moore, who wanted me to serve on a leadership team as a consultant in the area of psychology. This new committee was Zeta Organizational Leadership (ZOL). My life, service, and commitment to Zeta have grown in leaps and bounds as a result of that phone call. I treasure the relationships cultivated with each member of the team. I had personal experience with the academic approach to framing a program from Dr. E. Fran Johnson; the political considerations to selling an idea from Grand Basileus Eunice Thomas; and, the overall organization, management, and leadership abilities of Grand Basileus Moore. Zeta has yet to realize all of the bounties to be gained from Grand Moore and her planning and implementation of the ZOL program. On the ZOL team I was also fortunate to work with National First Anti-Basileus Valerie Hollingsworth-Baker, a partnership that has lasted almost 14 years. She is a visionary who brings out the potential in all with whom she works. The role of social sciences within Zeta is yet to be fully realized.

"For unto whomsoever much is given, of him shall be much required," (Luke 12:48). My pursuit of knowledge and the goals I have set for myself have matured over time. Raised to attend church as a child, I read the Bible from cover to cover when I was 14 years old. Once finished, I did not feel that I needed to pick it up again. Now that I am older, more experienced, and wiser, I keep a Bible with me everywhere I go and look to it for knowledge, wisdom, and comfort. I look on my life experiences and realize how blessed I am and have been. It is through God's mercy and blessings that I have accomplished what I have in life. I never stopped to think that I couldn't do something or fear that I would fail. All of my life events have prepared me to look towards giving back and to use my time and talents to make the world a better place for my having been here. Zeta is my vessel to accomplish that.

A Trailblazing Road to Excellence

Yvette F. Clark-Blake, M.A.

I, too, have chronicled many firsts. Not only am I the first member of my family to join a Greek organization, I'm the first college graduate in my family. I'm proud to have created this educational legacy in my family. My cousins, nieces, and nephews have pursued interests in many career fields from the delicate fabric of interior design to the hard laboring efforts in construction.

It's exciting to me to inspire the next generation of servant leaders in my family and beyond. I explain to them that it is important to motivate and assist others as well as pay it forward for those who follow them. My belief system in education has led me to mentor and teach the future generations in my communities. As an elementary educator in Prince George's County Public Schools and previously, in Los Angeles Unified School District, it's important to me to motivate and support students to future contributing citizens in our communities.

In my pursuit for educational excellence, I participated in California's Miss Inglewood Scholarship Pageant (1989). The experience was invaluable, as it forced me to embark on a new encounter and embrace another layer of support and endurance. I stand proud to declare that I completed a Bachelor of Arts in Psychology (1995), Master of Arts in Behavioral

Sciences in Gerontology (2000), Master of Arts in Education: Educational Administration (2006) at California State University, Dominguez Hills (CSUDH) in Carson, California. I obtained a Professional Clear Multiple Subject Teaching Credential (2004) and Tier I

Administrative Services Credential (2006) at CSUDH. Due to high scholastic achievement, I received the 1995-1996 Outstanding Student Award and was awarded membership in the Honor Society of Phi Kappa Phi (1997), Alpha Kappa Delta, International Sociology Honor Society (2000) and Pi Lambda Theta, International Honor Society and Professional Association (2005). I became a two-year recipient of The Who's Who Among America's Teachers award (2004 and 2005). I received a Certificate of Recognition as the recipient of the Hearst Fifth Year Scholarship at CSUDH (2005). Also, I joined Phi Delta Kappa International, a Professional Association in Education (2005). As I continue my personal quest for academic excellence, I am completing my doctoral degree in Education in Organizational Leadership at Pepperdine University in California.

Yvette F. Clark-Blake
M.A. in Education:
Educational Administration
California State University,
Dominguez Hills – May 2006
Graduation Photograph

I dedicate this trailblazer's page to my wonderful and supportive parents. My mother and late father, who were instrumental in ensuring that my brother and I were knowledgeable, skillful, and ready to engage in our communities as servant leaders.

A Weekend in Ghana

Charbet M. Duckett, C.P.A., C.G.F.M.

"Akwaaba" means welcome in Ghana and I felt very welcomed by the men and women whom I met there. It was very apropos that Black History month, February 2005, began while I was on a business trip to Ghana, for its Gold Coast abounds in history.

I learned about the Andikra symbols, the making of Kente cloth, and the uses of various trees. I walked in the rain forest and crossed a rope bridge strung among the 130-foot tall trees. I visited two of the most famous slave castles, Elmina Castle owned by the Portuguese, Dutch, and British, and the Cape Coast Castle, owned by the British.

The castle guide brought to life the women and men from northern Ghana, Togo and Benin, who were forced to walk for months from their homelands to the coast, then sold to foreigners and subsequently, housed in cement and iron cells. For three to four months, our ancestors, were forced to live in these cramped cells with little ventilation, minimal light, inadequate facilities, and bits of food. Men or women who were too powerful or obstinate were killed by their captors. When the time came to be transported, these men and women walked through dark, dank tunnels chained together to a gated hole in the wall through which they had their last glimpse of their Africa before they were loaded onto ships as merchandise, never to return.

Against the backdrop of this misery, darkness and evil, the slave traders attempted to justify themselves through religion and built a church inside the prison walls for themselves. I believe that God was there not to justify the traders, but to strengthen the remnants: those intended to survive the long walk through slavery; live in the dank, dark, diseased prison cells; survive the passage to North and South America and the far East; endure plantation life and and Jim Crow laws; and, persevere in spite of unfair practices, laws, and discrimination in every form. As a descendant, I celebrated and welcomed my return to Mother Africa.

As a result of my trip to Accra, I learned that the strength and fortitude of our forefathers and foremothers is without measure, and the favor of God is unmatched. It reminded me that when tests and trials come, and they will, I am of a favored people! I am of a lineage of strength in mind, body and spirit.

The Lessons My Mom Taught Me

jordyn joAnna eubanks

In my 17- going-on-18 years of living, my wonderful mother has taught me a lot. She taught me the importance of family and the significance of self-respect. She taught me to always do my best, to treat everyone equally, and to not give up when things get hard. She taught me right from wrong and how to handle my feelings. My mom taught me that morals are more important than success, that being a good person is much more important than being a celebrity, and that virtue is the most valuable asset I could possess.

I learned from her that giving is harder than taking, but the outcome is much more rewarding. My mom says giving makes one happy. I am sure she is right because half of her life has been spent giving me what I need, yet in spite of all those years of giving, she is happy. And when I make decisions, she might not always agree but she is always supportive because she wants *me* to be happy. She reminds me to at all times be honest because, in the end, lies always hurt more. And that no matter what circumstances I encounter, there will always be opportunities for growth.

So far my mother has taught me all I needed to live my life as a 17-year-old teenager. I know she has more to share.

The Marginalized Mind

Lisa G. Eley

During a respectable 30-year career, I've been responsible for culturing and keeping cells alive from the laboratories of Johns Hopkins University to the National Institutes of Health.

Soror Eley sharing her career as a Lab Associate with fourth and fifth graders at Glenallan Elementary School in Silver Spring, MD.

I've handled almost every type of cancer cell known, including the incredible human cervical HeLa cancer cells, taken from Henrietta Lacks of Baltimore, MD after her death in 1951. When I work with cells, I often think of Mrs. Lacks, a poor black tobacco worker who died from something that is readily treatable today if detected early enough. Cells such as those from Mrs. Lacks have proven invaluable to scientific research and medical breakthroughs. Today, through my lab work culturing cells, albeit behind the scenes, I provide a service to mankind while, on the front lines, brilliant scientists and doctors help underserved patients like Mrs. Lacks improve their quality of life by eradicating some of these diseases.

But not so long ago, I remember sitting in my college advisor's office where the following discourse unfolded …

"You don't have the GPA to go to medical school, but because you're black maybe they will make an exception." Can you imagine hearing these words from your college advisor? I knew I didn't have what it took to be a medical doctor. Family aspirations were set high for this first generation college student who wasn't even sure she would graduate. I lacked ambition, I lacked direction, and I often didn't finish what I started. I discovered very late in my major I had an aversion to the sight of blood and the smell of labs.

My parents really struggled putting me through college, so I didn't have the heart to tell them I should have majored in something other than biology or that I wanted to start all over with a different major. My grades were marginal, my accomplishments were marginal, and now in the formative moments of my vanishing adolescence, I'd been told my mind was marginal . . . because of my race. My marginalized mind thought in that instance that if I couldn't earn it, then I didn't want it. I determined to work for mine, and that's what I did. I graduated with a degree in biology, earned a place in Beta Beta Beta, the National Biological Honor Society, and even landed a job right out of college. That's what a not-so-marginalized mind can do.

The students were eager to feed the mock cells Soror Eley brought to the classroom.

"You can do anything you put your mind to!" is one of the most enduring motivational one-liners in existence. No one is in a position to marginalize your mind or define its depths as if they know your mind better than you do. It breathes, it thinks, it drives, it dreams, it desires, and it acts. The mind and its wisdom extend beyond scholarly pursuits. Intelligence gained is knowledge learned. And the whole of humanity benefits from that knowledge when we are gracious enough to share it.

> *"Men have a respect for scholarship and learning greatly out of proportion to the use they commonly serve."*
>
> – Henry David Thoreau

Time Is Always Moving

Neffie Gatewood

Soror Neffie Gatewood receives
a Zeta of the Year Award.

I had taken a break from working on my degree and I was working for Nike at the employee store. During that time, most of my friends had completed their degrees and I was invited back to my university for a reunion. I was ashamed to attend it because it made me feel like a failure. I communicated this with one of the customers who owned his own business. He said to me, "Time is always passing; it is about what you do with that time. You are going to get older and life will continue to move. Whether you are doing anything to advance yourself or not, go back to school and as time moves, so will you and eventually, you will accomplish your goal." Since that moment, I have completed by undergraduate degree and graduate degrees, and own several businesses. That moment in time has and continues to change my life.

The Legacy of
Soror Ola Hill Lives On!

Tracee J. Howard

Soror Ola Hill was born on August 26, 1934 in Atlanta, Georgia. She attended Booker T. Washington High School, but did not gain a passion for education immediately upon graduation. Her pursuit of teaching and education began in the mid 1960's when her children were young. She began volunteering at their elementary school on a regular basis. Soror Hill eventually worked her way up to the role of substitute teacher. Her profound love of children and education kept her in the Atlanta Public School System serving many years as a teacher's assistant at various schools. After raising four children, she made the decision to further her own education while also continuing to work full time. In May 1975, she received a Bachelor of Arts degree from Clark Atlanta University, proving it's never too late to pursue a college education. She then accepted a fulltime position at P.L. Dunbar Elementary as a kindergarten teacher.

Soror Ola Hill

Soror Hill's teaching career spanned more than 30 years! One of her most memorable quotes was, "One of *the greatest joys is to have students that I taught in kindergarten return to me as college graduates.*" She never wanted to teach any other grade because she believed the most important years were those when children were young and first entering school. During these early stages, the most formative foundation could be built. Her lifelong dream was to start a child daycare center so that she could impart her experience, knowledge and love of learning to children at risk.

Soror Ola Hill joined Zeta Phi Beta Sorority, Incorporated in 1991 as a charter member of Omicron Kappa Zeta Chapter in College Park, Georgia. She found an organization whose beliefs and commitment to the principles of Scholarship, Service, Sisterhood and Finer Womanhood most aligned with her own lifelong passions and beliefs. Soror Hill passed away in September of 2001, but her legacy did not end when she was called home to the Great Boulé in the sky.

Soror Hill was a pioneer for education and held the principle of Scholarship near and dear to her heart. To continue this legacy, Omicron Kappa Zeta Chapter established a scholarship in memory of our beloved Triumphant Soror. Each year we award graduating high school seniors with scholarships to celebrate their individual accomplishments and desire to pursue a higher education. Candidate applications are scored based on a strict and standardized rubric. Once winners are chosen, we celebrated their accomplishments by hosting a reception in their honor. Omicron Kappa Zeta Chapter has provided thousands of dollars in scholarships and will continue to do so in our beloved Soror's honor. Soror Ola Hill's legacy will continue to live on by our chapter's commitment to continue her passion for helping students reach their full potential.

Unexpected Advice from an Unexpected Source

Barbara J. Johnson, Ph.D.

As the first person in my family to attend graduate school, as I applied to doctoral programs, I was under the mistaken impression that there were few differences in a Ph.D. and Ed.D. I recall my supervisor and Soror, Velma Watts, saying a Ph.D. is associated with research while an Ed.D. was for practitioners. I wanted to be a Vice President of Student Affairs, so getting an Ed.D. seemed like the appropriate degree to pursue. It was not until I entered the Ed.D. program in higher education at Vanderbilt University which ranked number 7 in higher education in the United States at that time, that I realized there was indeed a distinction between the Ed.D. and Ph.D. programs. I was not dissuaded from my Ed.D. track. However, it was an administrative assistant, Ms. Ophelia, in the Office of Graduate Admissions in which I served as a 10-hour-a-week graduate assistant, who provided advice that would make me change my perspective about pursuing a Ph.D.

In the fall of the first year of my doctoral program, Ms. Ophelia overheard a conversation between students about the differences between the Ed.D. and the Ph.D. but she did not engage in discourse with us. A few days later, when none of my peers were around, she pulled me aside after glancing around to ensure there was no one within earshot, and said to me in a matter-of-fact tone, "You need to switch to the Ph.D. program." I responded, "The Ed.D. and Ph.D. have pretty much the same curriculum, but the major difference is the dissertation requirement." Her response was unexpected, "You are a Black woman, and you do not need to give anyone a reason to pass you up for an opportunity. I have worked at many institutions and I have seen that not having a Ph.D. will be used against you." These words hit me like a ton of bricks, and at that very moment, I knew she was right. As a native of the South with a strong accent, I did not need to give anyone the power to eliminate me from consideration because of the type of degree I held, if it was in my power to do something about it. I instantly knew that I had no choice but to apply to the Ph.D. program. There would be enough 'missed' opportunities because of my gender, skin color, and possibly my southern twang, but not having a Ph.D. would not be another thing held against me. I applied to the Ph.D. program and received a scholarship because of the strength of my application. Eighteen months later, I walked crossed the stage to receive my Ph.D.

I will always be eternally grateful to Ms. Ophelia for taking the time to help me understand in very "real" terms what was at stake. While Ms. Ophelia was not a Soror, she exhibited true sisterhood by caring enough to tell me in no uncertain terms what I needed to know. While Ms. Ophelia's advice was unexpected, it was welcomed. I am practicing what I learned that day; taking the time to help another along the way.

A Zeta Journey Paved by Community and Scholarship

Veronica Fields Johnson

My first up close and personal experience with Zeta Phi Beta Sorority, Incorporated was a family affair, in more ways than one. My husband, Daniel Johnson, pledged Tau Chapter of

Phi Beta Sigma Fraternity, Incorporated as a student at the University of Louisville. His sister, Marla Johnson Polk, pledged Delta Theta Chapter of Zeta Phi Beta Sorority, Incorporated at the same school. Daniel and I met in Atlanta during my senior year at Clark Atlanta University (CAU) and started dating shortly after we'd both graduated from our respective schools. Both Daniel and Marla were very active in Sigma and Zeta and whenever there was an activity that either organization had that coincided with my visits to Louisville, Daniel and I attended together.

Soror Veronica Fields Johnson

As a writer I observe and listen, and what I found was camaraderie between the fraternity and sorority that went beyond socializing together. Watching the two organizations support each other as, together, they supported the community impressed me, especially the way they handled challenges that came up as they continued working together to achieve their overall goal. Though not a member, I always felt welcomed by the Royal Blue and White family in Louisville. I joined them in some of the community service projects and social affairs that the respective chapters sponsored.

After we married, my husband was elected president of the Louisville graduate chapter, Epsilon Beta Sigma. On several more occasions, I was able to note, enjoy and appreciate that

Brother Daniel and Soror Veronica Johnson

same camaraderie either while participating in a joint march supporting AIDS-awareness or while watching my husband and his fraternity brothers mentor members of the Sigma Beta Club, their youth auxiliary.

We moved back to Atlanta in 1996, and within a few years, I had struck up a friendship with a coworker, Sandra Marshall Murray. We initially bonded over having attended CAU at the same time. Although we knew some of the same people, we had never met there. Later I learned she was a Zeta and told her about my husband's affiliation with Sigma. She invited Daniel and me to the Metro Atlanta Joint Founders' Day program. We attended and, yet again, I experienced the same warmth and welcoming spirit from the Atlanta-area Royal Blue and White family that I had in Louisville. During one of our casual conversations, Sandra asked me if I had ever considered joining Zeta. I had, but had never acted on it.

Afterwards, I decided to look more closely at Zeta Phi Beta Sorority. What I found was an organization steeped in a rich history, one with which I wanted to affiliate. I am also an avid reader, so I was overjoyed to learn that one of my favorite authors, Zora Neale Hurston, was a Zeta. I called other Zetas I'd met along the way and asked why they had joined the sorority. They shared similar stories of how they were embraced by an organization that holds fast to the founding principles of Scholarship, Service, Sisterhood and Finer Womanhood. Those stories captivated me.

On May 10, 2008, Veronica Williams and I joined the illustrious Zeta Phi Beta Sorority, Incorporated, Omicron Kappa Zeta Chapter in College Park, Georgia and became V-Squared – The Diva and the Scribe and, soon after we joined, we were immersed in the work of Zeta. My chapter's Zetas Zumba for Education is one of my favorite events. We promote healthy living and raise money for the Ola Hill Memorial Scholarship, which we award annually to deserving high school seniors in memory of one the chapter's charter members. The members of Omicron Kappa Zeta do great work in the community, and I've had the good fortune to meet and learn from many of them, including the late Bettye Shelling, a Zeta Dove and an Atlanta-area educator who shaped minds yet remained humble about her accomplishments. I have been very fortunate to meet Sorors who not only promote scholarship for the local community but also invest in themselves, pursuing advanced degrees and other certifications.

These women do much more than obtain titles; their sustained dedication to scholarship multiplies their contributions to society as leaders and mentors. Joining Zeta Phi Beta in my 30s has been, and continues to be, an enriching, rewarding, and character building experience, and I am blessed to be a part of this Sorority.

Damascus Road

Paula A. Kay

I like to compare my journey towards scholarship to Saul's experience on the road to Damascus. On my journey, I encountered my own 'Saul moments'—akin to that three-day period when, although blinded by the light, he gained valuable insights regarding his life's purpose. He was later converted and became Paul, the apostle. As I journeyed, I was not physically blinded but I was sometimes overwhelmed by what I learned about myself and others. I have since come to appreciate those obstacles as stepping stones toward my success and opportunities to build my character.

Words to share: Embrace every opportunity to learn and enjoy each step of your Damascus Road as you take blinded moments to change the course toward your true DESTINY.

Of Pleasing the Masses

Danielle Nicole McNeil

What is happiness?

Is it a warm embrace?

The smile on your child's face?

A warm wind blowing through your hair?

The home you and your loved ones share?

For happiness is sought after as a reward

For pain and heartache one may have endured.

To lose its feeling we cannot afford

Once it is found our faith is restored

But have you ever stopped to ask yourself

Am I happy?

Happiness with self is most important of all

Without it our flesh is reduced to a pall.

Concealing the emptiness in our soul

Preventing our lives from feeling whole.

There was a time in my own life

When within myself I dealt with a strife.

Trying to please everyone in my path

Blind to foreseeing the aftermath

And I realized I never stopped once to ask

Am I happy?

It wasn't until I had a moving conversation

With the man responsible for my creation.

He made me realize the flaw in my ways

When he told me that from all I would never receive praise.

He said most important is that I am happy inside

And to this day those words serve as my guide.

As I navigate this life through trials and tribulations

No longer will I slave to meet others' expectations

And every so often I will stop to ask

Am I happy?

Now thanks to the man that has raised me from birth

I understand now that my happiness comes first.

So when the question arises I no longer guess

Because I know that the answer will always be yes.

Dr. Totten's #1 Student:
A Tribute to a Master Educator
Who Took Me under His Wing

Alberta G. J. Mayberry

2015! I'm an old oak tree now. I've done it all. Education – Check! Marriage – Check! Children –Check, Check, Check and Check! Career success – Check! World Travel – Check! – AND not necessarily in that order. I'm an old oak tree that started from seeds planted during my early years in Houston (Fifth Ward), Texas. Even now, I stand in the shadow of a giant redwood.

While still a sapling, ready to graduate from high school, headed in my head and heart to Thurgood Marshall's Howard University in Washington, D.C. to become Houston's next Barbara Jordan; into my life walked Dr. Herman L. Totten. Yes, he was a charmer; speaking all the right words to me about high expectations, quality academic

My first son, Dr. Totten
and my dad with my grandchildren.

performance, dedication, leadership, integrity and hard work. He espoused the virtues of higher education; of lifting as we climb; of preparing for a life of high moral and intellectual standards. He had me at "full scholarship" – an Equal Education Opportunity grant – even though I had never heard of Wiley College in Marshall, Texas.

Dr. Totten is that "someone" in my life who saw my potential, recognized my intense desire to succeed, and then nurtured me through my higher education endeavors. Not only did he recruit me to Wiley College and serve as my college librarian, but he was also an ever-present epitome of excellence. After three years as a work study student under his tutelage in the T. Winston Cole Library, and as I prepared to graduate from Wiley College, with a child, Dr. Totten orchestrated my being awarded a Ford Foundation graduate fellowship to study library science at Atlanta University with a stipend for my son.

Three more children and one divorce later, I telephoned Dr. Totten on a teary-eyed afternoon in 1983 to discuss my future. (Oh, woe is me; whatever shall I do; what must I do next with my life?) As fate would have it, my continuing educational guru had been trying to get in touch with me to invite me to be a part of the initial class of the doctoral degree program, fully funded plus a living stipend, at the North Texas State University School of Library and Information Science. I held the distinction of being designated "Student Number One" in the accreditation request for approval of the University of North Texas School of Library Science and Information Services Interdisciplinary Doctoral Program, based on a plan that I developed for my doctoral studies with the full support of Professor Totten. Years later when I decided to pursue the Master of National Security and Strategic Studies at the U. S. Naval War College funded by the DOS, of course I sought and received the blessings of and a glowing recommendation from Dr. Totten. I am degreed four times over because of Herman Totten – and the Grace of an Almighty God.

There comes a time to demonstrate the value of all that "book-learning." I so fondly recall the assurance with which Dr. Totten recommended me to the Director of Libraries for my first professional position: "You would be foolish not to hire her." I worked hard to make that proclamation a truth. Over the years, other potential employers were challenged likewise by Dr. Totten to take me on as a stellar addition to their institutional staffing patterns. I knew that I could never fail, for failure would bring disrepute to my mentor. I soared through the ranks in the academic library field with determination and dedication to serving histori-cally black colleges and universities at which I could provide guidance and mentoring for up and coming success stories as Dr. Totten had done for me. My professional experiences at Texas Southern University (Houston, TX), Bishop College (Dallas, TX) and Langston University (Langston, OK) included a huge dose of "payback" to Dr. Totten and many other inspirational professors who propelled me into the sphere of success that I have come to enjoy. My teaching and administrative work at Ahmadu Bello University (Zaria, Nigeria) and Emory University (Atlanta, GA) proved beyond a doubt that my historically black col-lege and university education equipped me well to work with and in international and ivy-league universities.

In 1993, I switched tracks and joined the U.S. diplomatic corps, traveling professionally to seventeen nations with long-term assignments in five of them. During my tours of duty abroad, I referenced Herman Totten in most of my public speeches on education, overcoming

barriers, mentoring and supporting young people, commitment to individual and community advancement, and self-improvement through higher education. I have excelled in every professional position I have held to ensure that my parents, my four sons *and Dr. Herman L. Totten* would be proud of me.

As he approaches retirement from an exemplary career, I know that Dr. Totten has impacted generations of librarians, information specialists, and students in

My grandchildren, front with my dad, me and Dr. Totten.

various other academic or professional disciplines. That is who he is, and that is what he does! I know that, like me, many of those students have gone on to be outstanding and renowned leaders in their chosen fields. Still, in my mind, I rank as #1 among this distinguished group.

I am Herman Totten's #1 student! I am the student he taught by continued example to be grateful, responsible, committed, loyal and accountable enough always to give back. Since that fateful, seed-planting day in 1966 at Kashmere Gardens High School in Houston, Texas, Dr. Totten has been a blessing in my life. He opened doors, propelled me forward, removed barriers of indecision, fear, and self-doubt, strengthened my resolve, countered my aggressive ambition and temperament and set extremely high standards that I had to meet or exceed!!

I thank God that He used Herman Lavon Totten to convey so many of His blessings to me – and to so many others! I have continued to say "Thank you" to Dr. Totten by "practicing intentional community, extended community, spiritual community, creative community." I will continue to give "love and work and investment" to others as my thank you gifts to my Dr. Totten.

Happy Retirement, Chief!!

Her Legacy:
A Scholar and Educator

Geraldine G. Taylor Peeples

Mrs. Irene Harris Taylor

The **Irene Harris Taylor (IHT) Memorial Scholarship** was the first sponsored scholarship of Theta Lambda Zeta Chapter. It was developed in 2006 and was funded by gifts from family and friends of the honoree. Irene Harris Taylor died at the age of 92 and was a 55 year resident of the Metro-East (Illinois-Missouri) Area leaving a legacy of love and commitment to education, excellence, community service and finer womanhood. The scholarship was established as the chapter's first-ever sponsored scholarship to recognize and support students who demonstrated perseverance and academic resilience.

Irene Harris Taylor's life was a testimony to academic excellence and the principles of scholarship. As the family reflected upon the life of Mrs. Irene Harris Taylor, it was clear that her life reflected the resilience and perseverance principles that characterized Theta Lambda

Zeta's scholarship offering. Mrs. Taylor was Mother to Soror Geraldine G. Taylor Peeples and Grandmother to Soror Carla Z. Peeples.

Irene Harris was born and raised in rural Mississippi just about 40 miles south of Memphis, Tennessee. She grew up as part of a sharecropper family and in a home where education was very important but very difficult to come by for Negro children male or female. The father-figure in her life was her beloved Grandfather who helped to raise her after her own Father died shortly after returning from active service in World War I. "Pa" was a meticulous scholar and instilled in her the value of an education.

She had persevered in her quest for an education as a youngster in racially segregated rural Mississippi. Irene and her siblings attended a one room elementary school between "field times." She learned in the cotton fields not only to endure tough situations, but also how to overcome them. Keeping in mind the lessons from her Grandfather, she learned how to set goals and stick to them. This was evident in her determination to stay in school. She repeated the eighth grade three times rather than stay at home because there was no high school for colored children in her area. Her teacher allowed her to help with the younger children with their lessons. This is when Irene developed her love for teaching.

When Johnson High School was finally built for colored children 20 miles away, Irene worked throughout high school to pay room and board and for school supplies. She left home again to attend the CME Methodist funded Rust College in Holly Springs, Mississippi to obtain her teacher training and certification. While there she endured the death of her younger sister due to a gangrene infection. Shortly after beginning to teach, the untimely death of her only brother was another painful episode in her life. She enjoyed teaching immensely at a school she had been recommended for before leaving to raise her family of eight children alongside her husband, Willie B. Taylor. Mr. Taylor had been prevented from getting an education in rural Mississippi as was the common scenario for especially colored boys. He also was a determined young man but only achieved a 3rd grade education—yet with his knowledge and perseverance; he became a self-taught master automobile mechanic whose abilities and skills were widely regarded far and wide throughout Madison County Illinois where the family relocated to.

Irene and Willie both showed grit and determination by leaving all that was familiar in 1951 and moved up North from the oppressive South when she and Willie were pressured to send their three sons to the cotton fields instead of to the classroom for an education. Once settled in their new home area, Mrs. Taylor applied for positions to teach in area school districts but was told that "coming from a southern Black college, her degree and training was not sufficient." After many such disappointing responses she remained a devoted wife and Mother to care for her family and children. Mrs. Taylor re-entered college after the last of her children started school and accepted a position as a Teacher's Aide in the Venice Illinois Public School District at 56 years of age. She believed in preparing oneself for the work he or she had to do—and was motivated to do whatever it took to make that happen—including returning to college for additional training.

During her 92-year lifetime, Irene Harris Taylor was an inspiration to her family, husband, her children and the students she later had the privilege to work with. Mrs. Taylor was known in her Madison County home town as a strong advocate for the education of young people. She is remembered by her Venice School community as a knowledgeable, patient, trusted and compassionate teacher and friend. She was especially attentive to students that seemed to have been "written off" by others. Not only did Mrs. Taylor encourage and support all eight of her children, she was a strong advocate for other children and made it known that she felt every child should have opportunities through education.

Mrs. Taylor was active in her church throughout her life and served in numerous ministries. She received certificates of completion in many areas of Christian education studies. She also taught classes in adult and youth ministries. In her community, Mrs. Taylor was selectively active in community projects that improved the quality of life especially for the youth. The Eagle Park Neighborhood Improvement Association which she helped to lead was responsible for building and equipping a community park and center where kids could play safely and engage in organized sports. The regal oak trees she personally planted in the park stand in salute to her contributions.

In 2006 the year of her death, two scholarships were awarded as well as in 2007. In 2008, three students received the scholarships. Each year subsequently, at least one scholarship is presented. The scholarship is awarded on the basis of Theta Lambda Zeta Chapter's resilience criteria with first preference given to graduating high school students from Madison and Saint Clair Counties (Metro East); secondly to Metro East undergraduate students currently enrolled at the University of Illinois; and finally, to Champaign County adult students who have returned to college to complete undergraduate degrees in spite of extraordinary personal and academic challenges.

My 52 Weeks at Cook County Jail in Chicago, Illinois

Connie V. Pugh, M.B.A., M.H.R.M., MA..

I was an excogitative child, questioning Sister Mary Francis' every word. Many years later, little did I know, discovering my passion for education would unveil itself as I sat in the county jail. Reflecting on this defining moment in my life as it relates to education and educating others, I find myself ruminating on the 52 weeks that I spent volunteering at the Cook County Jail. The jail's educational facility provided skills to inmates so that they might change the trajectory of their lives upon release.

My experience in and of itself was remarkable. I tutored non-violent inmates in developing basic skills in preparation for their General Education Diploma test as a college student. They looked forward to the tutoring sessions week after week. After a couple of months of instructing, I had a life-altering experience. I walked in ready to begin my math lesson and little did I know, I would played a major role in a student's life that fateful day. I was working with a student named "Tony" (not his real name).

After the formalities and pleasantries, I said, "Today, we will begin with a simple math problem." We both smiled. I asked, "How many times does 100 go into 200?" I was expecting another smile, a laugh, a smirk, or a bit of sarcasm. After the longest 3-4 seconds in my life, I noticed he had drawn the division bracket and was desperately working to provide the answer to this simple question I had posed. My heart sank. I was speechless, humbled, devastated, and slightly embarrassed (not for him, but for me). Time froze for me as my mind filled with wonderment. I wondered about this young man's story. I wondered had the educational system failed him. I wondered if anyone ever took the time to talk to him about life, about education, or about his future. Most of all, I was moved and, therefore, pondered my course of action.

I left the tutoring session with one definite answer. My mission from that moment forward focused on educating others. I have spent countless hours volunteering in programs geared toward providing education to individuals throughout the Chicago area, as well as, those created on the Illinois State Leadership Academy geared toward providing a broad range of personal and professional workshops for Sorors, Zeta Amicae, and Youth Affiliates.

Having read, studied, and researched various components of education as part of my formal educational requirements, I find it intriguing that researchers often note the third grade as the determinate of one's educational outcomes. In an *Education Week* article, a report compared the reading scores and graduation rates of almost 4,000 students. "A student who can't read on grade level by third grade is four times less likely to graduate by age 19 than a child who does read proficiently by that time. Add poverty to the mix, and a student is 13 times less likely to graduate on time than his or her proficient, wealthier peer." Given that statement, it is important to engage young people in conversations about education, not for the sake of recapitulating information, but more so as a means of aiding them in understanding that education is a blueprint for life.

In closing, I often wonder what became of "Tony." It is my hope that he too is telling a similar story. Telling a story of the college student tutoring him and how that interaction changed his life, and it started with a "simple" math question. "How many times does 100 go into 200?"

An Unexpected Hero

Michelle W. Russell

While growing up, I never applied myself in school. I was an average student without trying. Upon graduation, I had no intention of going to college, but my high school counselor suggested that I consider Bowie State University (BSU). I still was not interested, but my stepfather, Sterling, said to me, "You are going to college." I in turn applied to and enrolled at BSU. While at BSU, I still did not apply myself. This resulted in average grades, changes in my major, and a five-year graduation plan. When I received my undergraduate degree, I said, "I'm never going to graduate school," but after my son was born, I decided to go back to school. I ended up with two MBA's and graduated with a 3.98 GPA. That was a paradigm shift compared to undergraduate school. I not only graduated with honors, but I finished my course of study in less than two years. I started my scholarship journey as an average student but finished the journey as an honor student. My unexpected hero did not have a college degree; however my mother and grandfather did. I believed that Sterling experienced hardships and struggles from not having a college degree. He saw the scholar in me that I could not see. Sterling has gone on to be with the Lord, but he will always be my "unexpected hero." Because of my experience with my step-dad, I told my son the following: "Not going to college is "not" an option." My step-dad's legacy of scholarship lives on.

Gratitude

Lynette R. F. Smith

Growing up in Philadelphia, Pennsylvania in the 60's was really a lot of fun. I enjoyed my time in elementary, junior high and high school. However, the period that made the most impact on my intellectual life was my time in elementary school, specifically, sixth grade. I attended George G. Meade Elementary School and my 6th grade teacher was named Mrs. Rose Martin. Mrs. Martin was a poet and had a passion for famous African Americans. Her poetry was always about famous African Americans. This was her teaching tool and she chose five of her best students, of which I was one, to learn and recite her poetry. At first we recited her works at school assemblies but she later began to carry us to various and sundry churches all around Philadelphia to recite her poetry. Little did I know at the time this would be the genesis of my love of poetry and African American history. Mrs. Martin also expressed to us the necessity of learning every stanza of the Negro national anthem, *"Lift Every Voice and Sing."* I have shared that necessity with my children as well.

I have often thought about the poems Mrs. Martin wrote and taught to us and whether or not any of them were ever published. I owe her such a debt of gratitude. So, Mrs. Martin, wherever you may be, "Thank you. Thank you for your love of poetry. Thank you for your sharing your gift with us students. Thank you for introducing us to the richness of our culture, for being proud of who we are as a people are and for celebrating what we have accomplished. Thank you!"

AMICAE TO ZETA: LIGHT BLUE, ROYAL BLUE AND WHITE

PROUD *to now call you Soror!*

Donnie Faye Hull, National Director, Amicae Affairs
Renee S. Byrd and Bobbie J. White,
Regional Amicae Coordinators

These are the stories of Sorors we once called Friends.

Atlantic Region – Janell M. Lavender

Atlantic Region –
Janell M. Lavender

Soror Janell M. Lavender was initiated into Zeta Phi Beta Sorority, Inc., Beta Delta Zeta Chapter in 2010, and served on the Board of Trustees as recording secretary. In 1991, prior to her initiation, she joined the Zeta Amicae Auxiliary of Philadelphia, where she served as president and editor of the Auxiliary Newsletter. During her service in the Zeta Amicae Auxiliary and Beta Delta Zeta Chapter, she attended multiple Boules, Atlantic Regional Conferences, and State Leadership Conferences. Currently, she serves as a Zeta sponsor for Zeta Amicae Auxiliary of Philadelphia and Z-HOPE sponsor.

Janell retired from Temple University after 34 years of dedicated employment and began her academic journey and ministry as Coordinator for the Department for Pastoral Care for Persons with Disabilities, Archdiocese of Philadelphia. She received her B.S. in Business Communication from Chestnut Hill College, May 2009, and will receive her Master of Arts in Theology from St. Charles Borromeo Seminary on May 18, 2016. Janell was also selected for membership in Sigma Beta Delta Honor Society.

Janell is the Executive Director of the Martin de Porres Foundation. The goal of the Foundation is to develop lay leadership among African American/Black Catholics. In her affiliations, she is a member of the National Catholic Partnership on Disability (NCPD) and serves as Recording Secretary for AFSCME Philadelphia District Council Retiree Chapter 47. She is a member of St. Martin de Porres Catholic Church (40 yrs.), Chair of the Advisory Committee on Persons with Disabilities and founder of the SMDP Catholic Church Library (in progress).

Soror Janell M. Lavender was a member of the Woman's Army Corp (WAC). She is married to Harold B. Lavender, Retiree (MSgt-USAF) WW II Veteran.

Great Lakes Region – Lynnette T. Williams

Great Lakes Region –
Lynnette T. Williams

Mrs. Lynnette T. Williams was introduced to Zeta Phi Beta Sorority, Inc., when her oldest daughter became a Zeta. Upon accepting an award for her daughter from her Sorority, two ladies, Mrs. Thelma Murray-Skyes and Mrs. Arletha Hardin, approached her and told her about the Zeta Amicae Auxiliary. The rest is history. She became a member of the Xi Mu Zeta Amicae Auxiliary in 1995, and in 2005 a member of the Tau Psi Zeta Amicae Auxiliary of Alsip.

Lynnette graduated from Copernicus Elementary School in 1958 and Englewood High School in 1962. Later she attended Wilson Junior College (now Kennedy-King) and Harold Washington City College, graduating from Chicago State University with a board of governors major and a minor in African American studies on December 19, 2013. Though she found it hard to leave the Amicae, she fulfilled her dream and was inducted into Tau Psi Zeta Chapter on November 15, 2014.

She has been married for more than 40 years to her husband Percy. They have two daughters, Yolanda, an academic advisor at Eastern Illinois University and an active member of Tau Psi Zeta Chapter, and LaTanya, a licensed practical nurse. She also has two grandchildren, Isis and Israel and enjoys scrapbooking and stamp collecting,

Lynnette was employed by the Chicago Board of Education for 25 years, two years as a teacher's assistant, and 23 years as a vision and hearing technician. She also served at the Chicago Teachers Union for 20 years in the capacity of delegate, district supervisor, functional vice president, and trustee before retiring in February of 2004.

South Central Region – Barbara Marbley

Soror Barbara Marbley is the Amicae Coordinator for the State of Arkansas. She is the mother of three beautiful children and nine grandchildren. She has been married for 41 years, and is a member of God's Elect and Chosen Few Intercessory Prayer Ministry. In the ministry she serves as Sunday School teacher and assistant pastor. She is employed as a home-based parent educator, working with children up to 3 years old.

South Central Region –
Barbara Marbley

Barbara joined the Amicae in 1983 and was active 21 years with the Epsilon Zeta Zeta Chapter Amicae Auxiliary in Pine Bluff, Ark., before becoming a member of Zeta Phi Beta Sorority, Inc. Barbara loves the Amicae and what they accomplish with their Zeta friends. As an Amica, she was selected local, state and regional Amicae of the Year, and was secretary for her local auxiliary for five years.

Barbara's daughter, Loukisha Marbley Lewis, served as the president for her Amicae auxiliary in Denver, Colorado. Also her sister, Cathy Hunt, is an Amicae in Pine Bluff, who serves as Amicae State President for Arkansas and Amicae President for the South Central Region.

Barbara went back to college as a nontraditional student, graduating in 2002 with the highest GPA in the School of Agriculture, Fisheries and Human Sciences. She graduated summa cum laude with a Bachelor's degree in Human Sciences. She also received her Master's degree in Addiction Studies in 2009.

Barbara became a member of Zeta Phi Beta Sorority, Inc., in 2004. She has been a Zeta now for 12 years, and serves as the Amicae sponsor for the Pine Bluff Amicae Auxiliary as well as the State Amicae Coordinator for Arkansas. Having been an Amica, she has a high respect for the magnificent ladies of the Amicae Auxiliary, their leadership abilities, their willingness to cooperate with their Zeta friends, and their love and passion for their auxiliaries. Barbara loves being a Zeta and she is truly honored to serve the Amicae.

Southeastern Region – Bonnie G. Belford

My journey to Zeta began when I attended a Zeta Amicae meeting at the invitation of a dear friend. I was impressed with what I witnessed and supported the ideals put forth, so shortly after the birth of my daughter, I became a member. (My daughter was a Pearlette, Amicette and Archonette and hopes to be a Zeta one day.) I became active immediately and attended my first State Leadership Conference shortly after becoming a member. I served the Manatee/Sarasota Auxiliary as secretary, vice president and then president for several terms. Our auxiliary was very involved in the Florida State Leadership Conference, and was an

Southeastern Region –
Bonnie G. Belford

award-winning group. I was elected to serve on the state level as secretary, vice president and president, serving two terms in each position.

I was also active in the Southeastern Region, serving as the Queen's Contest coordinator and as chaplain. During her tenure as Florida State Amicae Coordinator, Triumphant Soror Margaret Redvict encouraged me to go back to school by suggesting that I prepare to take her position as coordinator. Under her direction, I was instrumental in revising the bylaws and in writing a policies and procedures manual. In July 2004, at the age of 50, I began my studies in the Bachelor of Science in Criminal Justice Administration program at the University of Phoenix. I had been employed with the Manatee County Probation Office since May of 1977, retiring in May, 2011. I completed my studies in November 2008 with a 3.48 grade point average while working fulltime and suffering the loss of my father, the week before my classes started, my mother in November 2005, and a sister in February.

My journey to Zeta was completed on February 21, 2009, when my nine intake sisters and I became members of Zeta Phi Beta Sorority, Inc., Tau Pi Zeta Chapter, Riverview (Tampa), Florida. What a proud moment that was! The day was made even better as the Florida State Leadership Conference was hosting its annual Undergrad Retreat and Zeta Amicae Summit in Tampa that weekend. The State of Florida Zeta Amicae presented me with a plaque for my outstanding service and commitment to the Auxiliary, and I had an audience on that day with International Grand Basileus Sheryl P. Underwood.

In 2009, I completed my Zeta Organizational Leadership certification and have since completed additional certification classes for the Membership Intake Process and the Zeta Amicae and Youth auxiliary sponsors. I have attended a Basilei Retreat and served my chapter as recording secretary, Blue Revue chair, Zeta Amicae sponsor, and currently as public relations chair. It was a long road to Zeta, but a journey I wouldn't trade for anything.

My Journey: From Amicae to Soror

Addie Cole as told to Janice M.T. Johnson

"A wise man will hear will and increase learning, and a man of under-standing will attain wise counsel."

– Proverbs 1:5

My journey began a long time ago. My mother died when I was 20 months old and I was raised by my aunt. I graduated from high school in 1945 with a strong desire to attend college. There was a program for children without parents that offered money for college and I was a recipient of that money. However, God had other plans for me. About the time I was to go to college, there was a lot of sickness and death in my family. With the money that would have been used to send me to college, my aunt had to pay for medical expenses and funerals. Although I couldn't go to college at that time, I was determined to further my education. I enrolled in Berean Institute, a business school in Philadelphia, Pennsylvania, established for African Americans. I enrolled in the clerk typist and secretary program. During my years at Berean, I met many new friends. We had many adventures on our train rides to and from Philadelphia. One fond memory I have is of meeting Mary McCloud Bethune. My friends and I saw her on the train and I said, "Isn't that Mary McLeod Bethune?" As we were whispering back and forth trying to decide who was going to go up to her, she looked at us and smiled. She looked just like her picture. She was very nice to us and shared that she was on her way to New York. Those friends and I became lifelong friends. After completing my studies at Berean, I held a job as a clerk/typist for the Department of Welfare.

During that time, race relations in the city of Wilmington, Delaware were not good. We were still on the back of the bus and couldn't go to school with whites. I was inspired to join in the fight for civil rights. I joined others in marching around the Governor's office. We marched around real estate brokers' offices for fair housing rights. We did a lot of marching and praying for equal schooling, fair housing and change. It was just like we were in the south.

During that time, I was attracted to the Amicae of Wilmington when I heard about their involvement in civic activities. They were doing beautiful work in the city. They worked in supporting the homeless and offering scholarships; they did so many things to help people. They had a beautiful fellowship with one another too. Once I joined them, I began working right away and I have many fond memories of those times. I remember my first plane ride was when the Amicae sent me to represent our chapter in Boston, Massachusetts at a regional conference. During my time as an Amicae, I had a beautiful experience. I was very excited to serve and it was very satisfying. Always looking to do more and to grow the organization, I was instrumental in reactivating the Amicae chapter of Morristown, NJ and that was a great feeling. I also served in various leadership positions as an Amicae which was very fulfilling. I even served as an Atlantic Region Amicae President and was recognized at the 56th Atlantic Regional Conference Amicae Luncheon as a Past President with other past Amicae presidents. I was so honored and humbled.

As a result of our civil rights marches and efforts, a bill was passed for desegregation in Delaware schools. I thank God I lived to enjoy what I marched for and to see the progression of it. Because of that bill, a program was set up that allowed minorities to attend the community college. In that program, we could take 12 credits and if we maintained an A average, we could then attend the University of Delaware.

Twenty-six years later in 1971 that desire to go to college was still in me. The community college was across the street from the Welfare Office where I worked and I decided to take a course. I enrolled in Sociology 1 and I earned an A. Then I enrolled in Psychology 1 and earned an A. I thought to myself, if I can get an A at the community college, then I could surely get a C at the University of Delaware. I showed the people at the University my grades and was accepted into the School of Sociology. Now that school was no longer across the street from work, and my classes at the university started soon after work ended, I had to learn how to drive. I enrolled in driving school, learned how to drive and then bought a car. My first car was an MG Midget convertible (I was riding in style). My boss was so supportive and gave me time off so I could get to school on time. Everyone worked with me to support my efforts. In my last year at the University of Delaware, I decided to take an independent study course in the summer. I worked with an Alcohol Abuse Counselor. I did my research by going to Al-Anon meetings with the counselor and wrote a paper on my research. I earned a B on that paper.

One day the Alcohol Abuse Counselor said to me that he'd like to see an Al-Anon meeting on the West Side for African Americans and encouraged me to start a group. Initially, I said no. However, the Spirit told me I was called to do something. So, in 1978, I went to my church and asked to start an Al-Anon group and was told no, but I did not give up. In 1982, I started a group at 8th Street Baptist Church and that served over 200 people. When I got married, my husband joined me and he began directing the meetings. That program is still going on today and I celebrate the fact that from one group, 4 other groups were started at other nearby churches.

In 1981, at 55 years of age, I graduated from the University of Delaware with a degree in Sociology and was promoted as a Social Worker. The local paper ran a story on me being a nontraditional student with determination who worked hard to get my degree. I then had a decision to make. Now that I had a degree, I could no longer be an Amicae.

I am grateful that the Sorors of Epsilon Rho Zeta Chapter, our sponsoring chapter, who invited me to be a member of Zeta Phi Beta Sorority, Inc. I was able to maintain my ties to the Sorority and the Amicae. Since becoming a Zeta, I have really enjoyed being a member. At that time the chapter was small with about 10 – 15 members. I am pleased to have witnessed the growth of the chapter over the years; we now have over 50 members. I am so pleased with the programs and service the chapter provides to the community, such as our Stork's Nest, scholarships, book drives and several other projects. I am overwhelmed with a great love for the sisterhood especially since I never had any biological sisters and was an only child. I am honored by the young ladies in the chapter who always look after me and treat me so well. This year, the chapter chose my church for our annual Finer Womanhood worship service. Not only did the Sorors present a donation to the church's scholarship fund, but they presented me with a beautiful bouquet of roses.

My journey from Amicae to Soror has been paved with lots of exciting and interesting experiences. I thank God for the journey and for the sisterhood of Zeta Phi Beta Sorority, Inc.

Once an Amicae, Now a Soror!

Jacquelyn Bobb

The late Amica Rosa Brunson, my mother, encouraged me to become an Amicae which was ultimately, the start of my journey. In August of 1999, I was inducted into Gamma Phi Zeta Chapter's Amicae Auxiliary. As an active Amicae, I held the offices of secretary, vice president and president. During my tenure, I also served as Florida State Amicae Secretary and Florida State Amicae Vice President.

Onboard the Carnival Cruise Ship for the 2009 Florida State Leadership Conference to the Bahamas, I was installed as President of the Florida State Zeta Amicae. I have since served as the Southeastern Regional Zeta Amicae Financial Secretary.

I was an active and financial Amicae for twelve years, and loved it dearly. In January 2010, I graduated with my Bachelor's degree and became a graduate member of Gamma Phi Zeta Chapter, Polk County. I was later appointed by Florida State Director Erna Foushee as the C-Coordinator of the Amicae and continued my work with them. I have served as secretary of the local chapter and currently serve as Basileus. I was recently was elected as Florida State Trustee under Florida State Director Karen Blount.

SCHOLARSHIP: ACTION THAT SPEAKS LOUDER THAN WORDS

Reflections of Elizabeth Duncan Koontz

Deedee (Dorris) Wright

Elizabeth Duncan Koontz

Soror Elizabeth Duncan Koontz had many firsts in her life. Soror Koontz was a leading advocate in the Nixon Administration for programs aimed at improving the status of women in the labor force. She was the Deputy Assistant Secretary of Labor and Special Counselor to the Secretary for Women's programs and she held the highest administrative post of any woman in the Nixon Administration. Soror Koontz was appointed to her key Labor Department post in 1972. At that time she was also serving as the Director of the Women's Bureau.

During her distinguished career, Soror Koontz was a member of the U.S. Delegation to the United Nations and the first African American president of the National Education Association (NEA). Soror Koontz also served as the first African American Assistant Superintendent for the Department of Public Instruction in the State of North Carolina and was a strong defender of equal rights for women when she was one of the founders of *Working Women.*

Both an educator and governmental official, she dedicated herself to destroying the myths and stereotypes that fostered discrimination against women, minorities and those that were handicapped.

She was a woman of unusual ability and immense energies, who loved students and saw their needs as the most critical aspect of her educational career. She started her career as a teacher for students who she would call "slow learners." (Today they would be referred as special needs). There is no barometer to adequately measure her worth as an educator or women rights advocate and, her love for seeing the best in those who wished to achieve high scholarship.

Soror Koontz was an educator, no matter what else she achieved. There was always an opportunity to teach. During my visit on holidays, one of my jobs was to make appointments during Christmas for students who came home and would want to share with her their successes and thank her for her guidance and support when they were in high school.

As an honorary member of Zeta Phi Beta Sorority, Inc., she always wanted to do more for the sisterhood. She served as chair for honorary members and would always talk about being of service. Her family was one of royal blue and white. Her three brothers were members of Phi Beta Sigma Fraternity and all of her sisters-in-laws were Zetas. She knew that Zeta Phi Beta was the way to go after being asked by other sororities.

When I talked about joining Zeta she would have a lot of questions. I remember her saying what do you have to offer: Competence? Integrity? Leadership or Management know how? Organizational acumen? Team Spirit? Compassion? Tenacity? A sense of justice? Fairness? Soror Koontz, when she was asked to be a member of Zeta Phi Beta Sorority, studied the precepts and its involvement in the community and thought that they well represented our sisterhood.

Soror Koontz also asked if I could be: Magnanimous without being condescending? Goal-oriented without being inhumane? Wise without being all-knowing? Female without being a clinging vine? She said more but those where the things that she said to me to make me want to be a member of Zeta Phi Beta Sorority.

She always saw young women as leaders and she told me that if I were ever in a position of leadership that the things she said to me she believed would take me far as a young woman.

Finally, Soror Koontz believed that you were either living by choice or living by accident. She believed that to create a fulfilling life, you should be purposeful in the decisions you make. You should know your purpose and live it every day.

Zora Neale Hurston

Doris McAdams Stokes

In the December 1945 ARCHON's Silver Anniversary edition, an article title reads, *"Zora Neale Hurston Receives Zeta's National Scholarship Award."* The Executive Board had awarded the internationally famous writer a scholarship to study folk music and dance in Central and South America. Her writings and anthropological research were highly respected. It was stated, perhaps by Soror Nancy Bullock Woolrige McGhee, the 1945 Antapokritis:

> *"In light of her enviable reputation as a scholar and writer, Soror Hurston easily exemplifies the Zeta ideal of scholarship. Her accomplishments serve as an inspiration to every young Negro woman, and Zeta sorors will follow with pride her activities as she travels and studies, and will be happy to share, even vicariously, in her experiences."*

Soror Hurston began her studies in 1918 and earned an asscociate degree at Howard University, where she was an early initiate of Zeta Phi Beta Sorority, Inc. In 1924, she won a scholarship to study at Barnard College and was awarded a bachelor's degree in anthropology. Her writing career began at Howard as co-founder and writer for *The Hilltop,* the student newspaper. Her first novel, *Mules and Men,* was published in 1935. She authored three more novels (*Their Eyes Were Watching God* (1937) was the most popular), and more than 50 short stories, plays and essays before her death in 1960.

Born on January 7, 1891 in Alabama, her family moved to Eatonville, Florida, the first all-black town to be incorporated in the United States. Eatonville houses the Zora Neale Hurston Museum of Fine Arts and celebrates her life with an annual festival.

The Pearl Foundation

Dr. Taneen D. Brinson, Chair

The Pearl Foundation is the charitable arm of Xi Mu Zeta Chapter of Zeta Phi Beta Sorority, Inc. **The Pearl Foundation** takes a holistic approach to servicing the community by exemplifying the ideals of scholarship. **The Pearl Foundation** strives for academic excellence among youth by awarding $9,000 annually, three scholarships and two book awards. The *Bonita Woods Scholarship* is provided to a member of Xi Mu Zeta youth auxiliary, the Archonettes, and is distributed to the graduating seniors. The *Debbie Gayden Lavizzo Scholarship* is provided to high school graduates within the south suburban area. The *Charlene Drake Scholarship* is awarded to an undergraduate member of Zeta Phi Beta Sorority, Inc.

The Pearl Foundation awards two $500.00 book awards. The *Dr. Jylla Moore Tearte Book Award* is presented to a graduating high school student who meets the application criteria. In order to be eligible for the Award, the applicant must submit the completed application, write an essay that highlights her commitment to community service, and discusses her career goals. *The Pearl Foundation Book Award* honors a selected youth who has demonstrated outstanding leadership and commitment to their community.

The Pearl Foundation is committed to continually exploring ways to secure funds to support the educational endeavors of a deserving student.

Z Community Foundation

Zoe L. Grant
Zeta Zeta Zeta Chapter Scholarship Program
Denver, Colorado

ABOUT US And OUR CAUSE

Zeta Phi Beta Sorority, Incorporated
ZETA ZETA ZETA CHAPTER
PO Box 220284
Denver, Colorado 80220

The Z Community Foundation was organized in 1999 as a 501(c)(3) non-profit group of Zeta Zeta Zeta Chapter, Zeta Phi Beta Sorority, Inc. The Z Community Foundation operates with a Board of Directors which includes members of the Zeta Zeta Zeta Chapter and the Denver Amicae Auxiliary. The Z Community Foundation receives and distributes funds that support the chapter's scholarships and community programs.

The Z Community Foundation was established to help improve the quality of life of citizens living in the metropolitan Denver area by providing community services and programs that focus on education, health awareness, youth, elderly and social issues that impact the community as a whole. The Foundation also fosters alliances with other charitable organizations that share the same vision of impacting the community in a positive manner.

With the cost of a quality education and the rising cost of books, the Foundation seeks donations to help offset some of that cost for graduating senior high school young ladies in the Denver metropolitan community to help them accomplish their goals.

This is important to us because helping young ladies pursue their dreams through a higher education and hopes of accomplishing their career choices, we help launch greater leaders in the community; positive attitudes; and, healthier relationships in the home. Since 1967 we have generated hope for many deserving recipients.

Annual scholarships awarded by Zeta Zeta Zeta to graduating high school seniors total over $61,000 since inception.

Visit our complete list of scholarship recipients at: *www.zphibzzz.org/scholarship.php*

Signature Programs

Scholarships are presented at our signature program each year during Finer Womanhood month and often involve our Archonette and Amicette youth affiliates while engaging the community through community service awards.

Girls 2 Pearlz & Pearlz 2 the World

Girlz 2 Pearlz & Pearlz 2 the World is a program of Zeta Zeta Zeta Chapter and works through the Z Community Foundation. The program is designed to introduce young ladies to dining etiquette, community service, and provide a support network for their self-esteem and academic progress in school.

The young ladies in the program are 9-18 years old and live in the Denver metropolitan area. They are encouraged to build up their community, one girl at a time, through caring about their appearance, how they treat others, and their academic success. Because some of the participants are financially disadvantaged, to provide all young ladies the opportunity of participating in the program, each young lady may have her program costs funded through sponsors. The program begins in October and ends in June of each year. As part of the program's curriculum, participants are required to participate in community service projects with Archonette and Amicette auxiliaries. They attend a health and beauty class, complete a dining etiquette class, and perform a song or dance routine keeping Finer Womanhood in mind.

The Z Community Foundation's other signature scholarship programs include:

- Finer Womanhood Scholarship Tea
- Gospel Brunch
- Bluetillion and
- Scholarship Receptions

Pledges and Tax Donation Contributions

Z Community Foundation is grateful for donations of any amount by July 31st of every year.

Centennial Scholarships

Since The Official National Centennial launch in 2015, Z Community Foundation has presented
three $1000 Centennial Scholarships to deserving female high school graduates,
Alexandra Matthews (Archonette), Nyat Ogbazghi and Franchesca Neal (Archonette).
In 2016 we presented another three $1000 Centennial Scholarships to
Jordan Fuselier (Archonette), Anifa Musengimana and Zuri Wright (Archonette).

The Gamma Zeta Zeta
Education Foundation, Inc.

Monique A. Hall, Esq., Chair

The Gamma Zeta Zeta Education Foundation, Inc. (GZZEF) is the non-profit charitable arm of Gamma Zeta Zeta Chapter in Columbus, Ohio. Whereas, nearly a century ago, the Founders of Zeta Phi Beta Sorority became trailblazers for those who believe in making change through action; The GZZEF is determined to preserve the Founders' legacies by promoting social change, service, and education in our community.

Since the 2005 inception of the foundation as a public charity, the GZZEF has striven toward educating, empowering, uplifting, and enriching the lives of humankind, by addressing specific community needs through service opportunities and educational programming. To that end, the foundation is charged with securing charitable contributions, gifts, donations, and other resources, which are used to promote the GZZEF mission of fostering youth development, promoting healthy prenatal behaviors among low-income women, and providing educational programs and services that improve the quality of life for communities in Ohio.

These objectives are manifested through the support, underwriting, and execution of various grassroot programs, including: community baby showers and workshops to benefit at-risk mothers in underserved populations; Archonette, Amicette, and Pearlette enrichment and mentoring; college preparedness workshops for local high school students; scholarship awards to deserving scholars; and, the acclaimed *From Girls to Pearls* program — an annual thirteen-week rite of passage program for eighth-grade girls, designed to aid adolescents in their matriculation to young adulthood through the promotion of physical, social and cultural awareness, and intellectual, character, and emotional development.

As the Sorority continues on her journey toward 100 years of Scholarship, Service, Sisterhood, and Finer Womanhood, the GZZEF will continue to respond to the call of Zeta by blazing new paths, being catalysts of change in our community, and upholding the banner of our beloved Founders.

The current GZZEF Board of Directors are Rita A. Barksdale, Bertie Ford, Monique A. Hall, Cathy Mock, Ashley L. Montgomery, Carla A. Robinson, Arlene MJ Taylor, and chapter President, Deborah D. Woodly (Ex officio).

The Tearte Family Foundation

Jylla Moore Tearte, Ph.D.

The Teartes with Mrs. Rachel Robinson at the 2014 Jackie Robinson Foundation Dinner in New York.

The Tearte Family Foundation (TFF) was founded in 2012 with initial funding by Curtis and Jylla Moore Tearte. The 501(C) (3) Foundation works through partnerships to identify students with academic promise and leadership potential to become Tearte Scholars. The scholars receive leadership training, personal development through coaching and mentoring, and financial awards to complete high school and pursue post-secondary education and career goals. Their goal is to know the Tearte Scholars personally. The Foundation also presents seminars and panels related to Global Business Trends and Leadership Skills Development.

Partners have included Brandeis University, Livingstone College, the Jackie Robinson Foundation, the Consortium for Graduate Study in Business, Emory University, the Goizueta School of Business Mid-Semester Global Study Program, The Posse Foundation, Inroads, Teach for America, 100 Black Men Metro North Atlanta Chapter, Phi

Dr. Tearte with Tearte Scholar Leigh Dunewood

Beta Sigma Centennial, The Naismith Award with the Atlanta Tipoff Club, and Hallahan Catholic High School for Girls in Philadelphia, Pennsylvania.

Dr. Tearte hosts Atlanta area undergraduate Sorors.

The Foundation supports several initiatives of Zeta Phi Beta Sorority, Incorporated. As the 20th Past International President of Zeta and the 2020 Centennial Chair, Dr. Tearte is an advocate of scholarship as a founding principle of Zeta. Thus, the following chapters and members have received support for their scholarship initiatives from the Foundation:

- Xi Mu Zeta Chapter, Markham, Illinois – The Pearl Foundation Archonette Scholarship and support for the youth affiliates programs
- Sigma Kappa Zeta Chapter, Brooklyn, New York – Oratorical Contest Scholarship
- Gamma Zeta Zeta Chapter, Columbus, Ohio – Girls to Pearls Program Scholarship
- Omega Eta Zeta Chapter, Quincy, Massachusetts – Business Scholarship
- Centennial interns (3) for 2016 Boule
- Documentary Filming in Guatemala Scholarship for a Zeta
- Zeta Organization Leadership - Great Lakes Undergraduates Sponsorship

The Teartes are major donors to the Smithsonian Museum of African American History and Culture as well as members of the United Way Tocqueville Society.

The Tearte Family Foundation sponsors the "Global Insights" panel discussion at Emory University Goizueta School of business.

The Atlantic Region

Janet Y. Bivens, Esq., Director
Andrea Todman, Regional Scholarship Coordinator

The Atlantic Region, States and Chapters take our precept of Scholarship very seriously with an estimate of $45,000 in scholarships paid throughout the region by our chapters from 2013 – 2015. Various scholarships offered by the Region, States and our International Chapters:

THE ATLANTIC REGION

Arizona C. Stemons Scholarship

Three scholarships totaling $6000 were awarded during the Biennial Atlantic Regional Leadership Conference in October 2015. Each scholarship is a one-time only award.

DELAWARE

Martha Sims-Wilson with LaDale Walker

First awarded in 2013, the State of Delaware awards the **Althea W. Armstrong Scholarship** annually. It is named in honor of Soror Armstrong, the 3rd Delaware State Director, a retired educator who served as Basileus in both of the Delaware graduate chapters, Epsilon Rho Zeta Chapter in Wilmington before chartering Theta Zeta Zeta Chapter in Dover, her city of residence. The criteria is a female graduating senior from a Delaware High School based on academic excellence and financial need. Award amounts range from $600 - $1000.

MARYLAND

Danielle R. Green with Tamika Daniels

The **Issie Jenkins Scholarship** was the vision of Soror Gwenneth Corujo, Immediate Past Maryland State Director. This Maryland State Scholarship is in its fifth year. Each year, two $2,000 awards are presented to one (1) Undergraduate or graduate Soror and one (1) graduating high school senior. The scholarship, which is given directly to the recipients for their educational endeavors. The recipients are invited to the Maryland State Leadership Conference to receive their awards.

NEW JERSEY

Gina Merritt-Epps, Esq. with Billie J. Bailey

Biannually, the State of New Jersey awards scholarships to New Jersey Sorors in 2 categories: The General State Scholarship - funded by New Jersey Chapters with $3,500, awarded to Sorors based on scholastic achievement and service to Zeta. In 2016, in honor of the Year of the Undergrad, the scholarships will be awarded to undergraduates.

Deborah Cannon Wolfe Life Members Awards – is funded by New Jersey's Life Members on a voluntarily basis, to Sorors pursuing graduate degrees or certifications. While funded by the Life Members, the scholarship is open to all financial Sorors.

In 2014, the State of New Jersey lost **Soror Natalie Goode** of Zeta Delta Zeta Chapter. Her family asked that in lieu of flowers, donations be made to the State of New Jersey Scholarship Fund. In 2016, a scholarship will be awarded to a Soror seeking a degree or employed in the field of education.

NEW YORK

Shannel L. Robinson with Katrina Banks

The Dr. Deborah Canon Wolfe Scholarship

The New York State, Dr. Deborah Cannon Wolfe Scholarship is awarded biannually to a financially active member of the Sorority and is announced during the New York State Leadership Conference. It recognizes the academic achievements, educational pursuits, and the personal qualities of its applicants. The amount awarded is $1200.

The New York State Pamela Profit Scholarship

Soror Pamela Profit was a teacher and dedicated leader of an Archonette Club in New York City. Her efforts in helping girls ages 14-18 develop on a cultural, educational, and personal level were timeless. It is in her memory that this New York State Scholarship for Archonettes is named. It recognizes the academic achievements, educational pursuits, as well as special personal qualities of an Archonette. Scholarships are awarded to active members of Archonette Clubs of Zeta Phi Beta Sorority, Inc. in New York State, who are graduating seniors planning to attend college.

PENNSYLVANIA

Barbara A. Cousar with LyTanja Jones-Beulah and Dana Moore

Arizona Cleaver Stemons Returning Scholars Award (Community Award)

This award is presented to a Pennsylvania resident with a 3.0 cumulative GPA on a 4.0 scale who completes an essay and has service and character letters of recommendation. This award of $2550 will be presented at an event of the graduate chapter which is in closest proximity to the recipient.

Barbara Bradley Young Memorial Scholarship (Soror Only Award)

Successful recipients must financial at all levels and a member of a PA graduate or undergraduate chapter.

The amount awarded is $4,000.

TRI-STATE

Annette Draper-Moore with Natalie Roach

A. Doris Banks Henries Scholarship

Soror Henries was the first Regional Director in Africa, appointed in 1949. The amount awarded is $500.

GERMANY

Janet Y. Bivins, Esq. with Miranda Lee

Mu Theta Zeta Chapter awards scholarships on an annual basis to Department of Defense Education Activity High School Seniors throughout Europe. Last year, a total of $4,000 was awarded, $1000 each, to four deserving high school seniors. Each year the chapter develops essay questions based upon current events. This year's topics included questions on the role of social media in social justice and social injustice issues; the importance of diversification in colleges and universities; and, the perception of today's immigration laws and their impact on equality or inequality.

In 2016, Germany initiated the Reach Back program, to keep in contact with recipients and encourage them in their future endeavors. After the first semester, the recipients will be provided a $300 book stipend providing they maintain a 3.0 grade point average.

The Eastern Region

T. Diane Surgeon, Esq., Director

The Eastern Region has named two scholarships in honor of two Sorors. The region awards scholarships to deserving students in honor of Soror Esther Peyton and Soror Edna S. Anthony. The Region also supports the National Educational Foundation's Nancy B. McGhee Scholarship.

The Legacy of Esther Peyton - Leadership Scholarship

Triumphant Soror Peyton was a very active Soror at every level of Zeta Phi Beta Sorority, Inc. She served as Chair of the National Executive Board, Eastern Regional Director, Chair of Regional Directors, First Chair of Life Members, and Co-Director of the National Project on Juvenile Delinquency, to name a few of her Zeta leadership roles. She was a very influential educator by profession. With tremendous gratitude, the Eastern Region is honored to pay special tribute to Soror Esther Peyton with this Leadership Scholarship named in her honor as a powerful leader in Zeta's legacy.

Each year, the Eastern Region selects an aspiring undergraduate Soror who exemplifies exceptional leadership skills and who has demonstrated outstanding leadership on the campus, in the state and region. The search for the most worthy candidate to receive the Esther Peyton scholarship is very competitive. At the 71st Eastern Regional Leadership conference in Charleston WV (March 3-6, 2016), Soror T'Keyah Johnson was the recipient.

The Legacy of Edna S. Anthony - Friendship Scholarship

Triumphant Soror Anthony was initiated into Nu Chapter at VA Union University in 1963. She transferred her membership into the Alpha Phi Zeta graduate chapter where she served Zeta faithfully until her untimely death.

Soror Anthony is most remembered for her significant contributions to Zeta Amicae of the Eastern Region. She served as advisor to Zeta Amicae of Richmond for many years. Beyond the local level, Soror Anthony served as Amicae Coordinator for the State of VA and as Amicae Coordinator for the Eastern Region for many, many years. Soror Anthony was 100% committed to Zeta and in particular, Zeta Amicae. In fact, at the time her death, Soror Anthony was attending a Virginia State Leadership Conference performing her duties as the Virginia State Amicae Coordinator. Soror Anthony died doing what she loved.

In her memory, the Eastern Region established the Edna S. Anthony Friendship Scholarship to be given annually to a deserving student. The Zeta Amicae of the Eastern Region have donated funds to the National Educational Foundation in memory of Ms. Margaret Breaux, the National President's mother.

The Legacy of Nancy B. McGhee - National Scholarship

Past National President Soror Nancy B. McGhee was a strong national leader who served our sisterhood from the Eastern Region. The Eastern Region proudly supports the Zeta National Educational Foundation by contributing to its Nancy B McGhee Scholarship.

The Eastern Region:
The Blue Hat Society

T. Diane Surgeon, Esq., Director

Grand Basileus Wright and members at the
Eastern Region's Blue Hat Society

The 71st Eastern Regional Leadership Conference was the backdrop for *The Blue Hat Society,* a new fundraising initiative launched by Zeta National Educational Foundation (Z-NEF) in March 2015. *The Blue Hat Society* is the brainchild of Dr. Alice McCullough-Garrett, Z-NEF Chair and Eastern Regional Director T. Diane Surgeon, Esq. with the goal of raising scholarship funds for deserving students throughout the United States. The Eastern Region includes the District of Columbia and the states of North Carolina, Virginia and West Virginia.

On Friday evening during the Night of Performing Arts, in beautiful West Virginia, Basilei from chapters in the Eastern Region each adorned in a blue hat, paraded one by one to the front of the ballroom with money orders, checks and cash to fill a beautiful blue hat held by Dr. Garrett. Undergraduate chapters contributed $25 to $50 while graduate chapters contributed $100 or more. Between performing artists' presentations, individual Sorors and Life Members representing over 40 chapters and Amicae from seven auxiliary groups contributed. International Grand Basileus Mary B. Wright made a donation in memory of her mother, Mrs. Margaret Breaux.

In the end, like a church fundraising program, the hat was emptied and passed around to reach the goal set by the Z-NEF Chair. When the hat returned to the chair, the members of the Eastern Region had far exceeded their goal. *The Blue Hat Society* total collected was $12,000! In one evening, with one program, Z-NEF was able to garner funds for at least twelve scholarships. Tears flowed from Dr. Garret and others in the room; hands clapped and joyous shouts rang out! Everyone celebrated.

Dr. Alice McCollough-Garrett, NEF Chair with the Blue Hat.

The Great Lakes Region

Michelle Porter Norman, Director
Geraldine G. Peeples, Regional Scholarship Chair

Soror Ida B. King

The "Greater" Great Lakes Region remains a mighty region of leadership and creative scholarship models. A number of Great Lakes Region leaders brought recognition to the region's scholarship efforts. The 8th Grand Basileus Violette N. Anderson (1935 -36), appointed Carolyn J. Cain as the West Central Region (name changed to Great Lakes in 1947) Director to serve from 1935–1936. Soror Cain brought with her her experience as past National Scholarship Chair and Soror Ione H. Gibson presented the first regional scholarship in 1963. The seven states that comprise the Great Lakes Region honor their own legacies through scholarship while celebrating the trailblazers who have served the region and the Sorority well. A brief synopsis of the scholarship awards presented to undergraduate, graduate, Amicae and public/private high school students in the Great Lake Region includes:

The IDA B. KING MEMORIAL SCHOLARSHIP pays tribute to the Great Lakes Region's "Grand Lady" Ida B. King, an outstanding Sorority leader who served at the state, regional and national levels, and most certainly, her Gary, Indiana chapter. Education and scholarship are the cornerstones of Zeta Phi Beta Sorority and it was the wish of Soror King that Zeta Phi

Beta Sorority play important roles in equipping today's youth with the necessary tools for a proper education. The scholarship named in her honor was established after her death in 1989. Her Sorors honored her for her powerful role as a Sorority leader, one who modeled Finer Womanhood, Scholarship and Service. She left a legacy for other Sorors to follow.

The Ida B. King Memorial Scholarship is awarded to active, financial members of Zeta Phi Beta Sorority who are undergraduate and graduate students in the Great Lakes Region. It is funded by an allocation in the region's operating budget. A successful funding proposal to the Ford Motor Corporation and General Motors in the late 1980's provided funds for this scholarship as well as the Ione Hartley Gibson Memorial Scholarship. Scholarships are presented at the annual Great Lakes Region Conference held in one of the seven states within the region and disbursed in the next academic term.

Soror Ida B. King's service in Zeta Phi Beta Sorority Incorporated was outstanding:

1948 – 1954	Elected and served as National Phylacter.
1954 – 1959	Elected and served as National Grammateus.
1961 – 1970	Elected and served as National Executive Board Chair.
1976 – 1980	Elected and served as National Executive Board Chair.
1980	Named "Soror of the Century" by Grand Basileus Janice G. Kissner for outstanding service to Zeta.

Yes, Soror King served two different terms as Chair of the National Executive Board. In the Great Lakes Region, she served as Historian and chaired the region's Constitution Committee which resulted in the region's first constitution that was adopted in April, 1969.

Her service took place during periods dynamic growth in the Sorority and Soror King's leadership was a valuable resource to numerous committees. The Great Lakes Region also recognized Soror King's meteoric career in Zeta by raising funds and purchasing a chair to place in the National Executive Board room at National Headquarters. This was done immediately after her last term as Chair of the National Executive Board when she was named National Executive Board Chair Emeritus. Soror Jylla Moore Tearte succeeded Soror King and became the first Executive Board Chair to occupy the chair that is now known as the Ida B. King Chair.

Soror Ida B. King served with distinction as a high school educator and counselor in her native Gary, Indiana. This very proper, dignified, eloquent and very elegant Soror was the epitome of Finer Womanhood. When she spoke, many listened. Countless Sorors in the region attribute their knowledge of and passion for Zeta, particularly the precise conduct of Zeta business, to Soror King.

The 2015 Ida B. King Memorial scholarships were presented to two undergraduate Sorors and two graduate Sorors. The undergraduate Sorors were Cortney Cosby (Indiana) and

Mariah Gerald (Michigan). Graduate recipients were Ebony Turnbow (Michigan) and Angelyn Anderson (Illinois). The April 2016 Great Lakes Region Conference was held in Louisville KY and the recipients were: undergraduate Soror Samantha G. Binion (Xi Gamma Chapter) in Ohio and Soror Chelsea K. Appiah (Xi Rho Chapter) in Ohio; and, graduate Soror Leslie Buckner (Tau Psi Zeta) in Illinois and Soror Charmayne L. Jackson (Upsilon Omega Zeta) in Indiana.

Soror Ione H. Gibson

The **IONE HARTLEY GIBSON REGIONAL MEMORIAL SCHOLARSHIP** honors a Soror who made significant contributions to the Great Lakes Region and Zeta Phi Beta Sorority, Inc. The scholarship was established after her death in March 2004. At that regional conference held in Detroit, the scholarship proposal, presented by Scholarship Chair Connie V. Pugh of Illinois was adopted as a rotating scholarship based on the location of the regional conference each year and was designated for graduating seniors enrolled in public or private high schools. This action served to reach a larger number of communities within Illinois, Indiana, Kentucky, Michigan, Minnesota, Ohio and Wisconsin. The scholarship is funded by an annual allocation in the region's operating budget. As the conference site is established each year, the state in which the conference is held is responsible for the outreach to public and private high schools within the state. The student must be matriculating in a four-year college or university. The scholarship is awarded at the regional awards banquet and disbursed the next academic year.

The Ione Hartley Gibson scholarship is a fitting tribute to a Soror who had served her State of Michigan, the Great Lakes Region, and the Sorority with honor and distinction. Though short in stature, Soror Gibson was oversized in personality, a confident leader, and a model of Finer Womanhood who was committed to excellence in all roles she served in. Some of her accomplishments:

1962	Appointed Director, Great Lakes Region by Grand Basileus Deborah P. Wolfe.
1963	Presented the first Great Lakes Region scholarship to Evelyn Reid.
1966	Initiated the *Zeta Zest*, the Great Lakes Region newsletter.
1967	Initiated the first Amicae breakfast and Life Member lunch in the region.
	Established a committee to draft the regional bylaws.

1968	Inducted the largest line in the region, 62 Sorors, at Central State University.
	Hosted the Boule in Chicago.
	Led a pilgrimage to Birch Haven.
1969 - 1972	Elected National Board of Trustees.
1974	Elected Chair, National Executive Board
1992 – 2004	Appointed Resident Agent, Birch Haven, Idlewild, Michigan by Grand Basilei Jylla Moore Tearte, Barbara West Carpenter and Barbara C. Moore.

Soror Ione Hartley Gibson was a native of St. Louis MO and attended Tennessee State University. It was there that she and her sister, Thelma Hartley Fisher became members of Zeta. When she married, she made her home in Detroit, Michigan. She served as Basileus of Beta Omicron Zeta and was a charter member and Basileus of Kappa Rho Zeta. Soror Gibson truly is a legacy and Soror Gibson's Zeta legacy includes four daughters, a granddaughter and cousin.

The 2015 Ione Hartley Gibson Memorial Scholarship was awarded to Kyilah M. Terry from Chicago. Kyilah is attending the University of California—Los Angeles. At the April 2016 Great Lakes Region Leadership Conference in Louisville, Kentucky, the high school scholarship was awarded to Ambria H. McCowan from Danville, Kentucky.

State of Illinois

Connie V. Pugh with Donna Fuller

The state of Illinois has championed the cause of providing service and scholarship for African Americans and members of other minority ethnic groups since the sorority's inception in 1920.

Sorority members and the auxiliary members are heavily involved in servicing the community; upholding the ideals of scholarship; sisterhood; and Finer Womanhood. Honoring its commitment service, the state of Illinois has formed alliances with various organizations such as the March of Dimes; American Cancer Society; American Lung Association; Urban League; United Nations; United Negro College Fund; and the National Pan Hellenic Council, Incorporated to name a few.

The community-conscious, action-oriented organization has evolved to meet the ever-changing needs of our society. The state of Illinois works tirelessly under the consolidated founding principles of **Z-HOPE**, (**Z**etas **H**elping **O**ther **P**eople **E**xcel, through the mind, body, and spirit). The state is especially proud of our programs geared toward educating individuals. Our goals revolve around identifying individuals in need of assistance and providing that assistance on a continual basis. Our mission encompasses raising the standard of excellence, through the mind, body, and spirit.

Alice Quinn Memorial Scholarship

Alice Quinn hails from the St. Louis, Missouri and East St. Louis area. Having held membership in Xi Zeta Chapter in St. Louis, she saw the need to charter a graduate chapter near her home, across the state line in Illinois.

She lobbied for a graduate chapter to address the needs of individuals living within the southeastern part of the state. After gathering additional like-minded individuals, she became a charter member of Eta Kappa Zeta Chapter in East St. Louis, Illinois.

She served the sisterhood untiring as the State Representative-at-Large, as well as, provided extensive service throughout the state. The state's first scholarship was named in her honor. The honor was befitting and well-deserved as she spent her life as an Educator.

Soror Quinn held membership in Eta Kappa Zeta Chapter until her death.

M. Ann Prendergast Scholarship (established January 2013)

M. Ann Prendergast served as Director of the state of Illinois. She was an advocate for education and social change. She fought for equal justice and women's rights.

Under her tutelage at the helm of the state, she served with elegance, grace, and a great will. The state's membership and auxiliaries grew tremendously under her leadership. Today, the state of Illinois continues to grow based on the foundation upon which she stood as a leader.

Life Member M. Ann Prendergast has been a dedicated member of Zeta Phi Beta Sorority, Incorporated for decades. She was part of the **"Fabulous 57"** chartering Zeta Tau Zeta Chapter in 1966. Soror Prendergast's knowledge of the sorority and feistiness are unmatched. She served in various leadership capacities, including President of Zeta Tau Zeta Chapter. She worked closely with the **Past International President of Zeta Phi Beta Sorority, Incorporated, Dr. Janice G. Kissner**. Soror Prendergast is a member of Xi Mu Zeta Chapter in Markham in Illinois.

The lifelong educator has impacted the lives of others for nearly 90 years. **In honor of her 90th birthday on January 1, 2015, she donated $2,500.00 to Zeta Phi Beta Sorority, Incorporated in the state of Illinois in order to provide additional funding for M. Ann Prendergast Scholarship. Ms. Carol Pazos was the 2016 recipient.**

The Isabel Connelly Taylor Memorial Scholarship (established January 2013)

Isabel C. Taylor lived a remarkable 104 years! Similar to the organization that she joined 40+ years ago, she has been a champion for change. She stood in the trenches arm to arm with current and past civil rights leaders; spent over 40 years educating children in classrooms from Holly Springs, Mississippi to Chicago, Illinois; published literary works; and continually provide service to Zeta Phi Beta Sorority, Incorporated.

She was an advocate for education and social change. The author and poet was born Queen Isabel Connolly in Savage, Mississippi to Lena and Toney Connelly. Her house became a classroom as she was taught by her grandfather, Mr. Jackson Connelly. She followed in her family's footsteps by becoming an Educator. At that time, aspiring teachers could take a test to teach prior to obtaining an official degree. In 1930, Ms. Connelly (Taylor) took and passed the state of Mississippi teaching test and was assigned a position. While teaching, she attended Mississippi Industrial College in Holly Springs. She continued teaching until her retirement in 1959.

Soror Taylor held membership in Zeta Tau Zeta Chapter (Chicago, Illinois) until her death in 2015.

State of Indiana

Susan D. Johnson, Ph.D. with Danielle Griffin

The Indiana State Organization awards one scholarship in the name of Soror Ida B. King and one Book Award in honor of Soror Ida Armour Gamble. The **Ida B. King Scholarship** and **Ida Amour Gamble Book Award** are paid directly to the institution on behalf of the student. Soror Gamble was the longest serving Indiana State Director, serving from 1974 – 1980 under the leadership of Grand Basileus Janice G. Kissner and from 1980–1986 under Grand Basileus Edith V. Francis. Indiana State scholarships are funded by yearly chapter scholarship assessments based on chapter size and are announced at the Annual State Leadership Conference in October. The 2015 recipient was graduate Soror Adrienne Woods of Iota Zeta Chapter.

State of Kentucky

Keisha D. Smith with Kimberly Newbern

The Kentucky State Association annually presents the **Soror Bobbie Qualls Book Scholarship** to two graduate or undergraduate students. These awards were developed as a benevolent initiative by Soror Bobbie Qualls, Past State Director. The 2015–2016 recipients were Mercedes Samuels, of Delta Theta Chapter at the University of Louisville and Bria Staten-Favors, Delta Theta Chapter, University of Louisville. In the event that no graduate applicants apply for the scholarships, two undergraduate Sorors may receive the scholarship.

State of Michigan

Tonia Jenkins with Leslie Wilson-Smith

The Michigan State Organization presents three scholarships at its Founders' Day Observance. The scholarships are slated for two undergraduate students and one graduate student. The **Frances Faithful Scholarship** is presented to an undergraduate student in honor of Soror Frances Faithful, the daughter of Founder Myrtle Tyler Faithful. Soror Frances Faithful is an active member of Zeta Beta Zeta Chapter in Flint, Michigan. The recipient for this year was Gwendolyn Morgan, an undergraduate at Wayne State University. The **Annye P. Roberts Scholarship** is given in honor of Soror Annye P. Roberts of Saginaw, Michigan. Soror Roberts served with distinction as a Past State Director and the 16th Great Lakes Regional Director. The 2016 recipient was Eboni Turnbow, a Ph.D. student. The third scholarship is presented as a tribute to all **Past State Directors of Michigan** and is a revolving scholarship among them. This year, the honored State Director was Soror Jeffrey P. Williams. There was no applicant for the scholarship this year and the funds were contributed to the Wilberforce University scholarship fund. The Michigan scholarships are funded by a nominal member assessment from the per capita paid by State of Michigan Sorors.

State of Ohio

LaRita Smith with Felicia Ocdise

Two scholarships are given each year at the Ohio State Organization's annual Leadership Conference. The **Legacy Trail Blazer Scholarship** was initiated to honor Hester Shoto and is given to a graduate Soror. Soror Shoto, who served as a National Phylacter, from 1982 - 1984, was recognized for her compassionate and sisterly work with older Sorors. The undergraduate scholarship, **The Evelyn J. Robinson Scholarship**, is presented in honor of Soror Evelyn J. Robinson who was the first Assistant Regional Director (later changed to State Director) in Ohio, appointed in 1958. She served a second term from 1980 – 1986. Ohio scholarships are funded by the dues of state members and various fundraising efforts. The undergraduate recipient was Shayrice Rand in 2016.

Sponsored Scholarships – A Path Blazed by Theta Lambda Zeta Chapter

Geraldine G. Peeples

CHAMPAIGN-URBANA, ILLINOIS – **Zeta Phi Beta Sorority, Incorporated** stands on its legacy of scholarship and service and at the national level, there are numerous examples of scholarship and service initiatives. Local chapters emulate the efforts of the national level as well as initiate ones of their own. Theta Lambda Zeta Chapter in Champaign-Urbana, Illinois initiated its "sponsored scholarships" in 2006 following the death two of its members' mother. This initiative was timely for both the chapter as well as for the family. The chapter's scholarship funds were supplemented when the Taylor family channeled contributions from family and friends of its loved one into a scholarship in honor of her life's service. This philanthropy served as an example to other chapter members and appealed to community individuals that wished to honor a loved one or to provide a tribute in honor of someone. This scholarship and others are appropriate and long lasting ways to honor special individuals associated with the Blue and White family.

The **Irene Harris Taylor (IHT) Memorial Scholarship** was the first sponsored scholarship in Theta Lambda Zeta Chapter. It was established in 2006 and funded by gifts from family and friends of the honoree, Irene Harris Taylor died at the age of 92. She was a 55 year resident of the Metro-East (Illinois-Missouri) area and left a legacy of love and commitment to education, excellence, community service and Finer Womanhood. The scholarship in her name recognized and supported students who demonstrated perseverance and academic resilience. Irene Harris Taylor's life was a testimony to academic excellence and the principles of scholarship. Mrs. Irene Harris Taylor's life reflected the resilience and perseverance, principles Theta Lambda Zeta wanted exemplified in its scholarship. Mrs. Taylor was mother to Soror Geraldine G. Peeples and grandmother to Soror Carla Z. Peeples.

Mrs. Taylor was known in her home town as a strong advocate for the education of young people. She had persevered in her quest for an education as a youngster in racially segregated rural Mississippi. Reared by her paternal grandfather and her mother after her father died post World War I, she repeated the eighth grade four times rather than stay at home until a high school was built for colored children 20 miles away. She worked throughout high school to pay room and board and purchase school supplies. After attending Rust College, she taught school before leaving to raise her family of eight children with her husband, Willie B. Taylor. Mr. Taylor had been prevented from getting an education in rural Mississippi and only achieved a 3rd grade education yet he became a self-taught master automobile mechanic whose abilities and skills were widely sought after throughout Madison County Illinois. Mrs. Taylor re-entered college for a refresher course after the last of her children started school and accepted a position as a teacher's aide in the Venice Illinois Public school district. She believed in preparing oneself and was motivated to do whatever it took to make that happen. In 2006 and 2007, two scholarships were awarded. In 2008, three students received scholarships. Each year thereafter, at least one scholarship is presented.

The initial effort of TLZ's sponsored scholarship paid dividends as a model for chapter scholarships. The **Wilson Family Memorial Resilience Scholarship** was presented first in 2007 and again in 2008 with the same criteria as the chapter's other Resilience Scholarship. In honor of David and Thelma Wilson, parents of Soror Gayle Jeffries and grandparents to Soror Andrea Jeffries, the family paid tribute to a couple who through 50 plus years demonstrated resilience in caring for their five children and making sure that each one graduated from college. Though neither David nor Thelma graduated from high school, they provided a nurturing home and encouragement to their children. Even in the face of adversity and tragedy, they never wavered but demonstrated to their children that "God will make a way in spite of your circumstances." Both parents worked and raised the family then secured General Educational Development credentials. Thelma Wilson was went on to complete a bachelor's degree and then a master's degree and worked as a clinical social worker.

The third chapter sponsored scholarship was setup in 2010 when one of its Sorors passed away in January. The Sorors voted to assess themselves each year to fund the scholarship. **The Carla Z. Peeples Memorial Resilience Scholarship** was a tribute to the excellence in service Soror Carla Peeples gave to the chapter. Carla had celebrated 20 years as a Zeta in September 2009 and was active in Phi Gamma Chapter at Michigan State University as an undergraduate student. She temporarily relocated to Champaign-Urbana, Illinois and became a member of Theta Lambda Zeta chapter. Carla had a phenomenal history in her short life as a fashion and hair model, radio and television employee, and national and international traveler that shaped her life. She was a National Sorority of Phi Delta Kappa Xinos Club member, Zeta debutante, youth member at her church, oratorical and drama contestant (and winner) in the Pan Hellenic contests, NAACP youth member, and NAACP Afro-Academic, Cultural, Technological and Science (ACT-SO) contestant and a national winner. A communications major, she eagerly put her talents to work in Theta Lambda Zeta Chapter when she temporarily relocated to Champaign-Urbana to assist her mom with caregiving tasks.

She held several chapter offices (Tamias-Grammateus, Antapokritis, Epistoleus, First Anti-Basileus), and a trio of positions, as communications chair, publications chair and web master at the regional level in 2009. During this time, she researched the life of Soror R. Lillian

2011 Scholarship Winners:
Teneshia Smith and Morgan Lett.

Carpenter (Director, Great Lakes Region, 1930 – 33), provided the photo, and wrote the bio-sketch of her to include in the 75th Great Lakes Region Anniversary Conference souvenir program booklet held in Minneapolis.

Carla's legacy lives on in the excellent work she gave in publicizing the chapter's activities, designing media materials, preparing award winning chapter scrapbooks and reports at all levels and, "putting the Carla on it" in materials that represented the chapter and Sorority. She was also a valuable and able assistant to the undergraduate chapter advisor, Soror D'wania Clark-Turner, with her knowledge of undergraduate culture. Her work was always characterized by excellence and quality. She was a resourceful Soror that gave credit to her mentors and teachers including Soror Annye P. Roberts (her "Super Zeta") and her grandmother, and mom. As a final tribute to Soror Carla, the Sorors also agreed to wear hats at Finer Womanhood celebrations because she had always been known as the "Diva." This scholarship was renamed in 2015 after the death of charter member Valerian A. Summerville in September 2014. The **Blue and White Scholarship** was geared toward children of active chapter members and Zeta Youth Auxiliary members. In 2015, the scholarship was awarded to Archonette, Aliya Savage.

The Reverend Dr. Lundy W. and Mrs. Carolyn M. Scott Savage Memorial Scholarship was given in 2011 in the memory and honor of a kind and generous Zeta partner It was funded by gifts from the Savage family. Pastor Savage lived the life that he advocated. Pastor and Mrs. Savage lived out the principles found in 1 Timothy 3:1-13 and Proverbs 31:10-31. Pastor and Mrs. Savage cherished the wonderful relationships built with family, friends and community leaders. Pastor Savage especially loved the youth of his church and community and his words of encouragement and motivation were distributed in generous measures. Pastor Savage was a champion for Christian and secular education and readily befriended Zeta Phi Beta Sorority in its efforts to generate scholarship funds for deserving students. The Mount Olive Missionary Baptist Church ("The Mountain") rallied at his leadership call and opened their doors for five successive years for the annual GospelFest musical which opened the year of giving for Zeta's scholarship and service fundraising. Pastor Savage gave his generous personal gift and one from the church first. When the first scholarship was awarded, the family said, "We hope this scholarship award highlights a wonderful legacy. We also hope that it serves to encourage students to persevere and aspire to a life lived with character and of service."

These sponsored scholarships not only celebrate the accomplishments of the students but also encourage them toward greater achievements. In awarding the scholarship, preference is given to students determined to complete college degrees despite of extraordinary personal and academic challenges. Grade point averages are important and must be considered, however, Theta Lambda Zeta blazed new paths and included students that needed that "extra" encouragement and acknowledgement. The door is still open for others to follow in the path of charitable giving in the name of Zeta and in honor and memory of others whose lives represent Zeta's principles of scholarship, service and Finer Womanhood.

Doris L. McAdams Memorial Scholarship

Doris McAdams Stokes
Beta Zeta Zeta Chapter, Cincinnati, Ohio

Doris L. McAdams, right, at the 1967 graduation of her daughter (and soon to be Zeta legacy), Doris McAdams Stokes, left.

This scholarship is given in her name by Beta Zeta Zeta Chapter in Cincinnati, Ohio. Soror McAdams became a member of Zeta Phi Beta Sorority in 1943 at Shaw University, Raleigh, North Carolina. The graduate chapter in the city, Omicron Zeta, awarded her a $25 scholarship which paid for her first year's tuition. The following year, she was initiated in Omicron Chapter, Zeta Phi Beta Sorority, on Shaw's campus. She transferred to the Great Lakes Region in 1957, to continue a career in education. She was a natural leader; her dedication to and love of the Sorority was evident. She held numerous positions and served as the 2nd State Director of Ohio from 1962 – 1969.

A consummate Zeta, Soror McAdams lived and practiced the Sorority's ideals and was determined that all other chapter members do so too. She was unwavering in her efforts to make her life, "An example for others to follow." She held three academic degrees and encouraged others, in and out of the Sorority, to continue their education. Scholarship was the one ideal she embraced over the others because it provided opportunities and opened doors.

At her insistence, Beta Zeta Zeta Chapter began awarding scholarships in the 1970s at a public, often Finer Womanhood program. Today, over 40 graduating high school seniors have been recipients of the chapter's scholarship. The award was named after her in 2011, following her death, to recognize her 68 years of active membership in the Sorority and her role in Beta Zeta Zeta Chapter. The 2016 recipient was Kezia Pennington.

Soror Marie Dorsey Memorial Scholarship

Tonya W. Conley
Beta Psi Zeta Chapter
Omaha, Nebraska

Soror Marie Dorsey was a charter member of Beta Psi Zeta Chapter in Omaha, Nebraska. She was a Life Member and always maintained her financial standing with Zeta Phi Beta Sorority, Inc. even after she could no longer participate. She was always dedicated to scholarship and supported one of our chapter scholarships individually from her retirement income. She passed on May 16, 2015 at age 87 after more than 50+ years of dedicated service to Zeta.

Oklahoma Brings Sunshine by Giving PB&J (Pajamas, Books and Joy)

Artisha J. Harris-Woody
Xi Nu Zeta Chapter, Oklahoma City

Snacks, new pajamas, and books that were provided to students at the PB&J event.

Xi Nu Zeta member reading to students.

Seven years ago, the women of the Xi Nu Zeta chapter of Zeta Phi Beta Sorority, Inc. committed to increasing proficient literacy within our local community. Since then, Xi Nu Zeta Chapter has annually hosted "PB&J," our signature program, at inner city elementary schools around the Oklahoma City, metropolitan area. The acronym "PB&J" stands for Pajamas, Books, and Joy.

The primary goals of the PB&J program are to: serve as a catalyst for positive, joyful, childhood memories and quality time spent reading with a parent or guardian; promote literacy; and, give needy children items they might enjoy. Xi Nu Zeta adopts one or two kindergarten or first grade classrooms and then provides each child a book and a pair of new pajamas.

To promote education, chapter members spend time reading to students and encourage the children to read to them. Afterwards, the children take their new books home to read at their own leisure. Xi Nu Zeta counts it a true honor to have been able to bring PB&J to so many children. PB&J is a real simple concept, but it has had a tremendous impact on our children!

A student reading to Xi Nu Zeta members during the PB&J event.

Xi Nu Zeta members supported by Phi Beta Sigma Brothers (Delta Beta Sigma Chapter)
as book donations were given to an inner city elementary school at the conclusion of a PB&J event.

The South Central Region

Ernestine Wilson, Director

One of Zeta Phi Beta Sorority Incorporated's ideals is scholarship! The Unconquerable South Central Region Scholarship Program continues *building on the principles of Zeta while blazing new paths* through scholarship. The South Central Region Scholarship Program supports the Sorority's mission while recognizing student achievement and excellence in and out of the classroom; commitment to community service; and, demonstrated leadership.

The regional scholarship program has reached new horizons in 2014 – 2015. With modern technology, regional scholarship applications are accepted hardcopy and electronically. Since this innovation, the submittal of applications has increased by 200%. Another expansion in the last few years has been the addition of the regional graduate scholarship. The South Central Region has awarded tens of thousands of dollars in scholarships to many deserving and talented Sorors. It is the duty of our dedicated scholarship committee to determine the most outstanding collegiate Zetas to receive the undergraduate and graduate scholarships.

To this end, the goal is to make the dream of a higher education possible by annually awarding scholarships at the South Central Regional Conference. The Unconquerable South Central Region Scholarship Co-Chairpersons are Dr. Theresa Green and Soror Carla Hamilton.

Alabama State Association Scholarships

Mary Foster, Scholarship Chair

In honoring the principles of our Five Founders, the Alabama State Association realized we were not implementing one, Scholarship. In 2008, under the leadership of Soror Veronica Moore-Vinson, State Director, and the Executive Board it was decided that Sorors would benefit from a scholarship offered at the state level. The official name given to this scholarship was:

"Zeta Phi Beta Sorority, Incorporated, Alabama Association." Soror Ida Crawford was appointed as Scholarship Chair in 2008 and served in this position until 2014.

This scholarship is awarded to undergraduate Sorors in the State of Alabama and provides funds for books, school supplies or other necessities for college.

The first scholarship was presented at the 2008 Alabama State Leadership Conference. In keeping with our standard of excellence in education, $1,000 scholarships have been offered since 2008 or at times, $500 book scholarships have been available, along with any television advertisement, newspaper articles and other publications used to promote the Alabama State Scholarship.

Recently another scholarship was introduced to the Alabama State body. The name of this scholarship is "The Alabama State Association Foundation Scholarship". This scholarship is not affiliated with the Alabama State Association Scholarship. The Foundation Scholarship has its' own governing board and will require a separate application process. This scholarship is offered to all students in the state of Alabama, including both high school students and undergraduate Sorors. Scholarships were presented by the Foundation at the 2015 Alabama State Conference.

There are also a number of scholarships offered at the local level by individual chapters throughout the State of Alabama. Applicant(s) will have to contact the chapter(s) in which they are seeking a scholarship for the appropriate application.

State of Arkansas Scholarships and Programs

Kathy R. Tatum, Arkansas State Director

Alpha Mu Zeta Chapter of Little Rock, Arkansas – Profiles of Academic Excellence Scholarship Program

(Formerly, the "Mi Ladi's Scholarship Brunch")

In 1976, the Alpha Mu Zeta Chapter began making plans to host the South Central regional meeting of Zeta Phi Beta Sorority, Inc. It was determined that a fundraising project would be needed to defray the expenses. Soror Levada P. Mason, Alpha Mu Zeta Chapter, dreamed of having an opportunity to sponsor a brunch similar to the one she had observed while working as a home economics teacher in Crittenden County, Arkansas and she presented her idea which was accepted. The *"Mi Ladi's Scholarship Brunch"* became a reality.

Today, the brunch is named "Profiles of Academic Excellence Scholarship Program" which spotlights young women who are high school seniors with a cumulative grade point average of 2.5 or higher, in addition to being actively involved in school, church, and community activities. The Alpha Mu Zeta Chapter is proud of this scholarship program and it is the chapter's goal to consistently promote Scholarship, Service, Sisterhood and Finer Womanhood.

The scholarships are awarded in four categories: academic excellence, essay writing, talent, and community service. Applicants must participate in the Profiles of Academic Excellence program. Awards are presented each spring.

Eta Sigma Zeta – Miss Blue Revue Scholarship Program – North Little Rock, Arkansas

Chartered in 1974, members of Eta Sigma Zeta quickly began to brainstorm ideas about fundraisers and ways to make an impact in the North Little Rock community. The chapter unanimously agreed to sponsor the Miss Blue Revue Pageant, a signature event of Zeta Phi Beta Sorority. Girls in kindergarten and through 8th grade, are highlighted at a pageant, in the areas of talent, interviewing, and poise. A portion of the proceeds raised are used to fund the **Eta Sigma Zeta Scholarship**. Since the inception of Miss Blue Revue, Eta Sigma Zeta has provided scholarships totaling in excess of $70,000.

Applicants must have a minimum grade point average of a 2.5; must be a female senior at an Arkansas High School, graduating that spring; must enroll in and attend an accredited 4 –year Arkansas College or University the next fall semester; and, must attain a minimum ACT score of 19. The criterion used for selecting recipients include: academic achievement, community service and leadership, letters of recommendations, financial need, and interview responses.

Epsilon Zeta Zeta – Pine Bluff, Arkansas

In 1966, Epsilon Zeta Zeta established and currently maintains a permanent Scholarship Fund. Originally a scholarship was awarded each year to a young lady who attends or plans to attend the University of Arkansas at Pine Bluff. In 2010, the Epsilon Zeta Zeta Chapter expanded its scholarship offering to include a book scholarship to a young lady who plans to attend or is attending Southeast Arkansas College. Applicants must have a 3.0 grade point average or higher, community service hours and demonstrate a need. Applications are received, reviewed and awarded during Finer Womanhood month. To date, approximately $70,000 has been awarded to young ladies in Pine Bluff, Arkansas.

Sigma Gamma Zeta – Jonesboro, Arkansas

The Sigma Gamma Zeta Chapter offers a Robert E. Stafford Community Achievement Scholarship. The scholarship provides a nontraditional student with the opportunity to fulfill his or her educational and career goals. The scholarship award is $1,000 paid directly to college and/or university within a 50 mile radius of Jonesboro, AR. This scholarship was created in memory of our chapter's First Anti Basileus' late husband Robert E. Stafford who was very supportive of the chapter and mentored nontraditional college students. Our chapter funds the scholarship through donations, fundraisers, and a portion of all chapter members' local dues.

Applicants must not have attended a college and/or university right after high school; be at least 25 years old and/or have children; and, plan to attend Black River Technical College, Arkansas State University-Jonesboro, or Arkansas State University-Newport (includes campuses in Marked Tree and Jonesboro).

Upsilon Pi Zeta – West Memphis, Arkansas

The Shanto L. Foster Scholarship was implemented in March 2008 in memory of her high achievements in higher education, community service, and charity. The Shanto L. Foster Scholarship provides assistance to citizens who are high school or college students who participate in community service activities and serve as role models for others. The recipient must excel academically. The UPZ Chapter Shanto L. Foster Scholarship is dedicated to providing monetary assistance in addition to serving as a resource for obtaining other financial support towards education. To be eligible, applicants must be high school seniors residing in the Crittenden or Mississippi Counties; perform at least ten hours of community service; have at least a "B" average or a grade point average of 3.0; write a 500 word autobiographical essay; submit two letters of recommendation; and, be interviewed..

Alpha Alpha Nu Zeta – Augusta, Arkansas

Alpha Alpha Nu Zeta, chartered in 2014, offers two book scholarships to deserving high school students.

Theta Gamma Zeta – West Helena, Arkansas

Theta Gamma Zeta offers book scholarships to students on an as needed basis.

The Southeastern Region

Yvonne Jefferson-Barnes, Ph.D., Director

Zeta Phi Beta Sorority's Southeastern Regional Conference, as a body, has established a number of scholarships in honor of distinguished Triumphant Sorors. These scholarships are awarded annually to undergraduate and graduate Sorors who meet the qualifying criteria, and application guidelines which focus on Academic Performance, Finer Womanhood, and Service. General academic scholarships are also awarded by the Region's Amicae Auxiliary.

The **Marian H. Shannon Scholarship** is awarded annually to one undergraduate and one graduate Soror in the amount of $1,000.00 each. Triumphant Soror Marion H. Shannon pioneered the development and growth of the structural model implemented in every region of Zeta Phi Beta Sorority, Incorporated (concept of state meetings). Soror Shannon, Associate Director of the State of Florida under Grand Basileus Lullelia W. Harrison, developed the concept of geographical areas to increase involvement at the grass-roots level in the business and function of Zeta.

Additionally, a scholarship was established in memory of Dr. Eunice S. Thomas, 19th International Grand Basileus and esteemed member of the Southeastern Region, who instituted the first leadership training for chapter presidents. Two $1,200.00 scholarships are given in her name to undergraduate and graduate Sorors.

The Southern Region enhances the Sorority's objective of scholarship through financial support to deserving students in their endeavors to further their educational studies.

The Florida State Leadership Conference

Karen Blount, Director

The Soror Marian H. Shannon Scholarship

In 1946, Marian H. Shannon became a member in the first class of new members for Beta Tau Zeta Chapter in Miami, Florida. In 1948, Nancy B. Woolridge heralded a new emphasis of identifying leadership in the states for the purpose of rendering greater service to individual Zeta chapters within each state. Under the leadership of Sue Jenkins, Associate Director for Florida, informal meetings and gatherings were held at the home of Soror Marian H. Shannon during the summer sessions. Zetas in attendance would congregate to discuss the possibilities for a conference to take care of the concerns for all chapters in Florida. During one of these meetings on the front porch of Soror Shannon's home, the idea blossomed for a statewide conference for Zetas. Soror Shannon was named Associate Director for State of Florida. During her leadership, she developed the concept of geographical areas. Our beloved Soror passed on August 9, 2011. Triumphant Soror Marian H. Shannon was a Diamond Life member.

Under the tenure of Erna M. Foushee, State Director, Florida and the Bahamas Islands, the Marian H. Shannon Scholarship was approved by the Florida delegation in May 2012. Each year the scholarship is awarded to a deserving Florida **graduate** member of Zeta Phi Beta Sorority, Incorporated, who is seeking a post graduate degree in business, education or communications field.

The Soror Laura Saunders Scholarship

Laura Saunders graduated from Florida A&M University in 1945. She was a member of Beta Tau Zeta Chapter until 1983. Soror Saunders and six other members who lived in the South Dade Area thought it was time to charter a chapter to meet the needs of families in the various communities in South Miami-Dade County. On May 28, 1983, Mu Gamma Zeta Chapter was chartered under the sponsorship of Beta Tau Zeta. Laura served as the first Basileus.

As an educator, Laura started as an elementary school teacher. However, she retired as principal of A.L. Lewis Elementary School. The school was re-named in her honor. From 1984 – 1988, she served as a City Commissioner in Florida City. She passed in August 1993. In her honor, the Laura Saunders scholarship was established. It is open to all financial under-**graduate sorors** of Zeta Phi Beta Sorority, Incorporated in the state of **Florida** with a 3.0 GPA or higher

Kappa Iota Zeta Book Scholarship Still Touching . . . Southeastern Region

Tecia M. McKay, Ed.D.
Atlanta, Georgia

Left to right: Soror Tecia McKay, Soror Jenelsia Lovejoy Belt and Dr. Mildred McCoy.

A legacy continues as Kappa Iota Zeta (KIZ) continues to lift the community by shining a light for tomorrow. The chapter has awarded the Marynette Bonner Lovejoy Book Scholarship since 1998. Currently the scholarship is awarded during a reception at the Sigma Zeta Foundation in collaboration with other chapters of Phi Beta Sigma Fraternity and Zeta Phi Beta Sorority.

The KIZ scholarship was originally initiated during the leadership of past chapter president, Soror Linda Isabel. During Soror Isabel's tenure, Soror Lovejoy, a charter member and an ongoing pillar of the chapter, passed. She was a faithful chapter member until the end. In that same year, a suggestion was made that the chapter book scholarship's name be changed to the Marynette Bonner

Lovejoy Scholarship to honor her memory. Given Soror Lovejoy's legacy as a librarian, her volunteerism at the DeKalb and Atlanta community libraries, and, her Zeta contributions (charter member, longest serving regional Amicae Coordinator), the chapter embraced the idea of changing the name. Many Sorors shared stories of the "good Zeta times" held at the home of Soror Lovejoy.

Historically, the chapter implemented the international Zeta tradition of holding a Little Miss Blue Revue pageant as a scholarship fundraiser. During pageant preparation, the participants

engage in meaningful cultural activities as they raise money for the scholarships that they too could receive as high school seniors. In addition to the financial contribution the chapter has always given, the Lovejoy family decided to commit to always giving the gift of reading by giving each recipient a book, the way their mother would have wanted as she believed in everyone being a lifelong learner.

2015 Scholarship Recipients and family members

The chapter began giving away four scholarships annually to high school seniors and over the years, this has expanded to financial KIZ Sorors pursuing graduate degrees, as well as returning young ladies that were previous recipients but are still pursuing bachelor's degrees. As the scholarship committee leadership transitions from Soror Jenelsia Lovejoy Belt, daughter of Lovejoy, (subsequent chairs have been Sorors Thelma Lester, Patrice Joseph, and Dr. Terri Williams) to Soror Tecia McKay, the chapter will award 5 scholarships to high school recipients.

In almost 20 years of book scholarships, under the current leadership of chapter president, Shannon McGuire Lee, KIZ approaches the $50,000 mark in scholarship support. While members secretly hope all recipients will become Zeta ladies, as was the case with two recipients, Sorors Jermise Benefield and Courtney Brooks, we rejoice in the contributions of all recipients and the lives they will touch in the future.

2014 - 16 Scholarship Committee members
Standing: Sorors M. Riley, A.Williams, M. Blount, Dr. M. McCoy, President S. McGuire Lee, T. McKay, J. Ward Williams, O. Holloway, Dr. L. Harris.
Seated: Soror L. Isabel. Front: Soror C. Paige

Phi Omicron Zeta Chapter Southeastern Region

Dorothy Ruffin Moss
Covington-Conyers, Georgia

2010 Scholarship Program, left to right: Gloria Fallings, Evon Mazyck, Sandra Speaks, Chelsea Darrnell (scholarship winner) Tia Cofield (scholarship winner), Audrey Williams, Gladys Gordon, Kathryn Williams, Dalphine Browder and Dorothy Moss.

Phi Omicron Zeta gives two $500.00 scholarships each spring to seniors graduating from high school in Covington or Conyers. The deadline for complete applications is February 28th or 29th. Our past scholarship recipients are Tia Cofield and Chelsea Darnell (2010); Morgan Lett and Teneshia Smith (2011); Darius Stephens and Tiffani Brown Smith (2012); Torri Cofield and Kaycee Wilson (2013); Ifeoma Egbulem and Charles Crowner (2014); and Taylar Reid and Craig Thomas (2015). Phi Omicron Zeta's website is http://zphibpozeta.org.

2014 Scholarship Program, left to right: Dorothy Moss, Tara Seright, Twannekia Glenn, Dalphine Browder, Ifeoma c. Egbulem (scholarship winner), Charles C. Crowner (scholarship winner), Kathryn Williams, Margie Evans, Gloria Fallings and Evon Mazyck.

The Southern Region

Kay Jones-Rosebure, Director

The Southern Region enhances the sorority's objective of scholarship through financial support to deserving students to help in their endeavors to further their educational studies.

The region awards the Southern Region Roberta Bell Scholarships to undergraduate applicants at the region's undergraduate leadership retreat-one recipient from East Texas, one from West Texas and one recipient from Louisiana.

The Zeta Amicae of the Southern Region award three scholarships each year at the Zeta Amicae Regional Leadership Workshop. The awards are: one to Texas honoring Lullelia Walker Harrison, in the amount of $1,500; one to Louisiana honoring Gertrude Jimson, in the amount of $1,500; and one honoring Hazel Wilson, the initiator of Amicae workshops, in the amount of $1,000 to recipients living in the area of the local auxiliary hosting the workshop.

Life Members in the Southern Region present two scholarships during regional conference years. The scholarship for the Texas recipient is named after Past Grand Basileus Lullelia Walker Harrison. The scholarship recipient from Louisiana receives an award named after the first regional director, Roberta Bell.

Noteworthy Accomplishments

In our 96th anniversary year, several Sorors serve as college or university presidents. We salute:

      Dr. Algeania Warren Freeman, Wilberforce University, Wilberforce, Ohio

      Dr. Elmira Mangum, Florida A&M University, Tallahassee, Florida

      Dr. DeRionne P. Pollard, Montgomery College, Rockville, Maryland

We also salute:

Soror Tommie Morton-Young, author and founder of the African American Genealogical and Historical Society of Tennessee. Her book, the *Afro-American Genealogy Sourcebook* (Garland) is nationally recognized among her nine publications.

SCHOLARSHIP REGISTRY

Introduction

Around the world, Sorors, chapters, states and regions plan and implement programs to raise thousands of dollars to fund scholarships that are awarded to students in their communities. This listing recognizes those efforts as voluntarily reported by 54 chapters on the Centennial Website of more than $164,000 for 2015 and/or 2016 in this 96th anniversary year of Zeta Phi Beta Sorority Incorporated. We applaud them and their efforts to perpetuate our national ideal of **Scholarship**.

HOST CHAPTER	REGION	CITY	STATE
Delta Zeta Zeta	Atlantic	Prince George's County	Maryland
Tau Delta Zeta	Atlantic	Laurel	Maryland
Kappa Epsilon Zeta	Atlantic	Bronx	New York
Iota Pi Zeta	Atlantic	Poughkeepsie	New York
Tau Eta Zeta	Atlantic	Baltimore	Maryland
Psi Mu Zeta	Eastern	Charlotte	North Carolina
Nu Xi Zeta	Eastern	Alexandria	Virginia
Eta Phi Zeta	Eastern	Chapel Hill	North Carolina
Phi Gamma Zeta	Eastern	Hopewell	Virginia

HOST CHAPTER	REGION	CITY	STATE
Beta Nu Zeta	Eastern	Greensboro	North Carolina
Tau Theta Zeta	Eastern	Pineville-Matthews	North Carolina
Gamma Zeta Zeta	Great Lakes	Columbus	Ohio
Xi Mu Zeta	Great Lakes	Markham	Illinois
Beta Zeta Zeta	Great Lakes	Cincinnati	Ohio
Tau Xi Zeta	Great Lakes	Forest Park	Illinois
Kappa Beta Zeta	Great Lakes	Milwaukee	Wisconsin
Upsilon Psi Zeta	Great Lakes	Oak Park	Michigan
Eta Zeta	Great Lakes	Louisville	Kentucky
Sigma Iota Zeta	Great Lakes	Reynoldsburg	Ohio
Zeta Zeta Zeta	Midwestern	Aurora	Colorado
Chi Zeta	Midwestern	Oklahoma City	Oklahoma
Zeta Zeta Zeta	Midwestern	Denver	Colorado
Xi Zeta Zeta	Pacific	San Jose	California
Pi Eta Zeta	Pacific	Seoul	Armed Forces Pacific
Alpha Psi Zeta	Pacific	Los Angeles	California
Pi Zeta Zeta	Pacific	San Bernardino / Inland Empire	California
Epsilon Zeta Zeta	South Central	Pine Bluff	Arkansas
Kappa Tau Zeta	South Central	Greenville	Mississippi
Rho Nu Zeta	South Central	Kosciusko	Mississippi
Delta Omega Zeta	South Central	Huntsville	Alabama
Nu Kappa Zeta	South Central	Vicksburg	Mississippi
Alpha Mu Zeta	South Central	Little Rock	Arkansas
Epsilon Zeta Zeta	South Central	Pine Bluff	Arkansas
Pi Zeta	South Central	Antioch	Tennessee
Nu Kappa Zeta	South Central	Vicksburg	Mississippi

HOST CHAPTER	REGION	CITY	STATE
Gamma Phi Zeta	Southeastern	Polk County	Florida
Eta Gamma Zeta	Southeastern	Brunswick	Georgia
Iota Omicron Zeta	Southeastern	Belle Glade	Florida
Phi Phi Zeta	Southeastern	Jasper	South Carolina
Delta Epsilon Zeta	Southeastern	West Palm Beach	Florida
Kappa Iota Zeta	Southeastern	Atlanta	Georgia
Beta Omega Zeta	Southeastern	Albany	Georgia
Chi Pi Zeta	Southeastern	Hinesville	Georgia
Sigma Mu Zeta	Southeastern	Stone Mountain	Georgia
Tau Kappa Zeta	Southern	Slidell	Louisiana
Alpha Pi Zeta	Southern	San Antonio	Texas
Delta Sigma Zeta	Southern	Gainesville	Florida
Mu Omega Zeta	Southern	Natchitoches	Louisiana
Omicron Gamma Zeta	Southern	Clear Lake	Texas

(Compiled from information submitted to www.zphib2020.com)

ZINGERS, QUOTATIONS and SAYINGS

Introduction

Geraldine G. Peeples

The "old sayings" we have heard throughout our lives serve as reminders on how to live, how to prepare ourselves for life in general and/or, prevent ourselves from falling into unwanted situations. Unexpectedly, and often to end a conversation, our grandparents or parents would zap us with them and there would be nothing else that could be said. These words of practical advice for daily living were repeated so often that even today, we still hear the voices of those who stated them in our heads. Zingers are sometimes humorous, other times laden with stern warnings, yet, always full of insight. One just has to "dig a little deeper" or "just live long enough" to extract their meaning. "He is not so wise as he who will not see."

Glory Days – Charise R. Bennett

After my first semester in college, I was in the doldrums. Going from being a 4.0 GPA high school senior to a 2.5 GPA college freshman was a blow to my confidence and made me realize just how much I didn't know as a first generation college student. All I wanted was to turn back the hands of time and go back to my high school "glory days," but it was my grandmother who admonished me to "Get out of my way and make better glory days!" Those words stuck with me, and I have done my best to do just that! Every challenge or trial is an opportunity to create a new glory moment. It's not healthy to dwell on what was, when each day is a new "glory" waiting to happen!

Brittany N. Bilbrew

Be proud of yourself and from where you came.

Taneen D. Brinson, Ed.D.

"Being finer is having a heart for service and the desire to serve."

Dr. Taneen
Brinson

Mother's Wisdom – Kathy F. Collins

My mother always told me, "Just go to school and get what they (the teachers) have to offer." During the mid-1970s, Memphis City Schools began desegregation steps just as I was beginning the tenth grade. African American students were bussed from all black schools, across the city to all white schools. I was one of many students to experience bussing.

Kathy F. Collins

Needless to say, as a fifteen-year-old student, I was unhappy that I could not attend the neighborhood school that I had looked forward to going to since junior high school. Many of my friends went on to attend our neighborhood school and those who did not, used other addresses or signed up for vocational courses, so they could go to the neighborhood school. My mother and uncle both had top positions within the Memphis City Schools and I did not have that option.   I did not enjoy my high school, but I still enjoyed my high school years. I was able to enjoy school social activities with my friends from the neighborhood. I did everything my mother told me to do which well prepared me for college.

My mother continued to instill in me daily, "Kathy, just go to school and get what they have to offer. They (the teachers) are going to teach their own." I did what she told me in a school that, at the time, was known as one of Memphis City Schools' highest academically performing schools. With her words of encouragement, I graduated from high school as an honor roll student, and from college with no academic problems, remedial classes, or class withdrawals. I also graduated in exactly four years and described my college years as "A breeze."

I am now a retired educator, having taught thirty-three years with the Memphis City Schools. I passed my mother's words of wisdom to my students, "Just get what I have to offer." Some career achievements of my former students include: teachers, careers in the military, a model in New York, a high school salutatorian, political candidates, and a guidance counselor for inner city students in Los Angeles, CA. Three of my students are now members of Zeta Phi Beta Sorority, and one is a member of the Amicae auxiliary. My mother's wisdom is the most precious of all life's gifts.

Your Role, Your Choice – LaRita Dalton

In everything we do, there is a process. In this process, we must possess ambition and discipline. We must use ambition and take the necessary steps get moving and the discipline to stay the course and keep going. As has been said, "The world is a stage, and we all have a role to play; it's up to us to try them (the roles)." The roles are limitless. We must find the role that is best for each of us and play that role to the best of our ability. We must understand that there will be successes and failures as we find ourselves perfecting that role but we must never give up. Remember that through it all "all will be well and will continue to be so." In the words of Oprah Winfrey, "What I know is, that if you do work that you love and the work fulfills you, the rest will come." The choice to be excellent begins with aligning our thoughts and words with the intention to require more of ourselves. Whatever our goal, we can get there if we're willing to work. Let her words motivate us to achieve success in whatever we choose to do. The choice is ours and ours to make. All we have to do is give it a try.

Shatonya Latrice Flowers

My parents always said and still say:

"Always go with your first thought. That way you won't have any should've could've would've (thoughts or regrets) down the road." And, "God doesn't take things away to be cruel. He takes things away to make room for other things. He takes things away to lighten us. He takes things away so we can fly."

Janet L. Hearns
Gardner, Ed.D &
Jimmie Hearns (Mother)

Janet L. Gardner, Ed.D.

My mother always said, "God has things for you to do in this life. Do them well."

A Look In The Mirror – Tina L. Johnson

When my siblings and I struggled with a decision we made or would make, my father would always say, "Have you looked in the mirror? Are you going to like the person that you see?" If I look in the mirror and feel good about the person looking back at me, the right decision was made. When my spirit is troubled by the person I see in the mirror, I must determine why. At the end of

Left: Soror Tina L. Johnson, January 17, 2016
Right: My Father, Isaiah Johnson, February 2015

the day, I have to live with my decision and the person in the mirror because that person in the mirror is me!

Learning Is For Life – Rev. Pamela N. Lewis, M.Div.

It is my belief that learning is a lifelong process that should never end, and we should strive to learn something daily. If you don't learn something daily, don't waste deodorant by getting up, taking showers, getting dressed and interacting with others. Make your deodorant count.

Tecia M. McKay, Ed.D.

Left: Picture taken almost 25 years ago. Some of my dearest Clark Atlanta University and DeVry Institute friends teaching me life lessons . . . we are still friends today. (Pictured are V. Pearson, T. McKay, T. Johnson, and Dr. Y. Horton)

Determination is Nothing Without Education: I Didn't Graduate From Clark, but . . .

As a member of a family filled with educators (mother, a retired educator, board member, committee member on many education focus groups, and has a scholarship in her name at Oglethorpe University and nephew and niece, both first year educators), I am a district level administrator and consistently serve on my chapter's scholarship committee, I certainly value all of education and the essence of it. As a woman of Zeta Phi Beta Sorority, I've had the chance to make lifelong friends, many of whom are educators. I also served for several years as an undergraduate advisor, locally, and undergraduate coordinator at the state and regional levels.

Right: Clark Atlanta University Homecoming with Psi Chapter Alumni. Most of these ladies are still active in Kappa Iota Zeta Chapter. (Pictured are M. Riley, Y. Horton, M. Evans, C. Hickman, T. McKay, K. Thompson, K. Scarlet, O. Holloway, and M. Brown)

Although I am a charter member at West Georgia State University (Omicron Nu Chapter), graduate of Fort Valley State (Delta Beta Chapter), with postgraduate degrees from Georgia State University, my words to live by have been adopted from my well-informed friends of Clark Atlanta University (Psi Chapter).

Thank you to my Clark Atlanta U friends. Their college motto is now my own:

"I didn't graduate from Clark, but I know how to Find a Way or Make One."

Might Makes It Right – Maxine Moore-Allen

Soror
Vera M. Moore

My Zeta Mother, Past Eastern Regional Director Vera McIlwaine Moore, always instilled in her children that we must always put our best foot forward and give 110% to everything we hoped to accomplishment. With tenacity and unwavering fortitude, she always said:

"All that you do; do with your might. Things done by half are never done right."

As I look back, those words of wisdom were the guiding light and compass that shaped the lives of her children and she was a Legacy of which I am proud.

Rosanna Nelson

"If you've got time to do it again, you've got time to do it right the first time!"

Said most often around midnight, by my persistent mama to my disgruntled sister as she schlepped back to the kitchen to wash the dishes… again!

"If the fox hadn't stopped to ___, he'd have caught the rabbit."

Said by my father after he'd heard just about all of the excuses he was going to tolerate on a given day.

"Are you going to believe me or your lying eyes?"

This was one of my sister's favorites. I always loved watching the reaction of the person she was speaking to as they began to process what they'd heard.

"You should have left sooner."

I say this most often when someone pulls up on my tail, then starts blinking their lights and blowing their horn.

"I should have left sooner."

The variation I use when I pull up on someone, start blinking my lights and blowing my horn!

"If you don't change your direction, you may end up where you are going."

I first heard this in a meeting of service providers at the VA Hospital in Fort Thomas, KY. I liked its double-entendre and used it often with my students to suggest reconsideration or encourage resolve.

"And this, too, shall pass."

This one, another double-entendre, is my all-time favorite and I've needed to repeat it often to assure that I fully appreciate my good times and remain open to learning from my challenges.

"A lack of planning on your part does not constitute an emergency on mine."

I first saw this ditty one day when, even though I was already running late, I thought I would just run by the Shriners' business office, drop off my rent and be on my way. As I entered the office, a prominently placed sign warned against leaving without a receipt for all transactions. The clerk, with her phone at her ear, had given a quick nod and made a face indicating a difficult caller. She proceeded to work on other items while the call continued and didn't look my way again for quite some time. The longer I stood at the counter, the angrier I became; however, just as I was about to smart off, I glanced down. Amid the Shriner paraphernalia on display was a single sheet of paper with that quote. As soon as the call ended, she turned to me and smiled welcomingly. I cooled my jets, paid my rent and, while she prepared my receipt, jotted down those words. When I finally got to work, I typed the quote on a sheet of paper and posted it on my door as a reminder for my students and myself!

Wisdom – Reatha Nesbitt

Words of wisdom should be ways of wisdom. If you believe in yourself and what you are trying to achieve, ACT like it. Give your goals the attention they deserve.

Geraldine G. Peeples

My mother repeated these sayings often.

The common sense you carry in your purse can't be bought, but you pay a huge price when you don't have it.

Books and boys don't mix!

I may not be as smart as you think I should be, but I passed by the "sense hole" and *looked* in!

My head doesn't screw on and off.

Parents have the mountain top view on life.

Be wary…a little bit of knowledge in the hands of a fool can be a dangerous thing.

In all thy ways acknowledge the Lord and He will direct your path.

The early bird catches the worm.

If you don't have what you want, take what you have and make what you want out of it.

When you don't see a way, make a way!

You don't get to be old and not learn *some*thing.

When they were passing out brains, you must have thought they said 'rain" and went for cover!

Money does not grow on trees.

A Passionate Teacher – Bobbie Nell Crudup Qualls

ON EDUCATION -

"An exemplary teacher leader has a compassionate heart and an authentic desire for every student to succeed. This leader makes a significant difference in the life of every student. She does not let her students 'fall through the cracks.' As a servant leader, she challenges, stimulates, teaches and guides students to *excellence*. Oh, how she loves teaching!"
– May, 1974

"Teach a child to read and you will have a lifelong learner." – August, 1990

"Each child is unique and endowed with a special type of intelligence; I believe every child has something to offer and can learn. We must, therefore, provide the opportunity for all students to receive appropriate instructional strategies and a humanistic approach to learning."
– July, 1997

"Give our children compassionate role models, empower our children to be great leaders, teach our children the power of learning, and our children will give back to the community".
– September, 1997

"Scholarly love is sacrificing one's time, money, experience, knowledge and wisdom for the betterment of humanity." – August, 2014

"Three crucial traits… to always exhibit as an exemplary coach are confidentiality, integrity, and character." – June, 2012

"There are two invaluable gifts I am thankful for – the gift of a biblical foundation of love (charity) and the gift of teaching and educating youth. …my focus was not discipline but teaching and learning. Engaging students with compassion in the learning process was of the utmost importance. Thus, my passion and love for education still lingers…"

ON ZETA --

"Every Zeta has a gift. How will I use my treasure to uphold our Sorority?" – October, 2008

"Sisters, what kind of seeds are we sowing?" – October, 2008

"As I mature more spiritually, I pay less attention to what Sorors say and focus more on their actions." – August, 2013

"I must uphold with integrity the objectives of this world class organization and share resources (human and fiscal) for the love and benefit of Zeta..." – July, 2014

"Visionary, don't rush your journey; allow it to keep expanding and evolving. Time has its own CEO — challenges, experiences and opportunities. The moment of destiny can only be traveled one second at a time. Enjoy your journey!"

ON SELF--

"Strive daily to surround yourself with a clutter free environment; this strategy provides a clutter-free mind, body and soul." – September, 2013

"Align your purpose with your passion. This alignment will create action steps toward your destiny." – March, 2014

"Giving generously from one's heart is a true sign of humility." – September, 2015

"Don't seek recognition, don't boast of what you do or give. Let your work and character speak for themselves." – Catherine Moore Lovelady-Crudup (Bobbie's Mom)

"Thank you God for other people's assistance with *my* bootstraps; I am a testimony... I didn't make it on my own..." – Ms. Q 2016

My First Zeta – Natasha G. Reynolds

In elementary school, I was extremely shy. My brother had recently graduated from the same school and had left a negative imprint on the teachers and staff. I wanted to avoid being seen and was fearful of teachers learning our connection. I often walked with my head down and my eyes on my feet, making no contact with anyone. In the fourth grade, my teacher, Mrs. Brown stopped me in the hallway and said, "Hold your head up. How can you see where you are going? But more importantly, how can you see what is coming?" From that moment, whenever I saw her, I made sure I was looking straight ahead. Eventually, I was always looking straight ahead. Mrs. Brown was my first Zeta, but not my last.

Dawn Marie Sealy, Ed.D.

Receiving my doctorate from St. John's University has been my greatest accomplishment to date. This journey has taught me so much about not only believing in myself, but in the notion that dreams do come true. I leave my Sorors with this verse: "For with God, nothing shall be impossible," Luke 1:37 (KJV).

Doris McAdams Stokes

"It's a poor rat that has one hole."

Soror Doris L. McAdams, my mother, repeated this old saying often to remind me that life or plans do not always happen as you want them to. She further advised that the wise woman needed options or choices - contingency plans - for everything she did. Understanding this nugget of wisdom kept me from falling flat on my face many times. Take a moment to make your plans, then make a plan for if those plans don't work. You will minimize any future disappointments or unmet expectations!

"If you are going to run with the big dogs, learn to pee in tall grass."

Many people seek positions of greater responsibility or power but often forget that when you move up, you have to act differently. At one point in my life, I found myself promoted to another position annually. There would always be different people, different rules and different ways of acting, and I had to follow suit if I wanted to remain in the position, and cash that heftier paycheck. My father, Ernest F. McAdams, often stated this quote when I would complain about the requirements of my position.

Maureen Walker

Always keep trying to do your best, never tiring in your efforts. Even when you want to quit, it's okay to take a breather and then continue. No one ever said it was going to be easy or happen overnight. Life is full of ups and downs. Just ride the waves and get back in there.

Leigh-Ann S. Williams

My mom always says, "Failure to prepare is preparing to fail."

ACADEMIC REGISTRY

Introduction

"Scholarship, we all have a bit," is true. It is a known requirement that members minimally have a bachelor's degree (or be working towards one) to join Zeta Phi Beta Sorority, Incorporated. Many Sorors continue their coursework and research to earn academic or professional degrees, or both, in countless programs throughout the world, after their first degree is conferred. Many toil an additional 2 –15 years on average, juggling families and careers, to earn an advanced degree and joyfully shout "hallelujah" the day it is complete.

In this the 96th anniversary year of Zeta Phi Beta Sorority Incorporated, we acknowledge those members who voluntarily reported their accomplishments.

Academic Registry

TRACY ABBOTT
Ed.S. - Education Specialist
University of Missouri-Kansas City
Specialty: Elementary Administration
Chapter: Upsilon Zeta Zeta
Grandview, Missouri
Region: Midwestern

CYNTHIA AIKEN
M.S., MEd
M.S.Ed. - Master of Science in Education
University of the Incarnate Word
Specialty: Higher Education
Chapter: Alpha Pi Zeta
San Antonio, Texas
Region: Southern

NANDI ALEXANDER
M.S.C.J. - Master of Science in Criminal Justice
Virginia State University
Specialty: Domestic Violence Against Women
Chapter: Omicron Phi Zeta
Washington D.C., District of Columbia
Region: Eastern

RUTH D. ALLEN
M.H.A. - Master of Health Administration
Capella University
Specialty: Health Administration
Chapter: Sigma Nu Zeta
New York, New York
Region: Atlantic

SHAWNIKA ANDERSON
Ed.S. - Education Specialist
Abraham Lincoln Memorial University
Specialty: Supervision, Curriculum and Instruction
Chapter: Rho Xi Zeta
Kennesaw, Georgia
Region: Southeastern

DONNA E. ANDERSON, Esq.
J.D. - Doctor of Jurisprudence
Hofstra University School of Law
Specialty: Labor Law, Administrative Law, Education Law
Chapter: Delta Beta Zeta
Long Island, New York
Region: Atlantic

DEANNA R. ANDREWS
C.P.T., M.S., R.N., C.N.O.R.
M.S. - Master of Science
Touro University
Specialty: Health Science-Public Health
Chapter: Eta Mu Zeta
Tacoma, Washington
Region: Pacific

BRANDY ARCHIE
O.T.D., O.T.R./L.,C.L.V.T., C.D.R.S.
Doctor of Occupational Therapy
Creighton University
Specialty: Certified Low Vision Therapist,
Certified Driving Rehabilitation Specialist
Chapter: Upsilon Zeta Zeta
Grandview, Missouri
Region: Midwestern

SHANEESA N. ASHFORD
M.A. - Master of Arts
University of Georgia
Chapter: Omicron Kappa Zeta
College Park, Georgia
Region: Southeastern

AMANDA AUGUSTE-ROBERTS
M.B.A. - Master of Business Administration
Davenport University
Chapter: Theta Rho Zeta
Lansing, Michigan
Region: Great Lakes

TONJA R AUSTIN
M.D., F.A.A.F.P.
M.D. - Doctor of Medicine
Xavier University of Louisiana and
Northwestern University Mesical School
Specialty: Family Medicine
Chapter: Xi Mu Zeta
Markham, Illinois
Region: Great Lakes

MELISSA L. BAILEY
M.A. - Master of Arts
College of Mount Saint Joseph
Specialty: Middle Childhood Education
Chapter: Beta Zeta Zeta
Cincinnati, Ohio
Region: Great Lakes

TIARA D. BANKS
M.S.W. - Master of Social Work
The University of Illinois at Chicago
Chapter: Tau Psi Zeta
Alsip, Illinois
Region: Great Lakes

JESSICA BANTOM
M.A. - Master of Arts
Marymount University
Specialty: M.A. in Interior Design; Thesis: Color
Education in the Interior Design Curriculum
Chapter: Nu Xi Zeta
Alexandria, Virginia
Region: Eastern

KORTNEE BARNETT
M.S. - Master of Science
University of Tennesee, Knoxville
Specialty: Statistics
Chapter: Sigma Rho Zeta
Cary, North Carolina
Region: Eastern

RAMONA M. BECK
Assistant Dean of Instruction
M.Ed. - Master of Education
Miami University-Oxford
Specialty: Education Leadership
Chapter: Beta Zeta Zeta
Cincinnati, Ohio
Region: Great Lakes

DR. TERRI N. BELL
Ph.D. - Doctor of Philosophy
Capella University
Specialty: Leadership for Higher Education
Chapter: Alpha Alpha Kappa Zeta
Newnan, Georgia
Region: Southeastern

MICHELLE NICOLE BENJAMIN
M.B.A. - Master of Business Administration
University of Texas at Arlington
Specialty: Concentration: Management
Chapter: Kappa Zeta
Dallas, Texas
Region: Southern

SARAH M. BERRY
M.S. - Master of Science
Cardinal Stritch University
Specialty: M.S. in Management, Capstone
Thesis: Women in Management: Does gender
still matter?, December 2009
Chapter: Alpha Gamma Zeta
New Orleans, Louisiana
Region: Southern

HELEN BETEET
R.P.H., M.H.A.
Master of Health Management (Policy)
University of Kansas
Specialty: Pharmacist (clinical management and
consultation); M.S., RA,PsA, Crohn's, HIV, and
oncology
Chapter: Alpha Epsilon Zeta Chapter
Overland Park, Kansas
Region: Midwestern

SHAWNTA N. BIBB
M.S.H.R.M.
Master of Science in Human Resources
Management
Troy University
Specialty: Human Resources
Chapter: Alpha Rho Zeta
Montgomery, Alabama
Region: South Central

ELLEN M. BILLARD
M.B.A., P.M.P.
M.B.A. - Master of Business Administration
University of Dallas
Specialty: Health Services Management, Project
Management
Chapter: Kappa Zeta
Dallas, Texas
Region: Southern

SARAH F. BIVINS
M.S. - Master of Science
University of Wisconsin
Specialty: Family Economics; "Rural Home
Facilities of Macon County, Alabama"
Chapter: Beta Delta Zeta
Philadelphia, Pennsylvania
Region: Atlantic

TAKISHA DENISE BLACK
M.S.F.S. - Master of Science in Forensic Science
The George Washington University
Specialty: Crime Scene Investigation
Chapter: Beta Zeta
Washington, District of Columbia
Region: Eastern

SCARLET H. BLACK
M.Ed. - Master of Education
University of North Carolina at Charlotte &
Clemson University
Specialty: First Master's Degree in Counseling
& Supervision; Second Master's Degree in
Administration & Supervision
Chapter: Nu Delta Zeta Chapter
Travelers Rest, South Carolina
Region: Southeastern

KIMBERLY BLACKWELL
M.Ed. - Master of Education
Texas A&M University-Commerce
Specialty: Educational Administration
Chapter: Kappa Zeta
Dallas, Texas
Region: Southern

MORGAN A. BLOUNT
M.A. - Master of Arts
Webster University
Specialty: Human Resources Management
Chapter: Nu Upsilon Zeta
Temple Terrace, Florida
Region: Southeastern

CUTIA M. BLUNT
Ed.S. - Education Specialist
Kennesaw State University
Specialty: Instructional Technology
Chapter: Rho Epsilon Zeta
Marietta, Georgia
Region: Southeastern

CUTIA M. BLUNT
M.Ed. - Master of Education
Kennesaw State University
Specialty: Educational Leadership
Chapter: Rho Epsilon Zeta
Marietta, Georgia
Region: Southeastern

ANGELA LEE BOLDEN
Ph.D. - Doctor of Philosophy
Howard University
Specialty: Counseling Psychology—Stress,
Coping, African American Women
Chapter: Sigma Rho Zeta
Cary, North Carolina
Region: Eastern

RYUSHIQUE R BONNER
M.S. - Master of Science
The College of New Rochelle
Specialty: Guidance and Counseling
Chapter: Delta Beta Zeta
Queens, New York
Region: Atlantic

CHANDRA L. BOONE
M.Ed. - Master of Education
University of Texas at Arlington
Specialty: Educational Leadership and Policy
Studies
Chapter: Upsilon Nu Zeta
Lancaster, Texas
Region: Southern

SHONDA S. BOSTON
M.Ed. - Master of Education
University of North Texas Dallas
Specialty: M.Ed Curriculum and Instruction
Literacy-Grand Canyon University; M.S. Human
Relations and Business
Chapter: Kappa Zeta
Dallas, Texas
Region: Southern

GLORIA TAYLOR BOUKNIGHT
M.B.A. - Master of Business Administration
American Intercontinental University
Specialty: Healthcare Management, Human
Resources Management
Chapter: Chi Lambda Zeta
Bartlett, Tennessee
Region: South Central

CHANTEL D. BOWIE
M.S. - Master of Science
Florida A & M University
Specialty: Software Engineering; Thesis
Title: Natural Interaction & Communication
Environments
Chapter: Epsilon Beta Zeta
Plant City, Florida
Region: Southeastern

TOWUANNA PORTER BRANNON
Ed.D. - Doctor of Education
Fordham University
Specialty: Executive Leadership, Administration,
and Policy
Chapter: Delta Beta Zeta
Queens, New York
Region: Atlantic

LaCRETIA BRAZZLETON
Bachelor of Science
Eastern Illinois University
Chapter: Tau Psi Zeta
Alsip, Illinois
Region: Great Lakes

BOBBIE BRIDGES
M.A.Ed. - Master of Arts in Education
University of Arkansas
Specialty: Learning Disabilities and
Administration Certification 4-12 Arkansas
Department of Education
Chapter: Epsilon Zeta Zeta
Pine Bluff, Arkansas
Region: South Central

BRITTANY BILBREW
Composite Degree: Physical Wellness
Hope College
Chapter: Tau Psi Zeta
Alsip, Illinois
Region: Great Lakes

BRANDI E. BROWN
M.P.A. - Master of Public Administration
University of Texas at Arlington
Chapter: Theta Mu Zeta
Longview, Texas
Region: Southern

LANIEL M. BROWN
M.B.A. - Master of Business Administration
Strayer University
Specialty: Human Resource Management
Chapter: Rho Eta Zeta
Glen Burnie, Maryland
Region: Atlantic

LEELA M. BRYANT
M.P.A. - Master of Public Administration
Keller Graduate School of Management
Chapter: Rho Xi Zeta
Kennesaw, Georgia
Region: Southeastern

MAXINE C. JONES BRYANT
M.A. - Master of Arts
Morgan State University
Specialty: Music Education; Thesis - "Resource
Materials On Mahalia Jackson: A Chronicle of
Her Life, . . ."
Chapter: Alpha Zeta
Baltimore, Maryland
Region: Atlantic

LESLIE BUCKNER
M.P.T. - Master of Physical Therapy
Marquette University
Specialty: Critical care, women's health, and
wound care
Chapter: Tau Psi Zeta
Alsip, Illinois
Region: Great Lakes

TAMEKA NICHOLE BUFFORD
M.B.A. - Master of Business Administration
Keller Graduate School of Management
Chapter: Tau Psi Zeta
Alsip, Illinois
Region: Great Lakes

ALISA EDMONSON
Associate of Science in Nursing (ASN)/
Bachelor of Science in Nursing (BSN)
Clayton State University/Medical College of
Georgia
Specialty: OB Nursing
Chapter: Sigma Mu Zeta
Stone Mountain, Georgia
Region: Southeastern

MARY GORDON BURTON
M.Ed. - Master of Education
Southern University
Specialty: Administration and Supervision
Chapter: Mu Zeta
Baton Rouge, Louisiana
Region: Southern

MARTHA S. BUTLER
M.A. - Master of Arts
Millersville University
Specialty: M.A. in English; Enrolled in Doctoral
Program at Widener University (Chester, PA):
Teacher Mentoring
Chapter: Epsilon Rho Zeta
Wilmington, Delaware
Region: Atlantic

LaKEESA S. BUTLER
M.S.M.
M.S. - Master of Science
Troy University
Chapter: Alpha Rho Zeta
Montgomery, Alabama
Region: South Central

RENEE' M BUTLER
M.S. - Master of Science
Troy State University Montgomery
Specialty: Counseling and Human Development
Chapter: Alpha Rho Zeta
Montgomery, Alabama
Region: South Central

MARTHA S. BUTLER
M.A. - Master of Arts
Millersville University
Specialty: M.A. in English; Enrolled in Doctoral
Program at Widener University (Chester, PA):
Teacher Mentoring
Chapter: Epsilon Rho Zeta
Wilmington, Delaware
Region: Atlantic

RENEE S. BYRD
M.S.Ed. - Master of Science in Education
Chicago State Universtiy
Specialty: Teaching in a Non-School Setting
Chapter: Tau Psi Zeta
Alsip, Illinois
Region: Great Lakes

SHARON CALHOUN-GETER
M.A.Ed. - Master of Arts in Education
Ohio State University
Specialty: Early & Middle Childhood Education;
Elementary & Middle Childhood Supervisor
Chapter: Gamma Zeta Zeta
Columbus, Ohio
Region: Great Lakes

BENITA A. CANGE
M.S. - Master of Science
University of South Florida
Specialty: Human Resources Management
Chapter: Rho Xi Zeta
Kennesaw, Georgia
Region: Southeastern

STACEY BANFIELD-CAPERS
M.A. - Master of Arts
The Ohio State University
Specialty: Comparative Politics and
International Political Economy - Latin America
and Sub-Saharan Africa
Chapter: Tau Delta Zeta
Laurel, Maryland
Region: Atlantic

SHIRLEY CARO
J.D. - Doctor of Jurisprudence
Northeastern University School of Law
Chapter: Sigma Nu Zeta
Manhattan, New York
Region: Atlantic

JENNETHA C. CARROLL
M.S. - Master of Science
University of Southern Mississippi
Specialty: The Re-Opening of Civil Rights
Cases from the 1960's: Justice Delayed or
Conscience Clearing
Chapter: Lambda Kappa Zeta
Hattiesburg, Mississippi
Region: South Central

KIMBERLY P. CARTER
M.S.N. - Master of Science in Nursing
Morgan State University
Specialty: Nursing Education
Chapter: Tau Eta Zeta
Baltimore, Maryland
Region: Atlantic

KALILAH WILKINSON CATLETT
M.S.E. - Master of Science in Engineering
Johns Hopkins University
Specialty: Systems Engineering
Chapter: Tau Delta Zeta
Laurel, Maryland
Region: Atlantic

TAMELA NICOLE CHAMBERS
M.L.I.S. - Master of Library & Information
Studies
University of Illinois Urbana-Champaign
Chapter: Xi Mu Zeta
Markham, Illinois
Region: Great Lakes

REV. DR. JALENE C. CHASE-SANDS
Doctor of Ministry - Urban Ministry
Wesley Theological Seminary
Specialty: Living In Community: Using the
Policy of the UMC to Order and Revitalize a
Local Church Community
Chapter: Delta Zeta Zeta
Prince George's County, Maryland
Region: Atlantic

JOY KELLOM-CHEATHAM
M.S.Ed. - Master of Science in Education
Purdue Calumet University
Chapter: Zeta Theta Zeta
Gary, Indiana
Region: Great Lakes

CHERYL A. B. CHRISTIE
M.P.A. - Master of Public Administration
The Ohio State University
Specialty: Public Finance; Public Health
Chapter: Gamma Zeta Zeta
Columbus, Ohio
Region: Great Lakes

ANGELA M. CHRISTIE
M.B.A. - Master of Business Administration
Florida A&M University
Specialty: Finance Concentration
Chapter: Gamma Zeta Zeta
Columbus, Ohio
Region: Great Lakes

GWENDOLYN WEBB CLARK
M.Ed. - Master of Education
Xavier University
Chapter: Beta Zeta Zeta
Cincinnati, Ohio
Region: Great Lakes

TIFFANY SIMONE CLEMMONS
M.A. - Master of Arts
Chicago State University
Specialty: Community Counseling
Chapter: Xi Mu Zeta
Markham, Illinois
Region: Great Lakes

TIFFANY CLEMMONS
M.S.Ed. - Master of Science in Education
College of Staten Island and College of Saint
Rose
Specialty: MS Ed- Education Administration;
MS Ed- Special Education
Chapter: Tau Eta Zeta
Baltimore, Maryland
Region: Atlantic

SAUNDRA M. COCHRAN
M.A.
M.A.Ed. - Master of Arts in Education
The Ohio State University
Specialty: Gifted Education, Reading, Reading
Supervisor
Chapter: Gamma Zeta Zeta
Columbus, Ohio
Region: Great Lakes

VANESSA COLE
M.P.H. - Master of Public Health
New York University
Chapter: Delta Beta Zeta
Queens, New York
Region: Atlantic

DANIELLE M. COLEMAN
M.S.N., R.N.
M.S.N. - Master of Science in Nursing
Governors State University
Specialty: Clinical Nurse Specialist
Chapter: Tau Psi Zeta
Alsip, Illinois
Region: Great Lakes

KATHERINE GLOVER-COLLINS
Dr.P.H. - Doctor of Public Health
McHarry Medical School
Specialty: Breast Cancer - BRA Ca-1 Res.
Chapter: Epsilon Zeta Zeta
Pine Bluff, Arkansas
Region: South Central

KATHY F. COLLINS
M.A.Ed. - Master of Arts in Education
Lemoyne -Owen College
Specialty: Elementary Education
Chapter: Alpha Eta Zeta
Memphis, Tennessee
Region: South Central

YULONDA R CONLEY
M.Ed. - Master of Education
Grand Canyon University
Specialty: Education Administration
Chapter: Kappa Zeta
Dallas, Texas
Region: Southern

ANDRIA L. COOK
M.B.A. - Master of Business Administration
Strayer University
Specialty: Finance
Chapter: Nu Xi Zeta
Alexandria, Virginia
Region: Eastern

MARY A. COOLEY-LIDDELL
Ed.S. - Education Specialist
Capella University
Specialty: Leadership Administration
Chapter: Epsilon Zeta Zeta
Pine Bluff, Arkansas
Region: South Central

ROBBIN COOPER
M.B.A. - Master of Business Administration
Concordia University Chicago
Specialty: Leadership and Change Management
Chapter: Xi Mu Zeta
Markham, Illinois
Region: Great Lakes

JOSEPHINE COPELAND
M.B.A. - Master of Business Administration
Franklin University
Specialty: Master of Business Administration;
Focus: Leadership
Chapter: Gamma Zeta Zeta
Columbus, Ohio
Region: Great Lakes

SHIRLEY FITZGERALD CORRY
J.D. - Doctor of Jurisprudence
Nashville School of Law
Chapter: Psi Phi Zeta
Thompsons Station, Tennessee
Region: South Central

BRITTANY N. COURSE
C.S.M., M.B.A.
M.B.A. - Master of Business Administration
Belhaven University
Specialty: Concentration: Leadership
Chapter: Alpha Eta Zeta
Memphis, Tennessee
Region: South Central

SAMANTHA TUBBS-CREWS
Mental Health Counseling
Nova Southestern University
Specialty: Mental Health Counseling/
Psychotherapy
Chapter: Nu Upsilon
Temple Terrace, Florida
Region: Southeastern

ASHLEY DALE
M.A. - Master of Arts
Concordia University
Specialty: Educational Administration
Chapter: Tau Psi Zeta
Alsip, Illinois
Region: Great Lakes

ANGIE DALEY
M.B.A. - Master of Business Administration
Roosevelt University
Specialty: Marketing and Integrated Marketing
Communications
Chapter: Tau Psi Zeta
Alsip, Illinois
Region: Great Lakes

IANA J. DANIELS
M.S., M.A.
M.A. - Master of Arts
Webster University
Specialty: Management and Leadership, and
Human Resources Development
Chapter: Rho Xi Zeta
Kennesaw, Georgia
Region: Southeastern

IANA J. DANIELS
M.S., M.A.
M.S. - Master of Science
Georgia Institute Of Technology
Specialty: Building Construction and Facilities
Management
Chapter: Rho Xi Zeta
Kennesaw, Georgia
Region: Southeastern

JENNIFER R. DAVIS, Esq.
J.D. - Doctor of Jurisprudence
New York Law School
Specialty: Intellectual Property & Transactions
Chapter: Delta Beta Zeta
Queens, New York
Region: Atlantic

MONIQUE I. DAVIS
J.D. - Doctor of Jurisprudence
Southern University Law Center
Chapter: Beta Epsilon Zeta
Shreveport, Louisiana
Region: Southern

JULIE MARKS DICK
M.A. - Master of Arts
Ball State University
Specialty: Student Personel Administration in
Higher Education. Praticum in Multicultural
Affairs.
Chapter: Gamma Zeta Zeta
Columbus, Ohio
Region: Great Lakes

KELLIE M DIXON
M.S. - Master of Science
Longwood University
Chapter: Omega Beta Zeta
Farmville, Virginia
Region: Eastern

CAROLYN D. DOZIER
M.S. - Master of Science
Wilmington University
Specialty: Human Resource Management and
Public Administration
Chapter: Epsilon Rho Zeta
Wilmington, Delaware
Region: Atlantic

CHARBET M. DUCKETT
C.P.A., C.G.F.M.
Certified Public Accountant
James Madison University
Specialty: accounting
Chapter: Delta Zeta Zeta
District Heights, Maryland
Region: Atlantic

TRACEY M. DUNCAN
Ed.S., Ph.D., LPC, ACS
Ph.D. - Doctor of Philosophy
Drexel University
Specialty: Research- Family Therapy,
Addictions Counseling, Multicultural
Counseling Competencies with Clients
Chapter: Eta Omicron Zeta Chapter
Plainfield, New Jersey
Region: Atlantic

DEEDRA DEYER-MINTER
M.S.W. - Master of Social Work
University of South Carolina
Specialty: Social Work
Chapter: Gamma Zeta Zeta
Columbus, Ohio
Region: Great Lakes

BRITTANI EARL
M.P.A. - Master of Public Administration
Bellevue University
Chapter: Sigma Gamma Zeta
Jonesboro, Arkansas
Region: South Central

PAMELA EASON
M.P.A. - Master of Public Administration
Western Michigan University
Specialty: Community Health/Health
Administration
Chapter: Beta Zeta
Washington, District of Columbia
Region: Eastern

JOCELYN EDEL, CPA
M.S. - Master of Science
Portland State University
Specialty: Financial Analysis
Chapter: Rho Epsilon Zeta
Marietta, Georgia
Region: Southeastern

DAWN C. EDWARDS
Pharm.D. - Doctor of Pharmacy
Xavier University of Louisiana
Chapter: Xi Mu Zeta
Markham, Illinois
Region: Great Lakes

QUEEN EKOBENA
M.S., L.P.C., N.C.C., Q.M.H.P.
M.S. - Master of Science
South Dakota State University
Specialty: Clinical Mental Health, Sex Therapy,
Marriage and Family Therapy
Chapter: Kappa Zeta
Dallas, Texas
Region: Southern

MISTY B. ELLERBY
M.S. - Master of Science
Langston University
Specialty: Rehabilitation Counseling
Chapter: Beta Phi Zeta
Langston, Oklahoma
Region: Midwestern

JANICE S. EVANS
M.A. - Master of Arts
State University of New York at Stony Brook
Specialty: Urban and Policy Science
Chapter: Nu Upsilon Zeta
Temple Terrace, Florida
Region: Southeastern

DEBRA P. EVANS
Master's in Management
George Washington University
Specialty: Program Management
Chapter: Omega Pi Zeta
Evanston, Illinois
Region: Great Lakes

DEBRA P. EVANS
M.M.E. - Master of Mechanical Engineering
University of Illinois
Specialty: Fracture Mechanics
Chapter: Omega Pi Zeta
Evanston, Illinois
Region: Great Lakes

ANISSA EVANS BUCKNER
D.Sc. - Doctor of Science
Purdue University
Specialty: Molecular Biology; Dissertation:
HIV-1 Gene Regulation; Research: Ocular
Virology
Chapter: Epsilon Zeta Zeta
Pine Bluff, Arkansas
Region: South Central

M. SHAYLA EVANS LEE
Dr.P.H. - Doctor of Public Health
University of Arkansas for Medical Sciences
Specialty: Public Health
Chapter: Epsilon Zeta Zeta
Pine Bluff, Arkansas
Region: South Central

M. SHAYLA EVANS
Dr.P.H., C.H.E.S.
Dr.P.H. - Doctor of Public Health
University of Arkansas for Medical Science
Specialty: Program Evaluation & Health Policy
Chapter: Epsilon Zeta Zeta
Pine Bluff, Arkansas
Region: South Central

MARCIA MOTEN EXUM
M.A. - Master of Arts
The Catholic University of America
Specialty: Secondary Education
Chapter: Beta Zeta
Washington, District of Columbia
Region: Eastern

NATALIE R. EXUM-PETERS
M.B.A. - Master of Business Administration
American Intercontinental University
Specialty: Project Management/General
Management
Chapter: Sigma Zeta Zeta
Jersey City, New Jersey
Region: Atlantic

KIMBERLYN M. FAULKNER
M.Ed. - Master of Education
University of North Carolina at Greensboro
Specialty: Special Education K-12
Chapter: Eta Pi Zeta
Silver Spring, Maryland
Region: Atlantic

TIFFINI BYRD FERDINAND
Pharm.D. - Doctor of Pharmacy
Florida A&M University-College of Pharmacy
& Pharmaceutical Sciences
Specialty: Pharmacy, Pharmacy Practice
Residency-Miami VA Medical Center, Humana
Pharmacy Champion
Chapter: Upsilon Alpha Zeta
Pembroke Pines, Florida
Region: Southeastern

SHARON H. FLETCHER
D.Min.
Doctorate in Religious Counseling
GMOR Theological Institute
Specialty: Religious Counseling, Biblically
Based Therapy Contrasted With Psychotherapy,
Societal Norms
Chapter: Epsilon Zeta Zeta
Pine Bluff, Arkansas
Region: South Central

ARIELA FLORENTINO
M.A. - Master of Arts
CUNY-Brooklyn College
Specialty: Mental Health Counseling; Advance
Certificate in Grief Counseling
Chapter: Sigma Nu Zeta
Manhattan, New York
Region: Atlantic

ANIKA STERLING FLOREZ
M.A. - Master of Arts
Northeastern Illinois University
Specialty: Inner City Studies; I researched the
history of sexism in the Black Church.
Chapter: Tau Psi Zeta
Alsip, Illinois
Region: Great Lakes

SHATONYA LATRICE FLOWERS
M.S. - Master of Science
Roosevelt University
Specialty: Journalism
Chapter: Tau Psi Zeta
Alsip, Illinois
Region: Great Lakes

ANJYLLA Y. FOSTER
M.A. - Master of Arts
University of Cincinnati
Specialty: Communication with a focus on urban
media and its perceptions in society
Chapter: Alpha Alpha Mu Zeta
Kenton County, Kentucky
Region: Great Lakes

KAREN A. FRANKLIN
M.B.A. - Master of Business Administration
Keller Graduate School/DeVry University
Specialty: Marketing
Chapter: Xi Mu Zeta
Markham, Illinois
Region: Great Lakes

MIRIAM JACKIE HINES FRY
M.A., M.S.
M.A. - Master of Arts
Tuskegee University - Clark -Atlanta University
Specialty: M.A. - Thesis: The Black
Woman As Viewed In African-American
Newspapers-1875-1895.   (Atlanta Univ)
Chapter: Zeta Theta Zeta
Gary, Indiana
Region: Great Lakes

NATASHA GREEN
M.S.Ed. - Master of Science in Education
College of Saint Rose
Specialty: School Administration
Chapter: Delta Beta Zeta
Queens, New York
Region: Atlantic

NATASHA GREEN
M.Ed. - Master of Education
Queens College
Specialty: Secondary Education
Chapter: Delta Beta Zeta
Queens, New York
Region: Atlantic

SHAROLYN A. GAILLIARD
M.Div. – Master of Divinity
Howard University
Chapter: Delta Zeta Zeta
Prince George's County, Maryland
Region: Atlantic

JANET L. GARDNER
Ed.D. - Doctor of Education
Roosevelt University
Specialty: The Relationship Between 3rd Grade
Reading Scores & Direct Instruction Based On
Teachers' Attitudes
Chapter: Xi Mu Zeta
Markham, Illinois
Region: Great Lakes

MELRITA M. GARRETT-JOHNSON
M.S.W. - Master of Social Work
University of Arkansas at Little Rock
Chapter: Epsilon Zeta Zeta
Pine Bluff, Arkansas
Region: South Central

NEFFIE GATEWOOD
M.Eng. - Master of Engineering
Christian Brothers University
Specialty: My degree is Master of Engineering
Management M.E.M.
Chapter: Psi Beta Zeta
Southaven, Mississippi
Region: South Central

MATTIE GLOVER
M.S. - Master of Science
Alabama A&M University
Specialty: Cytogenetic, in the field of
Argiculture; The production Of Wheat and Rye
Amphiploids
Chapter: Epsilon Zeta Zeta
Pine Bluff, Arkansas
Region: South Central

KATHERINE GLOVER-COLLIN
Ph.D. - Doctor of Philosophy
Meharry Medical College
Specialty: Cancer Biology; Nuclear Export of
BRCA1occurs During Early S Phase and is
Calcium -dependent
Chapter: Epsilon ZetaZeta
Pine Bluff, Arkansas
Region: South Central

VESTA GODWIN CLARK
M.A. - Master of Arts
William Paterson University
Specialty: Non Profit Management; Thesis - The
Church - The Pillar of the Community
Chapter: Eta Omicron Zeta
Plainfield, New Jersey
Region: Atlantic

AVIS Y. GORDON
C.E.M., M.M.P.A.
M.P.A. - Master of Public Administration
Roosevelt University
Specialty: Utilization of Social Media in
Nonprofit Organizations to Recruit and Retain
Members
Chapter: Tau Psi Zeta
Alsip, Illinois
Region: Great Lakes

ALEXIS C. GRAHAM
Ed.S. - Education Specialist
Oakland University
Chapter: Lambda Rho Zeta
Pontiac, Michigan
Region: Great Lakes

AMBROSIA K GRANT
M.Ed. - Master of Education
University of Holy Cross
Specialty: Master of Education Leadership
Chapter: Omicron Sigma Zeta
Baton Rouge, Louisiana
Region: Southern

ISIDRA GRANT
Master of Arts in Community Health Promotion
Adelphi University
Chapter: Delta Beta Zeta
Queens, New York
Region: Atlantic

CAROL M. GRANT, LMSW
M.S.W. - Master of Social Work
Adelphi University
Specialty: Clinical social work with children
and families. Child welfare and Behavioral
Health Integration.
Chapter: Delta Beta Zeta
Queens, New York
Region: Atlantic

GRACE N. GRIFFIN
M.S. - Master of Science
Kettering University
Specialty: OPERATIONS MANAGEMENT
Chapter: Beta Zeta Zeta
Cincinnati, Ohio
Region: Great Lakes

MIRANDA GRIFFIN
M.B.C. - Master of Building Construction
Auburn University
Chapter: Omicron Pi Zeta
Niceville, Florida
Region: Southeastern

ALLISON E. GROOMES, CPA
M.B.A. - Master of Business Administration
Florida A & M University
Specialty: Accounting
Chapter: Rho Xi Zeta
Kennesaw, Georgia
Region: Southeastern

PAMELA GUTTER
M.B.A. - Master of Business Administration
St Xavier University
Specialty: Financial Fraud Examination for Non Profit
Chapter: Xi Mu Zeta
Lynwood, Illinois
Region: Great Lakes

LeQUANDRA RANIECE HALE-BANKS,
L.M.S.W.
M.S.W. - Master of Social Work
Georgia State University
Specialty: Child Welfare, Mental Health & Substance Abuse, Child & Family, Community Based, Medical Health
Chapter: Kappa Iota Zeta
East Point, Georgia
Region: Southeastern

COURTNEY HALL
M.S. - Master of Science
The University of Southern Mississippi
Specialty: Medical Laboratory Science
Chapter: Theta Psi Zeta
Panama City, Florida
Region: Southeastern

MONIQUE HALL
J.D. - Doctor of Jurisprudence
The Ohio State University
Chapter: Gamma Zeta Zeta
Columbus, Ohio
Region: Great Lakes

SHERITA HALL
M.A. - Master of Arts
Norfolk State University
Specialty: Public Relations, How to Increase Attendance at Female Sporting Events.
Chapter: Psi Mu Zeta
Charlotte, North Carolina
Region: Eastern

LORI A. HALL-DIAZ
M.B.A., M.P.M.
Master of Project Management
Keller Graduate School of Management
Chapter: Gamma Zeta Zeta
Columbus, Ohio
Region: Great Lakes

LORI A. HALL-DIAZ
M.B.A., M.P.M.
M.B.A. - Master of Business Administration
Keller Graduate School of Management of DeVry University
Chapter: Gamma Zeta Zeta
Columbus, Ohio
Region: Great Lakes

DeETRA LaSHAN HANKINS-TRUE
M.A.T. - Master of Arts in Teaching
Liberty University
Specialty: Elementary Education
Chapter: Rho Xi Zeta
Kennesaw, Georgia
Region: Southeastern

CHAKITA SHANTE HARGROVE
Ph.D. - Doctor of Philosophy
Capella University
Specialty: The Affect of Antisocial Behavior and Self-Concept on Adolescent Females Reoffending
Chapter: Epsilon Beta Zeta
Plant City, Florida
Region: Southeastern

E. JEAN HARPER
Ph.D. - Doctor of Philosophy
University of Akron
Specialty: Dissertation Title: An Empirical Study of Teacher Perceptions of Their Role in Curriculum Change...
Chapter: Gamma Zeta Zeta
Columbus, Ohio
Region: Great Lakes

DONNA LYNN HARRIS
M.A. - Master of Arts
Chicago State University
Specialty: Psychology / Community Counseling
Chapter: XI Mu Zeta
Chicago, Illinois
Region: Great Lakes

ARTISHA J. HARRIS-WOODY
M.B.A. - Master of Business Administration
Oklahoma Christian University
Chapter: Xi Nu Zeta
Midwest City, Oklahoma
Region: Midwestern

TANYA "T. LYNN" HARRISON
M.A. - Master of Arts
Bellevue University
Specialty: Leadership
Chapter: Kappa Zeta
Dallas, Texas
Region: Southern

SHERIEE K. DAVIS HART
J.D. - Doctor of Jurisprudence
Georgia State University College of Law
Chapter: Kappa Iota Zeta
Atlanta, Georgia
Region: Southeastern

MARISSA HARVEY
M.B.A. - Master of Business Administration
Saint Leo University
Specialty: Specialization in Accounting
Chapter: Rho Xi Zeta
Kennesaw, Georgia
Region: Southeastern

LaSHAN A. HAYES
M.S. - Master of Science
Amridge University
Specialty: Human Services
Chapter: Pi Eta Zeta
Seoul (Korea), Armed Forces Pacific
Region: Pacific

DIANE RENEE HEATH
M.B.A. - Master of Business Administration
Trident University
Specialty: Concentration in Human Resources
Chapter: Alpha Alpha Gamma Zeta
Phenix City, Alabama
Region: South Central

DIANE HEATH
M.B.A. - Master of Business Administration
Trident University
Specialty: Master's degree in Business
Administration with a concentration in Human
Resources
Chapter: Alpha Alpha Gamma Zeta
Phenix City, Alabama
Region: South Central

DEIRDRE JOY HENDERSEN
M.S. - Master of Science
Indiana Institute of Technology
Specialty: Management Science
Chapter: Xi Mu Zeta
Markham, Illinois
Region: Great Lakes

KIARA S. HENDERSON
B.A. Elementary Education
Aurora University
Chapter: Tau Psi Zeta
Alsip, Illinois
Region: Great Lakes

LaSHONDA HENDERSON
L.M.H.C., M.C.A.P., M.A.
M.A. - Master of Arts
Webster University
Specialty: Mental Health and Addiction
Counseling
Chapter: Zeta Eta Zeta
Fort Pierce, Florida
Region: Southeastern

CONSTANCE SMITH HENDRICKS
Ph.D., R.N., F.A.A.N.
Ph.D. - Doctor of Philosophy
Boston College
Specialty: Clinical Nursing Research/Health
Promotion
Chapter: Psi Gamma Zeta
Auburn, Alabama
Region: South Central

DENISHA L. HENDRICKS
Ed.D. - Doctor of Education
Auburn University
Specialty: Higher Education Administration/
Sport Management
Chapter: Tau Psi Zeta
Alsip, Illinois
Region: Great Lakes

JOELLA HENRY
M.B.A. - Master of Business Administration
Franklin University
Specialty: Leadership
Chapter: Gamma Zeta Zeta Chapter
Reynoldsburg, Ohio
Region: Great Lakes

ALEESHA LEE HERRING
M.A. - Master of Arts
Webster University
Specialty: Counseling w/ an emphasis in mental health.
Chapter: Alpha Alpha Phi Zeta
Laurinburg, North Carolina
Region: Eastern

ANGELYA HIGGINBOTHAM
M.P.H. - Master of Public Health
Saint Louis University
Specialty: Environmental & Occupational Health/Biosecurity and Disaster Preparedness
Chapter: Zeta Beta Zeta
Flint, Michigan
Region: Great Lakes

DIANA LISA HILAIRE
M.Pr.S. - Master of Professional Studies
Georgetown University
Chapter: Delta Beta Zeta
Queens, New York
Region: Atlantic

RHEA HILL, LCSW
M.A. - Master of Arts
The University of Chicago School of Social Service Administration
Specialty: Clinical social work; mental health and veteran services
Chapter: Rho Xi Zeta
Kennesaw, Georgia
Region: Southeastern

YEISHA HINDS
M.S.W. - Master of Social Work
Yeshiva University
Chapter: Sigma Nu Zeta
New York, New York
Region: Atlantic

BIANCA DANIELLE HOWELL
M.S. - Master of Science
University of Wisconsin-Madison
Specialty: Educational Leadership and Policy Analysis
Chapter: Kappa Beta Zeta
Milwaukee, Wisconsin
Region: Great Lakes

SHAE M. HUDSON
M.S.Ed. - Master of Science in Education
SUNY OSWEGO
Specialty: Childhood Education 1-6
Chapter: Rho Epsilon Zeta
Marietta, Georgia
Region: Southeastern

FLORENTINE HUMPHREY
M.A.Ed. - Master of Arts in Education
University of Arkansas at Fayetteville
Specialty: Vocational Business Education
Chapter: Epsilon Zeta Zeta
Pine Bluff, Arkansas
Region: South Central

ISI IKHAREBHA
M.P.H. - Master of Public Health
The Ohio State University
Specialty: Population Health Management
Chapter: Sigma Iota Zeta
Reynoldsburg, Ohio
Region: Great Lakes

NELL WILLIAMS INGRAM
Ph.D. - Doctor of Philosophy
University of North Texas
Specialty: Adult/Continuing Education, major; Vocational Education, minor; Personnel Relations (related area)
Chapter: Kappa Zeta
Dallas, Texas
Region: Southern

SANDRA C. INGRAM-JOHNSON
M.A. - Master of Arts
George Washington University
Specialty: Universite de Paul Valery, Montpellier, France; GWU: Secondary Vocational Special Education
Chapter: Beta Zeta Chapter
Washington, District of Columbia
Region: Eastern

NASTASSIA IRELAND-MERRIWEATHER
M.S.J.P.S. - Master of Science in Justice and
Public Safety
University of Phoenix
Specialty: Master of Science in Administration
of Justice and Security
Chapter: Epsilon Zeta Zeta
Pine Bluff, Arkansas
Region: South Central

HANNAH DAVONNE JACKSON
D.V.M. - Doctor of Veterinary Medicine
University of Georgia College of Veterinary
Medicine
Chapter: Beta Zeta Zeta
Cincinnati, Ohio
Region: Great Lakes

SHERRI JACKSON
M.S. - Master of Science
Capella University
Chapter: Sigma Nu Zeta
New York, New York
Region: Eastern

DEMETRA JACKSON WILLIAMS
Ed.S. - Education Specialist
Lincoln Memorial University
Chapter: Sigma Omega Zeta
Clayton/Henry Counties, Georgia
Region: Southeastern

PHYLLIS JEANS, Assistant Professor
M.S.N. - Master of Science in Nursing
Union University
Specialty: Images of Caring from non-traditional
BSN students in an accelerated program
Chapter: Alpha Eta Zeta
Memphis, Tennessee
Region: South Central

TAMARA SHANAE JEFFER
M.Ed. - Master of Education
Lamar University
Specialty: School Counseling
Chapter: Kappa Zeta
Dallas, Texas
Region: Southern

ROBBIE L. JEWELL
M.A.T. - Master of Arts in Teaching
National-Louis
Chapter: Tau Psi Zeta
Alsip, Illinois
Region: Great Lakes

DAWN YOUNG ROMAIN JOHNS
M.Ed. - Master of Education
Howard University
Specialty: School Psychology and Sociology
Chapter: Beta Zeta
Washington, District of Columbia
Region: Eastern

DEIRDRA R. JOHNSON
M.S. - Master of Science
Ohio State University
Specialty: Master of Science in Food Science
and Nutrition; Thesis: Electrostatic Powder
Coating of Snack Foods
Chapter: Epsilon Zeta Zeta
Pine Bluff, Arkansas
Region: South Central

BARBARA J JOHNSON
Ph.D. - Doctor of Philosophy
Vanderbilt University
"Specialty: Higher Education; Research: Faculty
socialization at Historically Black Institutions"
Chapter: Zeta Tau Zeta
Chicago, Illinois
Region: Great Lakes

SARAH MARIE JOHNSON
M.P.A. - Master of Public Administration
Troy University
Specialty: Public Administration
Chapter: Omicron Pi Zeta
Niceville, Florida
Region: Southeastern

COURTNEY C. JOHNSON
Bachelor of Liberal Arts and Science
University of Illinois at Chicago
Specialty: Gender and Women's Studies
Chapter: Tau Psi Zeta
Alsip, Illinois
Region: Great Lakes

JANICE M.T. JOHNSON
M.Ed. - Master of Education
Wilmington University
Specialty: Elementary and Secondary School
Counseling
Chapter: Epsilon Rho Zeta
Wilmington, Delaware
Region: Atlantic

TINA L. JOHNSON
M.Ed.
M.A.Ed. - Master of Arts in Education
Converse College, Wheelock College, and
University of South Carolina
Specialty: Wheelock - Elementary Ed; Converse
- Gifted Ed; USC Columbia - Educational
Administration
Chapter: Mu Pi Zeta
Beaufort, South Carolina
Region: Southeastern

KELLYE JOHNSON
M.B.A. - Master of Business Administration
University of Phoenix
Specialty: Accounting
Chapter: Xi Nu Zeta
Midwest City, Oklahoma
Region: Midwestern

ALISHA L. JOHNSON
M.S. - Master of Science
Central Michigan University
Specialty: Human Resources Administration
Chapter: XI PSI ZETA
Honolulu, Hawaii
Region: Pacific

DANNÉ L. JOHNSON
J.D. - Doctor of Jurisprudence
George Washington University, National Law
Center
Chapter: Chi Zeta
Oklahoma City, Oklahoma
Region: Midwestern

SHANNON TENNILLE JOHNSON
M.P.A. - Master of Public Administration
Western International University
Specialty: Thesis Title: Satisfaction Issues in
the Tempe Police Department Communications
Bureau
Chapter: Delta Gamma Zeta
Phoenix, Arizona
Region: Pacific

CLAUDIA D. JONES
M.S.Ed. - Master of Science in Education
University of Dayton
Specialty: Educational Administration
Chapter: Gamma Zeta Zeta
Columbus, Ohio
Region: Great Lakes

DONNA PENNIE JONES
M.Ed. - Master of Education
University of Houston Victoria
Specialty: Counseling
Chapter: Gamma Omega Zeta
Houston, Texas
Region: Southern

CANDACE L. JONES
M.P.A. - Master of Public Administration
University of North Carolina at Charlotte
Specialty: Higher Education data analytics
Chapter: Psi Mu Zeta
Charlotte, North Carolina
Region: Eastern

VERLION JORDAN
M.A.Ed. - Master of Arts in Education
Florida A&M University
Specialty: Education
Chapter: Nu Upsilon Zeta
Temple Terrace, Florida
Region: Southeastern

CHRISTINA RAE JUNIOR
M.S.A.
M.S. - Master of Science
Trinity Washington University
Specialty: Human Resource Management -
Analysis of Entry Level programs in the Federal
Government
Chapter: Eta Pi Zeta
Silver Spring, Maryland
Region: Atlantic

PAULA A. KAY
M.A. - Master of Arts
University of South Florida
Specialty: Criminology/ Racial/Ethnic
Differences of Women in Florida Prisons
Chapter: Nu Upsilon Zeta
Temple Terrace, Florida
Region: Southeastern

KEISHA L KEMPER
M.Ed. - Master of Education
University of Cincinnati
Specialty: Health Education
Chapter: Beta Zeta Zeta
CINCINNATI, Ohio
Region: Great Lakes

KRISTINA D. KEYS
M.S., Ph.D., A.S.C.P.
Ph.D. - Doctor of Philosophy
Morehouse School of Medicine
Specialty: Doctor of Philosophy in Biomedical
Sciences; Microbiology/Virology/Molecular
Biology
Chapter: Omicron Kappa Zeta
College Park, Georgia
Region: Southeastern

MARKETA HUDSON KILLINGBECK
M.B.A. - Master of Business Administration
University of Phoenix
Chapter: Sigma Mu Zeta
Stone Mountain, Georgia
Region: Southeastern

YVETTE A. KINCHELOW-SMITH
M.A. - Master of Arts
Bowie State University
Specialty: Mental Health Counseling,
Psychologist Associate and Licensed Graduate
Practicing Clinician (LGPC)
Chapter: Beta Zeta
District of Columbia, District of Columbia
Region: Eastern

OLLIE KING
Ed.S. - Education Specialist
Arkansas State University (ASU)
Specialty: Leadership Administration
Chapter: Epsilon Zeta Zeta
Pine Bluff, Arkansas
Region: South Central

KAREN H. KING
M.B.A. - Master of Business Administration
Mercer University
Chapter: Rho Xi Zeta
Kennesaw, Georgia
Region: Southeastern

MICHELLE T. LANGHAM-ROBINSON, Esq.
J.D. - Doctor of Jurisprudence
Southern University Law Center
Specialty: Corporate Generalist; Commercial/
Residential Real Estate
Chapter: Kappa Iota Zeta
Atlanta, Georgia
Region: Southeastern

NICOLE LANGSTON
M.S.W. - Master of Social Work
University of Illinois at Chicago
Chapter: Tau Psi Zeta
Alsip, Illinois
Region: Great Lakes

LEAH BAILEY LANGSTON, Esq.
J.D. - Doctor of Jurisprudence
Depaul University College of Law
Chapter: Tau Psi Zeta
Alsip, Illinois
Region: Great Lakes

ZSHOAN M. LATHAN
M.S.Ed. - Master of Science in Education
Eastern Illinois University
Specialty: Educational Psychology of Guidance
and Counseling
Chapter: Tau Psi Zeta
Alsip, Illinois
Region: Great Lakes

JANNORA LAUDERDALE
M.Ed.
M.A. - Master of Arts in Education
Ferris State University
Specialty: Mathematics, Curriculum &
Instruction, Proposal and Grant Writing
Chapter: Zeta Beta Zeta
Flint, Michigan
Region: Great Lakes

LYNÉA N. LAWS
Ph.D. - Doctor of Philosophy
Capella University
Specialty: Educational leadership, special education, ESL, standardized testing, and achievement
gap
Chapter: Kappa Iota Zeta
Atlanta, Georgia
Region: Southeastern

RHONDA M. LAWSON
Doctoral Candidate
Northcentral University
Specialty: Doctorate of Business Administration
with an emphasis in Organizational Leadership
Chapter: Alpha Alpha Theta Zeta
Belgium, Armed Forces Europe
Region: Atlantic

MONICA M. LEAK
M.A., CCC-SLP
M.A. - Master of Arts
South Carolina State University
Specialty: Speech Language Pathology and
Audiology
Chapter: Nu Xi Zeta
Alexandria, Virginia
Region: Eastern

LEANNA LEVEL
M.A. - Master of Arts
Ball State University
Specialty: Student Affairs Administration in
Higher Education
Chapter: Iota Zeta
Indianapolis, Indiana
Region: Great Lakes

CAROL E. LEWIS
M.S. - Master of Science
Indiana University
Specialty: Elementary Education
Chapter: Mu Tau Zeta
Indianapolis, Indiana
Region: Great Lakes

REV. PAMELA N. LEWIS
M.Div. – Master of Divinity
Howard University
Specialty: Ministry
Chapter: Omicron Phi Zeta
Washington, District of Columbia
Region: Eastern

MRS. SONYA LOCKETT
M.L.S. - Master of Library Science
Texas Woman's University
Specialty: (not listed)
Chapter: Epsilon Zeta Zeta
Pine Bluff, Arkansas
Region: South Central

DAWN A. LOTT, Esq.
J.D. - Doctor of Jurisprudence
Benjamin N. Cardozo School of Law
Specialty: Employment and Labor Law
Chapter: Rho Omega Zeta Graduate Chapter
Great Neck, New York
Region: Atlantic

CRYSTAL A. LOTTERBERRY
M.H.S., L.C.D.C.
M.H.S. - Master of Health Science
Governora State University
Specialty: Addiction Studies
Chapter: Upsilon Nu Zeta
Lancaster, Texas
Region: Southern

ANNA LOVELACE WARE
MS.Ed.
M.Ed. - Master of Education
Chicago State University
Specialty: Curriculum & Instructions, Teaching
in a Non-School Setting. Correlation betw mom
weight & child wt
Chapter: Tau Psi Zeta
Alsip, Illinois
Region: Great Lakes

BERNARDINE E. LOWERY-CRUTE
M.L.I.S. - Master of Library & Information
Studies
Queens College, CUNY
Specialty: Library Media Specialist
Chapter: Sigma Nu Zeta Chapter
New York, New York
Region: Atlantic

GAYLE M. LYKE
M.T. (A.S.C.P.), M.S.H.A.
M.S.H.A. - Master of Science in Health
Administration
Southern New Hampshire University
Chapter: Delta Zeta Zeta
District Heights, Maryland
Region: Atlantic

MITZI J. MACK
Ed.D. - Doctor of Education
Argosy University
Specialty: Education, Instructional Leadership
Chapter: Nu Upsilon
Temple Terrace, Florida
Region: Southeastern

OLAYINKA O. MAJEKODUNMI
R.N., B.S.N.
M.S.N. - Master of Science in Nursing
The George Washington University
Specialty: Nurse Leadership and Management
Chapter: Omicron Phi Zeta
Washington, District of Columbia
Region: Eastern

BARBARA MARBLEY
Master of Addiction Studies
University of Arkansas at Pine Bluff
Chapter: Epsilon Zeta Zeta
Pine Bluff, Arkansas
Region: South Central

JASMINE NICOLE MARSHALL
M.A.T. - Master of Arts in Teaching
University of Chicago
Chapter: Tau Psi Zeta
Alsip, Illinois
Region: Great Lakes

ELISE J. MASON
M.B.A. - Master of Business Administration
Strayer University
Chapter: Rho Xi Zeta Chapter
Kennesaw, Georgia
Region: Southeastern

DAVONNE FELICIA MATTHEWS
M.P.A. - Master of Public Administration
Metropolitan College of New York
Specialty: Non-Profit Organization; THESIS-
New Employee Orientation
Chapter: Sigma Nu Zeta
New York, New York
Region: Atlantic

ALBERTA MAYBERRY
M.S. - Master of Science
U. S. Naval War College
Specialty: National Security and Strategic
Studies; Interagency information sharing and
strategic planning
Chapter: Beta Phi Zeta
Langston, Oklahoma
Region: Midwestern

ALBERTA G. J. MAYBERRY
Ph.D.
M.L.I.S. - Master of Library & Information
Studies
Atlanta University (now Clark Atlanta
University)
Specialty: Academic Library Management
Chapter: Beta Phi Zeta
Langston, Oklahoma
Region: Midwestern

ALBERTA G. J. MAYBERRY
Ph.D. - Doctor of Philosophy
University of North Texas
Specialty: Interdisciplinary Doctorate with
emphasis in Library, Information, and
Management Sciences
Chapter: Beta Phi Zeta
Langston, Oklahoma
Region: Midwestern

JACQUEL J. McDONALD
M.S.N., RN-BC
M.S.N. - Master of Science in Nursing
Walden University
Specialty: Nursing Informatics
Chapter: Gamma Nu Zeta
Camden, New Jersey
Region: Atlantic

MESHELL D. McGEE
Master's in Community Counseling
Argosy University
Specialty: Mental Health
Chapter: Tau Psi Zeta
Chicago, Illinois
Region: Midwestern

TECIA MCGRUDER MCKAY
Ed.S. - Education Specialist
Georgia State University
Specialty: Educational Leadership (School
Improvement / School Change)
Chapter: Kappa Iota Zeta
Atlanta, Georgia
Region: Southeastern

BRIDGET T. McRAE-BUTLER
M.H.R.M. - Master of Arts in Human Resources
Management
Webster University
Chapter: Delta Zeta
Charlotte, North Carolina
Region: Eastern

RASHUNDA SIMS MENDY
M.B.A., M.Ed.
M.A.Ed. - Master of Arts in Education
Dallas Baptist University, Louisiana Tech
University
Chapter: Upsilon Nu Zeta
Lancaster, Texas
Region: Southern

CHARLOTTE F. MILLER
M.Ed. - Master of Education
Mississippi State University
Specialty: Educational Leadership
Chapter: Rho Nu Zeta
Kosciusko, Mississippi
Region: South Central

CATHY COPELAND MOCK
M.P.A. - Master of Public Administration
Northeastern University
Chapter: Gamma Zeta Zeta
Columbus, Ohio
Region: Great Lakes

IEISHA MONTGOMERY
M.A. - Master of Arts
University of Manchester
Specialty: International Political Economy
Chapter: Xi Mu Zeta
Markham, Illinois
Region: Great Lakes

DEANNE S. MOORE
M.A. - Master of Arts
California State University Northridge
Specialty: K-12 Educational Administration
Chapter: Omega Iota Zeta
Kansas City, Missouri
Region: Midwestern

MICHELLE D. MORRIS
M.B.A. - Master of Business Administration
Keller Graduate School of Management
Specialty: Information Systems
Chapter: Tau Psi Zeta
Alsip, Illinois
Region: Great Lakes

TERRAE PARHAM MORRIS
Ed.S. - Education Specialist
University of Missouri at Kansas City
Specialty: Building Level Adminstration
Chapter: Omega Iota Zeta
Kansas City, Missouri
Region: Midwestern

BRENDA MOUNT
M.A. - Master of Arts
University of Phoenix
Specialty: Organizational Management
Chapter: Nu Upsilon Zeta
Temple Terrace, Florida
Region: Southeastern

MALIYKA A. MUHAMMAD
M.A., M.P.H.
M.P.H. - Master of Public Health
Benedictine University
Specialty: Health Policy and Administration
Chapter: Sigma Nu Zeta
New York, New York
Region: Atlantic

JENNIFER MUMFORD
M.P.H. - Master of Public Health
Trident University International
Specialty: Public Health Education/ Health
Disparities
Chapter: Mu Lambda Zeta
Jacksonville, North Carolina
Region: Eastern

TRINA DENISE MURPHY
M.B.A. - Master of Business Administration
Keller Graduate School of Management
Chapter: Xi Mu Zeta
Markham, Illinois
Region: Great Lakes

CAROLYN COLLINS MURPHY
M.P.A., M.C.R.P.
M.U.R.P. - Master of Urban and Regional
Planning
The Ohio State University
Specialty: Public Administration and Urban and
Regional Planning
Chapter: Xi Gamma
Columbus, Ohio
Region: Great Lakes

SANDRA MARSHALL MURRAY
M.L.I.S. - Master of Library & Information
Studies
Clark Atlanta University
Specialty: Special Libraries
Chapter: Omicron Kappa Zeta
College Park, Georgia
Region: Southeastern

LENICE NELSON
M.S. - Master of Science
Long Island University
Specialty: Sports Medicine
Chapter: Sigma Nu Zeta
New York, New York
Region: Atlantic

ROSANNA M. NELSON
M.Ed. - Master of Education
University of Cincinnati
Specialty: Curriculum and Instruction,
Specialization in Reading
Chapter: Beta Zeta Zeta
Cincinnati, Ohio
Region: Great Lakes

JENNIFER E. NELSON-CRISS
M.B.A. - Master of Business Administration
University of Phoenix
Specialty: Human Resource
Chapter: Sigma Mu Zeta
Stone Mountain, Georgia
Region: Southeastern

LETICIA NICHOLSON
M.B.A. - Master of Business Administration
Winston Salem State University
Chapter: Delta Kappa Zeta
Greensboro, North Carolina
Region: Eastern

DARCELL NORWOOD-BAUGH
M.B.A. - Master of Business Administration
University of St. Francis
Chapter: Tau Psi Zeta
Alsip, Illinois
Region: Great Lakes

KATE NKECHI OFIKURU
M.A., M.Div.
Master of Divinity & Master of Arts in
Curriculum & Teaching
Alliance Theological Seminary; Teachers
College, Columbia University
Specialty: Biblical & Theological Studies,
Hebrew (Alliance); Inclusive Elementary
Education (Teachers College
Chapter: Sigma Nu Zeta
New York, New York
Region: Atlantic

KEYONA OWENS
M.B.A. - Master of Business Administration
University of Phoenix
Chapter: Rho Xi Zeta
Marietta, Georgia
Region: Southeastern

LAVONIA A. PAGE
M.A. - Master of Arts
Eastern University
Chapter: Rho Chi Zeta
Chester, Pennsylvania
Region: Atlantic

ELIZABETH SHERON PARSONS
R.N., M.S.N., W.H.N.P., N.E.
M.S.N. - Master of Science in Nursing
University of South Alabama
Specialty: Women's Health Nurse Practitioner;
Nursing Education
Chapter: Alpha Alpha Gamma Zeta
Phenix City, Alabama
Region: South Central

THERESA D. PATTERSON
M.B.A. - Master of Business Administration
Jones International
Specialty: Financial Planning and Accountant
Chapter: Delta Beta Zeta
Queens, New York
Region: Atlantic

JOANNE McDOUGAL PATTERSON
D.N.P., M.S.N., P.M.H.N.P.
D.N.P. - Doctor of Nursing Practice
Brandman University, Part of the Chapman
University System
Specialty: Psychiatric Mental Health Nurse
Practitioner specializing in women's and infant
mental health
Chapter: Kappa Iota Zeta
Dacula, Georgia
Region: Southeastern

NICOLE R. PENNINGTON
M.B.A. - Master of Business Administration
Judson University
Specialty: Organizational Leadership
Chapter: Zeta Nu Zeta
Inkster, Michigan
Region: Great Lakes

LESLIE L. PERKINS
M.S. - Master of Science
Radford University
Specialty: Counselor Education, College Student
Personnel Concentration
Chapter: Tau Delta Zeta
Laurel, Maryland
Region: Atlantic

MINISTER DORRELL B PERRY
Bachelor of Business Administration Accounting
Major
Robert Morris University
Specialty: My Area of Specialization is in
Accounting and Management.
Chapter: Tau Psi Zeta
Alsip, Illinois
Region: Great Lakes

SYLVIA M. PERRY
Pharm.D. - Doctor of Pharmacy
Xavier University of Louisiana
Chapter: Kappa Zeta
Dallas, Texas
Region: Southern

BEVERLY JEAN PILLOW
M.I.S.,M.B.A.,M.S.L.
M.B.A. - Master of Business Administration
Grand Canyon University
Specialty: I have 3 Master's degrees: Master
of Information Science and Master of Science
Leadership with an MBA
Chapter: Beta Zeta Zeta
Cincinnati, Ohio
Region: Great Lakes

ROSHANDA RENEE PINSON
M.S. - Master of Science
University of Wisconsin-Milwaukee
Specialty: Higher Education Administration
Chapter: Nu Upsilon Zeta
Temple Terrace, Florida
Region: Southeastern

TUCCOA S. POLK
M.P.A. - Master of Public Administration
Golden Gate University
Specialty: Non profit Management
Chapter: Kappa Zeta
Dallas, Texas
Region: Southern

ROSALYN BECTON POPE
M.B.A. - Master of Business Administration
Tennessee State University
Specialty: Business Administration
Chapter: Psi Phi Zeta
Thompsons Station, Tennessee
Region: South Central

MICHELE E. POSEY-JOHNSON
M.S. - Master of Science
Roosevelt University
Specialty: Human Resources Management
Chapter: Xi Mu Zeta Chapter
Markham, Illinois
Region: Great Lakes

NAKKI ANGELA PRICE
B.S., M.P.H., P.M.P.
M.P.H. - Master of Public Health
University of South Florida
Specialty: International Health Management
Chapter: Nu Xi Zeta
Alexandria, Virginia
Region: Eastern

MONIQUE PURIFOY-ROJAS
M.B.A. - Master of Business Administration
Troy University
Specialty: Management
Chapter: Rho Xi Zeta
Kennesaw, Georgia
Region: Southeastern

BOBBIE CRUDUP QUALLS
M.Ed. - Master of Education
University of Louisville
Chapter: Eta Zeta Chapter
Louisville, Kentucky
Region: Great Lakes

JACQUELINE DOZIER RALLS
M.Ed. - Master of Education
The Ohio State University
Specialty: Educational Policy and Leadership
Chapter: Gamma Zeta Zeta
Columbus, Ohio
Region: Great Lakes

SHANTI N. RAY
M.B.A. - Master of Business Administration
University of Phoenix
Specialty: Business Administration
Chapter: Omicron Kappa Zeta
College Park, Georgia
Region: Southeastern

PAMELIA W. READUS
M.B.A. - Master of Business Administration
Nova Southeastern University
Specialty: Business and Entrepreneurship
Chapter: Delta Omega Zeta
Huntsville, Alabama
Region: South Central

CYNTHIA D. REDFEARN
M.S. - Master of Science
Central Michigan University
Specialty: Administration
Chapter: Tau Nu Zeta
Monroe, North Carolina
Region: Eastern

ELIZABETH REED-SMITH
M.Ed. - Master of Education
University of Texas at Arlington
Specialty: Curriculum and Instruction
Chapter: Upsilon Nu Zeta
Lancaster, Texas
Region: Southern

ANGELA L. REED JOHNSON
M.B.A. - Master of Business Administration
Keller School of Business
Specialty: Human Resources
Chapter: Nu Beta Zeta
Radcliff, Kentucky
Region: Great Lakes

ELIZABETH THOMAS REEVES
M.D. - Doctor of Medicine
University of Maryland, Baltimore
Specialty: FAMILY MEDICINE
Chapter: OMICRON THETA ZETA
Fairfax, Virginia
Region: Eastern

JOSETTE MONIQUE RICE
M.B.A. - Master of Business Administration
Texas A&M University-Texarkana
Specialty: Marketing
Chapter: Alpha Pi Zeta
San Antonio, Texas
Region: Southern

LORAINE K. RICHARDSON McCRAY
B.A., M.A., M.S., A.G.C., S.D.L.
M.S. - Master of Science
Stony Brook University
Specialty: Technological Systems Management -
Educational Computing
Chapter: Rho Omega Zeta
Long Island, New York
Region: Atlantic

KRATRINA RICHARDSON-COOPER
M.S.Ed. - Master of Science in Education
Walden University
Chapter: Upsilon Nu Zeta
Lancaster, Texas
Region: Southern

BRENDA DIANE CARROLL RITTMAN
M.Ed. - Master of Education
Capella University
Specialty: Educational Leadership
Chapter: Mu Pi Zeta
Beaufort, South Carolina
Region: Southeastern

CRYSTAL R. RIVERS
R.N., B.S., B.S.E.D., M.H.S.A.
Master of Health Services Administration
Xavier University
Chapter: Beta Zeta Zeta
Cincinnati, Ohio
Region: Great Lakes

SHANELL L. ROBINSON
M.Ed. - Master of Education
CUNY - Baruch College
Specialty: Education Administration/
Supervision; Nonprofit Management
Chapter: Delta Beta Zeta
Queens, New York
Region: Atlantic

SHANELLE RODRIGUES
M.P.A. - Master of Public Administration
John Jay
Specialty: Duel specialization in Criminal
policy & management & Operation
Chapter: Sigma Nu Zeta
New York, New York
Region: Atlantic

JERILYN ROGERS
M.B.A. - Master of Business Administration
Troy University
Chapter: Alpha Alpha Gamma Zeta
Phoenix City, Alabama
Region: South Central

VALINDA N SAMPLES
M.Ed.
M.A.Ed. - Master of Arts in Education
Texas Woman's University
Specialty: Special Education
Chapter: Kappa Zeta
Dallas, Texas
Region: Southern

KAREN WRIGHT SANDERS
M.B.A. - Master of Business Administration
Temple University
Specialty: General & Strategic Management
Chapter: Beta Delta Zeta
Philadelphia, Pennsylvania
Region: Atlantic

FELICE SANDERS-JOHNSON
D.Min.
M.L.A. - Master of Liberal Arts
Southern Methodist University
Chapter: Upsilon Nu Zeta
Lancaster, Texas
Region: Southern

WALTORIA SANKEY
M.S.H.R.M.
M.S. - Master of Science
Troy University
Specialty: Human Resources Management
Chapter: Alpha Rho Zeta
Montgomery, Alabama
Region: South Central

KOLLIE SAYGBE, LMSW
M.S.W. - Master of Social Work
Fordham University
Chapter: Sigma Nu Zeta
New York, New York
Region: Atlantic

LASHELLE SCOTT
M.P.M. - Master of Project Management
Keller Graduate
Specialty: Project Management
Chapter: Kappa Iota Zeta
East Point, Georgia
Region: Southeastern

ANNIKA SCOTT, LMSW
M.S.W. - Master of Social Work
Fordham University
Chapter: Delta Mu Zeta
New York City, New York
Region: Atlantic

ANDREA CHRISTINA SCOTT, LCSW
M.S.W. - Master of Social Work
Columbia University
Chapter: Delta Beta Zeta
Long Island, New York
Region: Atlantic

DAWN-MARIE SEALY
Ed.D. - Doctor of Education
St. John's University
Specialty: The Impact Professional Development
Involving Technology Has on the 8th Grade
Reading NAEP
Chapter: Delta Beta Zeta
Queens, New York
Region: Atlantic

CINNAMON SHEFFIELD
Ed.D. - Doctor of Education
University of North Texas
Specialty: Higher Education; "Preferred qualifi-
cations of collegiate athletic directors:..."
Chapter: Kappa Zeta
Dallas, Texas
Region: Southern

JALISSA T. SHELBY
B.A. Psychology
Chicago State University
Specialty: Mental Health
Chapter: Tau Psi Zeta
Alsip, Illinois
Region: Great Lakes

LaDONN SHELTON
R.N., M.S.N.
M.S.N. - Master of Science in Nursing
Walden University
Specialty: Nurse Educator for nursing practice
Chapter; TPZ
Alsip, Illinois
Region: Great Lakes

MARGE L. SIMS
M.Ed. - Master of Education
Western Governors University, Concordia
University Portland
Specialty: 5-9 Math Education; Educational
Leadership
Chapter: Kappa Zeta
Dallas, Texas
Region: Southern

VALERIE A. SINCLAIR, LPC
M.A. - Master of Arts
Webster University
Specialty: Human Resources Development;
Licensed Professional Counselor
Chapter: Alpha Alpha Phi Zeta
Laurinburg, North Carolina
Region: Eastern

VALERIE A. SINCLAIR, LPC
M.S. - Master of Science
Southern Christian University
Specialty: Marriage and Family Therapy; North
Carolina Licensed Professional Counselor
Chapter: Alpha Alpha Phi Zeta
Laurinburg, North Carolina
Region: Eastern

DR. BRANDI MICHELE SINGLETON
P.T., D.P.T., C.C.I.
D.P.T. - Doctor of Physical Therapy
Armstrong Atlantic State University
Specialty: Geriatrics. Thesis project presented at
APTA CSM Conference in 2012.
Chapter: Psi Mu Zeta
Charlotte, North Carolina
Region: Eastern

LYNETTE R. F. SMITH
M.S. - Master of Science
Howard University
Specialty: Research Microbiology/Immunology
Chapter: Beta Zeta
Washington, District of Columbia
Region: Eastern

NATASHA NICOLE SMITH
M.L.I.S. - Master of Library & Information
Studies
Wayne State University
Chapter: Sigma Iota Zeta
Reynoldsburg, Ohio
Region: Great Lakes

GWENDOLYN D. SMITH
M.Ed. - Master of Education
American College of Education
Specialty: Curriculum and Instruction
Chapter: Xi Mu Zeta
Markham, Illinois
Region: Great Lakes

GWENDOLYN D. SMITH
M.Ed. - Master of Education
American College of Education
Specialty: Educational Leadership
Chapter: Xi Mu Zeta
Markham, Illinois
Region: Great Lakes

ANGELA MH SMITH
M.S., B.S.N.
M.S. - Master of Science
Mount Carmel College of Nursing
Specialty: Nursing Education
Chapter: Gamma Zeta Zeta
Columbus, Ohio
Region: Great Lakes

NATASHA NICOLE SMITH
M.L.I.S. - Master of Library & Information
Studies
Wayne State University
Chapter: Sigma Iota Zeta
Reynoldsburg, Ohio
Region: Great Lakes

EUPHEMIA RENEE' SMITH
M.B.A. - Master of Business Administration
Kaplan University
Chapter: Mu Zeta
Baton Rouge, Louisiana
Region: Region:

LYNETTE ROBERTA FRANCIS SMITH
M.S. - Master of Science
Howard University
Specialty: Microbiology/Immunology;
Registered Patent Agent; United States Patent
and Trademark Office
Chapter: Beta Zeta Chapter
Washington, District of Columbia
Region: Southern

SHIRLEY RUTH STANSBERRY
Ph.D. - Doctor of Philosophy
University of Denver
Specialty: Thesis – Students' Achievement &
Attitudes in Geometry,1996; (Administration,
Curriculum, & Math)
Chapter: Chi Kappa Zeta
Benton Harbor, Michigan
Region: Great Lakes

ASHLEY C. STEWARD, LMSW
M.S.W. - Master of Social Work
Arkansas State University
Chapter: Epsilon Zeta Zeta
Pine Bluff, Arkansas
Region: South Central

JENELL B STEWART
M.A.Ed. - Master of Arts in Education
Brooklyn College CUNY
Specialty: Elementary Special Education
Chapter: Sigma Nu Zeta
Harlem, New York
Region: Atlantic

DR. ANJANETTE M. STEWART
Ph.D. - Doctor of Philosophy
Capella University
Specialty: An Examination of Bullying From
The Perspectives of Public And Private High
School Children
Chapter: Alpha Theta Zeta
Savannah, Georgia
Region: Southeastern

DORIS McADAMS STOKES
M.A. - Master of Arts
University of Cincinnati
Specialty: Employee and Labor Relations
Chapter: Beta Zeta Zeta
Cincinnati, Ohio
Region: Great Lakes

DEWANA STRAUDER
M.S. - Master of Science
University of Phoenix
Specialty: Master of Science in Curriculum and
Instruction Emphasis Computer Technology
Chapter: Xi Epsilon Zeta
Natchez, Mississippi
Region: South Central

JANINE I.G. STULTZ
M.S. - Master of Science
Columbia University
Specialty: Negotiation and Conflict Resolution
Chapter: Sigma Nu Zeta
New York City, New York
Region: Atlantic

SHERRY ANN STURGEON
M.P.A. - Master of Public Administration
Florida International University
Chapter: Eta Nu Zeta
Miami Gardens, Florida
Region: Southeastern

NAKIA R. STURRUP
Ed.D. - Doctor of Education
Nova Southeastern University
Specialty: Instructional Leadership
Chapter: Nu Upsilon Zeta
Temple Terrace, Florida
Region: Southeastern

NAKIA R. STURRUP
M.Ed. - Master of Education
University of West Florida
Specialty: Educational Leadership
Chapter: Nu Upsilon Zeta
Temple Terrace, Florida
Region: Southeastern

NAKIA R. STURRUP
M.B.A. - Master of Business Administration
Strayer University
Specialty: Human Resource Management
Chapter: Nu Upsilon Zeta
Temple Terrace, Florida
Region: Southeastern

MIRIAM SUMMERVILLE DUFER
M.F.A. - Master of Fine Arts
National University
Specialty: Creative Writing/
Thesis: Korean Voodoo
Chapter: Lambda Theta Zeta
Gordo, Alabama
Region: South Central

MIRIAM SUMMERVILLE DUFER
M.A. - Master of Arts
California State University Dominguez Hills
Specialty: Humanities with a concentration in
Literature. Published Thesis. Research: Identity
Theory in Race
Chapter: Beta Eta Zeta
Tuscaloosa, Alabama
Region: South Central

MICHELLE LYNETTE SWEAT, Esq
J.D. - Doctor of Jurisprudence
Salmon P. Chase College of Law
Chapter: Beta Zeta Zeta
Cincinnati, Ohio
Region: Great Lakes

DIEDRA N. TATE
M.S. - Master of Science
University of Tennessee-Knoxville
Specialty: Sports Studies/Management
Chapter: Tau Psi Zeta
Alsip, Illinois
Region: Great Lakes

ROBERTA M TAYLOR
Pharm.D. - Doctor of Pharmacy
Hampton University
Specialty: Clinical Pharmacist
Chapter: Sigma Psi Zeta
Fort Washington, Maryland
Region: Atlantic

CHARLOTTE DENISE TAYLOR
J.D. - Doctor of Jurisprudence
DePaul University
Specialty: Law
Chapter: Rho Omega Zeta
Great Neck, New York
Region: Atlantic

ARLENE MJ TAYLOR
M.S. - Master of Science
The Ohio State University
Specialty: Mathematics; Thesis Title -
Convergence and Summability in the Theory of
Fourier Series
Chapter: Gamma Zeta Zeta
Columbus, Ohio
Region: Great Lakes

JYLLA MOORE TEARTE
Ph.D. - Doctor of Philosophy
Benedictine University
Specialty: Organization Development; Cracking
the Transition Code: A Paradigmatic Framework
of Competencies that Construct the Reality of
50+ Black Executive Transitions
Chapter: Xi Mu Zeta
Markham, Illinois
Region: Great Lakes

JYLLA MOORE TEARTE
Ph.D.
M.B.A. - Master of Business Administration
Indiana University
Specialty: Marketing
Chapter: Xi Mu Zeta
Markham, Illinois
Region: Great Lakes

IZETTA N. THOMAS
M.Ed. - Master of Education
The Ohio State University
Specialty: Special Education/Early Childhood
Intervention Specialist
Chapter: Gamma Zeta Zeta
Columbus, Ohio
Region: Great Lakes

ANDREA THOMAS
Ed.D. - Doctor of Education
Nova Southeastern University
Specialty: Organizational Leadership-Early
Intervention Program in Georgia
Chapter: Sigma Omega Zeta
Clayton County, Georgia
Region: Southeastern

PATRICIA A. THOMAS
Ph.D.
M.A. - Master of Arts
George Washington University
Specialty: Clinical Mental Health Counseling
Chapter: Omicron Theta Zeta
Fairfax, Virginia
Region: Eastern

PATRICIA A. THOMAS
Ph.D.
M.A. - Master of Arts
Teachers College, Columbia University
Specialty: Curriculum & Teaching
Chapter: Omicron Theta Zeta
Fairfax, Virginia
Region: Eastern

PATRICIA A. THOMAS
Ph.D.
M.Ed. - Master of Education
Teachers College, Columbia University
Specialty: Curriculum & Teaching, with a spe-
cialization in Urban & Multicultural Education
Chapter: Omicron Theta Zeta
Fairfax, Virginia
Region: Eastern

PATRICIA A. THOMAS
Ph.D. - Doctor of Philosophy
Emory University
Specialty: Educational Studies, with special-
izations in Second Language Acquisition &
Multicultural Education
Chapter: Omicron Theta Zeta
Fairfax, Virginia
Region: Eastern

KATHLEEN TURNER THOMAS
M.A. - Master of Arts
Teachers College, Columbia University
Specialty: Elementary Education: Early
Childhood Education Specialty
Chapter: Beta Zeta
Washington, District of Columbia
Region: Eastern

MARY A. T. TILLMAN
M.D. - Doctor of Medicine
Howard University
Specialty: PEDIATRICS; FELLOW,
AMERICAN ACADEMY OF PEDIATRICS
Chapter: XI ZETA
St. Louis, Missouri
Region: Midwestern

CHEVON ANISE TOLER
M.S. - Master of Science
Central Michigan University
Specialty: Human Resources
Chapter: Gamma Zeta Zeta
Columbus, Ohio
Region: Great Lakes

SHANTA D. TOLIN
Pharm.D. - Doctor of Pharmacy
University of Michigan
Specialty: Clinical Pharmacist
Chapter: Zeta Nu Zeta
Inkster, Michigan
Region: Great Lakes

LAURIE A TUFTS
R.N., M.S.N.
M.S.N. - Master of Science in Nursing
Capital University
Specialty: School Health; Thesis: School Nurse
Knowledge of Sickle Cell Disease Pain
Chapter: Gamma Zeta Zeta Chapter
Columbus, Ohio
Region: Great Lakes

TONIA C. TURNER
M.A.T. - Master of Arts in Teaching
University of Phoenix
Chapter: Tau Psi Zeta
Alsip, Illinois
Region: Great Lakes

LINDA JOYCE BARNETT VAUGHN
Master of Speech Pathology
University of Mississippi
Specialty: speech/audiology
Chapter: Delta Zeta Zeta
District Heights, Maryland
Region: Atlantic

LINDA JOYCE BARNETT VAUGHN
M.Ed. - Master of Education
University of Mississippi
Specialty: Special Education
Chapter: Delta Zeta Zeta
District Heights, Maryland
Region: Atlantic

DR. CAROLYN C. WADLINGTON
Ed.D. - Doctor of Education
Argosy University
Specialty: Educational Leadership
Chapter: Tau Psi Zeta
Alsip, Illinois
Region: Great Lakes

KIMBERLY ANDREA WALKER
M.S.N., NP-C
M.S.N. - Master of Science in Nursing
Loyola University of Chicago
Chapter: Tau Psi Zeta
Alsip, Illinois
Region: Great Lakes

KRISHNA A. WALKER, Esq.
J.D. - Doctor of Jurisprudence
University of Notre Dame
Specialty: Business/Corporate Laywer
Chapter: Xi Zeta
St. Louis, Missouri
Region: Midwestern

MELISSA IRENE WALTON-JONES
M.B.A., C.I.A.
M.B.A. - Master of Business Administration
University of Missouri
Specialty: Finance & Accounting; Certified
Internal Auditor, CIA
Chapter: Omega Iota Zeta
Kansas City, Missouri
Region: Midwestern

TYEIS WASHINGTON
M.H.R.M.
M.A. - Master of Arts
Webster University
Specialty: Human Resource Management
Chapter: Psi Mu Zeta
Charlotte, North Carolina
Region: Eastern

RHETTA WASHINGTON McCOY
M.B.A. - Master of Business Administration
University of North Texas
Specialty: Strategic Management
Chapter: Kappa Zeta
Dallas, Texas
Region: Southern

TORI WATSON
M.A. - Master of Arts
John Jay College of Criminal Justice
Specialty: International Crime and Justice
Chapter: Sigma Nu Zeta
New York, New York
Region: Atlantic

MESHEA O. WEB
M.B.A. - Master of Business Administration
Shorter College
Chapter: Rho Xi Zeta
Marietta, Georgia
Region: Southeastern

RASHIDA SALIM WESLEY
M.B.A. - Master of Business Administration
University of Phoenix
Chapter: Xi Nu Zeta
Midwest City, Oklahoma
Region: Midwestern

GERTRUDE A. WEST
M.A.T. - Master of Arts in Teaching
Liberty University
Specialty: Special Education
Chapter: Epsilon Zeta
East Point, Georgia
Region: Southeastern

CATHERINE PEAKS WHITE
M.A.
M.Ed. - Master of Education
Howard University
Specialty: Area of Speciality: Reading and
Curriculum, Education
Chapter: Beta Zeta
Washington, District of Columbia
Region: Eastern

CATHERINE PEAKS WHITE
M.A.
M.Ed. - Master of Education
Howard University
Specialty: Area of Speciality: Reading and
Curriculum, Education
Chapter: Beta Zeta
Washington, District of Columbia
Region: Eastern

NIKOLA WHITE
M.B.A. - Master of Business Administration
St. John's University
Specialty: Finance
Chapter: Delta Beta Zeta
Queens, New York
Region: Atlantic

DEBORAH D. WILKERSON
M.S., M.A., M.A., LCDI
M.A. - Master of Arts
Amberton University
Specialty: Counseling, Psychology
Chapter: Kappa Zeta
Dallas, Texas
Region: Southern

LESHIA VIVIAN WILLIAMS
M.B.A. - Master of Business Administration
University of Illinois at Chicago
Specialty: Human Resources Management,
Management of Information Systems,
International Business
Chapter: Tau Psi Zeta
Alsip, Illinois
Region: Great Lakes

TONISIA WILLIAMS, LCSW
M.S.W. - Master of Social Work
Fordham University Graduate School of Social
Service
Chapter: Sigma Nu Zeta
New York, New York
Region: Atlantic

SHATYSH K. WILLIAMS
M.S. - Master of Science
Stevens Institute of Technology
Specialty: Telecommunications Management
Chapter: Nu Upsilon Zeta
Temple Terrace, Florida
Region: Southeastern

CHERJUAN WILLIAMSON
Master's in Education (in Progress)
Expected Graduation date is May 2017
Northern Illinois University
Chapter: Tau Psi Zeta
Alsip, Illinois
Region: Great Lakes

SHILENA M. WILSON
M.A. - Master of Arts
Kaplan Online University
Specialty: Psychology with a focus on
Addictions.
Chapter: Tau Psi Zeta
Alsip, Illinois
Region: Great Lakes

KENDRA L. WOODS
L.M.S.W., Ed.D.
Ed.D. - Doctor of Education
Argosy University
Specialty: Thesis – Does Counseling Impact
the Ability of Welfare Recipients to Engage in
Employment/Employment Training
Chapter: Pi Zeta
Nashville, Tennessee
Region: South Central

RITA WOODS
MS.Ed. - Master of Science in Education
Hofstra University
Specialty: Reading Instruction
Chapter: Delta Beta Zeta
Long Island, New York
Region: Atlantic

JOHNNIE MARIE WRIGHT
Ed.D. - Doctor of Education
Walden University
Specialty: Curriculum and Instruction
Chapter: Tau Omicron Zeta
Hephzibah, Georgia
Region: Southeastern

KATRINA J. WRISPER
M.B.A. - Master of Business Administration
Columbia Union College
Chapter: Nu Upsilon Zeta
Temple Terrace, Florida
Region: Southeastern

STEFANY S. WYNN
M.S.P
Walden University
Chapter: Gamma Zeta Zeta
Columbus, Ohio
Region: Great Lakes

Acknowledgments

Jylla Moore Tearte, Ph.D.

"Wisdom and Intellect for the 21st Century" is the second in a series of books that capture the thinking and perspectives of members. This project of the Centennial Commission focuses on the ideal of Zeta Phi Beta Sorority, Incorporated, *Scholarship*. It could not have been produced without the collective efforts of its contributors and those members who submitted information via the Centennial website. Thank you for your time and your creative energy! Special thanks to:

Doris McAdams Stokes and the team of editors and proof readers.

Sheryl Collins, National Director, Protocol

Norma C. Dartis, National Historian

Malica Fleming, Cover Design

Krishna A. Walker, Esq., Legal Advisor

Submitters and compilers for the registries and group sections.

Reginald Knox, Presyce Media

Daniel Barrozo, the Ink Studio

Proceeds from the sale of this book will be donated to the 2020 Centennial fund raising campaign of Zeta Phi Beta Sorority, Incorporated. Chapters, states and regions of the Sorority who order 25 or more copies from the Centennial Exchange will be credited with a 2020 Visionary contribution. For more information, visit the Centennial website at:

www.zphib2020.com/CentennialExchange

Many thanks to the Anthology contributors and we trust that this publication will be a lasting reminder of all that "Scholarship" means to the Sisterhood of Zeta Phi Beta Sorority, Incorporated.

Jylla Moore Tearte, Ph.D.
20th Past International President and
2020 Centennial Commission Chair
Zeta Phi Beta Sorority, Incorporated

CEO, Crystal Stairs, Inc.
Project Director

PERSONAL REFLECTIONS

Made in the USA
Monee, IL
28 October 2021

80959718R00243